AUTOCOURSE
CART™
OFFICIAL CHAMP CAR YEARBOOK

1999-2000

HAZLETON PUBLISHING

contents

publisher
RICHARD POULTER

editor
JEREMY SHAW

art editor
STEVE SMALL

production manager
STEVEN PALMER

managing editor
ROBERT YARHAM

business development manager
SIMON SANDERSON

sales promotion
CLARE KRISTENSEN

text editor
IAN PENBERTHY

chief photographer
MICHAEL C. BROWN

race car illustrations
PAUL LAGUETTE

AUTOCOURSE CART OFFICIAL CHAMP CAR YEARBOOK 1999-2000

*is published by
Hazleton Publishing Ltd.,
3 Richmond Hill,
Richmond, Surrey
TW10 6RE, England.*

*Color reproduction by
Barrett Berkeley Ltd., London, England.*

*Printed in England by
Butler and Tanner Ltd.,
Frome.*

ISBN: 1-874557-44-6

*U.S. advertising representative
Barry Pigot
2421 N. Center Street
PMB 128
Hickory, North Carolina 28601
Telephone and fax: (828) 322 1645*

acknowledgments

The Editor and publishers wish to thank the following for their assistance in compiling the *Autocourse CART Official Car Yearbook 1999–2000*: Andrew Craig, Randy Dzierzawski, Cathie Lyon, T.E. McHale, Ron Richards, Mark Tate, Mike Zizzo, Nancy Altenburg, Jody Bennett, Tom Blattler, Lisa Boggs, Susan Bradshaw, Holly Cain-Tritchler, Francois Cartier, Monica Davis, Kevin Diamond, Ben Edwards, Steve Fusek, Kika Garcia-Concheso, Deanna Griffith, Ashleigh Higgins, Alison Hill, Christine Horne, Paul Laguette, France Larrivee, Kathi Lauterbach, Brian Lawrence, Dan Luginbuhl, Sean Marchant, Kinnon Marshall, Brent Maurer, Eric Mauk, Scott McKee, Woody McMillin, Chris Mears, Chris Mergardt, Steve Nickless, Max d'Orsonnes, John Oreovicz, Paul Pfanner, David Phillips, Steve Potter, John Procida, Sid Priddle, Patty Reid, Scott Reisz, Amy Riley, Mark Robinson, Adam Saal, Alex Sabine, Mike Sack, Mike Smith, Elizabeth Swan, Rosa Elena Torres, Clayton Triggs, Brian Wagner, Melissa Watson, Kathy Weida, Carol Wilkins; and Tamy Valkosky.

This book is dedicated to the memory of fallen friends Greg Moore and Gonzalo Rodriguez.

photography

The photographs published in the *Autocourse CART Official Champ Car Yearbook 1999–2000* have been contributed by: Michael C. Brown; Allsport USA/Al Bello/Jon Ferrey/Robert Laberge/Jamie Squire/David Taylor, Diana Burnett, Barry Hathaway, John Morris/M-Pix, Motor Sport Images, Kazuki Saito, Nigel Snowdon.

DISTRIBUTORS

UNITED KINGDOM
Biblios Ltd.
Star Road
Partridge Green
West Sussex RH13 8LD
Telephone: 01403 710971
Fax: 01403 711143

NORTH AMERICA
Motorbooks International
P.O. Box 1
729 Prospect Ave., Osceola
Wisconsin 54020, USA
Telephone: (1) 715 294 3345
Fax: (1) 715 294 4448

NEW ZEALAND
David Bateman Ltd.
P.O. Box 100-242
North Shore Mail Centre
Auckland 1330
Telephone: (64) 9 415 7664
Fax: (64) 9 415 8892

REST OF THE WORLD
Menoshire Ltd
Unit 13, Wadsworth Road
Perivale
Middlesex UB6 7LQ
Telephone: 020 8566 7344
Fax: 020 8991 2439

EXpert handling.

foreword

by Juan Montoya
1999 PPG Cup champion

When I look back at the beginning of the 1999 CART season, the word that comes to my mind is 'expectations'. Although it was my rookie year, everyone had high expectations for me. Team Target had just won three straight titles, and I was taking the place of back-to-back champion Alex Zanardi.

I had much confidence in my ability, but I truly did not know what to expect from this season. The competition was great and the tracks were all new to me. Some of my goals at the beginning of the season were to finish races, try to win at least one race and, hopefully, win Rookie of the Year honors. Winning the PPG Cup never really even crossed my mind.

Although I did my best to keep realistic expectations back in March, everyone, including me, was interested to see if I could keep up the great Target/Chip Ganassi Racing tradition. It didn't take long for me to realize that 1999 could be another great season for Team Target.

I first realized how special our team was following the first race in Miami. I was very satisfied to finish tenth, but it wasn't my performance that helped my confidence – it was the entire team. From my teammate Jimmy, to Chip, to Morris, to my pit crew, to my friends at St. Jude Hospital and all of our sponsors. Everyone believed in me and quickly made me feel like part of the Team Target family. That is what made my adjustment to the CART series so easy.

I owe a big thanks to all of those people, and many more, for a very memorable season. I'm glad I was able to keep up the great tradition. Thanks for giving me the opportunity!

Photo: Michael C. Brown

5

Young Colombian prefers champagne over coffee.

Montoya

So much for beginner's luck.

Montoya

Good thing it wasn't the Milwaukee Mile and a half.

Tracy

Gas. Some drivers worry about it, de Ferran steps on it.

de Ferran

Rain delay at Cleveland Airport can't ground Montoya.

Montoya

Not even the Canadian Mounties could catch Franchitti.

Franchitti

We helped our drivers take home over a dozen first-place trophies.

At the U.S. 500, Kanaan wins by a nose.

Kanaan

Despite the debris, Franchitti swept the course clean.

Franchitti

Montoya adds some heat to the Mid-Ohio summer.

Montoya

Montoya blows competition away in Windy City.

Montoya

Montoya rains on the competition's parade.

Montoya

"Houston, Honda has landed."

Tracy

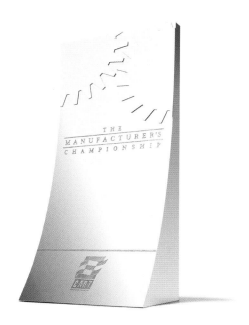

In return, they helped us earn this one.

It was another remarkable season for Honda-powered cars and teams in the CART series. Honda engines helped rookie Juan Montoya win more trophies this year than most drivers do in their entire careers. And they kept teammates Dario Franchitti and Paul Tracy at the top of the standings with excellent power and fuel mileage. Our racing turbo V-8 carried young Tony Kanaan to his first CART victory while continuing to aid veterans Jimmy Vasser and Gil de Ferran, as well as newcomer Naoki Hattori. When we counted up all our victories, the result was the 1999 Manufacturer's Championship trophy. And we must admit, it looks pretty good right next to our other two. For more **POWERED by** on the 1999 CART season and Honda's trophy room, visit us at www.honda.com. **HONDA**

Top: Side-by-side action at speeds reaching 240 mph provided an exciting spectacle for a full-house crowd in the Fontana finale.

Above left: The championship is won, but there is no joy for Juan Montoya or his father, Pablo *(left),* after the youngster is informed about Greg Moore's death.

Above, left and far left: The end of an era as the FedEx Championship Series bids adieu to the PPG Pace Cars, Goodyear and Valvoline. Even so, CART teams still boast annual sponsorship revenues in excess of $400 million.

TRIUMPH AND TRAGEDY

A CLEAR blue sky ensured picture-perfect conditions for the 1999 FedEx Championship Series finale at California Speedway on October 31. The imposing main grandstand was filled to capacity. The coveted PPG Cup trophy and an accompanying $1 million bonus was at stake. A similar sum was up for grabs to the winner of the day's Marlboro 500 Presented by Toyota.

The two title protagonists, Dario Franchitti and Juan Pablo Montoya, were at the wheels of similar Honda/Reynards fielded by their respective KOOL and Target-backed teams, Franchitti holding a slender nine-point advantage after a dominating performance in the previous race at Surfers Paradise, Australia.

The stage was set for a thrilling climax to the 20-race season.

Three hours later, Adrian Fernandez emerged to score a beautifully judged victory for Patrick Racing. The closest title-chase in Champ Car history ended with Montoya and Franchitti actually tied on points – but with the Colombian securing a record-setting fourth consecutive crown for Target/Chip Ganassi Racing by virtue of his seven race wins to Franchitti's three.

Tragically, the respective accomplishments of the two top-quality teams and drivers were totally eclipsed by the news that Greg Moore, one of the sport's promising young stars, had succumbed to injuries sustained in a crash earlier in the afternoon. The mood afterward was somber in the extreme.

The close-knit CART community – already reeling from the death of talented Uruguayan rookie Gonzalo Rodriguez at Laguna Seca only seven weeks earlier – was devastated by the double tragedy. Moore was an exceptional talent who had not yet fulfilled his potential. He was also an extremely likable, down-to-earth character, popular among his peers and with a forthright, well-balanced view on life.

The accident that claimed his life came as a cruel reminder of the sport's fickle nature. The last man to die in a CART-sanctioned event on an oval was Jim Hickman at Milwaukee in 1982. Since then there had been innumerable incidents on the ovals (and both Jovy Marcelo and Scott Brayton had perished at Indianapolis), yet due to the vast leaps in technology and overall safety standards – not to mention a liberal dose of good fortune – life-threatening injuries had been few. Sadly, it took the untimely demise of two extremely gifted youngsters to refocus attention on safety issues.

It seemed especially importune that calamity should strike on what promised to be an auspicious day for Champ Car racing. Yet such seems to have been the way of things these past few years.

During a roller-coaster 1999 season, for various reasons, several large corporations announced they would cease their involvement prior to the new millennium. First to make its intention public was Valvoline, which confirmed in early July the imminent end to its hitherto successful alliance with Walker Racing. Later, Budweiser elected not to extend an association with Della Penna Motorsports; Goodyear, one of the mainstays of Champ Car competition for at least the past quarter-century, bowed to pressure from its board of directors (not to mention the unequal struggle against long-time rival Firestone); and finally, a few weeks after the season had been concluded, PPG Industries, which had provided stability for CART virtually since its formation in 1978, also announced the cessation of its open-wheel sponsorship.

There is no doubt that the withdrawals could be attributable, at least in part, to the continuing impasse between Championship Auto Racing Teams, sanctioning body of the FedEx Championship Series, and the Indy Racing League, founded in 1996 by Indianapolis Motor Speedway President Tony George – and in particular the fact that the Champ Cars remained ostracized from the Indianapolis 500.

For a while during the summer, there seemed genuine hope of a rapprochement between the two factions, which according to the general consensus would have reaped enormous benefits for the sport of auto racing as a whole. CART President and CEO Andrew Craig was involved in lengthy discussions with Tony George. Numerous other parties – including the four engine manufacturers committed to CART (Ford, Honda, Mercedes and Toyota) – attempted to assist in the delicate negotiations. The mood in late August seemed especially upbeat, with rumors of the existence of revised technical regulations aimed at combining the best attributes of both series. A month later, however, George called an abrupt halt to talks. The IRL, he declared, would continue in precisely its present form...despite the fact that the vast majority of its teams were living a hand-to-mouth existence and that sponsorship opportunities were few and far between.

Separate series they would remain.

But don't for one moment be misled into believing it was all doom and gloom with the FedEx Championship Series. Far from it. The standard of competition remained at an extraordinarily high level in 1999, as evidenced by the single-season record total of ten different race winners. There were a dozen different pole-sitters (another record), while no fewer than 16 drivers secured at least one podium finish.

For the first time since 1996, the outcome of the championship remained undecided until the final lap of the final race. Montoya and Franchitti had waged a fascinating duel throughout the season, their individual fortunes ebbing and flowing as the races unfolded. Montoya displayed remarkable flair for one so young: he celebrated his 24th birthday on September 20, just a few days after extending his advantage over Franchitti to a season-high 28 points. But when he made errors in successive races at Houston and Surfers Paradise, the Colombian almost allowed his rival to sneak through and snatch the honors.

Franchitti, indeed, arrived at the Fontana finale with a slender lead of nine points. But it was not to be for the charismatic Scotsman. A problem with a wheel retaining nut cost him valuable time during a pit stop, causing him to fall two laps behind the leaders. Team KOOL Green tried valiantly to make up the deficit, but to

Dallenbach moves on

Michael C. Brown

THE season finale at California Speedway represented the end of an era – the swan song for CART Chief Steward Wally Dallenbach. An accomplished driver in his own right, with five Champ Car victories to his name, Dallenbach hung up his helmet at the end of the 1979 season, just one year after the formation of CART. He didn't go far. The following year he took on the role of CART's competition director, and in '81, added the duties of chief steward. He has remained in charge of CART's raceday activities ever since (apart from a brief hiatus in 1997 during a short-lived 'retirement').

Dallenbach has been a pillar of strength in the intervening 19 years. The unassuming, quietly-spoken Dallenbach earned a great deal of credit for the vast improvement in safety standards that took place during his tenure. It was an unhappy irony that he should have witnessed two fatalities within his final two months on the job.

Dallenbach made several controversial decisions over the years, but his ethics were beyond reproach. He will be missed – not least by many of the drivers.

'I have to thank Wally for what he did,' said Paul Tracy, who had more run-ins than most with Dallenbach. 'He changed my focus and made me a better driver.'

Added Michael Andretti, another frequent visitor to the stewards' room, 'I have known Wally all of my life. He has been a real friend to me and he is going to be missed. He helped make CART one of, if not the most competitive racing series in the world. Wally is fair and has a true passion for the sport.'

Gil de Ferran summed up Dallenbach's duties perfectly: 'He's got the toughest job in the world, because he's always making a call against somebody. His job is to make difficult judgments and difficult decisions, and he knows his decisions are going to be unpopular with at least part of the crowd. I think he's had everybody's respect. You can tell he's a racer at heart. He's a charming individual. His decision to retire is very personal and he'll be missed.'

Left: The Boss man no longer. Twice champion Al Unser Jr. endured a tough season in '99 and will seek pastures new in 2000.

Below left: The new faces of CART. Tony Kanaan tries to exert his authority over Brazilian buddies Helio Castro-Neves *(left)* and Cristiano da Matta.

Photos: Michael C. Brown

no avail. Montoya survived a couple of close calls in traffic and did precisely what he needed to secure the championship by the narrowest possible margin. It was close, but richly deserved. Montoya, clearly, was the outstanding driver in 1999. Merely one year after losing twice champion Alex Zanardi to Formula 1, team owner Ganassi had found another rough diamond and, with the crucial guidance of veteran race engineer Morris Nunn, had turned him into a gem.

Montoya's magnificent triumph ensured that Ganassi was able to break the previous record of three consecutive PPG Cup titles – achieved in 1981, '82 and '83 by Penske Racing. Truly, a new dynasty had been established.

For Roger Penske, by contrast, the memories of 1999 will forever be shrouded by anguish. The loss of Rodriguez in one of his cars was hard enough to bear. The despair deepened when Moore, who, along with proven race winner Gil de Ferran, had signed

to lead his team out of a depression in 2000, also was killed.

A hard-nosed businessman he most assuredly is, but Penske also is a dedicated family man – and he has an abiding passion for the sport. It was sorely tested in 1999. Even before the late-season calamities, his commitment to CART had been publicly questioned following the longest victory drought of his career as a car owner. By year's end, it had reached 50 races (dating from May 1997), precisely double his previous longest winless streak, which occurred in 1974–75.

Equally disappointing for Penske was the form of Al Unser Jr., who showed rare glimpses of the expertise that took him to 31 race wins and two PPG Cup championships during an illustrious 18-year career in Champ Cars. To be fair, Unser's equipment package was rarely on a par with his rivals, although a measure of his competitiveness could be gleaned from the fact that he was regularly outpaced by his far less experienced teammates.

After being informed that his services would not be required for the Y2K campaign, Unser, unable to secure an alternative ride, opted instead to prolong his career in the IRL. He would be missed, of course, as one of Champ Car racing's marquee names.

There has been a wholesale changing of the guard in recent years. Indeed, following Bobby Rahal's retirement in '98 and Scott Pruett's decision to pursue a new career path in NASCAR Winston Cup competition, Unser's lifelong friend and rival, Michael Andretti, remained as the undisputed blue blood of the FedEx Championship Series – at the relatively tender age of 37.

Yet fear not, there was plenty of youthful enthusiasm and charisma to carry the series forward. Brazilians Tony Kanaan, Helio Castro-Neves and Cristiano da Matta possess undoubted star quality with personalities to match. Ditto Franchitti and Max Papis. Christian Fittipaldi emerged as a bona fide championship challenger to go

along with his pin-up good looks. Paul Tracy, meanwhile, bounced back from a dismal 1998 season. The Canadian veteran also developed into an eloquent spokesman for the sport.

On the home front, the story of Californian Memo Gidley made compelling reading. The Toyota Atlantic graduate, in stark contrast to many of his contemporaries who relied on family support or wealthy benefactors, reached the pinnacle of the sport through sheer determination and hard work.

There was plenty more good news. FedEx had brought valuable credibility and a broader appeal to Champ Car racing since signing on as title sponsor in 1998. The addition of new backing from McDonald's (Forsythe Championship Racing), Pioneer Electronics (Arciero-Wells Racing), Alpine Audio (Walker Racing), Johns Manville and Menards (Team Gordon) also provided a measure of growth. Television viewing figures had been in steady decline since the CART/IRL split at the end of the '95 season, yet that trend was arrested in '99 with a modest increase.

'Our number one objective in 1999 was to reach more U.S. television viewers,' declared CART Vice President of Broadcast Services Keith Allo, 'and while our numbers are not yet at the level we wish, this is a positive achievement.'

The series continued to gather momentum in other ways, too. For example, the championship expanded to 20 races in 1999 with the addition of the sensational new Chicago Motor Speedway, which attracted a full-house crowd of 70,000 for the inaugural Target Grand Prix in August. The event was a huge hit. The well-established Surfers Paradise temporary circuit, on the Gold Coast of Queensland, Australia, played host to a record 250,000-plus fans in October, while several other venues were clamoring for the opportunity to host additional races. New 1.5-mile oval tracks were under construction – the Lausitzring, Germany, and Rockingham Motor Speedway in England – both with firm expectations of hosting Champ Cars in the not-too-distant future. Mexico also was campaigning hard for a fixture to highlight the ability of its two star performers, Adrian Fernandez and Michel Jourdain Jr.

Indianapolis or not, the FedEx Championship Series has continued to flourish.

Jeremy Shaw
Dublin, Ohio
December 1999

THE 24 h
CHALLENGE

SACHS RACE ENGINEERING

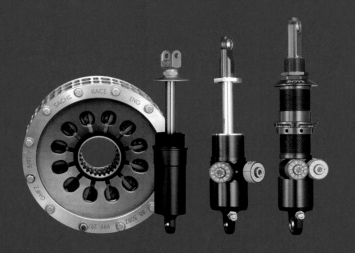

SACHS RACE ENGINEERING – is a German-based company specializing in the design, development, manufacture and world-wide service support of racing clutches and shock absorbers. It is an official supplier of Scuderia Ferrari (shock absorbers) and Sauber (clutch and shock absorbers). Sachs Race Engineering is also one of the leading manufacturers of performance dampers and clutches, servicing especially the international performance car and tuning industry.

Sachs Race Engineering GmbH · A Mannesmann Sachs company

Ernst-Sachs-Str. 62 · D-97424 Schweinfurt · Phone +49 9721 98 43 00 · Fax +49 9721 98 42 99

e-mail olaf.schwaier@sachs-ag.de · www.sachs-race-engineering.de

SACHS
RACE ENGINEERING

FROM the first green flag in Homestead to the final checkered flag in Fontana, the 1999 CART FedEx Championship Series unfolded as one of the most exciting championship battles in the history of open-wheel racing.

The 1999 season featured a record 20 events – on four different types of racetrack – spread out over five countries on four different continents. On any given weekend, the difference between winning and losing came down to split-second decisions by drivers and their teams.

In the business world, just like in a Champ Car race, success comes down to quick decisions and reliability. Over the past 27 years, FedEx has built its reputation as the world's leading express delivery company on these

principles and has made a habit of putting customer service first.

So whether it is a Champ Car driver winning a race or a FedEx courier making an on-time delivery, both rely on speed, reliability, precision, technology, safety and teamwork. Looking back on the second year of title sponsorship, it is evident that the relationship between FedEx and CART continued to evolve based on these shared synergies.

As part of the sponsorship, FedEx continued its role as the official transportation company of the FedEx Championship Series. In a sport in which the delivery and accessibility of parts are critical, FedEx provided time-definite, reliable service to meet the transportation and distribution needs of CART, its promoters and race teams.

Once again, the FedEx Championship Series enjoyed enormous success overseas as FedEx transported the entire series to race sites in Japan, Australia and Brazil. Throughout the whole season, FedEx was able to make crucial deliveries for teams through the on-track FedEx Ship Site.

• *Prior to the Miller Lite 225, FedEx delivered electronic equipment from Motorola Racing Radios in Atlanta to the Milwaukee Mile racetrack. The equipment enabled Motorola representatives to fit 20 helmets with receiving and transmitting capabilities for pit-crew members.*

• *The PacWest Racing Team and driver Mark Blundell called on FedEx when two Mercedes engines en route*

to Japan were unexpectedly delayed in Alaska customs prior to the Toyota Grand Prix in Long Beach, California. FedEx personnel were made aware of the situation on Friday, and after making calls to trace agents, the package cleared customs and was flown on a FedEx plane to Oakland, California. FedEx trucks met the plane in Oakland, and the engines were delivered to the Long Beach track early Saturday morning, in time to be fitted for Sunday's race.

• *In Detroit, Team Gordon and Robbie Gordon called on FedEx to save their race weekend. Following a crash in qualifying, Gordon had a replacement front wing shipped from his home base in Anaheim, California to Detroit in time for Sunday's race.*

These were some highlights of the 1999 CART FedEx Championship season:

• For the first time in its history, the series ended in a tie for the FedEx Series Championship points lead between Juan Montoya and Dario Franchitti, and a tiebreaker was required to break the deadlock. Montoya earned the championship based on his seven race victories to Franchitti's three wins.

• Michael Andretti added to his CART record for race victories by claiming his 38th at Gateway International Raceway on May 29. The win also allowed Andretti to tie Rick Mears' CART record for the most seasons (12) with at least one victory.

• Juan Montoya became the youngest Champion in FedEx Championship Series history, at 24 years, one month and 11 days. In doing so, he broke existing CART rookie records for victories with seven and laps led with 942. Montoya also matched Nigel Mansell's rookie record of capturing seven pole positions.

• The Target/Chip Ganassi Racing team won an unprecedented fourth consecutive championship.

• The 20-race FedEx Championship Series season produced ten different winners, a series record.

FedEx will continue its efforts to further build its relationship with CART and its partners, working from the foundation of the first two seasons toward success in the seasons to come.

Left: Champ Cars are loaded aboard a FedEx airplane. FedEx carried the entire series to overseas races in Japan, Brazil and Australia.

Below: Juan Montoya took the FedEx CART series by storm in his Target/Chip Ganassi Honda/Reynard.

Firestone Firehawk®
The Choice Of Champions.

1996 **1997** **1998** **1999**

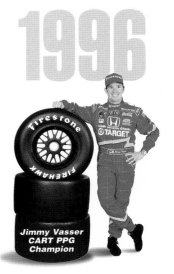

Jimmy Vasser
CART PPG
Champion

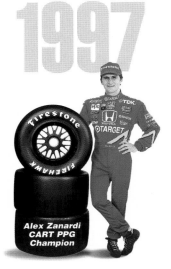

Alex Zanardi
CART PPG
Champion

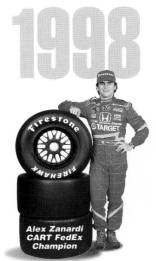

Alex Zanardi
CART FedEx
Champion

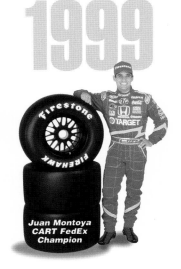

Juan Montoya
CART FedEx
Champion

THE LESSONS WE LEARN ON RACE DAY ARE IN THE TIRES YOU COUNT ON EVERY DAY.

With a record 50 wins at the Indy 500,® Firestone knows Indy® racing like no other tire company. And if we can develop the kind of quick acceleration, grip and stability required for **IRL** and **CART** racing tires, just imagine how well our line of Firehawk® street performance radials will perform for you. Firehawk performance tires are speed rated from S to Z and specifically engineered for crisp handling and legendary performance.

Firestone® Firehawk® SH30® With UNI-T®
High-Performance Street Tire
Get A Grip On Wet Cornering

We offer two Firehawk tires with **UNI-T,®** the **U**ltimate **N**etwork of **I**ntelligent **T**ire **T**echnology—the Firehawk® SZ50® and the Firehawk® SH30.® The Firehawk SH30 with **UNI-T** is an H-rated high-performance tire designed to deliver outstanding wet performance, especially wet cornering, while still providing excellent dry performance. Stop by your local Firestone retailer and check out the complete Firehawk line today.

Race-Winning Firestone® Firehawk®
Indy Racing Slick &
Firestone® Firehawk® SS10® Street Tire

America's Tire Since 1900

1-800-807-9555
www.firestone-usa.com

Race-Winning Firestone® Firehawk®
Indy Racing Rain Tire &
Firestone® Firehawk® SZ50® With UNI-T®
Ultra-High Performance Street Tire

Indianapolis 500,® Indy 500® and Indy® are registered trademarks of the Indianapolis Motor Speedway.

Drivers On Firestone Firehawks Continue Dominating CART Competition

JUAN MONTOYA

IN each of the last four years, drivers on Firestone tires have not only won the CART championship, but also won the majority of races, taken the most pole positions and led the most race laps.

- In 1999, Firestone-equipped drivers won 19 of 20 races, earned 18 of 20 poles, led 2,679 of 2,769 laps, swept the podium 16 times and won the season championship (Juan Montoya).
- In 1998, Firestone-equipped drivers won 18 of 19 races, earned 18 poles, led 1,837 of 2,549 laps, swept the podium nine times and won the season championship (Alex Zanardi).
- In 1997, Firestone-equipped drivers won 13 of 17 races, earned 11 poles, led 1,321 of 2,259 laps, swept the podium three times and won the season championship (Zanardi).
- In 1996, Firestone-equipped drivers won 10 of 16 races, earned 12 poles, led 1,077 of 2,005 laps, swept the podium three times and won the

season championship (Jimmy Vasser).

The accomplishments are stunning, even for a company with nine decades of racing under its corporate belt.

As early as 1909, The Firestone Tire & Rubber Company took to the racetrack to demonstrate its technical prowess and competitive spirit. When Ray Harroun won the inaugural Indianapolis 500® in 1911, driving a Marmon Wasp, he began a record of Indy 500® wins for Firestone that now stands at fifty—more than all other tire manufacturers combined.

The Firestone brand made its presence known in numerous motorsports venues, providing the now-legendary drivers with a foundation for winning. Among the early stars who won races while wearing the Firestone logo on their firesuits are such greats as Bobby Allison, Mario Andretti, Buddy Baker, Tony Bettenhausen, Jim Clark, Mark Donohue, Emerson Fittipaldi, A.J. Foyt, Dan Gurney, Graham Hill, Junior Johnson, Parnelli Jones, Richard

Petty, Dick Rathman, Fireball Roberts, Dick Simon, Jackie Stewart, John Surtees, Al Unser, Cale Yarborough and dozens more.

In 1990, Bridgestone and Firestone operations in the U.S. were consolidated as Bridgestone/Firestone, Inc. The arrangement allowed tire manufacturing concepts and information to be shared on a global basis, with technical centers in Akron, Ohio; Tokyo, Japan; and Rome, Italy, sharing information. The pooling of talent contributed to dramatic success in the marketplace and on the racetrack.

"The past four years have been amazing," said Al Speyer, Bridgestone/Firestone Motorsports Director. "In some of the world's toughest competitions, going head to head with other tire manufacturers, we've come out on top. To not only win, but dominate, is a powerful testament to the talent and commitment of our engineering team and our whole motorsports program."

*Indianapolis 500®, Indy 500® and Indy® are registered trademarks of the Indianapolis Motor Speedway.

NOT since the heady days of 1993, when Nigel Mansell overwhelmed a Michael Andretti-less Champ Car field, has a rookie had such an impact on the FedEx Championship Series as Juan Montoya. The difference is that Mansell was fully 40 years of age and the defending Formula 1 World Champion in '93. In contrast, Montoya was all of 24 and – in the eyes of many – a future World Champion when he won the '99 PPG Cup.

No matter. Montoya eclipsed Mansell's mark for victories (seven) and tied his record for poles (seven) in a rookie season, and led a greater percentage of laps (34 versus 29 percent) than 'El Leone', while amassing the fourth-highest points total since the current scoring system was adopted in 1983. Although it's true

that Montoya had more races (20) in which to score than any previous champion, most would agree he faced a field deeper in quality of drivers, teams and equipment than most of his predecessors.

'The competition's a lot tighter than when Nigel ran,' said Tom Anderson, Managing Director of four-time champions Target/Chip Ganassi Racing. 'In those days, it was basically Carl Haas versus Roger Penske and everybody else was kind of making up the show. To go from two dominant teams to probably eight teams that are extremely close, you've gotta say the competition is better.'

The facts support Anderson. The '99 season featured more different winners (ten) and pole-sitters (12) than ever before, not to mention history's closest competition for the PPG Cup – one

that ended in a mathematical tie between Montoya and Dario Franchitti, a tie resolved in the Colombian's favor based on his number of race wins (seven to three).

Given the stiff competition, Montoya's youth and relative lack of experience, few expected him to be a major factor this year. One man who was not surprised by his form, however, was Montoya himself.

'When he came in, he never thought about Rookie of the Year,' said Anderson. 'That wasn't his goal at all. He knew he had the ability to win, and you've never seen a winner who wasn't confident.'

To say Montoya is confident is like saying water is wet or the sun is bright. Misconstrued by some as 'cocky', the 23-year-old Colombian is simply very, very sure of himself. He's

good; he knows it, and he's disappointed in himself and his team when their efforts produce anything less than victory. Thus, he's taking the FedEx Championship in his stride; more as proof of a job well done than as an end in itself.

'To be honest, I haven't thought about it much,' he laughed. 'Sometimes I'll be sitting at lunch or something and think "Wow! I won the championship!" When I saw my car at the CART banquet with the number 1 on the side, that was very neat, but almost like a surprise too.

'I actually never expected to win it the first year. The competition was really hard, and being a rookie I had big disadvantages, but it seems it didn't affect me much.'

Although Montoya earned four of his seven wins on road and street

JUAN IN A MILLION

by David Phillips

Above: Juan Montoya leads Dario Franchitti at Nazareth.

circuits, it was his oval-track performances that were most impressive. Saddled with an oversteering car at Homestead, he set fifth-fastest lap and finished tenth. But for a fuel miscalculation, he might have won at Motegi, and he did win on the idiosyncratic Nazareth and Rio ovals as well as the sensational new Chicago track. He also took poles at Nazareth and Gateway, and came within 0.032 second of victory at Michigan.

'I think the ovals were good,' said Montoya. 'I like them; I enjoy them. It hasn't been difficult for me. I feel very comfortable driving them. It's funny, because I think I had almost as many points in the ovals as in the road courses.'

Actually, Montoya's final tally read 110 points in 12 road courses, 102 in eight ovals.

In part, Montoya's strong oval form resulted from a highly productive relationship with teammate Jimmy Vasser.

'The biggest thing there was Vasser,' said Anderson. 'We never went into an oval where Juan tested first. Most of the places were three-day tests and the first day and a half was Jimmy. So when you're getting into Jimmy Vasser's car on an oval, that's a pretty good starting point.'

Take nothing away from Montoya, however. Although Ganassi, Anderson, race engineer Morris Nunn, Vasser and Co. gave him the tools, it was Juan Pablo Montoya who hustled the #4 Target Honda/Reynard to the front.

'I came to realize throughout this season that the kid's not human,' said Vasser. 'I don't think anything he does surprises me anymore. He's done things this year that I didn't

think were possible for a racer, much less a rookie.'

Montoya was also sensational on the temporary circuits and road courses, scoring his first Champ Car win on the streets of Long Beach and adding victories at Cleveland, Mid-Ohio and Vancouver to his total. In retrospect, the Mid-Ohio triumph gave him the greatest satisfaction. There, Montoya qualified a lowly (for him) eighth on the grid, but went straight to the front on race day, catching his main championship rivals – Team KOOL Green's Dario Franchitti and Paul Tracy – on the race track, then taking the lead thanks to typically brilliant pit work by the Target/Ganassi team.

'Mid-Ohio was perfect teamwork: good on the track and in the pits,' he said. 'That's the kind of race you like to have every weekend.

'We were not that quick on the weekend until the race, and I think everyone thought it was going to be another win for Dario. But it didn't come out that way!'

It was not all plain sailing, however. There was a controversial clash with Andretti in practice in Japan, a bungled pit stop strategy in Detroit that, ultimately, resulted in a DNF, and crashes in Toronto, Houston and Australia. The final miscue set up a climactic showdown with Franchitti in the season's finale at California Speedway.

The fact that the championship went down to the final race of the season was a source of some frustration to Montoya, not only because of the fact that he had won so many races, but also because he well knew that he and his teammates were – at times – their own worst enemies.

Michael C. Brown

'We won seven races,' he said. 'Nobody else did that this year. We just had bad luck in other races. We gave away I don't know how many points by making simple mistakes. Very silly things. Everybody made mistakes; we had to pay for it. But that's the way it goes.

'You know, we had a problem in Houston, a miscommunication, and at Surfers Paradise I just made a single mistake. We gave away too many points to Dario – and he never let up on us.'

Under pressure not only to score his first FedEx Championship, but also to bring an unprecedented fourth straight PPG Cup to Target/Chip Ganassi Racing, Montoya drove flawlessly in the tragic Marlboro 500 to finish exactly where he needed to be to claim the title.

After a few weeks of R&R, it was back to business for Montoya and his teammates as they prepared for the challenges of a new millennium. Chief among those challenges is coming to grips with an all-new (for the team) engine package supplied by Toyota after a hugely successful four-year association with Honda. Toyota has yet to win in Champ Car competition; indeed, a Toyota-powered car has never so much as produced a CART podium finish. But if he had any doubts about repeating his CART championship victory, Montoya wasn't showing them.

'I look forward next year to win again,' he said. 'I'm not aiming to finish second. I can guarantee that.

'I think Toyota has a big compromise with us, but at the same time we have a big compromise with them because we are going to do our best

again. And to do our best, we have to win. It's going to be very interesting for sure, to be honest. They need a championship and we have proven we can win championships and races, so why would it be a different way? We were so quick at some races that I think we could have won some races for Toyota, even with this year's engine.'

Offsetting the challenge of a new and (as yet) winless engine package is the fact that, at the ripe old age of

24, Montoya will be familiar with all the tracks in the 2000 FedEx Championship. That should not only benefit his performances on the race weekends, but enhance his preseason preparation.

'I think we're going to be able to take it to a different level because of his familiarity with the race tracks,' said Anderson. 'Things we were having to focus on to make sure he got track time at certain places, we're not gonna

have to focus on as much. And in pre-season testing at Sebring, Homestead or wherever, he will be able to relate aspects of the test to specific circumstances he expects to encounter during the season at, let's say, Toronto, Cleveland or Nazareth.

'I think it'll make him a lot stronger. I think he has the confidence and the understanding of the people around him, so he's comfortable that way. And if we've got some power and reliability, then I think he's gonna have a pretty good chance to defend his championship.'

And beyond the 2000 season? Although Montoya prefers to focus his thoughts and words on the coming Champ Car season, the fact remains that he will likely be a very hot property on the Formula 1 front when talks turn to 2001. Team owner Chip Ganassi and Frank Williams have developed a cordial relationship in recent years, one that led to Ganassi's two-time CART champion driver Alex Zanardi moving to Williams last year in exchange for that team's test driver, Montoya.

Might 2000 be Montoya's final season in Champ Cars?

'No comment,' he laughed. 'I don't know. Of course, at sometime I want to go to Formula 1. That's no secret to anyone, and I'm sure everyone wants to end up there in their career. But also, I think if you are in Formula 1, you wonder if you'd like to come back to Champ Cars here and win like Mansell did, so you win everything.

'I don't know. I won here. I got another year here, so as long as I'm still quick we'll see. It'll be interesting.'

Grand Slam

FEW would have imagined, much less predicted, that Chip Ganassi had assembled a racing dynasty when the 1996 racing season began. His drivers included a Formula 1 cast-off turned CART rookie and a Champ Car veteran of four years who had yet to win his first race. The team's technical package included Honda engines, with one Champ Car win to their credit – one less than tire supplier Firestone – and Reynard chassis. True, Reynard, which Ganassi had enticed into Champ Car competition in '94, had won the '95 CART Constructor's Championship. But virtually the entire field was using Reynard chassis, so Ganassi's team hardly figured to enjoy an advantage on that front.

Four years, 30 wins, 23 poles and four PPG Cups later, Target/Chip Ganassi Racing is the unrivaled blue-blood of Champ Car racing.

The secret to its success?

'Three things,' said Ganassi. 'People, people and people. Everyone asks me how we've managed to have the success that we've had, and I just tell them I feel fortunate to have been associated with people of the quality of Tom Anderson, Mike Hull [team manager], Rob Hill [crew chief], Morris Nunn, Julian Robertson [race engineers] and everyone else in this organization.'

Ganassi's mantra will be put to the test in 2000 when Target/Chip Ganassi Racing switches from Honda to Toyota power. In a flash, his team will go from a partnership with an automotive manufacturer whose Champ Car success is but the latest chapter in one of the most storied legacies in all of motorsports, to one with a company that has yet to earn its first Champ Car win; indeed, which captured its first Champ Car pole in the season finale at Fontana.

While the Toyota RV8D and RV8E engines made tangible progress on the race track in '99, as always with Ganassi, it's the people who count.

'The Toyota engine has made significant strides recently and is experiencing a great deal of momentum heading into 2000,' he said. 'I've had the opportunity to get to know the people at Toyota, and I believe they're hungry to win.'

Amazingly, after a fourth straight FedEx Championship, so is everyone at Target/Chip Ganassi Racing.

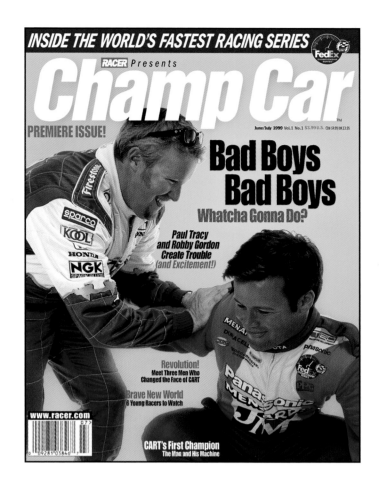

INSIDE THE WORLD'S FASTEST RACING SERIES

RACER Presents

Champp Car™

June/July 1999 Vol.1 No.1 $3.99 U.S.

PREMIERE ISSUE!

Bad Boys Bad Boys
Whatcha Gonna Do?

Paul Tracy and Robby Gordon Create Trouble (and Excitement!)

Revolution!
Meet Three Men Who Changed the Face of CART

Brave New World
6 Young Racers to Watch

CART's First Champion
The Man and His Machine

www.racer.com

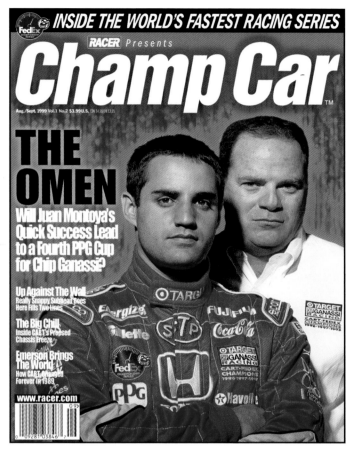

INSIDE THE WORLD'S FASTEST RACING SERIES

RACER Presents

Champ Car™

Aug./Sept. 1999 Vol.1 No.2 $3.99 U.S.

THE OMEN
Will Juan Montoya's Quick Success Lead to a Fourth PPG Cup for Chip Ganassi?

Up Against The Wall
Really Snappy Subhead Goes Here Fills Two Lines

The Big Chill
Inside CART's Proposed Chassis Freeze

Emerson Brings The World
How CART Changed Forever In 1989

www.racer.com

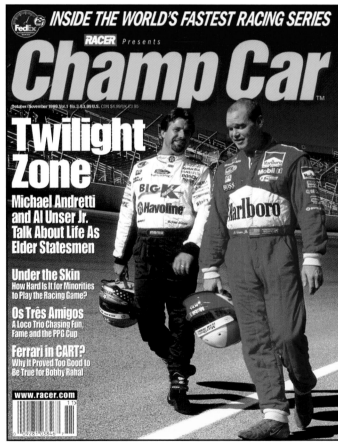

INSIDE THE WORLD'S FASTEST RACING SERIES

RACER Presents

Champ Car™

October/November 1999 Vol.1 No.3 $3.99 U.S. CDN $4.99/UK £3.95

Twilight Zone

Michael Andretti and Al Unser Jr. Talk About Life As Elder Statesmen

Under the Skin
How Hard Is It for Minorities to Play the Racing Game?

Os Três Amigos
A Loco Trio Chasing Fun, Fame and the PPG Cup

Ferrari in CART?
Why It Proved Too Good to Be True for Bobby Rahal

www.racer.com

INSIDE THE WORLD'S FASTEST RACING SERIES

RACER Presents

Champ Car™

December 1999/January 2000 Vol.1 No.4 $3.99 U.S. CDN $4.99/UK £3.95

Greg Moore
1975-1999

www.racer.com

A Remembrance

Get Inside the World's Fastest Racing Series

Call now for a free trial issue: Toll-free 1-800-999-9718

(Outside the USA and Canada call 714-259-8240)

Or visit our Web site: **www.racer.com**

In accordance with the *Autocourse* tradition, Editor Jeremy Shaw offers his personal ranking of the best of the best in the 1999 FedEx Championship Series, taking into account their individual performances, their level of experience and the resources at their disposal. Also per tradition, an appreciation of the late Greg Moore's career – and season – appears separately on page 34.

FEDEX CHAMPIONSHIP SERIES 1999

TOP TEN DRIVERS

Photographs by Michael C. Brown

juan montoya

1

Date of birth: September 20, 1975

Residence: Miami, Florida and Bogota, Colombia

Team: Target/Chip Ganassi Racing

Equipment: Honda/Reynard/Firestone

CART starts in 1999: 20

PPG Cup ranking: 1st

Wins: 7; Poles: 7; Points: 212

VETERAN race engineer Morris Nunn had been contemplating retirement after guiding Alex Zanardi to a pair of PPG Cup titles. The Englishman was persuaded to change his mind, however, after watching Juan Pablo Montoya in action for the first time during a Formula 1 test in Europe in the fall of 1998. Nunn was aware of Montoya's accomplishments, which included winning the 1998 FIA International Formula 3000 Championship, but was – in his own words – 'astonished' at the youngster's raw ability and level of commitment behind the wheel. Upon his return to the U.S., Nunn confided to Crew Chief Rob Hill, 'This kid could be a winner by Long Beach.'

The only apparent drawback was Montoya's lack of experience on the ovals. It proved not to be a problem. After a solid debut at Homestead, Montoya fought his way into contention for the lead at Motegi before a miscue in the pits saw him run out of fuel. Montoya, amazingly, won both of his next two oval races, at Nazareth and Gateway, after already making Nunn's prediction come true by romping to a clear victory at Long Beach.

Not since Nigel Mansell in '93 had a rookie driver adapted to the ovals with such apparent ease. In fact, by the season's end, Montoya had eclipsed many of the Englishman's records, including most wins (seven to Mansell's five) and total laps led (954 versus Mansell's 603) during a rookie campaign. Montoya also equaled Mansell's tally of seven poles.

It was a quite remarkable performance. Montoya never pulled out much of a lead in the championship and, in fact, almost allowed it to slip away following errors in consecutive races at Houston and Surfers Paradise. He finished tied on points with Dario Franchitti, but judged upon pure speed alone, there is no question that the right man won.

dario franchitti

2

Date of birth: May 19, 1973

Residence: Edinburgh, Scotland

Team: Team KOOL Green

Equipment: Honda/Reynard/Firestone

CART starts in 1999: 20

PPG Cup ranking: 2nd

Wins: 3; Poles: 2; Points: 212

MUCH was expected of Dario Franchitti in 1999. He had finished a strong third in the '98 title chase and, in the absence of Alex Zanardi (who preferred the greener pastures of Formula 1), was widely tipped as a potential champion. The amiable Scotsman came oh-so close to fulfilling his dream, even though frequently he was unable to match his less experienced rival Juan Montoya for pace.

The bare statistics tell the tale. Armed with identical Honda/Reynards and Firestone tires, each qualified faster than the other on ten (out of 20) occasions. Franchitti, though, earned two poles to Montoya's seven. Montoya accumulated a better average grid position, 5.0–5.6, and led an amazing total of 954 laps (in 15 different races) during the year (34.5 percent) against 272 (in ten races) for Franchitti. Ultimately, their respective win tallies (seven to three in favor of Montoya) would prove decisive in the championship tie-break.

Despite the statistical imbalance, Franchitti had his chances. A conservative pit strategy cost him a potential victory in the season opener at Homestead. A deflating rear tire resulted in him slipping from first to third at Mid-Ohio. Mechanical problems in successive events at Cleveland and Road America also cost valuable points. Then there was a rare driver error in Vancouver, where Franchitti spun off the road while attempting to pass the Colombian.

By and large, though, Franchitti was a model of consistency. He failed only three times to qualify among the top ten and was fast on all the differing types of race track. An oval victory continued to elude him, but five podium appearances in the first eight races – and 11 in all (against nine for Montoya) – helped him mount a stern challenge for the title. He was a gallant and characteristically gracious runner-up at season's end.

paul tracy

3

Date of birth: December 17, 1968

Residence: Las Vegas, Nevada

Team: Team KOOL Green

Equipment: Honda/Reynard/Firestone

CART starts in 1999: 19

PPG Cup ranking: 3rd

Wins: 2; Poles: 0; Points: 161

AFTER far too long in the wilderness, the *real* Paul Tracy proved a force to be reckoned with in 1999. It was a welcome return to prominence for the enigmatic Canadian, who has still not achieved his ultimate potential after eight years in the Champ Car ranks.

Team owner Barry Green deserves much of the credit for the resurgence, having stood by Tracy when his critics were enjoying a field day in '98. Green was anxious to find the key that would unlock Tracy's true talent. So, too, was Tony Cicale, who agreed to take on the challenge after a year's sabbatical. Cicale rejoined the fold initially as a consultant, but was obliged to take on more of a leading role when race engineer John Dick left to pursue an opportunity with Arciero-Wells Racing. The new partnership clicked almost immediately.

As the season unfolded, a new Paul Tracy emerged – one who was at peace with the world and able to focus entirely on his efforts to win races. The transformation was remarkable. He was far more relaxed than at any other time in his career. He discovered a penchant for amusing, penetrating quotes. More importantly, he put his accident-prone past behind him.

Tracy won twice – at Milwaukee and Houston – and added five more podium finishes. He was forced to sit out the season opener, the legacy of an incident at Surfers Paradise in '98, but quickly developed into a regular pacesetter. His qualifying average was bettered only by Montoya and Franchitti, and while there were a few miscues (including collisions with teammate Franchitti at Gateway and, more controversially, with Michael Andretti at Chicago), errors were kept to a minimum. It was a measure of the new respect engendered within the series that Tracy was voted 'Most Improved Driver' by his peers.

adrian fernandez

4

Date of birth: April 20, 1965

Residence: Paradise Valley, Arizona

Team: Patrick Racing

Equipment: Ford/Swift,

Reynard/Firestone

CART starts in 1999: 16

PPG Cup ranking: 6th

Wins: 2; Poles: 0; Points: 140

COMPARED to 1998, Adrian Fernandez finished one place lower in the overall PPG Cup rankings, but one notch higher in our estimation. And that was despite missing four races following an accident during practice in Detroit that left him with a broken arm. Fernandez's progress also was hindered by some indecision from Patrick Racing, especially in the early part of the season when he shuffled back and forth between Swift and Reynard chassis.

After winter oval testing with the new Swift proved disappointing, Fernandez switched to a '98 Reynard for the opener at Homestead. He qualified on the front row, only to crash in the race following an engine failure while running fourth. Three weeks later, in a hastily prepared and updated '97 chassis, he scored a finely judged victory at Twin-Ring Motegi – his second in two visits to Japan. Then at Long Beach he guided the Swift to a strong fourth-place finish.

Fernandez rose above the confusion by deciding that his best interests would be served by concentrating on the Reynard. He duly did so, although Pat Patrick's belated order for a brand-new 99I meant that its appearance had to wait until Round 8 at Portland. Fernandez was immediately competitive, although in Toronto he was forced to use another updated backup '97 car and produced one of the single most impressive drives of the season as he rose from 23rd on the grid to sixth. Despite the interruption due to injury, Fernandez never missed a beat, adding a second victory – once again in the '97 car – in the tragedy-marred finale at Fontana.

The amiable and hard-working Fernandez has established rapturous support in his homeland, where he is regarded as a major celebrity. As a result of his performances this year, his stock has risen dramatically, too, in the United States.

5

christian fittipaldi

Date of birth: January 18, 1971

Residence: Key Biscayne, Florida

Team: Newman/Haas Racing

Equipment: Ford/Swift/Firestone

CART starts in 1999: 15

PPG Cup ranking: 7th

Wins: 1; Poles: 1; Points: 121

CHRISTIAN Fittipaldi, like Paul Tracy, emerged from the wilderness in 1999. And unfortunately, in common with Adrian Fernandez, a mid-season injury prevented him from making a proper challenge for the PPG Cup title. Until then, Fittipaldi had displayed a new-found confidence that had been lacking virtually throughout his Champ Car career, which began in '95.

The ovals have always been a stumbling block for the personable Brazilian, and while the Rio track (named in honor of his uncle Emerson, who also served as race promoter in '99) might be somewhat unconventional, Fittipaldi provided a useful boost for his confidence by snaring the pole and running well to finish third. He drove a cautious race at Michigan Speedway, but finished on the lead lap in eighth, while at Fontana he enjoyed a spell in the lead before securing a podium result.

Fittipaldi's bread and butter has always been the road and street circuits, and after coming close to a win on numerous occasions, he finally took a well-deserved maiden victory at Road America. True, he had to rely on a mechanical problem for Juan Montoya to snatch the advantage, but Fittipaldi was clearly best of the rest that day in Wisconsin. The real measure of his ability came next time out in Toronto, where he qualified only fifth, but made an opportunist dive to the inside of teammate Michael Andretti at the first corner. At last, here was an example of the aggressive style that had marked him as a man to watch in the formative stages of his career in Europe. These days, as competitive as the FedEx Championship Series has become, a legitimate contender must be able to find the right balance between forcefulness and discretion. Judging by his form in 1999, Fittipaldi has what it takes to mount a serious championship offensive.

roberto moreno

6

Date of birth: February 11, 1959

Residence: Fort Lauderdale, Florida

Teams: PacWest Racing and
Newman/Haas Racing

Equipment: Mercedes/Reynard/Firestone
and Ford/Swift/Firestone

CART starts in 1999: 13

PPG Cup ranking: 14th

Wins: 0; Poles: 0; Points: 58

THE story of Roberto Moreno's season is about as unusual as one could imagine. The veteran was without a ride when the FedEx Championship Series began at Homestead. Worse, there were no real prospects for the 40-year-old Brazilian. He had undertaken a couple of tests for Bettenhausen Motorsports during the winter, but that door had been closed when several sponsorship possibilities failed to materialize. Instead Moreno grasped an opportunity to join the fledgling Truscelli Racing IRL team for the Indianapolis 500; but when PacWest's Mark Blundell was injured in a test at Gateway in early May, Moreno's recent (and past) oval-track experience made him the logical choice as a replacement for the forthcoming race at Rio. He wasn't able to repeat his front-row performance of two years earlier, when he filled in for Christian Fittipaldi at Newman/Haas Racing, but he did earn kudos for a fine drive to 11th after starting 23rd. Next time out at Gateway, Moreno took advantage of an excellent fuel strategy and led the Motorola 300 in his Motorola-backed Mercedes/Reynard before finishing fourth. It was just the tonic he – and the team – needed.

Moreno gelled immediately with the PacWest engineers, earning praise for his work ethic and technical feedback. After he finished fourth in Toronto, there were more than a few long faces when he left the fold following Round 12 at Michigan. Even then, despite not contesting the first five races, he had moved up to 12th in the points. He was not out of work for long. Ironically, just a few days after the U.S. 500, Fittipaldi was injured while testing at Gateway. 'Super Sub' was called upon again. He responded by out-qualifying team leader Michael Andretti in three of the next four races, culminating in a career-best second place at Laguna Seca.

michael andretti

7

Date of birth: October 5, 1962

Residence: Nazareth, Pennsylvania

Team: Newman/Haas Racing

Equipment: Ford/Swift/Firestone

CART starts in 1999: 20

PPG Cup ranking: 4th

Wins: 1; Poles: 1; Points: 151

THE retirement of Bobby Rahal following the 1998 season left Al Unser Jr. and lifelong friend and rival Michael Andretti as the most experienced contenders among the Champ Car field. In the previous few seasons, Andretti's hopes of adding a long overdue second PPG Cup title to his lone triumph in 1991 had been thwarted by a variety of technical issues. This time, after Newman/Haas Racing elected to make a late switch from Goodyear to Firestone tires, there could be no excuses.

It's true, the belated decision didn't allow the team's engineers much time to tune the Swift chassis to the different characteristics of the Firestones, but that didn't seem to be much of a handicap. In the opener at Homestead, Andretti cost himself a chance of victory by stalling in the pits. Ditto at Motegi. He accumulated useful points, finishing seventh and sixth, respectively, in the next two races, then was struck by a spate of rare Ford engine failures throughout the weekend at Rio, before bouncing back to score a fine victory at Gateway. After six races, Andretti lay a mere eight points adrift of series leader Juan Montoya. Everything was looking good. But at Milwaukee he was involved in a horrifying accident in the pit lane when he mistook Team Manager Ed Nathman's instruction and attempted to leave before his crew had finished its service, inflicting lingering injuries on fueler Ty Manseau.

It's hard to know whether or not Andretti was distracted during the summer by the imminent arrival of wife Leslie's first baby (Lucca was born on September 16), but the fact is he made far too many mistakes for a man of his experience. Consequently, while he possessed the speed, to his intense frustration, Andretti allowed his championship aspirations to slip away.

helio castro-neves

8

Date of birth: May 10, 1975

Residence: Miami, Florida

Team: Hogan Racing

Equipment: Mercedes/Lola/Firestone

CART starts in 1999: 20

PPG Cup ranking: 15th

Wins: 0; Poles: 1; Points: 48

HELIO Castro-Neves came of age in 1999 after three years spent largely in the shadow of close friend Tony Kanaan. The pair had joined Steve Horne's Marlboro/Tasman Indy Lights team together in 1996 after pursuing separate careers in Europe. Each displayed prodigious talent, but it was Kanaan who emerged ahead following that first North American campaign, and who secured the championship in 1997 after Castro-Neves allowed a handsome advantage to slip away in the final stages. They graduated into the Champ Car ranks together in '98, but once more it was Kanaan who held the upper hand as he claimed the coveted Jim Trueman Rookie of the Year Award – thanks in no small part to more competitive equipment.

But the momentum shifted in 1999. Okay, Kanaan was first to gain a pole (Long Beach) and a race win (Michigan Speedway), but while he retained a superior technical package with Forsythe Championship Racing's Honda/Reynard, it was Castro-Neves who earned more credit with his enthusiastic and skilled accomplishments with Hogan Racing's unfancied Mercedes/Lola.

After posting some promising times during winter testing, Castro-Neves was reduced to tears when Tony Bettenhausen told him shortly before the start of the season that he did not have enough sponsorship to proceed. Luckily, Carl Hogan came to the rescue. The youngster showed his gratitude with a string of fine performances. Sadly, he was often thwarted by technical problems, but not before making his mark. Highlights included passing Juan Montoya incisively twice at Nazareth and claiming the pole (plus a second place) at Milwaukee. His championship hopes were shattered by 12 DNFs. Only two, however, were self-inflicted. His positive attitude in the face of adversity was as impressive as his speed. There is much more to come.

max papis

9

Date of birth: October 3, 1969

Residence: Miami Beach, Florida

Team: Team Rahal

Equipment: Ford/Reynard/Firestone

CART starts in 1999: 20

PPG Cup ranking: 5th

Wins: 0; Poles: 1; Points: 150

MUCH was expected of the ebullient Italian, who, after three years of valuable experience with Arciero-Wells Racing, was invited to fill the breach left by the retirement of Bobby Rahal. Papis was undaunted by the prospect of filling the shoes of a three-time champion. He displayed considerable promise during winter testing and, after qualifying only 15th for the first race at Homestead, parlayed a sensible drive into a top-five finish. It was to set the tone for his season. He was out-qualified more often than not by teammate Bryan Herta (who placed fourth overall on average grid positions versus 11th for Papis), but frequently he made good progress in the races. Just two retirements (against eight for Herta) enabled him to score well in the points chase.

A seven-race sequence between Rio and Toronto saw Papis qualify among the top ten only once, but he drove well to garner four top-five finishes. Then he posted a magnificent performance in the U.S. 500, controlling the race until, cruelly, running out of fuel on the last lap. The manner in which he coped with the disappointment spoke volumes of his character. In tears as he pulled into the pits, he swiftly composed himself and graciously accepted his fate.

Curiously for one brought up on the road courses of Europe, it was the ovals that provided his best results. Papis secured his first pole at Chicago and was looking good at Fontana, too, until fuel strategy once more conspired against him. The ultimate result continued to prove elusive, but Papis added six top-five finishes from the final eight races, including a brace of runner-up placings at Surfers Paradise (where, ironically, an 'alternative' fuel strategy finally worked in his favor) and Fontana, to round out an entirely satisfactory campaign.

gil de ferran

10

Date of birth: November 11, 1967

Residence: Fort Lauderdale, Florida

Team: Walker Racing

Equipment: Honda/Reynard/Goodyear

CART starts in 1999: 20

PPG Cup ranking: 8th

Wins: 1; Poles: 2; Points: 108

EIGHTH in the PPG Cup standings represented a thoroughly disappointing result for Gil de Ferran, Walker Racing and Goodyear. Even though the tire giant had seen its representation dwindle to just four teams over the course of the previous three years, preseason expectations were high following some encouraging tests. De Ferran rebounded from a heavy crash (due to engine failure) in qualifying at Homestead to finish a strong sixth. He took the pole at Motegi and, despite spinning before the green flag, recovered to finish second. Paradoxically, given Goodyear's impressive record on the short ovals in recent years, de Ferran struggled on the one-mile tracks at Nazareth and Milwaukee, but was a pace-setter virtually everywhere else in the first half of the season. He won at Portland, taking full advantage of an excellent strategy conceived by Derrick Walker and his team. The victory was richly deserved, the reward for a great deal of hard work by the personable Brazilian and Walker Racing, which carried out the lion's share of Goodyear's development.

Following another second place at Cleveland (where de Ferran's tires were no match for Juan Montoya's Firestones in drying conditions), only the Colombian lay ahead in the PPG Cup points table. Then the wheels came off. De Ferran scored only 21 points from the final 11 races. He was forced out by engine failure at Road America. In Toronto, after claiming a second pole, he collided with Christian Fittipaldi in the pit lane and failed to finish. The remainder of the season was punctuated by some uncharacteristic errors (the most blatant of which occurred in Detroit, when he hit the wall during a pace-car period) as Goodyear failed to match the improvement managed by Firestone and he strove too hard to make up the deficit.

IF the success of Goodyear's 1999 CART season were judged solely on the number of wins posted by the race tire manufacturer, it would appear to a casual observer to be a disappointing season indeed. However, despite posting only one win in the 20-race 1999 season, Goodyear's race-tire engineers made significant progress in their development and performance efforts, even though the tiremaker was hampered by having only four CART teams running on Goodyear tires.

'At the conclusion of the 1998 CART season, we realized that while our tire performance on the oval tracks was competitive, our tire performance on the road and street courses had room for improvement,' said Stu Grant, Goodyear's general manager for global race tires. 'As a result, one of our goals going into this season was to improve significantly on our CART road and street course performance.'

Goodyear's CART engineering team worked throughout the winter and made extensive changes to its CART operations from last season in order to strengthen Goodyear's race-tire performance. The biggest, and most exciting change, was the tire technology gained from the company's Formula One successes. By transferring that knowledge and experience to its CART operations following the company's withdrawal from F1 competition in 1998, they were able to develop a more competitive product.

'What we learned over the years in F1 transferred very well to CART's road and street courses,' Grant added. 'The results posted by Goodyear-equipped teams on these types of courses speak for themselves.'

The highlight of Goodyear's road and street course performances was undoubtedly the Budweiser/G.I. Joe 500 at Portland International Raceway's permanent road course. It was here that Walker Racing's Gil de Ferran, driving on Goodyear Eagles, posted the tiremaker's CART win after an impressive third-place qualifying effort. Two weeks earlier at the Miller Lite 225 at Wisconsin's Milwaukee

Mile, de Ferran posted another podium finish by grabbing third place.

De Ferran's hot streak away from the ovals didn't stop with his Portland win. At the Medic Drug Grand Prix of Cleveland, he drove the Goodyear-equipped Honda/Reynard to a second-place qualifying and finishing position, followed closely by Marlboro Team Penske's Al Unser Jr. finishing in fifth position. Unser's Goodyear Eagle wet tires were credited with helping him drive from a starting position of 14th on the grid to a top-five finish in what can only be described as a wet and wild race.

Goodyear's good fortune continued when de Ferran grabbed the pole at Toronto's Molson Indy and then posted impressive performances by qualifying third at both the Texaco/Havoline 200 and the Detroit Grand Prix.

By the season's end, Goodyear-equipped drivers had claimed one pole, five top-three qualifying positions and two podium finishes on CART's road and street courses.

Goodyear's performance on the CART ovals was equally balanced, with de Ferran's pole and second-place finish at Motegi and a third-place finish at Milwaukee.

'Racing is, among other things, a numbers game,' Grant said. 'We made the best of a challenging situation, having only four or five Goodyear-equipped cars in a field of approximately 25 cars on race day. Couple those odds with a few crashes and mechanical problems, and the odds of a Goodyear-equipped car crossing the finish line first are reduced significantly.

'A lot of credit goes out to our team partners – Marlboro Team Penske, Walker Racing, Bettenhausen Motorsports and All American Racers – for their efforts, feedback and co-operation they provided us this season during the CART races and tire tests,' Grant added. 'The technological advances we made would certainly not have been possible without them.'

An exciting CART season was not without tragedy, however, following the deaths of CART drivers Gonzalo Rodriguez and Greg Moore in separate race accidents occurring barely a month and a half apart. 'The racing community lost two very promising young drivers,' Grant said. 'They will, undoubtedly, always be missed and remembered by the racing community,

their friends and family.'

Near the conclusion of the 1999 CART season, Goodyear announced it was taking a sabbatical from open-wheel racing in North America and would not return as a tire supplier to both the CART and Indy Racing League series, choosing instead to concentrate its efforts on the other forms of racing with which the company is involved.

'The company has enjoyed a long and successful history in motorsports competition around the world,' Grant said. 'Our long-standing commitment to racing has made this an agonizing decision. We are firmly committed to our successful supplier and marketing partnership with NASCAR, as well as our commitment to many other racing series to which Goodyear is a tire supplier.'

Despite its exit from both CART and IRL, Goodyear has left the door open for an eventual return to open-wheel racing in North America, as well as a return to F1 competition, at some point in the future. Until then, look for the Goodyear Racing Eagles to continue to fly high at racetracks around the country as able competitors in a variety of racing series.

Above: A change of Eagles for Valvoline Walker Racing's Gil de Ferran.

Over the years, Goodyear has been fortunate to have long-enduring partnerships with great racing teams such as Dan Gurney's AAR Eagle *(centre left)* and Roger Penske's Team Penske *(bottom left)*.

Al Unser jr *(top left)* retires from CART competition as two-time champion, whilst 1999 Portland winner Gil de Ferran *(near left)* takes over his ride at Penske.

Michael C. Brown

GREG MOORE, 1975–1999

The loss of Greg Moore, who sustained fatal injuries in a horrific accident during the early stages of the season finale at California Speedway on October 31, shocked the entire auto racing world.

Moore, 24, was an extremely likable young man, admired and respected both by his peers and his countless fans around the world. He was a fearless racer who was driving hurt, having sustained a broken bone and several lacerations to his right hand after being knocked from his motor scooter by an inattentive driver in the motor-home area the previous day.

Typically, after missing qualifying, Moore insisted on starting the race from the back of the grid. He refused to heed several advisers, including his father, Ric, who masterminded Greg's rise to prominence in the sport and always ensured that his son remained humble and loyal to his roots, despite his ever-increasing public visibility.

Greg Moore had a special talent. He developed his skills initially in karting and impressed from the first moment he climbed aboard a race car – at the tender age of 15 – with the Spenard David Racing School in Shannonville, Ontario. The following year, 1991, saw Moore claim Rookie of the Year honors in the extremely competitive Esso Protec Formula (Ford) 1600 Series in his native Canada. In '92, again as a rookie, he ventured south across the border to win the USAC Formula 2000

West Series. A special dispensation was required from CART before Moore could make his next step up the ladder, graduating directly into the PPG-Firestone Indy Lights Championship several weeks before his 18th birthday. He qualified seventh and finished fifth on his debut with his family-run team, and went on to place eighth in the championship. Two years later, after already earning support from the Player's Driver Development Program (through the recommendation of his first race car driving school instructor, Richard Spenard), Moore was snapped up and given a long-term contract by CART team owner Jerry Forsythe.

Moore displayed his gratitude in spades by dominating the Indy Lights field in 1995, winning all but two of the 12 races. The only exceptions were at Detroit, where he was narrowly beaten by 1992 series champion Robbie Buhl, and, ironically, in front of his home crowd in Vancouver, where he was inadvertently punted out of the lead following a mid-race restart.

Moore's graduation into the Champ Car ranks in '96 was equally meteoric. He might well have won on his debut at Homestead but for a controversial stop-go penalty assessed for a pit-lane transgression. Moore, though, fought back into contention, unlapping himself on race-winner Jimmy Vasser en route to a seventh-place finish. While a victory continued to prove elusive during his rookie campaign, a runner-

up finish at Nazareth and two more podium appearances cemented his status as a young man to watch.

For a variety of reasons, Moore did not achieve his ultimate capability during four years with the Player's/Forsythe Racing Champ Car team. He became the youngest man ever to win a Champ Car race when he triumphed at Milwaukee during his sophomore season – and backed up that success by winning again in Detroit the following weekend. Just as it appeared he might mount a concerted attack on the championship, however, his challenge collapsed due to a series of incidents and mechanical woes. Subsequent years progressed in a similar vein. In 1999, indeed, Moore began with a masterful display at Homestead by winning from the pole. Unfortunately, that was to remain the highlight of another disappointing campaign.

Yet for 2000 the prospects looked extremely bright. Moore had finally broken the umbilical cord with Forsythe, signing instead a lucrative new deal with a rejuvenated Marlboro Team Penske. Armed with the proven Honda/Reynard/Firestone package and joining forces with the most successful team in Champ Car history, he was expected to become a bona fide championship challenger and would surely have increased his tally of five wins and five poles. Tragically, his promise will remain largely unfulfilled.

Tributes

Championship Auto Racing Teams President and CEO Andrew Craig: 'Greg was one of the best and clearly had all the potential to be a series champion. He was also a fine individual who was much admired for his positive attitude and approach.'

Player's Ltd. President Jean-Paul Blais: 'Greg was more than an outstanding race car driver with a brilliant future. He had a passion for the sport and a zest for life. He was a person with an engaging personality, a friend to everyone in the racing community and a true ambassador for the sport.'

Player's/Forsythe Racing teammate Patrick Carpentier: 'I feel privileged that I had the opportunity to be Greg's teammate the last two seasons. I had a great deal of respect and admiration for him, both as a professional and as a person, and I think every driver in the CART series felt the same way.'

Michael C. Brown

WALTER PAYTON, 1954–1999

Merely one day after the death of Greg Moore at Fontana came news from Chicago that NFL Hall of Fame running back and Payton/Coyne Racing co-owner Walter Payton, 45, was dead – claimed in the end not by the liver disease he told the world about the previous February, but by cancer of the bile duct.

Payton, who holds several National Football League records – career rushing (16,726 yards), 100-yard games (77), most yards gained in a single game (275), and others – never disclosed the cancer that would deny him the liver transplant he said he needed. Doctors, detailing the pro football star's medical situation at the time of his death, explained that Payton was not eligible for a transplant because of his cancer.

The athlete called 'Sweetness' tacked a sporting chapter to his career history book following his retirement from the NFL in the late 1980s. He earned an SCCA competition license and showed great enthusiasm as a driver in both Sports 2000 and Trans-Am, although he was never able to step far enough away from his business commitments to think about racing full-time.

On the Chicago Bears team board of directors, he also owned the Walter Payton Roundhouse Complex and a part of both Walter Payton Power Equipment and Payton/Coyne Racing, the Illinois-based Champ Car team.

'Walter exemplified class, and all of us in sports should honor him by striving to perpetuate his standard of excellence,' said NFL Commissioner Paul Tagliabue. 'Walter was an inspiration in everything he did. The tremendous grace and dignity he displayed in his final months reminded us again why "Sweetness" was the perfect nickname.'

Added Champ Car team co-owner Dale Coyne, 'All of us in the racing community have lost a great friend and competitor. We will all remember the fun times that Walter brought to all of us.'

Loved and respected well beyond the borders of Chicago, Payton left behind wife Connie and two children, Jarrett and Brittney.

In Memoriam

Emil Andres, who attended every Indianapolis 500 since 1928 – and competed in nine of them – died July 20 following a fall at his home in Flossmoor, Illinois. His best result at Indy came in 1946, when he placed fourth and secured his largest-ever purse, $10,000. Andres scored his most important victory two years later at Milwaukee, driving an Offy-powered Kurtis, and retired after competing at the same track in 1950. He became an official with AAA and, later, USAC. Andres also served as President and Honorary Chairman of the 500 Oldtimers Club. He was 88.

Tom Binford, who succumbed to a cerebral hemorrhage January 14, at age 74, was the longest serving Chief Steward of the Indianapolis 500, holding the post from 1974 through 1995. He was a founder of the United States Auto Club in 1955, serving as president from 1957 until 1969, and remained as a director until his death. He was a hugely respected member of the Indiana business community through his own companies, Binford Lumber and D.A. Lubricant, and was active in many civic projects. He assisted in the formation of the Indiana Pacers pro basketball team.

Herb Porter, one of the sport's foremost engine builders, died June 16 at age 84. 'Herbie Horsepower' succumbed to injuries sustained 27 days earlier in an auto accident – the day before he was inducted into the Indianapolis Motor Speedway Hall of Fame. Born in Texas and raised in Kansas, Porter was around engines virtually all his life. His big breakthrough came at Indianapolis in 1968, when Bobby Unser earned his first '500' victory using a Porter-tuned Offenhauser. Later he founded Speedway Engine Development, Inc., based in Gasoline Alley, Indianapolis.

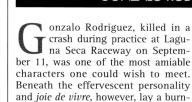

Robert Laberge/Allsport/USA

GONZALO RODRIGUEZ, 1962–1999

Gonzalo Rodriguez, killed in a crash during practice at Laguna Seca Raceway on September 11, was one of the most amiable characters one could wish to meet. Beneath the effervescent personality and *joie de vivre*, however, lay a burning desire to succeed.

The native of Montevideo, Uruguay, began racing karts at age 13 and was a champion in his first season. Seven years later, he moved to Europe to pursue his passion, starting out in the Spanish Formula Ford Championship, in which he won five races and placed second in the title chase in 1992. He soon graduated into Formula Renault, then switched his attention to England, competing again in Formula Renault and, later, Formula 3. He moved up to Formula 3000 in 1997, initially with the Redman Bright team.

After producing some startling results on a meager budget, he shifted to Team Astromega and emerged as a true front-runner toward the end of the 1998 season, posting the closest challenge to Juan Montoya and earning victories at two of the classic circuits, Spa-Francorchamps and the Nürburgring. The progress continued in 1999 as he added another win at the challenging Monaco street circuit.

Rodriguez's sights had been set initially on Formula 1, but later he switched his attention to the FedEx Championship Series. He was thrilled by the invitation to test last winter for Marlboro Team Penske and, after acquitting himself well, was even more delighted when asked to contest a couple of races in 1999.

'Gonzo' made a solid debut in Detroit, finishing 12th. He was disappointed by the bombshell news that Gil de Ferran and Greg Moore had been signed to drive for Penske in 2000, but pressed on cheerfully, anxious to prove his ability to other would-be employers. Indeed, he was on more than one team owner's shortlist prior to his untimely demise.

THE CHAMELEON

by David Phillips

EVEN for a man who's made a career as a substitute and test driver from CART to Formula 1, Roberto Moreno enjoyed a remarkable 1999 season. The year began, as so many have, with a sketchy plan to drive for an unproved entity – Truscelli Racing's fledgling Indy Racing League team – and concluded with a career-best 14th in the FedEx Championship Series standings.

All told, Moreno made a baker's dozen Champ Car starts – eight with PacWest Racing and five with Newman/Haas Racing in the wake of injuries suffered by Mark Blundell and Christian Fittipaldi respectively.

'I would have been skeptical if somebody had asked me if I was going to do that much this year,' said the 40-year-old Brazilian. 'I would say that I have been fortunate with other people's *un*fortunate situations. One thing I must say is, if somebody had to replace those drivers, I've been very honored that I was the one chosen. That comes to show that, once the teams have their finances into place and *they* can chose who *they* want, I come first on the list.'

The '99 season saw Moreno's second extended stay at Newman/Haas, as he had replaced Fittipaldi under similar circumstances in '97 (and for one race in '98). However, it was his run with PacWest that made people take notice. He earned two fourth-place finishes, led twice and brought the Motorola Mercedes-Benz/Reynard home in the points six times – this for a team whose best previous showing on the season had been Mauricio Gugelmin's seventh-place finish at Twin-Ring Motegi in April.

'What you saw there was the experience that I built up at Newman/Haas in '97, I was able to apply to my performance at PacWest,' says Moreno. 'And my relationships with [race engineers] Allen McDonald and Matt Borland were key factors to my performance as well. We exchanged information, we made progress within the team; and also my relationship with Mauricio [Gugelmin] was very important. We could, each of us, go in a different direction and at the end of the day analyze which changes were good and apply those in the next day.

'So that was two advantages I believe were good there. My experience had built up, and you could see

me perform really well in the ovals as the road courses, whereas in '97 I was in the middle of a big learning curve in the ovals with Newman/Haas.'

Moreno took the change in chassis, engines and teams in his stride when he went from PacWest's Mercedes/Reynard to Newman/Haas' Ford/Swift, promptly out-qualifying Michael Andretti at Detroit and scoring a career-best second place at Laguna Seca before Fittipaldi returned to action. Even more remarkable than his on-track performance, however, was the ease – and professionalism – with which he moved between the two camps.

'You would expect him to come around and say "This is what we did" or "This is how it felt" somewhere else,' says Newman/Haas engineer Todd Bowland. 'But I think he respects the position that he's in – that he really won't talk about what he did [with his previous team]. And I think he's learned that, because we weren't going to tell him anything about our set-up or the way we work if he came to us and said, "At PacWest, this is what we did."'

But there's more to Moreno's

Moreno made the most of the opportunities presented to him.

Opposite: The extreme speed at Michigan led Moreno to use a new style of helmet. For raceday, the entire PacWest team personalized the plain white 'hat' by adding their autographs.

Below: The Brazilian's vast racing knowledge proved a huge asset both to PacWest and Newman/Haas.

ROBERTO MORENO PROFILE

THE CHAMELEON

Togetherness with wife Celia.

Below: Moreno set the fastest lap at Chicago Motor Speedway.

professionalism than discretion. It takes a unique individual to come to a team at a moment's notice, fit in under difficult circumstances, give his enthusiastic best, and not act like – or be perceived as – a threat to the status quo.

'I think most guys would come in and try to be positive,' says Bowland, 'but he didn't come in and try to take Christian's place at all. He treads lightly. He doesn't want to go in this area if it's not his, and I think he understands his position. He wants to be really careful with that, and make sure we don't get offended and say, "You're not coming to take over for Christian here; he's our driver."'

Moreno's chameleon-like abilities are the product of a career that has seldom afforded him a full-time ride, but which has seen him log more miles – testing and pinch-hitting – than many a World Champion. His alma maters include, in no particular order, Benetton and Galles, Lotus and Bettenhausen, Penske and Ferrari, Payton/Coyne and Eurobrun, and now, of course, PacWest and Newman/Haas.

'I made a career out of being a substitute, yes, but I never thought about it,' he says. 'I always was a test driver, raising money that allowed me either to be in the right time or the right place for a break, or I even raised money to go racing.

'Racing is my life. That's how I motivate myself. I don't do anything else. That's difficult for people to understand. I've developed my career longer than other drivers, but in a different way – developing racing cars to be able to go racing, and in that process I became a good test driver. And that helps me fit into situations like this [at PacWest and Newman/Haas].'

It is perhaps fitting that Moreno's 'big chance' in Formula 1 came during 1990/91 when he replaced the injured Alessandro Nannini at Benetton, joining old friend and three-time World Champion Nelson Piquet on the team in time to earn a second-place finish at the '90 Japanese Grand Prix and gain a full-time ride for the following season. But mid-way through the '92 campaign, Moreno was out on the streets, replaced by a brash young German by the name of Michael Schumacher.

Talk to Moreno about the near misses in his career, and you won't hear a word of bitterness or regret.

'I don't call myself unlucky,' he says, without a hint of guile in his voice. 'If it wasn't because of my availability to be prepared for unusual situations, I would have never come this far... Being available this year certainly paid off much more than having a full-time ride with a bad team!'

Indeed. After waiting in the wings for so many years, Moreno appears to have finally landed a full-time ride for the new millennium. And not just any full-time ride: he seems set to drive alongside Adrian Fernandez at Patrick Racing, a team that has more than 40 Champ Car victories to its credit, including two by Fernandez in each of the past two seasons.

While Moreno is delighted with the prospects of driving for one of CART's most storied teams, he will take the same attitude into a 2000 season filled with promise as he did into an uncertain '99 campaign.

'I pray a lot for God to help me continue developing my career in a way that I can help others, like my kids and people around me,' he says. 'Somehow He's always showing me the way. Maybe it's harder than most, but there must be a reason for it and I've learned from it; and I became a better person to live life in the process.'

Not to mention a very remarkable race car driver in the bargain.

Photos: Michael C. Brown

ROBERTO MORENO PROFILE

TEAM KOOL GREEN

BUILDS TOWARDS A CHAMPIONSHIP THROUGH TEAMWORK

Above: Team owner Barry Green and his brother Kim (general manager) survey the situation from Team KOOL Green's position in the pit lane.

TEAM KOOL GREEN ran on a championship pace throughout much of the 1999 CART FedEx Championship Series. Everybody was pulling in the same direction, from Team Owner Barry Green and his brother, General Manager Kim Green, their drivers Dario Franchitti and Paul Tracy, the engineering staff and to every single crew member.

"We had a fantastic season, but I guess you can say we didn't quite put the icing on the cake when we had the opportunity," said Barry Green. "But I'm thrilled about the manner in which we showed what the strength of a team is all about. We had two great drivers and two great teams working as one – using each other to go faster."

I N any other year the tenacity of Franchitti and Tracy, who finished 2–3 in the series and who were dominant in three 1–2 victories, would certainly be an achievement envied by the competition.

Franchitti's 11 podiums were the most by any driver in the series, and he won poles at Mid-Ohio and Australia. Usually the fastest on the street circuits, Franchitti won at Toronto, Detroit and Australia, and finished second at Long Beach and Houston.

Franchitti and his fierce rookie rival Juan Montoya were the class of the field on every type of circuit in 1999. Their final showdown though came down to a 500-mile crapshoot on the large 2-mile oval at California Speedway. When it was over, Franchitti had brought the CART championship down to its closest finish ever, a 212–212 tie with Montoya. By virtue of Montoya's seven wins to Franchitti's three, the rookie from Colombia won the PPG Cup and its million-dollar bonus.

Tracy's third-place finish in the championship was all the more remarkable considering he began the season in the penalty box, serving a one-race suspension for alleged blocking tactics at Australia in October 1998. (Veteran driver Raul Boesel filled in for Tracy at Homestead.) Wins at

Milwaukee and Houston coupled with runner-up finishes at Toronto, Detroit and Mid-Ohio allowed Tracy to reestablish himself as a full-time front-runner. Besides finishing third, tying his highest finish in the series (1993 and 1994), he and his crew earned a pair of season-end awards. Tracy's pit crew won the season-long $50,000 Crafts-man Pit Crew Challenge and for the second time in his nine years in the CART series, Tracy was selected by his fellow drivers as the STP Most Improved Driver.

"They must have really thought I stunk last year," said Tracy. On reflection, Tracy ceased being flippant. "We worked really hard over the winter with a lot of testing that helped me better understand the car. That really has been the biggest difference, along with working with [engineer] Tony Cicale."

Tracy's career totals at season-end included 15 victories and 12 pole positions in 132 starts. To say he understands the value of teamwork in his job and in winning would be an understatement. Most sports fans don't really see auto racing as a team sport like baseball or football. According to Tracy, they really need to open their eyes. He says that just like the stick-and-ball sports, the star, or driver in this case, must have a strong supporting cast.

"I'm just the monkey they put in the car," laughs Tracy, making reference to early unmanned space missions. Tracy's car is no rocket, but it's as close as you can get on land when you consider the speeds he reaches with a powerful Honda engine and a fresh set of Firestones. His type of car has been clocked at more than 245 mph, higher than the speed needed for Boeing 747 jumbo jets to take off. So, he must have absolute faith in the car and in his crew that works on it.

"I cannot do what I do without having complete confidence in the people around me," he explains. "These guys are my teammates. Nobody can have a bad day on a Sunday if we are going to win races. It's not just me or the guy with the heaviest foot that comes out on top. It's the best team that wins. We have to have flawless work from the pit crew over the wall and an excellent race strategy from our engineering staff. A lot of teamwork goes into taking the checkered flag."

While the drivers get the credit – or sometimes take the blame – their race engineers like Don Halliday (Franchitti) and Tony Cicale (Tracy) provided the set-ups that are the key to success.

Tracy's season began with John Dick returning for a second year to engineer the #26 KOOL car. But Dick left the team

three races into the season (after Long Beach). Some teams would have fallen apart under similar circumstances. Barry Green, however, was able to rally the troops and turn Tracy's season around. Green persuaded Tony Cicale to step-up his involvement with the team and assume full engineering duties on the race weekends. Green also coerced the team's aerodynamicist (and former race engineer) Tino Belli to assume Tracy's engineering responsibilities at tests and assist at many races.

According to Halliday, this was the point the #26 and #27 teams started to work as one. That may have been just the right ingredient, missing from the previous season to get both Tracy and Franchitti consistently at the front in their Honda/ Reynard/Firestone package.

"At that point we really had to funnel the thought process of all concerned for the good of both drivers. Because of that we were then able to use both drivers' performance to reference better improvements... of the whole team. So after that point I think you saw the team on average grow in qualifying and races," explained Halliday.

Cicale put aside his other plans to remain with the team. He said, "Paul says that I've helped him a lot and certainly he's helped me a lot. It's always a two-way street. When you give something

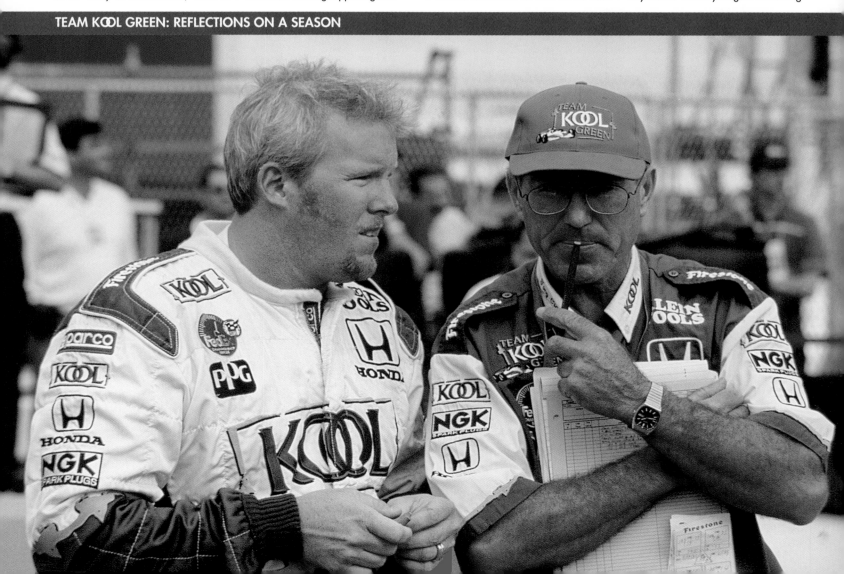

Below far left: Paul Tracy and his crew chief Tony Cicale. The pairing of the hard-charging racer and the seasoned professional paid dividends as the season progressed.

Left: Paul celebrates on the podium after his victory at the Milwaukee Mile.

Below left: Tucked into the cockpit and ready for business.

Below: Relaxing in the motorhome with wife Liisa.

you get something in return. I decided to stay on because I thought we were successful. Though I was helping him, he was helping the team."

Cicale's calm insight helped harness the raw energy that surged in Tracy. The driver is quick to credit his engineer. "When Tony came on board I knew what his credentials were, everybody does. He instantly gives you confidence."

They started a dialogue that not only helped Tracy but also helped the whole team take on the positive attitude that makes champions.

"I feel very comfortable criticizing him because I think that he realizes that I'm doing it not to criticize or praise him but to help make sure that he doesn't make that mistake down the road," added Cicale.

Halliday, who had a full season with Franchitti in 1998, was more than ready to take up the task of a championship battle. They were on the same wavelength.

"Over time you build up a rapport; I liken it to a sixth sense. I can sense what he's going to say. You see very little of the driver through the helmet, but you get a sense – from the eyes, the way the head is held and the way the hands move – of what he's trying to say. Not that he says very much, but it's enough typically to be able to do something to help him."

Green, the team owner, like his engineers has a strong track record of being able to get the most out of people around him, whether from a driver or a crew member. As a team manager beginning back in 1979, Green enjoyed a lot of success helping guide the careers of big name drivers like Danny Sullivan, Michael Andretti, Bobby Rahal, and Al Unser Jr. Making the jump to the ownership level in 1994, Green partnered with Gerry Forsythe to nurture a talented and brash rookie by the name of Jacques Villeneuve. One year later, Green parted ways with Forsythe and carried Villeneuve to an Indy 500 victory, as well as a CART PPG Cup championship.

"Keeping the chemistry right is a key factor in the success of any race team. Without it, it doesn't matter how good your drivers, engineers, crew or race car is," says the man who should know. Green has been involved in 30 CART victories as a manager or team owner. "Our type of racing is a highly competitive environment and we've got two of the best drivers and crews at Team KOOL Green. Naturally there will be an internal rivalry between Paul and Dario, as well as between their crews. That's good for the team. But the philosophy on my team is that it is a single team. We always work together."

Team chemistry has been put to the test a few times at Team KOOL Green. At Houston in 1998, Franchitti was leading the race and being chased by Tracy in second. The teammates bumped tires,

sending Tracy's car against a concrete wall. Tracy limped back into the pits and Franchitti was able to continue and win.

This past season, they tangled on the Memorial Day weekend race at Gateway International Raceway near St. Louis. This time, Tracy was running second and Franchitti was third when the two came together on lap 148 (of 236). Tracy's car hit the wall and he was unable to continue. Franchitti's car went into a slide, but he punched the throttle and saved his car from spinning. It was the kind of incident that can turn one team with two cars into two one-car teams, with everyone taking sides. Green would have none of it.

"After that one [in May], we had some very, very serious meetings," Green admitted. "Mistakes are OK, but you need to learn from them. I sat both drivers down and reminded them that the object of the game is to beat the other guys. I laid it out for both of them that we are a team and that they are teammates."

Franchitti added; "There was never any problem between Paul and myself.

The fact is we have equally fast cars and we are both capable of winning. It's only natural that at some point in a race, we'll find ourselves trying to pass each other. We just need to use our heads and consider all of the consequences in doing it."

Barry Green wasn't worried and it would turn out that things did get sorted out. Franchitti was able to continue, finishing third behind race-winner Michael Andretti and runner-up Helio Castro-Neves. It was his fourth podium and he closed to within four points of Montoya (69–65). But it might have been the low point of Tracy's season.

At the next race in Milwaukee, Tracy answered his critics and ended a two-year winless drought with his 14th career victory. And to do it, Tracy stretched his final 35 gallons of fuel over 101 laps. Green and his engineering staff had gambled with a two-stop pit strategy in the 225-lap race and needed to survive just five more laps.

"We took a big gamble and as soon as I went on the restart, the fuel-pressure warning light came on, and I said, 'Oh, #@#!$#@, we're going to

be out of fuel in a lap'," Tracy recalls. "We did the five laps and it was still running at the end. We were definitely running on fumes. It was a great call by Barry and Tony [Cicale]."

Teamwork paid off again in Toronto a few weeks later, as Green was able to enjoy the team's first of three 1–2 finishes by Franchitti and Tracy. Franchitti started second, but took the lead from Gil de Ferran at Turn 3 and led all 95 laps, jumping back into second in the point standings, just seven points behind Montoya (113–96).

In winning his first race of the season and fourth of his CART career, Franchitti chased away the jinxes that prevented him from finishing his earlier two appearances in Toronto. In 1998, he was leading with less than 8 laps to go when he spun out of the race due to a brake problem. He was on the pole in his rookie year of 1997 for Hogan Racing, but got taken out in the first corner.

"It's about time I finished a race in Toronto," said Franchitti. "I've made it difficult on myself the last couple of years and it was a great way to do it

for the team with a 1–2 finish."

Three weeks later in Detroit, Team KOOL Green did it again. Franchitti led Tracy home to another 1–2 finish, taking the championship lead (136– 131) from Montoya who crashed out and failed to score any points.

Over the next five races, Montoya stretched out to a comfortable lead in the standings with a 28-point advantage over Franchitti (199–171). At Round 18 in Houston however, Montoya was snake-bitten and the Team KOOL Green completed the hat trick with yet another 1–2 result. This time, Tracy led the way en route to his 15th career win. He led 85 laps, after pole-sitter Montoya made an unforced error, crashing into Helio Castro-Neves' stranded car on lap 13.

Once again it proved Barry Green's confidence in Tracy. And after the race, Tracy described his race in this colorful way: "I hate to say that any place owed me one, but I definitely stuck that boot [race winner's trophy] right in my ass last year. It's better to have the gold boot in my hand than in my butt. I got it right this year."

Skeptics were ready to hand Montoya the PPG Cup prior to Houston and as it turned out they were extremely premature. The next race in Australia was pure Team KOOL Green steamroller with Franchitti behind the wheel.

In the team's short but storied history, one of the few things that has eluded it is a win in Surfers Paradise, Australia – the Green family's native land. That changed in 1999 with a large part of the family in attendance.

As it turned out it was a perfect weekend for Franchitti, earning all 22 points for the pole (1), most laps led (1) and the victory (20) at the seaside street circuit. He regained the points lead (209–200) from Montoya who had another unforced error and scored no points.

"What can you say about that?" Dario asked rhetorically. "We came to Australia, hoping for a 22-point weekend. We were just working towards that and it happened. It's pretty amazing. I heard on the radio that there was a local yellow in Turn 9. When I found out Juan was out of the race, it was a big relief because of the points situation. It's never nice when something like that happens to a competitor, but we needed it."

The final weekend of the season at California Speedway in Fontana was billed as a title fight between Montoya and Franchitti. However, the race and championship became secondary with the tragic loss of Greg Moore.

Franchitti and Tracy were the best of friends with Moore, sharing a lot of good times together. They competed hard together on track and put racing behind them to have fun while away from the track. As hard as it is

to concede a title, the loss of a friend and respected rival overrode the day.

In the race, Franchitti and his crew experienced problems changing a right rear tire on lap 72 that required a stop under green and he lost two laps to the leaders. In the closing laps, Franchitti was told to drive it hard and he was charging through the field. He had made up one lap, but came up just a little short. He was running ninth when he needed to pit for a splash-and-go, which cost him one position and the championship to the tiebreaker. He finished 10th, while his teammate Tracy retired much earlier (lap 141) with an electrical problem. Montoya finished fourth to become 1999 PPG Cup champion.

About the missed opportunity of winning the championship, Green said, "We had a little mistake. During a stop, for whatever reason, a wheel wasn't put on right and Dario had to come back in the next lap. He was as fast as anyone and was running fifth at the time. I promise you, without that mistake, we would have won the championship.

"Remember this though, the same crew that made the mistake in the pits was the same team that got us to second in the championship. It was a mistake by one of the pit crew guys – probably the one that I would consider our best. You can be sure that even after the mistake, I wouldn't trade him for anyone."

Green added, "I think that the secret of Team KOOL Green is to make sure everyone understands that no one's bigger than the team, and that team is absolutely everything. We win or lose as a team and everybody here understands that."

Above left: Don Halliday and Dario in deep discussion during a practice session.

Above: The trappings of success. Dario enjoys a ride in his Ferrari.

Left: Another win for Franchitti and Team KOOL Green at Surfers Paradise.

Below: Jonny Kane listens to Dario Franchitti's advice on aspects of racecraft.

Bottom: The four Team KOOL Green drivers for 1999. Jonny Kane, Alex Gurney, Paul Tracy and Dario Franchitti.

CHAMPIONSHIP contenders can't rest on their laurels. In order to keep at the front, Team KOOL Green has its own farm system much like professional baseball teams.

Team owner Barry Green said, "It's been very important, not only trying to find future drivers of tomorrow for the Champ car program, but also to find personnel, mechanics, engineers and truck drivers."

The responsibility for overseeing the driver development program lies with Kim Green, general manager of Team KOOL Green. "When Barry and I are scouting drivers, we're looking for someone with the potential to be very successful in a Champ car. Dario Franchitti and Paul Tracy sit in our Champ cars now, but I'm sure that in a couple of seasons you'll see some young guys nipping at their heels."

The 1999 season saw Team KOOL Green working with two drivers with the sort of potential the "Greens" are looking for. Jonny Kane, who has been a champion at every level he has contested in his racing career, drove the Team KOOL Green's Indy Lights car. Kane was joined in the driver development program by Alex Gurney, who drove for TKG in the 1998 Barber Dodge Pro Series before stepping up to his Team KOOL Green ride in the 1999 KOOL/Toyota Atlantic Championship.

Kane, a native of Northern Ireland, came to America to further his racing career. From his early beginnings in karting to the British Formula 3 Championship, the wiry Kane has fought hard to win races and ultimately championships. In 1994, he displayed considerable skill to capture both British and European Formula Ford

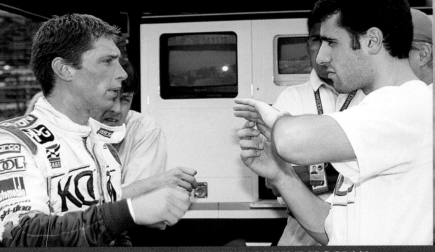

TEAM KOOL GREEN: DRIVER DEVELOPMENT PROGRAM

TEAM KOOL GREEN'S FARM SYSTEM

thinking about a racing career.

O.K., but why the University of Colorado?

"Number One, I got in!" laughs Alex. "Seriously, I was looking to get out of California and live away from home for a while. I had a few friends who were already going to the University of Colorado. I visited the campus and fell in love with the place.

"Boulder's a couple of thousand miles away from Southern California, but the lifestyles are very similar: laid-back, with lots of things to do out of doors," he says. "But the weather was a real shock. I learned real fast I don't like the cold."

Although the cold weather and presence of the nearby ski resorts enabled Alex to trade his surfboard for a snowboard, it wasn't long before his racing heritage surfaced.

"I spent most of my free time at a go-kart track near Boulder," he says. "It's out in the middle of nowhere, a mile long and it's the most awesome go-kart track I've ever seen."

His passion for karting was just the tip of the iceberg. By his senior year Alex had convinced his parents to let him try his hand at racing, and he promptly earned rookie of the year honors in the 1997 Skip Barber Midwestern Dodge Series. After graduating with a bachelor's degree in business administration, Gurney began his "post-graduate" work as a professional driver.

"I'm glad I went to college," he says. "It's an experience that a lot of people in racing don't have. Besides, in racing you can't get by anymore on just driving fast. With the importance of commercial sponsorship you've got to be on top of things business-wise as well."

In 1997, Gurney won 10 of 14 races in the Skip Barber Midwestern Dodge Series. For his efforts, he collected Rookie of the Year honors. More importantly, however, he thoroughly impressed the management of Team KOOL Green. He spent the 1998 season, running for Team KOOL Green by learning the ins-and-outs of the Barber Dodge Pro Series. He finished 10th in the series championship in a season highlighted by four top-10 finishes, including two top-fives and the first pole of his professional career at Homestead. He felt ready for the next step.

"Driving for Team KOOL Green in the Atlantic series last season was an awesome experience," said Gurney. "I showed my rookie colors at times, but that's part of the learning curve and I felt I improved every time I got in the car."

Gurney qualified in the top-10 eight times and posted five top-10 finishes, including a season-high fifth-place result at the Canadian Grand Prix in Montreal.

Gurney and Kane certainly appear to be on top of things as a part of Team KOOL Green's ongoing driver development program. It's clear that they are on the path for future success. Now all they have to do is keep working hard, be determined, learn and oh yeah... win races. They both know that winning and patience will lead to their next opportunity.

---

championships. Around this time, he caught the eye of his racing mentor and former Formula One champion Jackie Stewart. In 1995, Kane led Stewart's Formula Vauxhall team to the championship as a rookie. Like his friend Franchitti and F1 star David Coulthard before him, Kane won the BRDC/McLaren Autosport Young Driver of the Year Award for his efforts that season. Two years later, he won the 1997 British Formula 3 Championship.

"Winning races is a great feeling, but being consistent enough to win a championship is the ultimate reward," says Kane. "Having the opportunity to run in the Indy Lights Championship – as a development series for Champ Car – is very exciting. I think I acquitted myself well in my first season and I look forward to posting better results and making a serious run for the championship in 2000."

While the first half of his rookie season was frustrating for Kane as he struggled to come to grips with his new Indy Lights car, new team, new country and new tracks (including his first ever oval races), the second half of the season was most impressive.

In the last five races, Kane earned two

poles and finished on the podium three times, including his first win at the season-finale at the California Speedway. His stretch run, which also included 3rd place finishes at Detroit and Laguna Seca, vaulted him from 12th to fourth in the final point standings and clinched the Rookie of the Year honors.

Although Kane showed promise during the year, however, that elusive first win was frustrating.

"I think it had been too long in coming," said his race engineer Eddie Jones. "Jonny deserved more than one win this year. I know that he showed us his speed at most places. We let him down at one or two of the ovals when the car wasn't great. It's really rewarding for the whole team because every one had a hand in our car being quick on these superspeedways. Jonny got the pole position at both of them [Michigan Speedway in July and California Speedway in October] and he finished off the season with a truly professional drive."

"I'm so happy for the boys because they worked so hard all year long," added Kim Green. "They've been so close so many times. I think we'll see some really good races from Jonny next year. This was his

first year and it's a tough little series."

Gurney, like Kane, is an easy-going, fun guy looking to make good on his dreams. To fulfil his dreams, however, Alex will have to follow in the footsteps of his father, Dan Gurney. Alex recognizes full well the racing legacy of his father, who was a top road racing star in America, as well as one of the most popular Formula One drivers ever.

"Without question my father is my racing hero and my mentor," explains Alex. "I have my own dreams and goals for what I want to accomplish in racing. If I can even come close to achieving what he did, I'd count myself lucky.

"Right now, I'm just stoked to be doing what I'm doing. I've got a fantastic job in the family business. I'm grateful for all the support I've been given, especially from my parents."

Alex praises his parents, but they did not want their son to become a race car driver... at first. You'd think the career path of the son of one of the most famous figures in American motorsports would lead straight to the race track. However, Dan and Evi Gurney (who worked for Porsche motorsports when she and Dan met) insisted Alex attend college before even

#26 PIT CREW FOR TEAM KOOL GREEN IS THE BEST IN BUSINESS

TEAM KOOL GREEN: CRAFTSMAN PIT STOP CHAMPIONS

DESPITE his reputation as a hard charger on the track, Paul Tracy knows that good finishes depend on good pit work.

Tracy's crew, led by Tony Cotman, got a chance to show off the right stuff when they won the inaugural $50,000 Craftsman Pit Crew Challenge preceding the series finale in Fontana, California.

The season-long competition (determined by a points system in the 19 previous events based on total time spent in the pits) culminated in a contest for four finalists in a 10-minute session requiring each driver to make a minimum of two pit stops and change all four tires. No fuel was added.

The winner was declared following calculation of the total pit times accumulated by each team, divided by the number of pit stops made. Teams were permitted to make more than one stop in an effort to lower the average time spent on each stop.

"Our plan was to do two stops and evaluate," said Cotman, but two nearly perfect stops were all that was needed.

Being in synch with the crew means a driver gains track position rather than losing it, as was seen by the close finish in the season points race. Every place counts.

"It makes my job a lot easier," Tracy said. "It takes some of the anxiety out when it comes time to stop. Rather than thinking I may lose places, I know we're going to gain a spot or two every time."

Members of the winning crew were left front tire changer Steve Price; crew chief and right front tire changer Cotman; left rear tire changer Chuck Miller; right rear tire changer Eric Haverson; fueller Jeff Simon and vent man Jeff Stafford.

Top: Paul Tracy blasts away from another pitstop by the #26 Team KOOL Green crew.

Above: Paul's crew members jump for joy at yet another win by Team KOOL Green.

TEAM-BY-TEAM ●

review

A total of 17 different teams, employing 36 drivers, contested the 1999 FedEx Championship Series. In the following pages, Jeremy Shaw, David Phillips, Eric Mauk and Ben Edwards assess some of the strengths and weaknesses of each organization.

Race Car Illustrations by
PAUL LAGUETTE
RACER Magazine

Photographs by
MICHAEL C. BROWN

TEAM KOOL Green was expected to be one of the pace-setters in the 1999 FedEx Championship Series. Dario Franchitti, in particular, had emerged as a bona fide title challenger in 1998, and Paul Tracy, his vastly more experienced teammate, was set to emerge from the shadows after a desperately disappointing '98 campaign that promised much, but produced surprisingly little in the way of notable results. Both drivers rose to the challenge.

Team principal Barry Green and his brother Kim had assembled a comprehensive group of talented professionals over the years and, as ever, the stability in terms of personnel and equipment proved crucial. There was no learning curve to speak of. Franchitti had developed a fine rapport with Technical Director-cum-race engineer Don Halliday, while Crew Chiefs Kyle Moyer (Franchitti) and Tony Cotman (Tracy) were acknowledged as being among the best organized in the business.

Tracy was obliged to skip the first race at Homestead, the consequence of a contretemps with Michael Andretti at Surfers Paradise in '98, and it seemed the #26 car might continue to be dogged by misfortune when substitute driver Raul Boesel was involved in a first-lap wreck. Despite the slow start, Tracy became a consistent front-runner – thanks in no small part to the calming influence of vastly experienced race engineer/general guru Tony Cicale. Franchitti, too, was always in contention, and his magnificent charge in the final few races produced a thrilling climax to the season.

Team KOOL Green accumulated 18 podium finishes, including three 1-2 sweeps, and failed by the narrowest margin in CART history to clinch a second championship to go with Jacques Villeneuve's crown in '95. Come to think of it, if Barry Green had opted to invoke team orders at Houston, and instructed Tracy to move over to assist Franchitti's quest for the championship, the eventual outcome would have been different. Then again, as Franchitti pointed out, 'You can only expect so much. You either win it or you don't.' Next year, perhaps.

Base:	Indianapolis, Indiana
Drivers:	Dario Franchitti, Paul Tracy, Raul Boesel
Sponsors:	KOOL, Klein Tools
Engines:	Honda HRS V8
Chassis:	Reynard 99I
Tires:	Firestone
Wins:	5 (Franchitti 3, Tracy 2);
Poles:	2 (Franchitti)

PPG Cup points: 373
Franchitti 212 (2nd)
Tracy 161 (3rd)

dario franchitti

paul tracy

kim green

barry green

raul boesel

DARIO FRANCHITTI – KOOL HONDA/REYNARD 99I

PAUL TRACY – KOOL HONDA/REYNARD 99I

Chicago, Illinois USA

Klein Tools... for Professionals... since 1857®

A generation before an automobile ever took to the road and more than half a century before the first Indy 500, tools manufactured by the earlier generations of the Klein family were the choice of master tradesmen. Like their counterparts of yesteryear, today's professionals, whose reputation and livelihood depend on the tools they use, still demand the quality found only in Klein tools.

Klein, the mark of quality since 1857, is still the most sought after and recognized name among professional tool users. Today, the professional, who takes pride in and realizes the importance of quality tools, can select from more than 4,000 job-matched Klein tools.

Klein Tools is proud to be associated with and support the professionals of Team Kool Green, Paul Tracy and Dario Franchitti in their pursuit of excellence in the 2000 FedEx Championship Series.

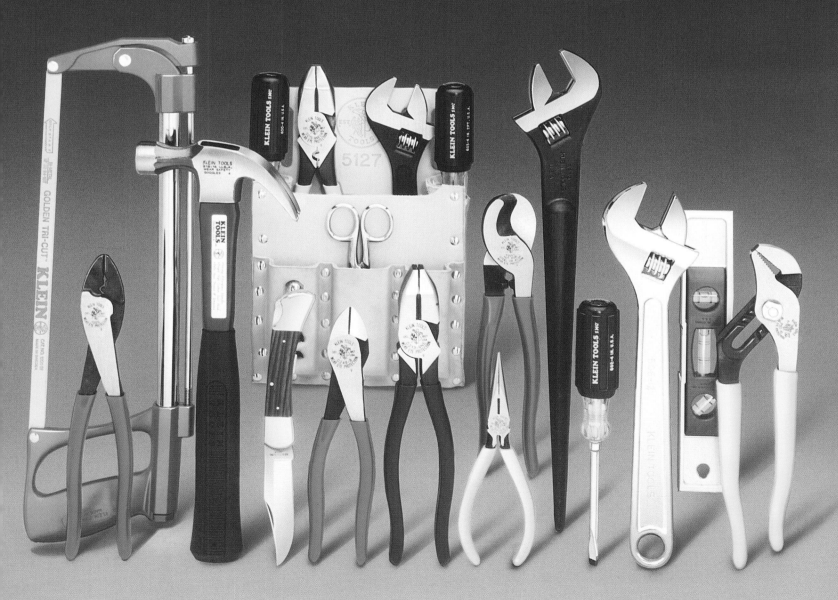

ABOUT the only people who didn't expect Target/Chip Ganassi Racing to backslide after a dominant 1998 campaign were those wearing the red shirts in the team's Indianapolis race shop.

Turned out they were right.

Seven trips to the winner's circle later, the record books needed a couple of new pages as the Ganassi team earned an unprecedented fourth straight crown.

Overcoming the defection of twice defending series champion Alex Zanardi to Formula 1, Ganassi made little noise when he tabbed Colombian F3000 star Juan Pablo Montoya in place of the Italian. In fact, most expected that the team's lone chance for a fourth consecutive championship lay with 1996 title holder Jimmy Vasser. But Ganassi is not only a shrewd judge of talent behind the wheel, he also knows ability in the pits and under the car. Managing Director Tom Anderson ran the day-to-day operation with the same acumen that had put the team on top. Mike Hull kept the crew tack-sharp, and for another season Ganassi had been able to keep veteran race engineer Morris Nunn from making good on his promise to retire to the golf courses of Florida.

Overall Crew Chief Rob Hill, ably assisted by Simon Hodgson (Montoya) and Grant Weaver and Ricky Davis (Vasser), helped maintain cars that would not give out under the hard-charging style of both drivers. As usual, the cars showed remarkable reliability, Montoya suffering just one DNF due to mechanical failure (Elkhart Lake), while Vasser's electrical problem at Rio was the lone mishap in the #12 car until gremlins attacked in two of the final three events of the year.

The team even drew from co-owner Joe Montana's expertise in performing with their backs to the wall, showing that never-say-die spirit in the season's final event. Down nine points to Dario Franchitti, Montoya finished fourth, while the Scot came home in tenth, tying the two for the points lead and giving the young Colombian the title on the strength of seven race wins.

Base: Indianapolis, Indiana

Drivers: Juan Montoya (R), Jimmy Vasser

Sponsor: Target Stores

Engines: Honda HRS V8

Chassis: Reynard 991

Tires: Firestone

Wins: 7 (Montoya); **Poles:** 8 (Montoya 7, Vasser 1)

PPG Cup points: 316
Montoya 212 (1st)
Vasser 104 (9th)

juan montoya

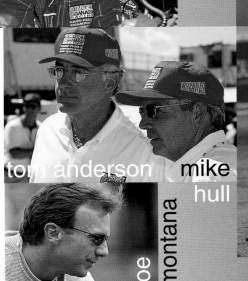

chip ganassi

jimmy vasser

tom anderson   mike hull

joe montana

JUAN MONTOYA – TARGET HONDA/REYNARD 991

JIMMY VASSER – TARGET HONDA/REYNARD 991

THE GUY WHO FILLS THE TANK IS EVERY BIT AS IMPORTANT AS THE GUY WHO EMPTIES IT.

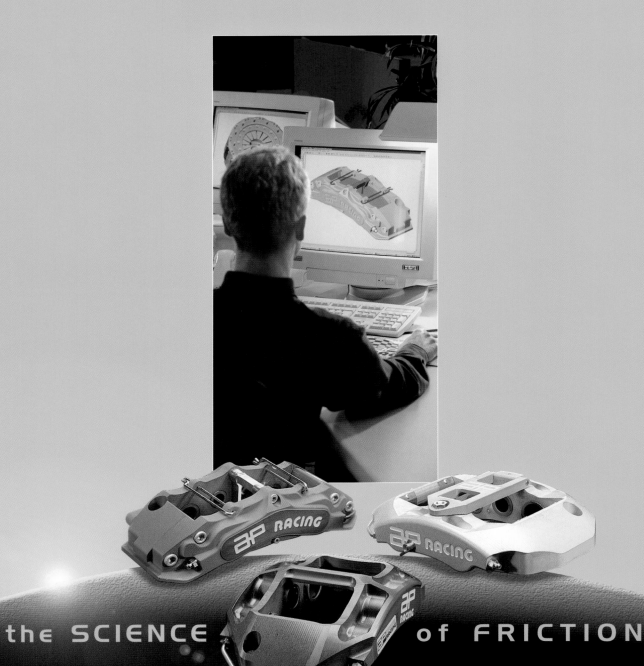

the SCIENCE of FRICTION

For over 50 years, **AP Racing** have pioneered advancements in clutch and brake technology. Today, the benefits of **AP**'s science are evident in a range of applications for every form of motorsport from CART to F1; NASCAR to World Sports Cars.

Capitalising on the science proven on the ovals and road circuits, **AP Racing** have developed clutch and brake systems suitable for a wide variety of high performance road cars. To realise the full potential of your engine, make sure you specify **AP** products to harness the power and effect.

AP Racing clutches and brakes. They're out of this world.

the SCIENCE of FRICTION

AP Racing, Wheler Road, Coventry, CV3 4LB, England. Tel +44 (0)24 7663 9595 Fax +44 (0)24 7663 9559
website: www.apracing.com   email: sales@apracing.co.uk

michael andretti

WHILE Patrick Racing, Team Gordon and Della Penna Motorsports all turned their backs on the latest Swift chassis, Newman/Haas Racing persevered to excellent effect. In fact, barring a succession of mishaps and mistakes – and despite (or perhaps even because of) a late switch from Goodyear to Firestone tires a mere two weeks before the first race at Homestead – another PPG Cup title appeared to be in the offing.

Michael Andretti had a strong season under Team Manager Ed Nathman, who was on board for Andretti's championship-winning year in 1991. Andretti proved his capabilities with a fine performance at Gateway, but a four-race run from Mid-Ohio to Laguna Seca netted just eight points, knocking him out of serious title contention. There were also far too many driver errors, ranging from stalling in the pits (at Homestead and Motegi) to crashing during a pace-car period (Vancouver).

Teammate Christian Fittipaldi, meanwhile, enjoyed by far his most impressive year. Heading to Round 13 in Detroit, after already recording the first pole (Rio) and race victory (Road America) of his career, he trailed Andretti by only 13 points. Sadly, a hard meeting with the Gateway wall during a test session with the new-for-2000 Ford Cosworth XF engine left the physically fit Brazilian on the sidelines for five races due to a head injury.

Roberto Moreno stepped in admirably – as he did during 1997 in similar circumstances. Indeed, Moreno's run to a second-place finish at Laguna Seca was the best of his career and put him in the top 15 in the final drivers' standings.

Changes abounded for the second straight year in the Newman/Haas garage as the vastly experienced Don Hoevel took over as Crew Chief on Andretti's car, while Todd Bowland stepped up to engineer Fittipaldi's Big Kmart machine after Brian Lisles opted to concentrate on his research and development duties. Nathman, furthermore, would quit shortly before the end of the year. Nevertheless, the Lincolnshire, Illinois-based outfit remained a force right through the season finale, where Fittipaldi capped his comeback with a third-place finish.

Base: Lincolnshire, Illinois	
Drivers: Michael Andretti, Christian Fittipaldi, Roberto Moreno	
Sponsors: Kmart, Texaco/Havoline	
Engines: Ford Cosworth XD	
Chassis: Swift 010.c	
Tires: Firestone	
Wins: 2 (Andretti 1, Fittipaldi 1);	
Poles: 2 (Andretti 1, Fittipaldi 1)	
PPG Cup points: 292 Andretti 151 (4th) Fittipaldi 121 (7th) Moreno 20 (of 58, 14th)	

paul newman

christian fittipaldi

roberto moreno

carl haas

mario andretti

MICHAEL ANDRETTI – KMART/TEXACO HAVOLINE FORD/SWIFT 010.c

CHRISTIAN FITTIPALDI – KMART FORD/SWIFT 010.c

It's in the blood

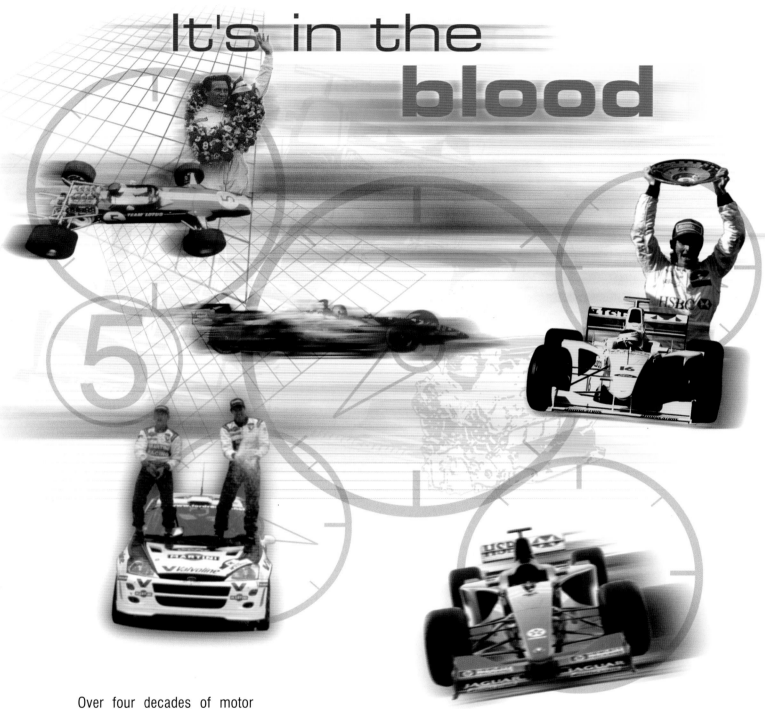

Over four decades of motor

racing heritage has given birth

to some of the world's most

successful racing engines.

Legendary partnerships: high-

performance future.

Visit our website **www.cosworthracing.com** for all the latest updates and info.

Cosworth Racing Limited, The Octagon, St. James Mill Road, Northampton, NN5 5RA

Tel: +44 (0)1604 598300   Fax: +44 (0)1604 598656   e-mail: cmanley@cosworth-racing.co.uk

BRYAN Herta dominated at Laguna Seca, winning from the pole to secure his – and Team Rahal's – only victory of the year. It was the highlight of a campaign that ended far short of initial expectations.

Always looking to improve his chances, Bobby Rahal had been notorious for tinkering with his technical package. But 1999 was the first year since '92 that his team would work with the same equipment for two years in a row. With the Ford Cosworth/Reynard/Firestone package firmly established – and preparation overseen by a veteran crew managed by Tim Cindric – Team Rahal looked for big things from Herta, who continued his partnership with race engineer Ray Leto and Crew Chief Larry Ellert. The Californian was expected to assume the veteran role in helping Max Papis become acclimated after replacing Rahal in the cockpit.

But after a third at Long Beach, Herta's fortunes went south. As has been the case in recent years, the team struggled to find a proper setup for the short ovals – to the intense frustration of both Herta and Rahal. The Shell car also was beset by all manner of niggling problems and miscues. Papis, meanwhile, quickly became the point man. The flamboyant Italian rapidly meshed with race engineer Tim Reiter and Chief Mechanic Jim Prescott, and the car became better at each stop with the help of one of the best pit crews in the sport.

A pole-winning effort at Chicago hinted at better things to come for Papis, while Herta and Rahal grew farther apart. Their relationship split irrevocably in August, Rahal telling Herta that he should look for a new job for the 2000 season. Meanwhile, Papis dominated the U.S. 500 before broken telemetry led to him running out of fuel within sight of the checkered flag. Six top-five finishes in the final seven races, including a pair of seconds to end the season, left confidence brimming as Papis finished fifth in the points race; but realistically the team ought to have had more to show for it.

Base:	Hilliard, Ohio
Drivers:	Max Papis, Bryan Herta
Sponsors:	Miller Lite, Shell Oil Products
Engines:	Ford Cosworth XD
Chassis:	Reynard 99I
Tires:	Firestone
Wins: 1 (Herta); **Poles:** 2 (Papis 1, Herta 1)	
PPG Cup points: 234 Papis 150 (5th) Herta 84 (12th)	

max papis

jim prescott

tim reiter

bryan herta

bobby rahal

MAX PAPIS – MILLER LITE FORD/REYNARD 99I

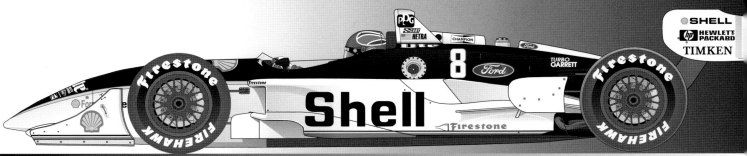

BRYAN HERTA – SHELL FORD/REYNARD 99I

adrian fernandez

pj jones

jan magnussen

pat patrick

Base: Indianapolis, Indiana

Drivers: Adrian Fernandez, PJ Jones, Jan Magnussen

Sponsors: Tecate, Quaker State, Visteon

Engines: Ford Cosworth XD

Chassis: Reynard 97/98/99I

Tires: Firestone

Wins: 2 (Fernandez); **Poles:** 0

PPG Cup points: 186
Fernandez 140 (6th)
Jones 38 (17th)
Magnussen 8 (24th)

CHANGE has never been a problem for U.E. 'Pat' Patrick, one of CART's founding fathers. It isn't a factor, because no matter what you throw at Patrick and General Manager Jim McGee, chances are good that they've seen it in some form before.

So when Scott Pruett left the team after the 1998 campaign and an expected move to the Swift chassis came a bit later than anticipated, the team never missed a beat. Under the watchful eye of McGee, who surpassed George Bignotti as the all-time winningest Champ Car Chief Mechanic-turned-Team/General Manager, and the steady hand of engineers Steve Newey and John Ward, plus Crew Chiefs Mike Sales and Donny Lambert, the team stood tall in the midst of change.

Following some disappointing preseason tests with the Swifts, however, Fernandez and new recruit PJ Jones drove year-old Reynards for the first two races. The 34-year-old Mexican defended his Motegi title with another fine victory, and followed that with a fourth a week later at Long Beach at the wheel of a Swift.

Jones stunned the CART community at Nazareth with a career-best second-place finish, and after six races both Patrick pilots were among the top ten in the points standings. However the second half of the season soon clouded the outlook.

At Detroit, Jones was replaced in the cockpit of the #20 Visteon machine by Denmark's Jan Magnussen. That same weekend, Fernandez suffered an accident that left him with a fractured right wrist and caused him to miss four races, putting Jones back in business. The team reverted to the Reynards, but Magnussen recorded only one top-ten placing (seventh in Vancouver) in his seven events.

Fernandez returned at Laguna Seca, but the four races he missed – and the four races he failed to finish before the accident – cost him any chance of challenging for the title. His win at the season-ending event at Fontana kept him in sixth place in the standings, but left most wondering what might have been.

john ward

jim mcgee

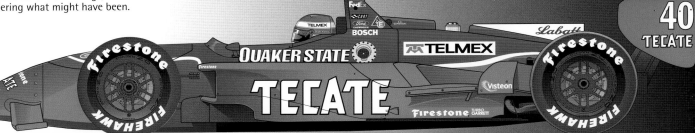

ADRIAN FERNANDEZ – TECATE/QUAKER STATE FORD/REYNARD 99I

PJ JONES – VISTEON FORD/SWIFT 010.c

greg moore

ACH of the late, lamented Greg Moore's four seasons with Jerry Forsythe's team proceeded in precisely the same manner. He would begin the year as a solid threat for championship honors, only to fade from contention. The 1999 campaign was no different. As in '98, though, the disappointment stemmed not so much from any shortcomings in either himself or the team, but from the relative lack of competitiveness of the latest Mercedes-Benz IC108E Phase III engine, which was no match for the Honda or the Ford in terms of horsepower, drivability and, even more importantly, reliability. Hence, for 2000, Forsythe will switch to Ford Cosworth motivation.

Vice President of Operations Neil Micklewright continued to run a tight ship, which had remained virtually unchanged for several years. Moore and Patrick Carpentier worked well with respective race engineers Steve Challis and Lee Dykstra, with able technical assistance from the likes of Alex Timmermanns and Michael Cannon. The equally experienced Buddy Lindblom took charge of the crew alongside Phil Le Pan and individual Chief Mechanics Chris Schofield (Moore) and George Klotz (Carpentier).

As the season progressed and the level of frustration increased, however, the seeds of change were sown. Firstly, Moore announced he would drive for Roger Penske in 2000. Then Challis, rather than moving with his countryman, whom he had guided from the youngster's earliest days in Formula Ford, opted instead for a future with Team Green. Challis was promptly given his marching orders.

The year will forever be overshadowed by Moore's tragic death in the Fontana finale. As ever, though, he proved himself a fighter. One victory (at Homestead) and two other podium finishes were not representative of his talent. Teammate Carpentier, meanwhile, emerged from the shadows in '99, especially after missing one race due to an injury suffered in Detroit. His drive to a career-best-equaling second place in the wet in Vancouver owed more to consistency than pace, perhaps, but it showed, too, that Carpentier has what it takes to win at this level.

Base:	Indianapolis, Indiana
Drivers:	Greg Moore, Patrick Carpentier
Sponsors:	Player's Ltd., Indeck
Engines:	Mercedes-Benz IC108E
Chassis:	Reynard 99I
Tires:	Firestone
Wins:	1 (Moore); Poles: 1 (Moore)
PPG Cup points:	158 Moore 97 (10th) Carpentier 61 (13th)

jerry forsythe

lee dykstra
patrick carpentier

GREG MOORE – PLAYER'S/INDECK MERCEDES/REYNARD

PATRICK CARPENTIER – PLAYER'S/INDECK MERCEDES/REYNARD

THE withdrawal of Goodyear from Formula 1 at the end of 1998 apparently boded well for the few Champ Car teams that had remained loyal to the Akron tire company. At least that's what Derrick Walker and Gil de Ferran were hoping as they entered the new season. Unfortunately, the anticipated advantage did not materialize.

Two cars were entered under the Walker banner at the first race, but Naoki Hattori's debut lasted as far as the first turn where he suffered a heavy accident that put him out of action for several months. His place was taken in four of the road-course races by fellow rookie Memo Gidley, who scored points at both Cleveland and Toronto. Hattori returned at Detroit, but was unable to emulate the Californian's feat.

That left de Ferran to carry the Walker flag, which he did impressively in qualifying for Round 2 in Japan by capturing pole position. Incredibly, he survived a spin at the start to finish in second place. The next few races saw varied fortunes, including a nasty pit-lane incident at Gateway where crewman Dave Stephens was injured, but it all came together at Portland where an inspired choice of a three-stop strategy (and a dose of luck in the shape of no caution flags) allowed de Ferran to score the team's first win since 1995. Another wheel-to-wheel dice with Montoya ensued at Cleveland, but the Firestones had the edge as the track dried out and the Brazilian had to settle for second. Pole position in Toronto and sixth places at Mid Ohio and Laguna Seca were the highlights of a disappointing latter part of the season, which was punctuated by too many driving errors, notably in Vancouver and Surfers Paradise.

Rob Edwards oversaw the running of the operation, as Tim Broyles had been elevated to the position of Crew Chief for de Ferran, who completed his final race for the team before leaving for Team Penske with a ninth place at Fontana.

Base: Indianapolis, Indiana

Drivers: Gil de Ferran, Naoki Hattori (R), Memo Gidley (R)

Sponsors: Valvoline, Cummins, Alpine

Engines: Honda HRS V8

Chassis: Reynard 98/99I

Tires: Goodyear

Wins: 1 (de Ferran); **Poles:** 2 (de Ferran)

PPG Cup points: 111
de Ferran 108 (8th)
Gidley 3 (of 4, 29th)

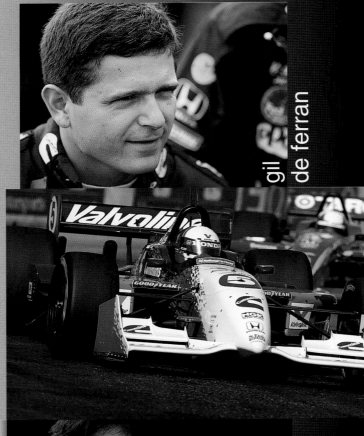

gil de ferran

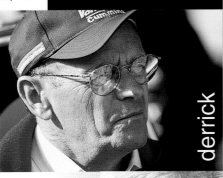

derrick walker

memo gidley

naoki hattori

GIL DE FERRAN – VALVOLINE CUMMINS HONDA/REYNARD 99I

NAOKI HATTORI – ALPINE HONDA/REYNARD 99I

THE WORKS

*Why buy hundreds of books
when one official work answers
all your questions ?*

Teams, Drivers, Cars, Key people, Mechanics, Engineers, Sponsors, Suppliers,
Engine manufacturers, Media, Tracks, Officials, Addresses, Fan clubs, Web sites, E-mail...

Who they are   What they do   How to reach them

www.who-works-in.com
Phone: +44 7000 WHO WORKS, or +44 1304 214494 Fax: +44 1304 212030

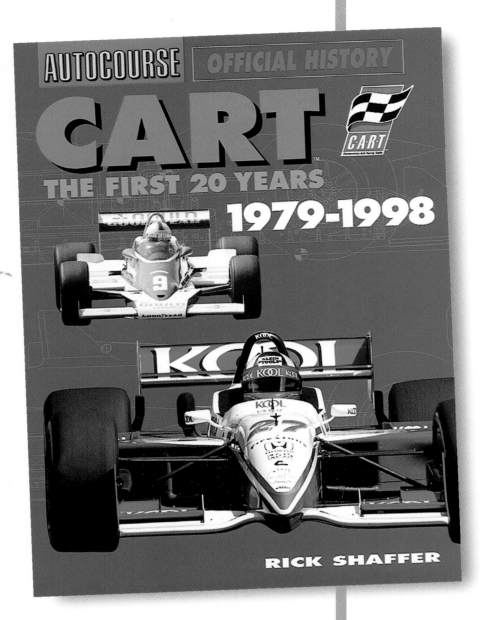

AUTOCOURSE OFFICIAL HISTORY

CART
THE FIRST 20 YEARS
1979-1998

RICK SHAFFER

AUTOCOURSE
CART
THE FIRST 20 YEARS
1979-1998
OFFICIAL HISTORY

In 1998, Championship Auto Racing Teams (CART) celebrated a milestone – it successfully completed its 20th year of competition.

To commemorate that occasion, we bring you CART: The First 20 Years 1979–1998. In reviewing the formation of the organization and its history to date, this beautifully illustrated book is a perfect companion to the previous AUTOCOURSE CART Official Yearbooks which have documented each season since 1993.

There is much to tell, such as stories of the Penske and Ganassi dynasties that serve as bookends for CART's first 20 years. The publication also examines CART's political structure and the involvement of major auto manufacturers, tire companies and race promoters.

It deals with companies such as March, Lola, Reynard, Ilmor and Cosworth. It looks at the champions, including Mario Andretti, Emerson Fittipaldi and Nigel Mansell, who transferred their winning ways from F1 to CART, as well as Jacques Villeneuve, who went on after his CART title to win the F1 crown.

Famous racing families and personalities are also covered as well as detailed statistics and race records, numerous features, and a year-by-year summary of the major developments in the sport.

20 glorious years of history for CART are all evoked in this detailed book.

RICK SHAFFER got his first opportunity in motor racing in 1987 when he was assigned to cover CART races for *The Indianapolis Star.*

In 1993, he went racing full time as publicist for Bettenhausen Motorsports. A self-proclaimed historian, he has been interested in the sport since 1962.

SPECIFICATIONS
• • • • • • • • • • • • • • • • • • • •
224 pages • 312 x 232 mm • over 250 stunning photographs • Hardback with dust-jacket
ISBN: 1 874557 14 4 • Available Now
Price: $39.95 U.S./£25.00 U.K.

To reserve your copy or for more information, please contact: Hazleton Publishing Ltd, 3 Richmond Hill, Richmond, Surrey TW10 6RE England. Tel: +44 020 8948 5151 ~ Fax: +44 020 8948 4111 in the U.K.; or Motorbooks International, PO Box 1, 729 Prospect Ave., Osceola, Wisconsin 54020, USA Telephone: (1) 715 294 3345 ~ Fax: (1) 715 294 4448 in the U.S.

AFTER a miserable 1998 season, Bruce McCaw's outfit was one of the first to take delivery of a Reynard 99I to ensure plenty of testing before the series opener at Homestead. Mark Blundell and Mauricio Gugelmin stayed for their fourth year together, and both scored points in Florida. That result was backed up by a strong performance from Gugelmin at Motegi, where he qualified on the front row and led until a poor pit stop dropped him back, ultimately to finish seventh. Blundell qualified fifth at Nazareth and was heading for the podium until an untimely pit stop put him out of the equation. There followed a dramatic downturn in fortunes that saw Gugelmin fail to finish in the top six until Vancouver at the end of August. Blundell, meanwhile, suffered a particularly nasty accident during a test session at Gateway that put him out of action until Detroit.

Roberto Moreno duly subbed for the Englishman and reaped the rewards of some intelligent and fuel-efficient driving, taking fourth at Gateway and Toronto, performances that brought him back to the attention of the leading team owners. His good relationship with Gugelmin and his similar driving style allowed Technical Director Allen McDonald to further develop the car, which still lacked horsepower (and, more importantly, drivability) from the Mercedes engine. Blundell returned at Detroit and went on to qualify on the front row in Chicago, but the last six races of the year brought just one finish, a 12th at Laguna Seca.

Gugelmin had a better run toward the end of the year, taking sixth at both Houston and Fontana, where he described his machine as 'one of the best cars I've ever driven.' His relationship with race engineer Ray McAuley seemed to gel throughout the course of 1999, and given a more powerful and more reliable engine package, there is no reason why this team should not get back to its race-winning form of 1997.

Base:	Indianapolis, Indiana
Drivers:	Mauricio Gugelmin, Mark Blundell
Sponsors:	Hollywood, Motorola
Engines:	Mercedes–Benz IC108E
Chassis:	Reynard 99I
Tires:	Firestone
Wins: 0;	**Poles:** 0

PPG Cup points: 91
Gugelmin 44 (16th)
Moreno 38 (of 58, 14th)
Blundell 9 (23rd)

mauricio gugelmin

bruce mccaw

roberto moreno

mark blundell

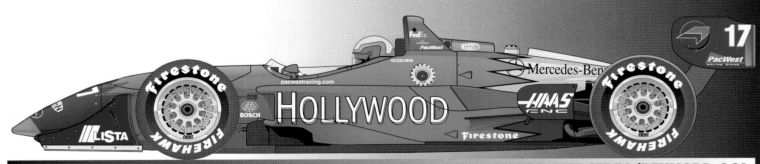

MAURICIO GUGELMIN – HOLLYWOOD MERCEDES/REYNARD 99I

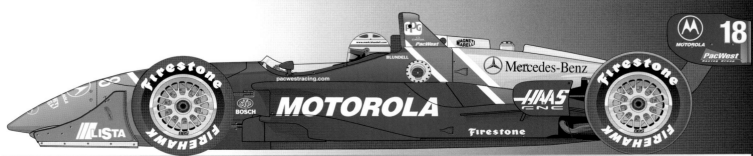

MARK BLUNDELL – MOTOROLA MERCEDES/REYNARD 99I

There are a handful of drivers who race Mercedes-powered cars.

And a million others who think they do.

Mercedes-Benz is the "Official Car of CART." All Mercedes road cars have something in common with every Mercedes-

powered car in Formula 1 and CART. They all set the pulse racing. So much, in fact, that we'd just like

to say to all our drivers out there (with the possible exception of the guys

behind the wheels of our actual race cars): Please, don't get too carried away.

Visit us on our Web site at www.MBUSA.com or call 1-800-FOR-MERCEDES

STAYING faithful to Toyota engines and Firestone tires, Cal Wells began the 1999 season with two new drivers, the experienced Scott Pruett having gained backing from Pioneer and being joined by exciting Champ Car newcomer Cristiano da Matta, who was entrusted with the MCI WorldCom-backed entry. The reigning PPG-Dayton Indy Lights champion soon struck up a rapport with engineer Iain Watt and stunned everyone with a third-row starting position for the first race at Homestead, Toyota's best effort to that date. He proved it was no fluke by running comfortably in the top six for much of the race, and then by finishing fourth at Nazareth a few weeks later.

Pruett, on the other hand, made a slow start to his tenth year in CART, scoring just three points in the first ten races. A solid seventh in Toronto, fifth on the grid at Michigan and eighth at the flag in Detroit picked things up a bit, but he saved his best until last. Having announced he was off to NASCAR in 2000, Pruett proceeded to qualify third in Australia and then snatch Toyota's first-ever pole position for the finale in Fontana. The fact that the engine gave up after 48 laps of the race (16 more laps than da Matta's unit managed) paled into insignificance.

If Montoya had not been on the scene, da Matta would have wrapped up the Rookie of the Year honors with his total of 32 points. A midseason spell of five non-finishes (through a mix of two accidents and three breakdowns) rather spoiled the momentum, but he was unfazed by a frightening looking accident in Detroit and came back to finish ninth next time out at Mid-Ohio. The lack of low-down horse-power from the Toyota engine hampered his qualifying attempts on the road and street courses, but all in all this was an impressive first season from the 26-year-old Brazilian, and the prospects for both him and the Richard Buck-managed team look extremely promising.

Base: Rancho Santa Margarita, California	
Drivers: Scott Pruett, Cristiano da Matta (R)	
Sponsors: Pioneer, MCI WorldCom	
Engines: Toyota RV8D	
Chassis: Reynard 99I	
Tires: Firestone	
Wins: 0; **Poles:** 1 (Pruett)	
PPG Cup points: 60 da Matta 32 (18th) Pruett 28 (19th)	

cristiano da matta

scott pruett

cal wells

gordon coppuck

CRISTIANO DA MATTA – MCI WORLDCOM TOYOTA/REYNARD 99I

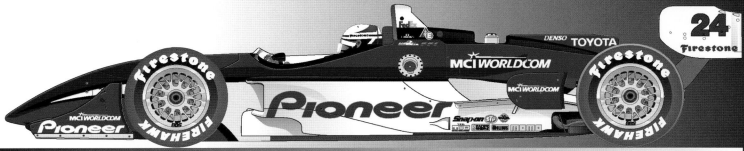

SCOTT PRUETT – PIONEER TOYOTA/REYNARD 99I

The competition is fierce.

Performance and reliability are key.

You need to take the lead and stay there.

It's nice to be part of something so familiar.

MCI WORLDCOM

MCI WorldCom is the Official Communications Company of **CART** www.mciracing.com

THE checks might have been signed by new owner Jerry Forsythe, but in reality McDonald's Championship Racing was the same Tasman Motorsports Group organization that Steve and Christine Horne, Jeff Eischen and Ben Dillon had built from the ground up over the previous six years.

The management team stayed the same, although there was some shuffling around within the engineering department as Diane Holl, Eric Cowdin (who worked successfully with Tony Kanaan in Indy Lights) and Martin Pare shared race engineering duties as the season unfolded. Kanaan was charged up about spending a second season with the proven Honda/Reynard/Firestone package, and when asked before the season if he would be disappointed not to win a race, the young Brazilian grinned and said yes, but then added that it wouldn't happen.

Kanaan was right, but his prophecy came true only after a win at the U.S. 500 fell from the sky when Max Papis ran out of fuel after dominating the race. That should not overshadow a strong performance by Kanaan and the Steve Ragan-led pit crew, who fought their way back into contention after an early delay due to a black flag.

Problems on the short ovals continued to plague the team, and some of the road-course events turned into fuel economy runs that never really worked out. Un-characteristic hiccups in the pits cost Kanaan a couple of good finishes, while mechanical problems (such as a fuel management glitch at Mid-Ohio and a broken shift linkage at Laguna Seca) also proved costly.

All in all, the season never lived up to the promise shown in 1998, when Kanaan earned Rookie of the Year honors and the team posted its first-ever top-ten finish in the season standings. A fifth at Rio was the best placing other than the Michigan win, and the Hilliard, Ohio-based outfit wound up a disappointing 11th in points.

Base:	Hilliard, Ohio
Driver:	Tony Kanaan
Sponsor:	McDonald's
Engines:	Honda HRS V8
Chassis:	Reynard 99I
Tires:	Firestone
Wins: 1; Poles: 1	
PPG Cup points: 85 (11th)	

steve horne

tony kanaan

jerry forsythe

diane holl

martin pare

steve ragan

TONY KANAAN – MCDONALD'S HONDA/REYNARD 99I

gonzalo rodriguez

al unser jr.

tarso marques

alex barron

roger penske

john travis

IT was a black year for the most successful team in the sport. Reduced to a singleton entry for Al Unser Jr. at the start of the season, it fared poorly when the twice champion suffered a broken ankle on the opening lap at Homestead. Brazilian Tarso Marques, who had tested impressively for Payton/Coyne Racing during the off-season, was called in at short notice and acquitted himself respectably, earning a ninth place in his third outing at Rio. Unser missed two races, crashed on his return at Nazareth, and then tested the Lola that Roger Penske had acquired in response to the disappointing performances of the Penske PC27B. In a blow to designer John Travis and the manufacturing team at Poole in England, Al raced the Lola at Gateway, finished in 12th and decided he liked it.

The team then concentrated on the Lola for road courses and short ovals, preferring the Penske for the superspeedways, although it wasn't always that clear cut. Alex Barron drove the second car at both 500-mile events, while Formula 3000 race winner Gonzalo Rodriguez made his debut with the team at Detroit. He had already made many friends in CART circles when he was tragically killed during practice for what should have been his second Champ Car start, at Laguna Seca.

Unser's best results came in the middle of the season with a fifth in the rain-affected Cleveland race and two ninth-place finishes at Road America and Toronto, but it was symptomatic of the year that a top-ten finish for a Penske entered car was a noteworthy achievement. By the end of the season, it was known that Unser would be leaving the team, but he signed off with an intelligent run to seventh at Fontana.

General Manager Clive Howell attempted to maintain morale in the camp, but a further blow was inflicted with the death of Greg Moore, who had signed to join in 2000 and whose aggressive style would have given the team the boost it so desperately needed.

Base:	Reading, Pennsylvania
Drivers:	Al Unser Jr., Tarso Marques (R), Alex Barron, Gonzalo Rodriguez (R)
Sponsor:	Marlboro
Engines:	Mercedes-Benz IC108E
Chassis:	Penske PC27B & Lola B99/00
Tires:	Goodyear
Wins: 0; **Poles:** 0	

PPG Cup points: 31
Unser 26 (22nd)
Marques 4 (28th)
Rodriguez 1 (32nd)

AL UNSER JR. – MARLBORO MERCEDES/LOLA B99/00

ALEX BARRON – MARLBORO MERCEDES/PENSKE PC27B

The 1999 season was a case of what might have been for Robby Gordon. CART's prodigal son took the bold step of establishing his own operation in partnership with business manager Mike Held and longtime open-wheel aficionado/acclaimed businessman John Menard. Arguably, he squandered the opportunity with a string of curious decisions, especially with regard to chassis choice.

He elected to start out with a new Swift, and despite taking delivery only a few weeks before the first race, immediately professed himself delighted after an initial road-course test. But when a subsequent oval test proved disappointing, he promptly purchased a pair of '98 Reynards with which to start the season. Gordon drove superbly in Japan to finish eighth, but later when results proved hard to come by, he bowed to inevitable pressure from Hiro Matsushita (the owner of Swift Engineering who also controlled associate sponsorship from Panasonic) and reverted to the Swift for Round 5 at Rio. To complicate matters further, Gordon subsequently was invited to test one of Dan Gurney's AAR Eagles during an open test at Mid-Ohio. After setting some rapid lap times almost right away, Gordon agreed to race the car at Chicago. He finished a strong tenth and elected to stick with the Eagle for four of the remaining five events. The exception was at Surfers Paradise, where he equaled his best finish of the year by placing eighth in the Swift. Go figure.

Gordon swapped race engineers with equal regularity and, in spite of the distractions, came extremely close to making our Top Ten list of drivers. The constant fluidity of cars and engineers – and lack of testing – meant he usually qualified poorly, but he displayed his class by frequently working his way forward. Indeed, he was the highest Toyota finisher on six occasions. Shortly after the end of the year, Gordon announced he was turning his back on CART – again – in favor of a return to NASCAR...

Base:	Orange, California
Driver:	Robby Gordon
Sponsors:	Johns Manville, Panasonic, Menards
Engines:	Toyota RV8D
Chassis:	Reynard 98I, Swift 010.c, Eagle 997
Tires:	Firestone
Wins: 0; Poles: 0	
PPG Cup points: 27 (20th)	

robby gordon

john menard

ROBBY GORDON – PANASONIC/MENARDS TOYOTA/SWIFT 010.c

ROBBY GORDON – PANASONIC/MENARDS TOYOTA/EAGLE 997

THE day after the final round at Fontana, Hogan Racing was formally wound up and a chapter was closed. Carl Hogan was a key player in CART throughout the 1990s, and his operation based at St. Louis was responsible for nurturing the talents of two potential champions: Dario Franchitti and Helio Castro-Neves.

The deal with Castro-Neves was completed only days before Spring Training, leaving a disgruntled JJ Lehto in the wings. Another change from 1998 was the use of Lola chassis, with full support from the revitalized British manufacturer. Mercedes power was retained, as were the Firestone tires, and it did not take long for everyone to sit up and take notice. The Ben Bowlby-penned car qualified fourth at Homestead and led 29 laps, ran comfortably in the top six in Japan, then battled for the lead at Nazareth as the only real opposition to Juan Montoya. Time lost in the pits led to frustration and ultimately an accident, but notice had been served both of the car's performance and Castro-Neves' electrifying talent.

Sadly, that talent was often wasted by poor reliability, which led to some scathing comments from Hogan later in the year. The highlights of the season came at one-third distance – the second place behind Michael Andretti at Gateway and pole position at the following race in Milwaukee – but initiated a run of six non-finishes. Helio's good natured optimism and excellent relationship with promising race engineer Casper Van Der Schoot helped maintain team morale, buoyed also by a fifth-place finish at Chicago. Castro-Neves also drove well to eighth in the wet in Vancouver, after starting at the very back of the grid following a host of engine failures in practice and qualifying.

A second car was entered for Luiz Garcia Jr. for several events before the money ran out, but it was Castro-Neves who carried the torch for the team, for Lola and, more often than not, for Mercedes. Unfortunately, Hogan's race winning dream remained just out of reach.

Base:	St. Louis, Missouri
Drivers:	Helio Castro-Neves, Luiz Garcia Jr. (R)
Sponsor:	Hogan Motor Leasing LLC
Engines:	Mercedes-Benz IC108E
Chassis:	Lola B99/00
Tires:	Firestone
Wins:	0; Poles: 1 (Castro-Neves)
PPG Cup points:	25 (20th)

helio castro-neves

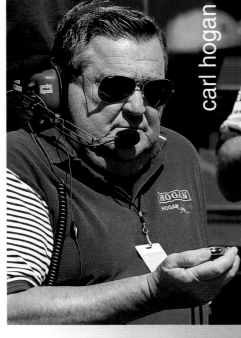

carl hogan

luiz garcia jr.

HELIO CASTRO-NEVES – HOGAN MOTOR LEASING MERCEDES/LOLA B99

LUIZ GARCIA JR. – HOGAN MOTOR LEASING MERCEDES/LOLA B99

THE death of Walter Payton at the end of the season, after a protracted illness, came as a sad blow to this hard-working team into which he had put so much enthusiasm after joining forces with longtime entrant Dale Coyne in 1995.

Michel Jourdain Jr. entered his third full season with Payton/Coyne armed with a pair of fully updated Lola chassis and Ford Cosworth engines, and duly achieved his best-ever result of seventh at Road America. Apart from a tremendous opening stint at Nazareth, however, the amiable young Mexican had precious little else to show for his efforts, which were punctuated by a high proportion of gearbox failures. Jourdain continued to work with experienced race engineer Dave Morgan, but the car never demonstrated the sort of pace that Hogan Racing was able to achieve with Helio Castro-Neves.

Tarso Marques had posted some sensational lap times during winter testing, but, sadly, could not procure the budget necessary to remain with the team. Instead, Florida's Dennis Vitolo and Brazilian rookie Luiz Garcia Jr. began the season with the intention of running partial programs using older Reynard chassis. Former Indy Lights and British Formula 2 runner Garcia began his campaign with a crash at Homestead and ended his association with the team with an off at Road America, while Vitolo, frankly, was out of his depth in this increasingly competitive series. His highlight was a sensible run to 11th at the U.S. 500.

Gualter Salles made a one-off appearance in a second Lola at Long Beach, while after Garcia's defection to Hogan Racing, Toyota Atlantic graduate Memo Gidley was granted an opportunity to drive a second Herdez-backed Lola in six races with the aim of providing more feedback for team leader Jourdain. Gidley posted several promising drives, which, with even a modicum of good fortune, would have resulted in comfortable top-ten finishes. As it was, the personable Californian had to be content with a solitary point for finishing 12th in Vancouver.

Base:	Plainfield, Illinois
Drivers:	Michel Jourdain Jr., Dennis Vitolo, Luiz Garcia Jr. (R), Gualter Salles, Memo Gidley (R)
Sponsors:	Herdez, Viva Mexico!, SmithKline Beecham, Tang
Engines:	Ford Cosworth XD
Chassis:	Reynard 97/98I, Lola T97/00
Tires:	Firestone
Wins:	0; **Poles:** 0

PPG Cup points: 10
Jourdain 7 (25th)
Vitolo 2 (30th)
Gidley 1 (of 4, 29th)

michel jourdain jr.

luiz garcia jr.

dennis vitolo

gualter salles

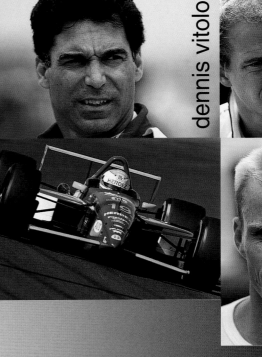

dale coyne

dave morgan

memo gidley

MICHEL JOURDAIN JR. – HERDEZ/VIVA MEXICO FORD/LOLA T97/00

DENNIS VITOLO – NICODERM CQ FORD/REYNARD 97I

MICHEL JOURDAIN JR.

THE HEAT IS ON.

HERDEZ® salsa, the authentic taste of Mexico is proud to sponsor Michel Jourdain Jr. on his quest for victory.

The French have an expression about things changing yet staying the same. This was all too true in 1999 for John Della Penna's team, which failed to progress in terms of results, despite changes in the engine and chassis departments. The winter switch from Ford Cosworth power to Toyota may reap benefits in the future, but there was no question that the Ford remained the superior unit throughout the '99 season.

Regarding chassis, Della Penna initially remained loyal to Swift – again on Firestone tires – but after failing to find the sweet spot with the California-built car (which remained more labor-intensive than most of its rivals), he opted to switch to Reynard after five races. In fact, the change was made possible in large part due to a direct swap with Team Gordon, which traded its ex-Team Rahal '98 Reynard for a '99 Swift prior to Round 6 at Gateway. Unfortunately, there was no sudden leap in performance – even after the first of two '99 Reynards was delivered in time for the race at Milwaukee.

Matters soon became even more complicated, since the original intention was to concentrate on developing the '99 car in concert with the new and significantly smaller RV8E engine, which required an entirely different chassis installation. The Les Channen-led crew, under the direction of equally well-respected Team Manager Phil Howard, continued to perform wonders as they swapped regularly between one configuration and the other. Eventually, Toyota decided to concentrate on the proven RV8D, although Hearn did finish a promising tenth in the RV8E's only other outing at Cleveland.

The constant juggling between engines proved to be a significant handicap, especially for hard-working race engineer Steve Conover, and Hearn had several big accidents as he strove to make up the deficit. Nevertheless, Hearn continued to show great promise, especially at Vancouver, where inspired timing on the switch to slick tires led to a season-best sixth-place finish.

Base: Indianapolis, Indiana
Driver: Richie Hearn
Sponsor: Budweiser
Engines: Toyota RV8D, RV8E
Chassis: Swift 010.c, Reynard 98/99I
Tires: Firestone
Wins: 0; Poles: 0
PPG Cup points: 26 (21st)

richie hearn

john della penna

RICHIE HEARN – BUDWEISER TOYOTA/SWIFT 010.c

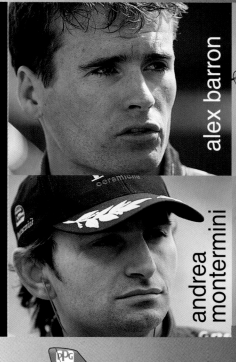

There were signs of desperation at Dan Gurney's team in 1999. A full campaign with the Eagle brought very little in terms of results, but it certainly gave a few drivers the opportunity to dust off their crash helmets. Alex Barron set the ball rolling for the first seven races. The promising sophomore managed a promising ninth-place finish at Nazareth before Gurney decided he needed a driver with more experience. Gualter Salles duly earned one point in his seven outings, but the under-rated Brazilian couldn't make any significant progress with the car, whereupon both Andrea Montermini and Raul Boesel were invited to make their contributions on road courses and ovals respectively. The Dave Bruns-developed car looked great, but Toyota horsepower and Goodyear rubber were not the most competitive elements to add to the package, and Dan Gurney's previous assertion that he was 'betting the farm' on the Eagle sounded distinctly unsafe.

Variety is the spice of life and more challengers to Reynard domination are welcome, but despite the best efforts of Gurney's extremely well-equipped team, this fractured campaign never really made progress.

Base: Santa Ana, California

Drivers: Alex Barron, Gualter Salles, Raul Boesel, Andrea Montermini

Sponsors: Denso, Castrol

Engines: Toyota RV8D

Chassis: Eagle 997

Tires: Goodyear

Wins: 0; Poles: 0

PPG Cup points: 9
Barron 4 (27th)
Salles 2 (of 5, 26th)
Montermini 2 (31st)
Boesel 1 (33rd)

ALEX BARRON – DENSO/CASTROL TOYOTA/EAGLE 997

BETTENHAUSEN MOTORSPORTS

The loss of longtime sponsor Alumax had serious implications for Tony Bettenhausen's team, which for the first time in nine years failed to attend all of the races. Unable to keep Helio Castro-Neves for a second season, the team was forced to run a limited program for Japanese journeyman Shigeaki Hattori. Although a race winner in Indy Lights, the 35-year-old rookie struggled to come to terms with a Champ Car and more often than not was a liability on the track. So much so that CART Chief Steward Wally Dallenbach withdrew his license before the end of the season. Gualter Salles stepped into the '98 Reynard for a one-off drive at Surfers Paradise and gave Tom Brown, Vince Kremer and the crew a welcome boost by scoring three points.

Even more frustrating was the fact that Bettenhausen had a brand-new Lola in the workshop that barely turned a wheel because of the lack of funds. Watching Castro-Neves performing brilliantly in the Hogan Lola in the early part of the season just served to rub salt into the wound.

Base: Indianapolis, Indiana

Drivers: Shigeaki Hattori (R), Gualter Salles

Sponsors: Epson, Refricentro

Engines: Mercedes-Benz IC108E

Chassis: Reynard 98I

Tires: Goodyear

Wins: 0; Poles: 0

PPG Cup points: 3
Salles 3 (of 5, 26th)

SHIGEAKI HATTORI – BETTENHAUSEN MOTORSPORTS MERCEDES/REYNARD 98I

MAKING only evolutionary changes to its V8 engine between the 1998 and 1999 seasons, Honda allowed its teams to focus on other aspects of their cars without having to worry about learning the characteristics of a new motor. The loss of twice series champion Alex Zanardi as Honda's standard-bearer left some wondering whether the manufacturer could maintain its lofty perch atop the standings. In fact, the transition was as smooth as could be. The FedEx Championship Series was again dominated by Honda as the Japanese automaker's latest HRS power plant swept the top three spots in the championship for the third straight season. The engine might have given away a little to Ford Cosworth in outright horsepower, but in tractability and consistency, it was no contest.

In fact, Honda eclipsed its previous best single-season victory total with 14, topping the mark of 13 established in '98. Only once, at Laguna Seca, did Honda fail to lead at least one lap. Its eventual tally of 1,577 laps led (56.95 percent of the total) represented an impressive statistic in light of the stiff competition, and the margin of victory in the Manufacturer's Championship over second-place Ford (383 points to 301) was even wider than in 1998 (365–293).

Honda

Production base:
Santa Clarita,
California

Wins: 14
(Montoya 7,
Franchitti 3,
Tracy 2, de Ferran 1,
Kanaan 1);
Poles: 13
(Montoya 7,
de Ferran 2,
Franchitti 2,
Kanaan 1, Vasser 1)

A LIGHTER, more reliable version of the venerable Ford Cosworth XD engine greeted teams in 1999. Its final tally of five race wins and four poles proved rather disappointing, especially considering its horsepower advantage. Ford earned oval-track wins at Motegi, Gateway and Fontana, and ended its season on a high note with a sweep of the Fontana podium. At the same time, with even a modicum of good fortune, there could (or should) have been many more victories – notably at Michigan Speedway, where Max Papis dominated until Team Rahal made a fuel miscalculation in the final stages. On several other occasions, Michael Andretti was in a position to win, only to be thwarted by a variety of ills.

Top-end power also was crucial at Road America, where Christian Fittipaldi headed another resounding Ford 1-2-3. The engineers worked hard over the winter to improve the motor's low-end power delivery – or 'drivability' – but in the majority of road- and street-course events, it remained a handicap, especially by comparison to the Honda. A notable exception came at Laguna Seca, where Bryan Herta once again asserted his superiority by scoring one of only two flag-to-flag wins all season.

Ford Cosworth

Production base:
Northampton,
England; U.S. base:
Torrance, California

Wins: 5
(Fernandez 2,
Andretti 1,
Fittipaldi 1, Herta 1);
Poles: 4
(Fittipaldi 1,
Andretti 1, Papis 1,
Herta 1)

THE latest Phase III version of the Mercedes IC108E engine made a handsome debut at Homestead as Greg Moore swept to victory. But that remained the Ilmor Engineering-developed unit's solitary success during a dismal campaign that netted only three more podium finishes – a second for Helio Castro-Neves at Gateway, a third for Moore in Detroit and a second for Player's/Forsythe teammate Patrick Carpentier in Vancouver.

The initial triumph was achieved with the '98 electronic management system after the new Magneti Marelli package failed to live up to expectations during testing. The Italian software was introduced eventually, but never performed to an acceptable level.

The compact engine performed respectably on the ovals, Moore and Castro-Neves claiming poles at Homestead and Milwaukee respectively. Castro-Neves, in particular, was often among the fastest contenders with Hogan Racing's Lola. In terms of horsepower, the IC108E wasn't too far off the mark. But it was no match for the opposition in the crucial mid-range power band. In addition to the 'peaky' power delivery, which made life difficult for the drivers, serious failures became increasingly common as the season progressed.

Mercedes-Benz

Production base:
Brixworth, England;
U.S. base:
Plymouth, Michigan

Wins: 1
(Moore 1);
Poles: 2
(Moore 1,
Castro-Neves 1)

THE light at the end of the tunnel proved not to be an oncoming train for Toyota Racing Development in 1999. Cristiano da Matta established the target right away by qualifying a magnificent sixth on his Champ Car debut at Homestead. A month or so later, the Brazilian finished a Toyota-best fourth at Nazareth.

The four Toyota teams (All American Racers, Arciero-Wells Racing, Della Penna Motorsports and Team Gordon) endured some tough times in midseason as TRD split its time between rebuilding the proven RV8D motors and trying to develop the new RV8E. Once the decision had been made to concentrate on the older unit, however, results began to improve dramatically. In fact, Toyota scored points in all except three of the 20 races, accumulating a respectable total of 80 Manufacturer's Championship points and ending the season on a high note as Scott Pruett qualified third on the road course at Surfers Paradise and then claimed a sensational pole at California Speedway. The joy didn't last long, however, as both Pruett and teammate da Matta saw their engines burn up less than 50 laps into the event; but Toyota at least had placed itself on the map following a tough four-year haul.

Toyota

Production base:
Costa Mesa,
California

Wins: 0;
Poles: 1 (Pruett)

FOR Firestone, the 1999 FedEx Championship Series was a case of almost total domination. Firestone-shod cars won all but one event on the Champ Car calendar (for the second successive year) and swept the top seven places in the championship. It was the fourth straight season that CART's champion had ridden Firestone rubber to the PPG Cup.

The bare statistics make impressive reading. Firestone's tally of 19 wins and 18 poles was shared among no fewer than 13 different drivers. Its Firehawk tires led in every one of the season's 20 races for a total of 2,669 (out of 2,779) laps – an astonishing 96.39 percent of the aggregate.

Under the circumstances, it might have been natural to expect Firestone to ease up on the intense pace of development. Not so.

'We were pushing very hard,' admitted Bridgestone/Firestone Motorsports Director Al Speyer. 'We did more testing than we had ever done, in any season. The combination of the competitiveness and having a whole flock of teams to do the testing resulted in us doing about ten percent more mileage of testing in '99 than we had in '98.'

The work clearly paid off. Following Round 9 at Cleveland, Firestone led every single lap of every race.

Despite the lopsided results, the season was no slam-dunk for Firestone. In the wake of its withdrawal from Formula 1 at the conclusion of '98, Goodyear marshaled considerable human and technical resources for its Champ Car program. Ironically, however, mirroring the problem when Firestone re-entered the Champ Car fray in 1995, following an absence of 20 years, Goodyear's efforts were stymied by the lack of numbers. Nevertheless, while Goodyear didn't always show on the results sheets, Firestone had its work cut out.

'The competitiveness of the two tire brands was probably closer this year than any year we competed against each other,' continued Speyer. 'I think Goodyear, tire-wise, had made significant gains. The problem they faced is that they were sometimes close, but never better...and being close or even equal wasn't enough. You need an advantage. People came to us early on in our Champ Car program [in 1995 and '96] and switched over because we were better.

'Race-in and race out in '99, we produced a tire that was capable of winning. There's no question that at any race this year, you could win on Firestones.'

Given Goodyear's decision to withdraw from Champ Car competition at the end of the season, there's also no question that the *only* way to win a Champ Car race in 2000 will be on Firestones. That is a mixed blessing for the company.

'We really wanted competition to continue,' said Speyer. 'It's real mixed emotion, because you look at it as the ultimate victory of winning the war – yet, as we always said, we didn't look at it as a tire war, but as a competition.'

Firestone			
Production base: Akron, Ohio, and Tokyo, Japan			
Wins:19		Poles:18	
(Montoya 7,	Andretti 1,	(Montoya 7,	Fittipaldi 1,
Franchitti 3,	Fittipaldi 1,	Franchitti 2,	Andretti 1,
Fernandez 2,	Kanaan 1,	Moore 1,	Vasser 1,
Tracy 2,	Herta 1)	Kanaan 1,	Papis 1,
Moore 1,		Castro-	Herta 1,
		Neves 1,	Pruett 1)

THE 1999 season brought the curtain down on The Goodyear Tire & Rubber Company's historic involvement in the North American open-wheel racing scene. From its first tentative forays into the Indianapolis 500 in the early 1960s, through the legendary tire wars with Firestone in the late '60s and early '70s, the benevolent monopoly of the '80s and early '90s, and the renewed tire 'competition' with Firestone beginning in '95, Goodyear has been an enthusiastic and staunch supporter of Champ Car racing.

Sadly, the harsh competitive, business and political realities of the day brought that support to an end with the checkered flag at the Marlboro 500 Presented by Toyota on October 31. Goodyear said the continuing schism between Championship Auto Racing Teams and the Indy Racing League – and the collapse of reconciliation efforts in October – was the principal reason for its decision. In the end, Goodyear could not justify the cost of competing in both the FedEx Championship and the Pep Boys Indy Racing League, developing tires for two open-wheel racing formulas.

'Our long-standing commitment to racing made this an agonizing decision,' said Stu Grant, Goodyear's General Manager for Global Racing. 'Our decision is based, in part, on open-wheel racing's present state of affairs in North America and the ongoing split between CART and IRL.

'Like many suppliers, we are certainly disappointed that no reconciliation is in sight and therefore believe it is in the best interests of our shareholders, customers and the racing division to take a sabbatical from the CART and IRL series.'

At the same time, even Goodyear's staunchest supporters would concede that Firestone had utterly dominated competition on the CART front for the past several seasons. Since mid-'97, in fact, Goodyear had just two wins and four poles to show for 50 starts. With fewer and fewer teams being able to justify their loyalty to Goodyear to sponsors looking for victories, the challenge of beating Firestone verged on the insurmountable.

The '99 season saw just three full-time teams on Goodyear – Walker Racing, Marlboro Team Penske and All American Racers – with Bettenhausen Racing running a partial season. Thanks to Goodyear's withdrawal from Formula 1, additional resources were made available for the CART program. Indeed, Gil de Ferran and Derrick Walker's team were competitive in the first half of the season – winning at Portland, taking pole at Motegi and Toronto, and qualifying in the top six no fewer than seven times.

However, de Ferran found the Goodyears took an inordinate amount of time to reach peak efficiency, so he was frequently unable to take maximum advantage of his good starting positions. Moreover, he generally lost ground on restarts following full-course yellows. Given the generally disappointing seasons experienced by Penske, AAR and Bettenhausen, carrying the fight to Firestone week-in and week-out proved an impossible task for de Ferran, Walker and, ultimately, Goodyear itself.

Goodyear
Production base: Akron, Ohio
Wins: 1
(de Ferran);
Poles: 2
(de Ferran)

REYNARD

**Production base: Bicester, England;
U.S. base: Indianapolis, Indiana**

Number of cars built in 1999: 46

Wins: 18
(Montoya 7, Franchitti 3, Fernandez 2, Tracy 2,
Moore 1, de Ferran 1, Kanaan 1, Herta 1);
Poles: 17
(Montoya 7, de Ferran 2, Franchitti 2, Moore 1,
Kanaan 1, Vasser 1, Papis 1, Herta 1, Pruett 1)

WHEN Barry Ward stepped into the Chief Designer position for Reynard Motorsport's Champ Car program, replacing Malcolm Oastler who concentrated most of his efforts on British American Racing's highly publicized entry into Formula 1, he knew that he didn't exactly have to re-invent the wheel to be successful. In building the 99I, Reynard's team of engineers simply made evolutionary changes to the '98 model that had won 18 of that season's 19 FedEx Championship Series events.

A pronounced inward curvature on the leading edges of the front wings was reminiscent of the '98 Swift, and the resulting change to the airflow necessitated a more obvious indentation to the sidepods. There were other subtle modifications to the all-important aerodynamics, while many minor changes were made in the name of driver safety, including a thickening of the sidepods.

'We didn't make any drastic changes,' said Ward, 'but we have made over 100 detailed, yet significant, improvements.'

Development, of course, continued during the season as several teams took advantage of Reynard's highly touted new wind tunnel, in Indianapolis, to hone their own cars. Consequently, the 1999 Reynard was every bit as strong as its predecessor, winning 18 events for the second straight year, along with 17 poles. Again there was strength in numbers, 21 of the 28 entries at the season opener being in the Bicester, England-based creations, although for various reasons that number had dwindled slightly to 19 of 27 by the Fontana finale.

The margin of victory in the Constructor's Championship was narrowed a bit in '99, but Reynard still was able to roll to its fifth consecutive crown with a 424–241 advantage over second-place Swift. (In '98, incidentally, the differential had been 408–166.) The 99I's superiority also was evident in the 'laps led' department, which showed Reynard out in front for a remarkable 2,334 of the season's 2,769 laps (84.3 percent).

SWIFT

Production base: San Clemente, California

Number of cars built in 1999: 15

Wins: 2 (Andretti 1, Fittipaldi 1); Poles: 2 (Fittipaldi 1, Andretti 1)

SWIFT Engineering produced some significant revisions in comparison to the car that won just one race in 1998, including an overall lengthening of the chassis by three inches. Technical Director Mark Handford found ways to make the car lighter and easier to work on, which proved to be a selling point, Patrick Racing and Team Gordon joining Della Penna Motorsports and Newman/Haas as customers during the off-season. A slightly longer nosecone and revised aerodynamics, including a two-element front wing and extended leading edges on the sidepods, differentiated the 010.c design from the preceding 009.c.

The car showed promise right away as Newman/Haas teammates Michael Andretti and Christian Fittipaldi set a fast pace in road-course testing. Adrian Fernandez was similarly delighted after trying out Pat Patrick's car for the first time before Christmas. But the Mexican wasn't nearly so happy following his first oval test at Homestead. After initially questioning the veracity of some negative feedback, Handford concluded that the aerodynamic balance for medium-length ovals was, indeed, sadly lacking. An update kit was beneficial, but not by enough of a margin to prevent Patrick Racing from wheeling out its updated Reynards for the first few races. Fernandez reverted to the Swift for Long Beach, where he finished fourth, but thereafter preferred to concentrate on the Reynards. By season's end, Gordon and Della Penna also had jumped ship.

Frankly, after some changes had been made, there didn't seem to be much wrong with the car. Andretti and Fittipaldi were consistently competitive, and while Fittipaldi missed five races due to injury, Andretti would have mounted a sterner title challenge had it not been for a series of mistakes and miscues. But the damage had been done. Handford left the fold before season's end, rejoining Lola, and Newman/Haas later followed suit.

LOLA

Production base: Huntingdon, England; U.S. base: Indianapolis, Indiana

Number of cars built in 1999: 7

Wins: 0; Poles: 1 (Castro-Neves)

LOLA Cars International took another step back toward the top of the Champ Car ladder in 1999. The staff, led by Technical Director Frank Dernie and Chief Designer Ben Bowlby, did not make many changes to the previous year's little-used model, relying instead on increased feedback from Lola's growing customer base. A newly-constructed wind tunnel at the company's base in Huntingdon, England, came on line in June, further enhancing the capacity for refinements.

The only noticeable change to the '99 edition of the Lola was the attachment of the rear wing by a vertical post rather than the canted strut seen in the previous season, although Chief Aerodynamicist Chris Saunders did produce several bodywork updates, including a new undertray.

Gerald Davis' small team had flown the Lola flag alone in '98 but, sadly, had been unable to raise sufficient sponsorship to continue. Nevertheless, spurred on by the promising results achieved in '98, Hogan Racing, Payton/Coyne Racing and Bettenhausen Motorsports all signed up to purchase new B99/00s. (The 'B' designation, incidentally, referred to accomplished Irish businessman Martin Birrane, who had rescued the famous name from bankruptcy in 1997.) Unfortunately, Bettenhausen never had the opportunity to run its car, due also to a lack of sponsorship, but eventually traded it on to Marlboro Team Penske, which later augmented its stable by purchasing two more cars.

It was Carl Hogan's team, though, that showed the B99/00's true capabilities, Helio Castro-Neves producing a string of excellent performances, including fastest race laps at Motegi and Nazareth, where he passed eventual winner Juan Montoya twice before retiring. The talented Brazilian also won the pole at Milwaukee, earning the top starting spot for the 75th time in the constructor's rich history and the first time since Andre Ribeiro took the honors in Toronto in 1996. A victory continued to prove elusive, and performances later in the year were masked by a series of engine problems, but the car's promise was plain for all to see.

DAN Gurney's superbly equipped manufacturing complex in Santa Ana, California, endured another difficult season in 1999, although once again its Eagle chassis produced some promising results. Swift co-founder David Bruns had joined Gurney's All American Racers group as Technical Director midway through the 1998 campaign, and once again he concentrated on some more fine-tuning of the promising 987 chassis, rather than a total redesign. The winglets in front of the rear tires were removed in favor of flip-up mechanisms, a la Penske, but many of the distinctive Eagle's unique features were retained, including the blunt nose cone, curved sidepods and triangular cutouts in the rear wing (designed to increase rear downforce during cornering).

Progress was hindered by the fact that the Toyota engine still was not on a par with the Ford, Honda and Mercedes opposition – at least in the early part of the season – plus the fact that budgetary constraints meant Gurney was restricted to running a singleton entry. Alex Barron showed prodigious speed in testing, especially on the short ovals, but for various reasons that was not translated into race results and the Californian's services were dispensed with after seven races. Gualter Salles, Raul Boesel and Andrea Montermini all tried to turn things around, but a lack of testing and unfamiliarity with the team, engine and the Goodyear tires all proved impossible handicaps to overcome. Ironically, Barron's ninth-place finish at Nazareth and a top-ten qualifying effort at Milwaukee were to remain as the year's best results.

Nevertheless, when Robby Gordon tested the car at Mid-Ohio in late-summer, he was immediately impressed, lapping considerably quicker than Salles with a bare minimum of mileage. Gordon fielded a second Eagle in five late-season races and scored points in two of them.

By year's end, the Eagles had accumulated 13 points, ensuring a position ahead of Penske in the Constructor's Championship.

EAGLE

Production base: Santa Ana, California

Number of cars built in 1999: 4

Wins: 0; Poles: 0

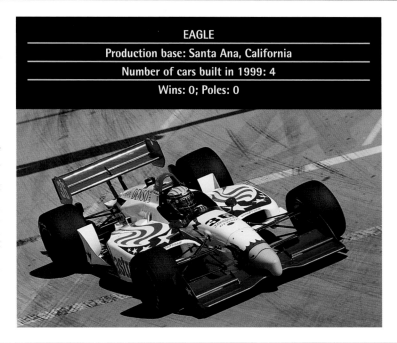

PENSKE

Production base: Poole, England; U.S. base: Reading, Pennsylvania

Number of cars built in 1999: 6

Wins: 0; Poles: 0

A YEAR that began with increased optimism for the Penske camp ended with nearly total abandonment as Al Unser Jr. switched to the Lola chassis after just five events, and Roger Penske announced major shakeups in the organization before the season-ending race in Fontana.

Chief Engineer John Travis, in his second year as Penske Cars' head designer, felt the team had made significant strides in eliminating what he described as 'fundamental aerodynamic problems' with the PC27, which had shown immense promise in '98 without producing the desired results. A resculpted undertray and a pronounced step on the chassis floor were among aerodynamic improvements to the PC27B. Wider end-plates on the front wing also were incorporated to influence airflow around the front tires following extensive wind-tunnel tests in Southampton, England.

As in '98, the Penske set new standards for the quality of workmanship on the Champ Car grid. Sadly, once again, there were no results to match. Part of the problem stemmed from Roger Penske's decision to concentrate on a solitary entry for Al Unser Jr., who's skills as a race car driver were undoubted, but who's developmental talents apparently left room for improvement. Worse, Unser was injured in the opening race, whereupon Brazilian rookie Tarso Marques was thrown in at the deep end after displaying some promise during testing. Marques' lack of experience led to numerous accidents, and when Unser returned and was given the opportunity to test a Lola, he immediately announced his preference for the latter chassis.

The Penske still showed well in back-to-back tests, but, curiously, was used only in the superspeedway events – to excellent effect by both Unser and Alex Barron – and in some late-season races after the tragic death of Gonzalo Rodriguez left only one serviceable Lola. Consequently, after finishing third in the constructor's race in '98, the team placed last in the five-car field with a dismal tally of just ten points.

Gil de Ferran

C·A·R·T·.com

MAN + MACHINE

FedEx
CHAMPIONSHIP
SERIES™

Richie Hearn

C·A·R·T FEEL THE SPEED

PPG CUP

Position	Driver	Car	Tires	Homestead	Motegi	Long Beach	Nazareth	Rio de Janeiro	Gateway	Milwaukee	Portland	Cleveland	Road America	Toronto	Michigan	Detroit	Mid-Ohio	Chicago	Vancouver	Laguna Seca	Houston	Surfers Paradise	Fontana	Points total
1	*Juan Montoya (COL)	Target/Chip Ganassi Racing Honda/Reynard 99I	FS	10	13	1	1p†	1†	1p†	11p	10†	2p	1p†	13	22	2	17p†	1	1†	1p†	8	25p	16	212
2	Dario Franchitti (GB)	Team KOOL Green Honda/Reynard 99I	FS	3	22	2	8	2	3	7	3	25	18	1†	5	1	3p†	2	10	25	2	1p†	10	212
3	Paul Tracy (CDN)	Team KOOL Green Honda/Reynard 99I	FS	–	11	21	3	15	19	1	5	4	11	2	3	2	2	23	18	4	1†	7	18	161
4	Michael Andretti (USA)	Newman/Haas Kmart/Texaco Havoline Ford Cosworth/Swift 010.c	FS	2	5	7	6	26	1†	15	10	3	2p	26	4	4	8	22	14	10	3	5	21	151
5	Max Papis (I)	Team Rahal Miller Lite Ford Cosworth/Reynard 99I	FS	5	16	9	13	4	5	13	8	16	5	5	7†	26	5	4p	23	3	4	2	2†	150
6	Adrian Fernandez (MEX)	Patrick Racing Tecate/Quaker State Ford Cosworth/Reynard 98I	FS	20	–	–	–	–	–	–	–	–	–	–	–	–	–	–	–	–	–	–	–	140
		Patrick Racing Tecate/Quaker State Ford Cosworth/Reynard 97I	FS	–	1†	–	5	20	21	5	–	–	–	6	–	–	–	–	–	–	–	1	–	
		Patrick Racing Tecate/Quaker State Ford Cosworth/Swift 010.c	FS	–	–	4	–	–	–	–	–	–	–	–	–	–	–	–	–	–	–	–	–	
		Patrick Racing Tecate/Quaker State Ford Cosworth/Reynard 99I	FS	–	–	–	–	–	–	–	4	19	3	–	6	NS	–	–	5	12	3	–	–	
7	Christian Fittipaldi (BR)	Newman/Haas Big Kmart Ford Cosworth/Swift 010.c	FS	9	3	5	7	3p	9	6	14	12	1	3	8	–	–	–	–	–	7	25	3	121
8	Gil de Ferran (BR)	Walker Racing Valvoline/Cummins Honda/Reynard 99I	GY	6	2p	6	15	10	25	3	1†	2	14	19p	24	22	6	13	26	6	17	27	9	108
9	Jimmy Vasser (USA)	Target/Chip Ganassi Racing Honda/Reynard 99I	FS	4	12	10	11	27	10	4	12	23	23	8	9p	5	4	3	18	20	18	5	–	104
10	Greg Moore (CDN)	Forsythe Racing Player's/Indeck Mercedes/Reynard 99I	FS	1p†	4	8	12	8	6	2	13	18	4	20	23	3	11	26	20	23	16	17	26	97
11	Tony Kanaan (BR)	McDonald's Championship Racing Honda/Reynard 99I	FS	21	6	22p†	23	5	7	18	15	22	6	17	1	6	23	11	9	21	9	6	8	85
12	Bryan Herta (USA)	Team Rahal Shell Ford Cosworth/Reynard 99I	FS	12	23	3	22	13	23	25	6	6	15	15	20	9	21	8	24	1p†	5	4	14	84
13	Patrick Carpentier (CDN)	Forsythe Racing Player's/Indeck Mercedes/Reynard 99I	FS	7	26	17	14	6	22	9	9	7	22	11	10	23	–	6	2	9	19	24	25	61
14	Roberto Moreno (BR)	PacWest Racing Group Motorola Mercedes/Reynard 99I	FS	–	–	–	–	11	4	12	7	8	19	4	19	–	–	–	–	–	–	–	–	58
		Newman/Haas Big Kmart Ford Cosworth/Swift 010.c	FS	–	–	–	–	–	–	–	–	–	–	–	–	14	16	9	15	2	–	–	–	
15	Helio Castro-Neves (BR)	Hogan Racing Hogan Motor Leasing Mercedes/Lola B99/00	FS	17	9	19	21	25	2	26p	26	26	16	27	25	7	7	5	8	26	26	21	20	48
16	Mauricio Gugelmin (BR)	PacWest Racing Group Hollywood Mercedes/Reynard 99I	FS	11	7	14	18	22	18	8	25	21	12	14	22	24	20	19	4	11	6	26	6	44
17	PJ Jones (USA)	Patrick Racing Visteon Ford Cosworth/Reynard 98I	FS	13	15	–	–	–	–	–	–	–	–	–	–	–	–	–	–	–	–	–	12	38
		Patrick Racing Visteon Ford Cosworth/Swift 010.c	FS	–	–	12	2	7	8	20	21	15	17	10	16	–	–	–	–	–	–	–	–	
		Patrick Racing Tecate/Quaker State Ford Cosworth/Reynard 97I	FS	–	–	–	–	–	–	–	–	–	–	–	–	–	–	15	7	21	–	–	–	
18	*Cristiano da Matta (BR)	Arciero-Wells Racing MCI WorldCom Toyota/Reynard 99I	FS	14	25	20	4	21	17	11	11	20	21	24	17	19	9	14	5	22	11	13	23	32
19	Scott Pruett (USA)	Arciero-Wells Racing Pioneer Toyota/Reynard 99I	FS	22	21	15	10	24	14	17	24	17	25	7	14	8	17	20	13	7	10	9	22p	28
20	Robby Gordon (USA)	Team Gordon Panasonic/Menards Toyota/Reynard 98I	FS	19	8	16	19	–	–	–	–	–	–	–	–	–	–	–	–	–	–	–	–	27
		Team Gordon Panasonic/Menards Toyota/Swift 010.c	FS	–	–	–	–	–	14	27	24	17	9	8	13	26	10	–	–	–	–	–	–	
		Team Gordon Panasonic/Menards Toyota/Eagle 997	FS	–	–	–	–	–	–	–	–	–	–	–	–	–	–	10	22	19	21	–	11	
21 =	Al Unser Jr. (USA)	Marlboro Team Penske Mercedes/Penske PC27B	GY	26	–	–	24	12	–	–	–	–	–	13	–	–	–	–	–	–	15	22	7	26
		Marlboro Team Penske Mercedes/Lola B99/00	GY	–	–	–	–	–	12	19	16	5	9	9	–	15	25	25	25	NS	–	–	–	
21 =	Richie Hearn (USA)	Della Penna Motorsports Budweiser Toyota/Swift 010.c	FS	23	10	11	20	19	–	–	–	–	–	–	–	–	–	–	–	–	–	–	–	26
		Della Penna Motorsports Budweiser Toyota/Reynard 98I	FS	–	–	–	–	–	–	13	–	22	–	–	–	–	–	–	–	–	–	–	–	
		Della Penna Motorsports Budweiser Toyota/Reynard 99I	FS	–	–	–	–	–	–	21	–	10	10	16	12	13	12	16	6	16	8	23	27	
23	Mark Blundell (GB)	PacWest Racing Group Motorola Mercedes/Reynard 99I	FS	8	24	13	17	–	–	–	–	–	–	–	–	10	13	21	19	12	24	19	16	9
24	Jan Magnussen (DK)	Patrick Racing Visteon Ford Cosworth/Swift 010.c	FS	–	–	–	–	–	–	–	–	–	–	–	–	18	–	–	–	–	–	–	–	8
		Patrick Racing Visteon Ford Cosworth/Reynard 98I	FS	–	–	–	–	–	–	–	–	–	–	–	–	–	14	24	7	17	13	11	–	
25	Michel Jourdain Jr. (MEX)	Payton/Coyne Herdez/Viva Mexico Ford Cosworth/Lola T97/00	FS	18	18	18	16	16	20	16	20	27	7	21	21	21	26	18	17	20	18	12	13	7
26	Gualter Salles (BR)	Payton/Coyne Refricentro Ford Cosworth/Lola T98/00	FS	–	–	27	–	–	–	–	–	–	–	–	–	–	–	–	–	–	–	10	–	5
		Bettenhausen Motorsports Epson Mercedes/Reynard 98I	GY	–	–	–	–	–	17	–	–	–	–	–	–	–	–	–	–	–	–	–	–	
		All American Racers Denso/Castrol Toyota/Eagle 997	GY	–	–	–	–	–	–	–	–	–	27	13	20	25	15	11	18	–	–	–	–	
27 =	Alex Barron (USA)	All American Racers Denso/Castrol Toyota/Eagle 997	GY	15	17	23	9	23	16	14	–	–	–	–	–	–	–	–	–	–	–	–	–	4
		Marlboro Team Penske Mercedes/Penske PC27B	GY	–	–	–	–	–	–	–	–	–	–	–	–	18	–	–	–	–	–	–	24	
27 =	*Tarso Marques (BR)	Marlboro Team Penske Mercedes/Penske PC27B	GY	–	14	25	–	9	26	–	18	–	–	–	–	–	–	–	–	–	–	–	–	4
		Marlboro Team Penske Mercedes/Lola B99/00	GY	–	–	–	–	–	–	–	–	24	–	–	–	–	–	–	–	–	–	–	–	
27 =	*Memo Gidley (USA)	Walker Racing Alpine Honda/Reynard 98I	GY	–	–	–	–	–	–	–	19	11	26	12	–	–	–	–	–	–	–	–	–	4
		Payton/Coyne Herdez/Viva Mexico Ford Cosworth/Lola T97/00	FS	–	–	–	–	–	–	–	–	–	–	–	–	–	–	20	22	–	12	13	14	
30 =	Dennis Vitolo (USA)	Payton/Coyne Nicoderm/Nicorette CQ Ford Cosworth/Reynard 99I	FS	16	–	–	NS	–	–	–	–	–	–	–	–	–	–	–	–	–	–	–	–	2
		Payton/Coyne Nicoderm/Nicorette CQ Ford Cosworth/Reynard 98I	FS	–	–	–	–	–	24	22	–	–	–	–	–	11	–	15	–	–	–	–	15	
		Payton/Coyne Tang Ford Cosworth/Reynard 97I	FS	–	–	–	–	–	–	–	–	–	–	–	–	–	18	–	–	–	–	–	–	
30 =	Andrea Montermini (I)	All American Racers Denso/Castrol Toyota/Eagle 997	GY	–	–	–	–	–	–	–	–	–	–	–	–	–	–	–	11	24	23	15	–	2
32 =	Raul Boesel (BR)	Team KOOL Green Honda/Reynard 99I	FS	27	–	–	–	–	–	–	–	–	–	–	–	–	–	–	–	–	–	–	–	1
		All American Racers Denso/Castrol Toyota/Eagle 997	GY	–	–	–	–	–	–	–	–	–	–	–	–	–	12	–	–	–	–	–	17	
32 =	*Gonzalo Rodriguez (URG)	Marlboro Team Penske Mercedes/Lola B99/00	GY	–	–	–	–	–	–	–	–	–	–	–	–	–	–	–	12	–	NS	–	–	1
	*Luiz Garcia Jr. (BR)	Payton/Coyne Racing Tang Ford Cosworth/Reynard 97I	FS	24	19	24	–	18	–	–	23	14	24	–	–	–	–	–	–	–	–	–	–	0
		Hogan Racing Hogan Motor Leasing/Tang Mercedes/Lola B99/00	FS	–	–	–	–	–	–	–	–	–	–	–	–	–	–	24	NS	16	15	NS	–	
	*Naoki Hattori (J)	Walker Racing Alpine Honda/Reynard 99I	GY	25	–	–	–	–	–	–	–	–	–	–	–	–	–	–	–	–	–	–	–	0
		Walker Racing Alpine Honda/Reynard 98I	GY	–	–	–	–	–	–	–	–	–	–	–	–	16	19	–	27	14	22	20	19	
	*Shigeaki Hattori (J)	Bettenhausen Motorsports Epson Mercedes/Reynard 98I	GY	NS	20	26	NS	–	15	23	28	–	–	23	–	–	–	17	–	NS	–	–	–	0

Bold type indicates car still running at finish

* rookie   † led most laps   p pole position   NQ did not qualify   NS did not start

Pole positions

1	Juan Pablo Montoya	7
2 =	Gil de Ferran	2
2 =	Dario Franchitti	2
4 =	Michael Andretti	1
4 =	Max Papis	1
4 =	Bryan Herta	1
4 =	Helio Castro-Neves	1
4 =	Christian Fittipaldi	1
4 =	Jimmy Vasser	1
4 =	Scott Pruett	1
4 =	Tony Kanaan	1
4 =	Greg Moore	1

Nation's Cup

1	Brazil	271
2	United States	264
3	Canada	248
4 =	Colombia	212
4 =	Scotland	212
6	Italy	152
7	Mexico	140
8	England	9
9	Denmark	8
10	Uruguay	1
11	Japan	0

Manufacturer's Championship

1	Honda	383
2	Ford	301
3	Mercedes-Benz	193
4	Toyota	80

Constructor's Championship

1	Reynard	424
2	Swift	241
3	Lola	69
4	Eagle	13
5	Penske	10

Jim Trueman Rookie of the Year

1	Juan Pablo Montoya	212
2	Cristiano da Matta	32
3	Tarso Marques	4
4	Memo Gidley	4
5	Gonzalo Rodriguez	1
6 =	Luiz Garcia Jr.	0
6 =	Naoki Hattori	0
6 =	Shigeaki Hattori	0

TOYOTA RACING DEVELOPMENT

LISTEN CAREFULLY AND YOU CAN
HEAR THE SOUND OF OUR ENGINEERS
COMMANDING YOUR RESPECT.

Back to back IMSA GTP championships. Over eighty off-road victories. The
fastest time ever at Pikes Peak. From the drawing board to the cockpit, at TRD
our minds are always racing. Visit www.toyota.com/trd and get up to speed.

TOYOTA | EVERYDAY

Michael C. Brown

HOMESTEAD

| 1 - MOORE | 2 - ANDRETTI | 3 - FRANCHITTI |

QUALIFYING

Everything old was new again at the Homestead-Miami Speedway as the 1999 FedEx Championship Series opened with the same pole-sitter as it had done one year earlier. Greg Moore snapped off a lap of 24.886 seconds, 217.279 mph, in Jerry Forsythe's Player's/Indeck Mercedes/Reynard to repeat his pole-winning effort from 1998.

'I'd be happy to end the championship right now,' quipped Moore, 'because I'm leading it.'

Posting the fastest morning practice lap allowed Moore to watch while the other 26 cars made qualifying attempts. The 23-year-old Canadian rose to the occasion with a lap only fractionally slower than his existing track record. Adrian Fernandez joined Moore on the front row. His Tecate/Quaker State Ford/Reynard was the only other competitor above 216 mph.

Moore's teammate, Patrick Carpentier, occupied third on the grid alongside the biggest surprise of the week, Helio Castro-Neves. The sophomore driver gave Lola its first top-ten starting position since the 1996 season finale at Laguna Seca, rounding the

1.502-mile oval at 215.581 mph.

Twice defending race champion Michael Andretti started fifth, while rookie Cristiano da Matta gave the Toyota engine program its best-ever starting position with a sixth-place run. Both Robby Gordon and Max Papis had gridded 13th last year for the previous high-water mark.

Gil de Ferran opened his season with a ruined car after an engine grenaded on his first qualifying lap. The result of the powerplant explosion pitched Derrick Walker's Valvoline/Cummins Honda/Reynard heavily into the Turn Two wall, ending the day, but not the weekend, for a bruised de Ferran.

Post-qualifying inspection claimed a pair of entries, as two of the three Payton/Coyne cars were disqualified. The rear wing on Michel Jourdain Jr.'s Lola was mounted too high according to inspectors, while Dennis Vitolo's Reynard carried its undertray (which had been repaired following a crash in testing) fractionally too low.

The new season is under way. Greg Moore (99) gets the jump on Adrian Fernandez as CART Starter Jim Swintal waves the green flag for the first time in 1999. Helio Castro-Neves, meanwhile, tries to make a move to the inside.

Inset: Greg Moore claimed the pole for the second successive year at Homestead. This time, flanked by Michael Andretti *(left)* and Dario Franchitti on the podium, he emerged victorious on race day as well.

NEW legal restrictions that prevented tobacco companies from advertising more than one brand meant that Forsythe Racing could not display its customary Player's logos on the Mercedes/Reynards of Greg Moore and Patrick Carpentier. The team had to find another way of leaving an impression on the Homestead crowd in the CART FedEx Championship Series opener, and Moore did just that in style. Starting from the pole for the second straight year, he dominated the latter part of the Marlboro Grand Prix of Miami Presented by Toyota, leading 96 of 150 laps en route to his fifth Champ Car victory.

Moore was fastest in Saturday's practice and came just 0.030 second short of breaking his own track record in qualifying. Teammate Carpentier occupied third position on the grid, the Forsythe cars sandwiching outside-pole qualifier Adrian Fernandez's Tecate/Quaker State/Patrick Racing Ford/Reynard 98I.

Moore led the first 16 laps at reduced pace after an opening-lap crash, when rookie Naoki Hattori lost control of his Alpine Honda/Reynard in Turn Two and was collected by Al Unser Jr.'s Marlboro Mercedes/Penske. Hattori suffered a double compound fracture of his lower left leg, while

Unser underwent surgery to repair a broken right ankle and a torn ligament in his left knee.

The #99 Forsythe car went on to lead under green-flag conditions seemingly as easily as it had under the yellow. Moore led 43 more laps at speed before pitting on lap 60.

Behind the 23-year-old Canadian, things remained fairly orderly. Brazilian Helio Castro-Neves showed that his fourth-place grid position was no fluke, easing his Hogan Motor Leasing Mercedes/Lola past Carpentier at the start and into third position. He would remain there until lap 42, when a resurgent Carpentier

stormed by on a charge back toward the front. Carpentier moved into second place a lap later, sweeping past Fernandez and setting off in pursuit of Moore.

Max Papis, making his first start aboard Team Rahal's Miller Lite Ford/Reynard, pushed his way into the top ten after starting 15th. Papis passed Jimmy Vasser's Target Honda/Reynard on lap 38 and didn't stop there. The 29-year-old Italian slid by Mauricio Gugelmin a lap later, then picked off rookie Juan Montoya on lap 41.

Tony Kanaan's sophomore year began with new colors, as McDonald's Championship Racing now controlled

the #44 Honda/Reynard. His season opener effectively came to an end on lap 48, however, when he pitted with the beginning of a fuel system malady and fell two laps behind. Kanaan finally dropped out on lap 98.

Kanaan's former Tasman Indy Lights teammate, Castro-Neves, began the first round of pit stops along with fellow Tasman graduate Cristiano da Matta (MCI WorldCom Toyota/Reynard) on lap 57. The first pit battle of the year was won by Team KOOL Green as Kyle Moyer's crew enabled Dario Franchitti to leapfrog Moore and Carpentier to take the lead on lap 67.

'My crew guys were just fantastic today,' said Franchitti. 'They gave me great pit stops.'

Michael Andretti also received solid service from his Newman/Haas Kmart/Texaco crew, emerging ahead of the Forsythe cars and behind only Franchitti's Honda/Reynard. But behind the #27 car is where Andretti would stay, as Franchitti had stormed to a 15-second advantage by the midpoint of the race.

Gil de Ferran, in the sole Goodyear-shod car to finish in the points, was the only driver to gain a spot for the next 13 laps. Rebounding from a nasty meeting with the Turn Two wall in Saturday's qualifying, de Ferran took Walker Racing's backup Valvoline/Cummins Honda/Reynard past Papis into seventh place on lap 76.

Scott Pruett single-handedly erased Franchitti's advantage on lap 80, when he slid his Pioneer Toyota/Reynard into the Turn Two wall. The resulting caution flag sent most of the leaders into the pits; but a brave pair dared to try a different strategy. Castro-Neves and de Ferran eschewed pit stops and reaped the benefits – at least temporarily. The Brazilian led 29 laps and was headed for a great result before an out-of-sequence pit stop and engine problems relegated Carl Hogan's team to the sidelines.

Despite the setback, Castro-Neves remained in upbeat mood. 'I'm so happy,' he said. 'I had a great car. I was just hanging in there, trying not to do anything stupid, trying to keep calm. I didn't understand the pit strategy and, of course, it was disappointing not to finish.'

Andretti was poised to show the way out of the pits after fast work by

The devil you know...

PATRICK Racing intended to field new Swift chassis in 1999, but decided only a few weeks before the first race to revert to its proven '98 Reynards – at least for the first few races. Initially, the team had been pleased with its Swifts following some promising tests on road courses.

During the traditional Spring Training session on the Homestead oval in early February, however, Adrian Fernandez and new teammate PJ Jones faced an uphill struggle due to excessive understeer (or push). It transpired that the Swift 010.c was producing plenty of downforce, crucial for the medium-length ovals, but with too much of a rearward bias. Thus, with insufficient front grip, the car tended to understeer into the corners.

Swift Technical Director Mark Handford admitted that, at first, he was skeptical of the Patrick engineers' doubts about the 010.c's effectiveness, which had first been raised during a test at Homestead before Christmas. Newman/Haas Racing had experienced no such difficulty; Michael Andretti and Christian

Fittipaldi were delighted with the new car. Instead, their concerns were tire-related and ultimately resulted in a switch from Goodyear to Firestone less than a month before the first race.

Immediately after Spring Training, Handford reconsidered the problem. Two weeks later, Pat Patrick's team returned to South Florida for more tests with a hastily redesigned underbody. Once again, the drivers were encouraged. The revisions were a step in the right direction, handling being improved and lap times becoming immediately almost a half-second quicker. But then Fernandez hopped aboard his trusty Reynard. Right away he was faster still, posting one of the fastest laps seen during preseason testing. Jones, too, felt more comfortable in his Reynard.

Fernandez was a factor throughout the race weekend, taking advantage of his previous experience with the car by posting the fastest lap on Friday and emerging second quickest after qualifying. He ran well in the race, too, before being let down by a rare XD engine failure.

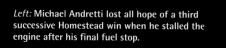

Left: Michael Andretti lost all hope of a third successive Homestead win when he stalled the engine after his final fuel stop.

Below: Dario Franchitti is dressed for action, while regular teammate Paul Tracy can only sit and watch.

Right: Most teams wore full-face helmets for the first time.

Below: Patrick Carpentier was in tune for qualifying, but slipped a little in the race.

Center: Rookie Cristiano da Matta compares notes with Tony Kanaan.

Bottom: Mark Blundell is ready for action.

FEDEX CHAMPIONSHIP SERIES • ROUND 1

Christian Fittipaldi describes the subtle sensations of pitch and roll as he attempts to improve the handling of his Newman/Haas Ford/Swift.

Donny Hoevel's crew. But the engine stalled abruptly, and by the time it was restarted, the Newman/Haas car had dropped to seventh.

'I don't know what happened. It was just a stupid mistake,' lamented Andretti. 'I dropped the clutch and it stalled. It was my fault. It cost us four [PPG Cup] points. Hopefully, they won't come back and haunt us.'

Papis had a strong restart, eclipsing rookie da Matta and Mark Blundell (Hollywood/PacWest Mercedes/Reynard) to claim eighth position on lap 93. Then Fernandez brought out the day's final yellow on lap 111, when his fourth-place run ended with an engine failure and consequent spin into the Turn Four wall. The caution enabled the fuel-starved Castro-Neves and de Ferran to head for the pits.

Franchitti had taken on fuel with everyone else during the second round of stops, but there was some doubt as to whether or not he could reach the finish without a splash-and-go stop. Barry Green's crew elected to err on the side of caution, and Franchitti dived into the pit lane for another few gallons, relinquishing the lead once again to Moore on lap 114.

Moore led Andretti to the restart, followed by Vasser, Papis, Blundell, da Matta, Carpentier, Franchitti and de Ferran. Castro-Neves, Christian Fittipaldi (Big Kmart Ford/Swift) and

Bryan Herta – who eschewed the opportunity to make a pit stop in his Shell Ford/Reynard to regain the lead lap – completed the unlapped runners.

Franchitti and de Ferran hooked up momentarily when the green flag flew, dropping Carpentier to ninth on lap 124. The #27 car powered on, making quick work of da Matta before going on to pick off Blundell and Papis on successive laps.

A strong opening run melted away for rookie da Matta in the late laps as a punctured tire condemned him to come home in 14th.

'It was a great experience,' said da Matta. 'The whole team did a great job during the entire weekend, and especially [during] the race. My first objective was to finish the race and we did that. I'm really happy with the way the engine and chassis ran all

day. I'm happy to have this one under my belt.'

Vasser held his grip on third place as Moore and Andretti pulled away. The 1996 PPG Cup champion had struggled with an ill-handling car during the early stages, but continual adjustments made both inside the cockpit and by his crew enabled Vasser to move steadily up the order and challenge for a podium finish. Ultimately, however, he had to give best to Franchitti, who concluded a fierce duel by slipping past into third with a strong maneuver in Turn One with only five laps to go.

'It was pretty tight. I had my eyes closed to be honest,' admitted Franchitti. 'But there was no way I was going to give the corner up. Jimmy's an experienced guy and he gave me enough room.'

Andretti saw his advantage over Franchitti shrink to just over a second in the waning moments as the Team KOOL Green star saved his best for last. A lap of 201.573 mph on lap 149 proved to be the fastest of the race; but it was not enough to overtake the #6 Newman/Haas car. Third place was the highest-ever finish on an oval for the Scottish driver.

'We played it very conservative and made an extra stop,' related Franchitti. 'We decided we'd be happy with a top-five finish. First race, podium, I'll take it.'

Papis gained fifth place in his first Rahal ride, followed by de Ferran, Carpentier (who earlier had been penalized for a pit-lane infraction), Blundell and Fittipaldi.

Nine cars finished on the lead lap. Target/Ganassi rookie Montoya earned tenth in his first race as replacement for reigning series champion Alex Zanardi, who opted for a return to Formula 1 with the Winfield Williams team instead of seeking a third successive PPG Cup title. The young Colombian lost two laps with a loose condition, but fought back to finish just one lap adrift. Gugelmin and Herta claimed the final two points-paying positions.

Moore won the race by 1.11 seconds and earned a maximum 22 points for doing so from the pole while also leading most laps.

'There are some times when you don't have the fastest car, but you have the breaks,' concluded Moore. 'This was a real team effort. We had to work on the car. It was extremely, extremely, extremely loose in the first stint, but we kept chipping away and it became good. I couldn't be happier.'

Jeremy Shaw/Eric Mauk

New faces, new places

AS usual, there were plenty of changes on race teams throughout the CART landscape prior to the new season. In fact, nearly half of the 27-car field had made some kind of major switch since the conclusion of the '98 campaign. The Homestead-Miami Speedway event provided the first true measure of the effectiveness of those moves.

Newman/Haas teammates Michael Andretti and Christian Fittipaldi switched to Firestone tires, for example, and both earned points in the season opener. Andretti finished second, a mere 1.11 seconds behind Greg Moore, while Fittipaldi came home in ninth.

Max Papis led those who changed teams entirely, battling from 15th on the starting grid to fifth in his first appearance with Team Rahal. The run matched his career-high finish at Houston in 1998. Former AAR stalwart PJ Jones just missed scoring a point, placing 13th in his first outing with Pat Patrick's Visteon Ford/Reynard. Helio Castro-Neves, formerly with Bettenhausen Motorsports, led a career-high 29 laps, but fell victim to an out-of-sync pit strategy that cost him any chance of being in contention

for a win on his debut with Carl Hogan's Hogan Motor Leasing Mercedes/Lola.

Rookies impressed in their first outings, led by Colombian Juan Montoya. Stepping into the Target/Ganassi ride after the defection of Alex Zanardi to Formula 1, Montoya finished tenth. Reigning Indy Lights champ Cristiano da Matta replaced Papis in Arciero-Wells Racing's MCI WorldCom Toyota/Reynard and ran among the top ten virtually throughout.

Michel Jourdain Jr. improved ten spots on his '98 Homestead finish in his first drive with a Lola chassis. Jourdain replaced his Reynard with a fully updated Lola T97/00, overcoming a sticking throttle and other problems to finish 18th.

Tony Kanaan raced under the McDonald's Championship Racing banner after Tasman boss Steve Horne sold his operation to Gerald Forsythe over the winter, while John Della Penna re-equipped Richie Hearn's Swift with Toyota (rather than Ford) engines. However, neither Kanaan nor Hearn made it to the finish line.

HOMESTEAD SNIPPETS

Photos: Michael C. Brown

• Team KOOL Green's **PAUL TRACY** became the first driver ever to be excluded from a CART event for disciplinary reasons when Chief Steward Wally Dallenbach sidelined the 30-year-old Canadian for the Homestead opener. Dallenbach benched Tracy after finding him guilty of 'blocking, unjustifiable risk and unsportsmanlike conduct' at the 1998 Honda Indy in Australia. Veteran **RAUL BOESEL** *(left)* stood in for Tracy in the #26 Honda/Reynard but, unfortunately, failed to complete a lap after being involved in the first-lap accident.

• Finnish driver **JJ LEHTO**, who made 19 starts for Carl Hogan's team in '98 with a best finish of fifth at Houston, was released from his contract less than six weeks before the first race. The likeable Finn filed a lawsuit against Hogan, which eventually was settled out of court. Lehto was replaced by gifted young Brazilian Helio Castro-Neves, who had been faced with unemployment after Tony Bettenhausen's sponsorship plans failed to reach fruition during the off-season.

• Former Indy Lights campaigner **SHIGEAKI HATTORI** was unable to start following a heavy crash during practice on Friday with Tony Bettenhausen's Epson Mercedes/Reynard. The accident in Turn Four was eerily similar to the one that cut short the rookie's run a month earlier in Spring Training. Hattori was detained overnight in the hospital for observation, but was released on Saturday with a concussion.

• **ROBBY GORDON** *(right)* had formed his own team over the winter, in partnership with long-time business manager Mike Held and veteran car owner John Menard. In common with Patrick Racing, however, Gordon was disappointed in the performance of his new Swift chassis, which was delivered less than a month before the first race. Instead, Gordon purchased a pair of '98 Reynards. He qualified an ex-AAR car 18th, second quickest among the Toyota contingent, but struggled in the race and eventually succumbed to engine woes.

• Jimmy Vasser's Target Honda/Reynard crew, headed by Grant Weaver, took an early lead in the newly instituted, season-long **CRAFTSMAN PIT CREW CHALLENGE** by spending least time in the pit lane during the race. Vasser's crew edged Mark Blundell's Motorola/PacWest crew by 68.371 seconds to 68.654.

• **JORGE KOECHLIN**, publisher of *AutoMundo* magazine and lead commentator for ESPN International's Spanish-language broadcasts, was named the first PPG Colorful Character of the new season. A former racer, Koechlin made one Champ Car start in 1983, when he placed 15th at Laguna Seca.

FEDEX CHAMPIONSHIP SERIES • ROUND 1
MARLBORO GRAND PRIX OF MIAMI PRESENTED BY TOYOTA

HOMESTEAD-MIAMI SPEEDWAY, HOMESTEAD, FLORIDA

MARCH 21, 150 laps – 225.30 miles

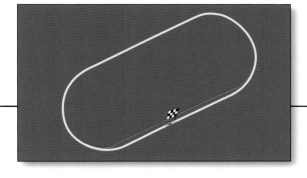

Place	Driver (Nat.)	No.	Team Sponsors Engine/Car	Tires	Q Speed	Q Time	Q Pos.	Laps	Time/Status	Ave. (mph)	Pts.
1	Greg Moore (CDN)	99	Forsythe Racing Player's/Indeck Mercedes/Reynard 99I	FS	217.279	24.886s	1	150	1h 38m 54.535s	136.671	22
2	Michael Andretti (USA)	6	Newman/Haas Kmart/Texaco Havoline Ford Cosworth/Swift 010.c	FS	215.358	25.108s	5	150	1h 38m 55.645s	136.646	16
3	Dario Franchitti (GB)	27	Team KOOL Green Honda/Reynard 99I	FS	214.554	25.202s	7	150	1h 38m 56.681s	136.622	14
4	Jimmy Vasser (USA)	12	Target/Chip Ganassi Racing Honda/Reynard 99I	FS	213.774	25.294s	9	150	1h 39m 03.713s	136.460	12
5	Max Papis (I)	7	Team Rahal Miller Lite Ford Cosworth/Reynard 99I	FS	212.656	25.427s	15	150	1h 39m 15.946s	136.180	10
6	Gil de Ferran (BR)	5	Walker Racing Valvoline/Cummins Honda/Reynard 99I	GY	no speed	no time	25	150	1h 39m 16.235s	136.173	8
7	Patrick Carpentier (CDN)	33	Forsythe Racing Player's/Indeck Mercedes-Reynard 99I	FS	215.071	25.068s	3	150	1h 39m 16.573s	136.166	6
8	Mark Blundell (GB)	18	PacWest Racing Group Motorola Mercedes/Reynard 99I	FS	213.184	25.364s	13	150	1h 39m 19.397s	136.101	5
9	Christian Fittipaldi (BR)	11	Newman/Haas Big Kmart Ford Cosworth/Swift 010.c	FS	212.439	25.453s	16	150	1h 39m 20.002s	136.087	4
10	*Juan Montoya (COL)	4	Target/Chip Ganassi Racing Honda/Reynard 99I	FS	213.850	25.285s	8	149	Running		3
11	Mauricio Gugelmin (BR)	17	PacWest Racing Group Hollywood Mercedes/Reynard 99I	FS	213.757	25.296s	10	149	Running		2
12	Bryan Herta (USA)	8	Team Rahal Shell Ford Cosworth/Reynard 99I	FS	213.757	25.296s	11	149	Running		1
13	PJ Jones (USA)	20	Patrick Racing Visteon Ford Cosworth/Reynard 98I	FS	208.531	25.930s	21	149	Running		
14	*Cristiano da Matta (BR)	25	Arciero-Wells Racing MCI WorldCom Toyota/Reynard 99I	FS	214.631	25.193s	6	148	Running		
15	Alex Barron (USA)	36	All American Racers Denso/Castrol Toyota/Eagle 997	GY	206.429	26.194s	23	148	Running		
16	Dennis Vitolo (USA)	34	Payton/Coyne Nicoderm CQ Ford Cosworth/Reynard 97I	FS	#no speed	no time	26	142	Running		
17	Helio Castro-Neves (BR)	9	Hogan Racing Hogan Motor Leasing Mercedes/Lola B99/00	FS	215.581	25.082s	4	138	Electrical		
18	Michel Jourdain Jr. (MEX)	19	Payton/Coyne Herdez/Viva Mexico Ford Cosworth/Lola T97/00	FS	#no speed	no time	27	136	Running		
19	Robby Gordon (USA)	22	Team Gordon Panasonic/Menards Toyota/Reynard 98I	FS	211.533	25.562s	18	112	Oil pressure		
20	Adrian Fernandez (MEX)	40	Patrick Tecate/Quaker State Ford Cosworth/Reynard 98I	FS	216.861	24.934s	2	110	Engine		
21	Tony Kanaan (BR)	44	McDonald's Championship Racing Honda/Reynard 99I	FS	211.566	25.558s	17	98	Fuel system		
22	Scott Pruett (USA)	24	Arciero-Wells Racing Pioneer Toyota/Reynard 99I	FS	206.484	26.187s	22	79	Accident		
23	Richie Hearn (USA)	10	Della Penna Motorsports Budweiser Toyota/Swift 010.c	FS	210.201	25.724s	19	36	Suspension		
24	*Luiz Garcia Jr. (BR)	71	Payton/Coyne Racing Tang Ford Cosworth/Reynard 97I	FS	196.020	27.585s	24	1	Accident		
25	*Naoki Hattori (J)	15	Walker Racing Alpine Honda/Reynard 99I	GY	213.479	25.329s	12	0	Accident		
26	Al Unser Jr. (USA)	2	Marlboro Team Penske Mercedes/Penske PC27B	GY	212.731	25.418s	14	0	Accident		
27	Raul Boesel (BR)	26	Team KOOL Green Honda/Reynard 99I	FS	208.877	25.887s	20	0	Accident		
DNS	*Shigeaki Hattori (J)	16	Bettenhausen Motorsports Epson Mercedes/Reynard 98I	GY	no speed	no time	–	–	DNS/accident		

* denotes rookie driver   # failed post-qualifying inspection

Caution flags: Laps 1–16, accident/Unser Jr., N. Hattori, Boesel and Garcia; laps 81–91, accident/Pruett; laps 110–120, engine/Fernandez. **Total:** Three for 38 laps.

Lap leaders: Greg Moore, 1–59 (59 laps); Patrick Carpentier, 60 (1 lap); Adrian Fernandez, 61–62 (2 laps); Michael Andretti, 63–64 (2 laps); Gil de Ferran, 65–66 (2 laps); Dario Franchitti, 67–84 (18 laps); Helio Castro-Neves, 85–113 (29 laps); Greg Moore, 114–150 (37 laps). **Totals:** Moore, 96 laps; Castro-Neves, 29 laps; Franchitti, 18 laps; Andretti, 2 laps; de Ferran, 2 laps; Fernandez, 2 laps; Carpentier, 1 lap.

Fastest race lap: Dario Franchitti, 26.825s, 201.573 mph on lap 149 (record).

Championship positions: 1 Moore, 22; **2** Andretti, 16; **3** Franchitti, 14; **4** Vasser, 12; **5** Papis, 10; **6** de Ferran, 8; **7** Carpentier, 6; **8** Blundell, 5; **9** Fittipaldi, 4; **10** Montoya, 3; **11** Gugelmin, 2; **12** Herta, 1.

OMEGA
OFFICIAL TIMEKEEPER OF CART

MOTEGI

FEDEX CHAMPIONSHIP SERIES • ROUND 2

1 - FERNANDEZ

2 - DE FERRAN

3 - FITTIPALDI

Far left: Mauricio Gugelmin receives service from the Hollywood/PacWest crew.

Below left: Gil de Ferran, race winner Adrian Fernandez *(center)* and Christian Fittipaldi acknowledge the plaudits of an enthusiastic Japanese crowd.

Bottom left: Fernandez celebrates victory surrounded by team members, photographers and race officials.

FOR Adrian Fernandez, the 1999 Firestone Firehawk 500 was subtly different from the previous year's event. Happily for the personable 33-year-old Mexican, the race ended with him standing on the same spot that he had occupied when CART made its historic first visit to Japan – atop the victory podium.

A year earlier, Fernandez had fought off the effects of a flu bug to capture his first Champ Car oval-track win at the imposing new Twin Ring Motegi. This time, a healthy Fernandez led more than half of the 201 laps (153) for the second straight year in guiding his Tecate/Quaker State Ford Cosworth/Reynard to the win. But while Fernandez showed the way for most of the race, clearly Lady Luck was on his side, because a couple of fortuitous yellow flags during the closing stages saved the day for Pat Patrick's team.

The last of the front-runners to make his first pit stop, Fernandez assumed the lead on lap 53 after the initial round of service from his Mike Sales-led crew. Fuel mileage continued to play a big part in his strategy as the other front-runners dipped into the pits for a few gallons of methanol in the waning laps. The Patrick car had fueled up on lap 143, when debris ensured a full-course caution. A total of 58 laps remained. No one had stretched a 35-gallon tank of methanol that far, and there was little indication that Fernandez would be able to do so.

As the laps ticked down, some of the contenders opted to make their pit visits early, banking on being able to run down those who would stop later. Michael Andretti, Paul Tracy and Tony Kanaan (whose McDonald's sponsor logos were painted on his car in Japanese) all gave up their track positions, but saw their plans go up in a cloud of Max Papis' tire smoke on lap 193. Team Rahal had ignored a directive from Firestone requesting that all teams change tires at each pit stop to compensate for uneven wear. As a result, Papis' Miller Lite Ford/Reynard promptly spun when his rear tire shredded on the exit from the pit road. By that time, only five cars remained on the lead lap.

Four of the five immediately dove to the pits for a splash of fuel. Fernandez, however, remained on the track. No one expected the #40 car to have a prayer of running four more green-flag laps, and all eyes were on the second-place Greg Moore, whose Player's/Forsythe Mercedes/Reynard took the green flag when mired behind some slower cars. On the restart, however, an aggressive move by Moore sent cars spinning, and the resulting yellow flag allowed Fernandez to coast home to the win behind the pace car.

'It was so close at the end,' said Fernandez. 'During the last two laps, I was half-throttle on the straights and I just saw the [fuel meter] number getting closer to the end. I didn't think we were going to make it.'

Gil de Ferran led the Honda contingent with his second-place finish, but the engine supplier was denied a win on its home ground for the second straight year. However, thanks to the efforts of de Ferran, the Japanese manufacturer once again was able to claim the small consolation of taking pole position.

But the qualifying spot was nearly for naught, as de Ferran lost control of his Valvoline/Cummins Honda/Reynard coming off Turn Four in preparation for the green flag. Leading 25 other cars toward the starting line, he seemed sure to ignite a momentous accident. Miraculously, though, the Brazilian spun 360 degrees and continued on his way, leaving a huge cloud of burnt Goodyears in his wake. The rest of the field did a stellar job of piloting through the turbulence and escaping unscathed.

'I actually started to slide when I was in Turn Four,' explained de Ferran. 'I started to slide toward [outside

Ruffled feathers

OVAL tracks are always fraught with potential calamity, especially for raw rookies. Target/Chip Ganassi Racing's new young charger, Juan Montoya, had begun the oval track portion of his CART career in nondescript fashion with a tenth-place finish in the season opener at Homestead, but he learned some lessons the hard way at Motegi.

Early in the second practice session on Thursday afternoon, Montoya scythed inside Michael Andretti, forcing both machines into the Motegi fence. Andretti was less than pleased and vented his spleen as the two drivers rode back to the infield care center for their CART-mandated check-up. He was further incensed when Montoya attempted to laugh off the incident.

'I'm not sure which disappoints me more, the move he pulled or the way he handled the situation afterward,' said Andretti. 'I hope he changes his attitude.'

CART Chief Steward Wally Dallenbach echoed those sentiments, promptly assessing a $5,000 fine for unsportsmanlike conduct and unjustifiable risk. Montoya was also placed on probation for an undetermined length of time.

Heated tempers were not confined to the CART safety vehicles. Andretti's car owner, Carl Haas, attempted to confront Montoya, only to have Chip Ganassi block his path by stepping in front of the 23-year-old driver. A brief shoving match ensued, during which Haas' trademark stogie was sent flying. The owners later patched up their differences over a drink in the Twin Ring Hotel.

Apparently, only feathers were ruffled in each camp. Andretti both qualified and finished in fifth position, while Montoya stormed through the field, climbing from 15th on the grid to shadow leader Adrian Fernandez for 61 laps. He passed Andretti on lap 80 without incident, but finished an unrepresentative 14th after running out of fuel on lap 142.

'It was an up-and-down weekend,' concluded Montoya. 'I learned a lot, but I'm disappointed because I think we had a winning car.'

QUALIFYING

When the FedEx Championship Series made its inaugural visit to Motegi, persistent rain denied Japanese fans the opportunity of witnessing CART's unique one-car-at-a-time qualifying session. This time, there were no such problems. Blue skies graced the magnificent motorsports complex on Friday morning, and the drivers responded by producing an exciting tussle for the coveted pole position.

Practice on Thursday had seen Adrian Fernandez at the top of the timing charts, posting a best of 216.711 mph in dismally cold and blustery conditions in his updated Ford/Reynard 97I. The vastly more hospitable weather conditions on Friday morning led to an immediate escalation in speeds, Fernandez again topping the list at 219.561 mph (25.398 seconds) – significantly quicker than Jimmy Vasser's unofficial best (217.964 mph/25.584 seconds) from the year before.

In general, lap speeds were a little slower in qualifying, due to the cool temperatures, but the tension continued to build as the faster contenders took to the track. Ultimately, the top 12 were separated by less than 0.2 second – not much more than a blink of an eye. Fastest of all, though, was Gil de Ferran, who secured his first-ever oval track pole – and Goodyear's first since Road America in 1998 – with a speed of 219.000 mph.

'This feels fantastic,' said the 31-year-old Brazilian. 'I was fairly confident that we had a good combination with Goodyear tires and the Honda engine, but to come out of here with the pole position is very special. Goodyear has been taking a lot of criticism over the past few years, so the pole position has a very sweet taste, and to win a pole for Honda feels good as well, as we have a lot of Honda friends around here this weekend.'

Mauricio Gugelmin (Hollywood Mercedes/Reynard) and Max Papis (Miller Lite Ford/Reynard) ensured that three manufacturers would be represented at the front of the grid. Robby Gordon was fastest of the Toyota contingent in 14th.

Mike Sales (partially obscured as he changes the right front wheel) and his Patrick Racing crew performed their usual sterling work in the pits to move Adrian Fernandez into a position to go for victory.
Photo: Michael C. Brown

Robert Laberge/Allsport

Christian Fittipaldi squeezes Gil de Ferran up against the pit wall as they battle for second position in the closing stages.

front-row qualifier] Mauricio [Gugelmin] and I said, "This isn't good!" Then I started to pinch it a little and the back just went around.'

'After that,' he added with a broad smile, 'I had to rely on my amazing car control skills.'

Since the race had not officially begun, CART reset the field, putting de Ferran back on the inside of the front row. The green flag then was waved with three caution laps already in the books. With a new lease on life, de Ferran made no mistake for the second time of asking and led the way cleanly into Turn One. Gugelmin's Hollywood/PacWest Mercedes/Reynard headed the chase, followed by Fernandez and Robby Gordon, who made up an astonishing ten places on the first green-flag lap to run fourth in his Panasonic/Menards/Johns Manville Toyota/Reynard 98I. Papis had earned the best starting spot (third) of his Champ Car career, but almost immediately began to experience excessive oversteer and fell to seventh position by lap ten.

De Ferran and Gugelmin shadowed each other through 25 laps before de Ferran's car also began to exhibit serious oversteer. The Brazilian tumbled back to fifth before stopping for service on lap 38. Gugelmin swept into the lead, where he would remain until making a pit stop on lap 47. The #17 car then fell prey to a grabbing rear brake on his stop, leaving Fernandez in the catbird seat.

Fernandez would lead all but one lap through the remainder of the race, although he was under pressure from Andretti and Juan Montoya throughout the second half. Interestingly, that pair had had a public battle after a crash in practice earlier in the weekend, when Montoya collected Andretti and put both cars into the Motegi wall.

Montoya cleanly passed the Kmart/Texaco Ford/Swift on lap 80 and set sail for the front. The Target Honda/Reynard quickly closed in on Fernandez and was poised to challenge before a miscalculation atop the war wagon cost Montoya a chance for his first Champ Car victory. The young Colombian's engine fell silent on lap 142 when he ran out of fuel, and he

lost several laps being towed back to the pits. Eventually, he finished an unrepresentative 13th.

'I learned a lot, but I'm disappointed because we had a winning car today,' said Montoya. 'The way we performed today, I think we are going to be winning races very soon.'

Teammate Jimmy Vasser, by contrast, had an awful day. The 1996 PPG Cup champion was never close to the pace and finished a lackluster 12th.

The race resumed again on lap 148, following a caution for debris on the track. A total of ten cars remained on the lead lap, but that became nine when Helio Castro-Neves was forced to pit Carl Hogan's rapid Mercedes/Lola on lap 151, serving a drive-through penalty for a pit lane infraction just 11 circuits earlier. Moore, meanwhile, had quietly moved into contention. Strong pit work allowed the Canadian to come off the pit lane right behind Fernandez, where he would stay for the next 37 laps.

Andretti was one of those eclipsed in the pit lane by Moore, but he reclaimed the spot with only 15 laps to

go. Then he decided that discretion was the better part of valor, and peeled off into the pits for fuel. The Nazareth, Pennsylvania, resident lost any chance of catching Fernandez when he stalled his car trying to rejoin the fray, having fallen victim to a broken first gear. Andretti recovered to finish fifth. 'The car was good and I really think we had a shot at the win,' he concluded.

Newman/Haas teammate Christian Fittipaldi also drove a strong race to finish third, behind de Ferran, who rebounded strongly from his early dramas. The Brazilians were followed home by Moore who, shredded tire and all, remained in fourth, despite his miscue. Andretti and Kanaan took the next two positions, with Gugelmin and Gordon the final two finishers to complete the full distance. Gordon, impressive all weekend, had suffered a setback during the first pit stop when he accidentally hit the kill switch instead of the fuel reset button. This mistake dropped him all the way to 20th place, but the 30-year-old Californian battled back to finish eighth.

Fernandez's win was the fourth of his career, and the third during his tenure with Patrick Racing. The former Mexican Formula 3 Champion won the race at a speed of 176.195 mph, tenth fastest in CART history and the quickest since Nigel Mansell's 1993 win at Michigan (188.203 mph).

Eric Mauk

Marques makes a mark

RESULTS are the most tangible indicators of how well a rookie driver performs, but Tarso Marques made his mark with Marlboro Team Penske at Motegi, despite placing 14th in the 26-car field. Making his first start in a Champ Car – as a replacement for Al Unser Jr., who was recovering from his first-lap crash in the season opener at Homestead – Marques ran on the lead lap in his Marlboro Mercedes/Penske PC27B until making his first pit stop on lap 44.

'Tarso has impressed everyone on the team with his consistent driving style and technical feedback,' said team owner Roger Penske. 'After just four days in our car [two of which came in testing at Nazareth], he was able to get up to speed quickly and run a good, clean race for us.'

The 23-year-old Brazilian had been similarly impressive during his climb up the racing ladder, which included six Formula 1 starts with Minardi in 1997. A veteran of South American Formula 3 and the European Formula 3000 series, Marques' 1995 win at Estoril established him as the youngest driver ever to win an F3000 event. He was slated to run selected events for Payton/Coyne Racing this season, before Penske offered the seat with his Marlboro-backed team on the strength of an extraordinarily promising test session at Nazareth Speedway.

As the youthful Marques watched CART races – and specifically national hero Emerson Fittipaldi – while growing up in his Brazilian home, he figured that anyone could run around in circles. But after sitting in the hot seat for nearly 200 laps of oval racing, he had a different perspective.

'It was very exciting to drive on the big oval for the first time,' said Marques. 'When I watched [oval] racing, I thought that it might be boring, but now I know that every oval is a unique challenge. You must always be driving on the edge.'

Michael C. Brown

MOTEGI SNIPPETS

Michael C. Brown

• Following a crash at Homestead, in which Adrian Fernandez's '98 Reynard was heavily damaged, **PATRICK RACING** rescued a '97 Reynard from show-car duties for use in Japan. Chassis 97I-007, with which Raul Boesel claimed the pole at Gateway in '97 for Patrick Racing in Brahma colors, was nicknamed 'Frankenstein' by team insiders in deference to its patchwork of '97, '98 and '99 components.

• Practice times gave a hint of the ever-increasing **COMPETITIVENESS** of the Champ Car field, the first session seeing the top 24 cars separated by less than a second. The trend held up in qualifying, when 18 drivers circumnavigated Twin Ring Motegi within a half-second of Gil de Ferran's pole-winning time.

• An eight-member committee was appointed by CART to assist in the search for a chief steward to replace **WALLY DALLENBACH**, who had held the position of top enforcer since the series' inception in 1979. Following Homestead, the well-respected former Champ Car driver had confirmed that he would be stepping down at the end of the season.

• Vastly experienced ace engineer **KENNY ANDERSON**, a long-time cohort of Robby Gordon, left Arciero-Wells Racing in favor of a position with Team Gordon. Anderson and Gordon had worked together off and on since Gordon's neophyte days with Target/Chip Ganassi Racing. Anderson was also slated to assist in Gordon's attempt to win the Indianapolis 500.

• The CART team owners held a meeting in Japan to address the concerns that several drivers had raised following the recent decision to mandate superspeedway-type wings for all short-oval events, beginning with the Bosch Spark Plug Grand Prix at Nazareth. Ultimately, however, it was decided to leave the **NEW RULE** unchanged. 'There was a lot of discussion from all parties, and it was decided to stay as we are,' explained Derrick Walker. 'We don't want anybody to get hurt. We also don't want 18-second lap times and cars going through the second turn at 185 mph. So we'll hope for the best and see what happens.'

• Excellent fuel mileage enabled Scott Pruett to lead a couple of laps before making his first pit stop on lap 52. It was only the second time a **TOYOTA** had led a race in FedEx Championship Series competition.

• Vintage High School senior Margot K Mendelson, of Napa, California, was named the winner of the **1999 JEFF KROSNOFF SCHOLARSHIP**. The scholarship was named in memory of the popular Champ Car driver who perished during the 1996 Toronto Molson Indy race. Mendelson will use the $10,000 award toward tuition expenses at Harvard, where she will study English and Political Studies.

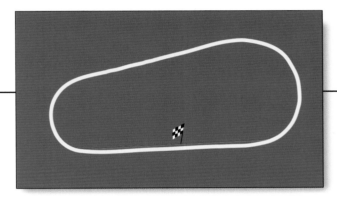

FEDEX CHAMPIONSHIP SERIES • ROUND 2
FIRESTONE FIREHAWK 500

TWIN-RING MOTEGI,
TOCHIGI PREFECTURE, JAPAN

APRIL 10, 201 laps – 311.349 miles

Place	Driver (Nat.)	No.	Team Sponsors Engine/Car	Tires	Q Speed	Q Time	Q Pos.	Laps	Time/Status	Ave. (mph)	Pts.
1	Adrian Fernandez (MEX)	40	Patrick Tecate/Quaker State Ford Cosworth/Reynard 97I	FS	218.212	25.555s	4	201	1h 46m 01.463s	176.195	21
2	Gil de Ferran (BR)	5	Walker Racing Valvoline/Cummins Honda/Reynard 99I	GY	219.000	25.463s	1	201	1h 46m 07.810s	176.019	17
3	Christian Fittipaldi (BR)	11	Newman/Haas Big Kmart Ford Cosworth/Swift 010.c	FS	217.760	25.608s	7	201	1h 46m 09.132s	175.983	14
4	Greg Moore (CDN)	99	Forsythe Racing Player's/Indeck Mercedes/Reynard 99I	FS	217.888	25.593s	6	201	1h 46m 39.490s	175.148	12
5	Michael Andretti (USA)	6	Newman/Haas Kmart/Texaco Havoline Ford Cosworth/Swift 010.c	FS	218.118	25.566s	5	200	Running		10
6	Tony Kanaan (BR)	44	McDonald's Championship Racing Honda/Reynard 99I	FS	215.122	25.922s	17	200	Running		8
7	Mauricio Gugelmin (BR)	17	PacWest Racing Group Hollywood Mercedes/Reynard 99I	FS	218.425	25.530s	2	200	Running		6
8	Robby Gordon (USA)	22	Team Gordon Panasonic/Menards Toyota/Reynard 98I	FS	216.955	25.703s	14	200	Running		5
9	Helio Castro-Neves (BR)	9	Hogan Racing Hogan Motor Leasing Mercedes/Lola B99/00	FS	214.857	25.954s	18	199	Running		4
10	Richie Hearn (USA)	10	Della Penna Motorsports Budweiser Toyota/Swift 010.c	FS	213.238	26.151s	21	198	Accident		3
11	Paul Tracy (CDN)	26	Team KOOL Green Honda/Reynard 99I	FS	217.514	25.637s	10	198	Running		2
12	Jimmy Vasser (USA)	12	Target/Chip Ganassi Racing Honda/Reynard 99I	FS	217.412	25.649s	12	198	Running		1
13	*Juan Montoya (COL)	4	Target/Chip Ganassi Racing Honda/Reynard 99I	FS	215.347	25.895s	15	197	Running		
14	*Tarso Marques (BR)	2	Marlboro Team Penske Mercedes/Penske PC27B	GY	212.507	26.241s	22	197	Running		
15	PJ Jones (USA)	20	Patrick Racing Visteon Ford Cosworth/Reynard 98I	FS	217.573	25.630s	9	196	Running		
16	Max Papis (I)	7	Team Rahal Miller Lite Ford Cosworth/Reynard 99I	FS	218.280	25.547s	3	196	Running		
17	Alex Barron (USA)	36	All American Racers Denso/Castrol Toyota/Eagle 997	GY	214.024	26.055s	19	195	Running		
18	Michel Jourdain Jr. (MEX)	19	Payton/Coyne Herdez/Viva Mexico Ford Cosworth/Lola T97/00	FS	206.878	26.955s	26	188	Running		
19	*Luiz Garcia Jr. (BR)	71	Payton/Coyne Tang Ford Cosworth/Reynard 97I	FS	208.729	26.716s	25	184	Engine		
20	*Shigeaki Hattori (J)	16	Bettenhausen Motorsports Epson Mercedes/Reynard 98I	GY	208.870	24.698s	24	140	Clutch		
21	Scott Pruett (USA)	24	Arciero-Wells Racing Pioneer Toyota/Reynard 99I	FS	214.008	26.057s	20	106	Fire		
22	Dario Franchitti (GB)	27	Team KOOL Green Honda/Reynard 99I	FS	217.480	25.641s	11	91	Suspension		
23	Bryan Herta (USA)	8	Team Rahal Shell Ford Cosworth/Reynard 99I	FS	217.726	25.612s	8	84	Electrical		
24	Mark Blundell (GB)	18	PacWest Racing Group Motorola Mercedes/Reynard 99I	FS	215.205	25.912s	16	78	Handling		
25	*Cristiano da Matta (BR)	25	Arciero-Wells Racing MCI WorldCom Toyota/Reynard 99I	FS	208.979	26.684s	23	39	Transmission		
26	Patrick Carpentier (CDN)	33	Forsythe Racing Player's/Indeck Mercedes/Reynard 99I	FS	217.073	25.689s	13	10	Fuel pressure		

* denotes rookie driver

Caution flags: Laps 1–3, spin/de Ferran; laps 88–95, accident/Franchitti; laps 139–147, debris; laps 193–197, spin/Papis; laps 199–201, accident/Moore and Hearn. **Total:** Five for 28 laps.

Lap leaders: Mauricio Gugelmin, 1 (1 lap); Gil de Ferran, 2–26 (25 laps); Gugelmin 27–46 (20 laps); Adrian Fernandez, 47–50 (4 laps); Scott Pruett, 51–52 (2 laps); Fernandez, 53–201 (149 laps).
Totals: Fernandez, 153 laps; de Ferran, 21 laps; Gugelmin, 21 laps; Pruett, 2 laps.

Fastest race lap: Helio Castro-Neves, 25.830s, 215.889 mph on lap 136 (record).

Championship positions: 1 Moore, 34; **2** Andretti, 26; **3** de Ferran, 25; **4** Fernandez, 21; **5** Fittipaldi, 18; **6** Franchitti, 14; **7** Vasser, 13; **8** Papis, 10;
9 Kanaan & Gugelmin, 8; **11** Carpentier, 6; **12** Blundell & Gordon, 5; **14** Castro-Neves, 4; **15** Montoya & Hearn, 3; **17** Tracy, 2; **18** Herta, 1.

Ω
OMEGA
OFFICIAL TIMEKEEPER OF CART

1 – MONTOYA

2 – FRANCHITTI

3 – HERTA

LONG BEACH

Once Tony Kanaan had squandered his lead, Juan Montoya (*left*) was able to march on to victory, despite the close attentions of Dario Franchitti and much to the delight of the Target/Chip Ganassi Racing team (*bottom left*).

Inset left: Famed guitarist Jeff Beck performed a rather different rendition of the traditional pre-race National Anthem.

QUALIFYING

Tony Kanaan established a new unofficial record during practice on Saturday morning, when a recurrence of Reynard's occasional gearbox glitch inadvertently allowed him to shift down two gears instead of one, as he had intended. Momentarily, his McDonald's Honda/Reynard reached an unprecedented 20,000 rpm! The motor, miraculously, survived, but it was changed as a precaution. The team wisely brought out the backup car for the final half-hour qualifying session, again as a precautionary measure. Kanaan responded by securing his first-ever Champ Car pole.

'It was a gamble [switching to the backup car], but it paid off,' said a delighted Kanaan. 'I am very happy and very proud of my Drive-Thru crew.'

Dario Franchitti, who earned the provisional pole on Friday with his #27 KOOL Honda/Reynard, also was forced to throw away his earlier lap time after a heavy crash on Saturday morning. He, too, paid tribute to his team after rebounding to claim the other front-row grid position.

'I'm frustrated not to be on the pole,' declared Franchitti, 'but the crew did an amazing job getting my spare [car] ready so fast. Second is great, but it's not the pole.'

Team Rahal's Bryan Herta and Max Papis shared row two in their Ford Cosworth-powered Reynards, followed by rookie Juan Montoya and Adrian Fernandez, who vindicated the decision to run one of Pat Patrick's new Ford/Swifts, despite winning at Motegi with an updated two-year-old Reynard.

'Driving the Swift is like meeting a new girlfriend,' explained the Mexican, a twinkle in his eye. 'She likes different things. We're still learning about the chassis, but every day we know more. We made a big change at the end of the session and it worked out well for us. What I really needed was one more lap.'

JUAN Montoya's first-ever Champ Car race on a street course produced a stunning victory in the 25th Anniversary Toyota Grand Prix of Long Beach. The 23-year-old belied his rookie status with a performance that was every bit as dominating as his predecessor in Chip Ganassi's #4 Target Honda/Reynard, Alex Zanardi, who garnered victory at Long Beach in both 1997 and '98. Montoya capitalized on a mistake by pole-sitter Tony Kanaan midway through the 85-lap race, which was run in glorious California sunshine, then galloped away toward the checkered flag. His final margin of victory was 2.805 seconds over the similar KOOL Honda/Reynard of preseason championship favorite Dario Franchitti.

'We did a quite good job,' said Montoya, with characteristic understatement. 'In Japan, we came very close to a win before we ran out of fuel. But [today] we did it absolutely right. The car was perfect.'

For the first 45 laps, Kanaan had seemed poised to break the Target team's winning streak. The Brazilian had claimed the first pole of his CART career on Saturday, hustling Jerry Forsythe's McDonald's Honda/Reynard around the revised 1.824-mile circuit in 1 minute, 1.109 seconds to edge out Franchitti and the two Team Rahal Ford Cosworth/Reynards of Bryan Herta and Max Papis.

Herta couldn't quite match his pole-winning form of a year earlier, but he did take the lead in opportunistic style under braking for Turn One, which this year was a hard left-hander due to the inauguration of a brand-new section of track around the parking structure of the impressive Aquarium of the Pacific. The Californian's maneuver was greeted by rapturous applause from the partisan crowd. However, he was unable to maintain his advantage. He had been obliged to use his backup car following a fuel pickup problem during that morning's warmup, and in the early stages it exhibited rather more oversteer than he liked. Kanaan duly wrested back the advantage on lap two with a clean move under braking for Turn Nine.

One lap later, Franchitti repeated the maneuver precisely at the end of Seaside Way. The original qualifying order was briefly restored, before Montoya moved into fourth at the expense of Papis on lap five. Herta, though, proved a tougher nut to crack. Montoya soon found himself stuck behind the Shell car, while Kanaan and Franchitti motored off into the distance.

'The start was okay,' said Montoya.

'I got around Max Papis – he wasn't that difficult to pass – but Bryan was the hardest guy to go by.'

Kanaan remained under strong pressure from Franchitti through the opening stages. By lap 12, however, the Brazilian had begun to make a break. The gap increased only gradually to begin with, but once the leaders began to lap some slower traffic, Kanaan extended the margin more convincingly. By lap 20, the separation had grown to almost seven seconds. Herta and Montoya remained tied together in third and fourth, a further three seconds or so adrift. Clearly, Montoya was the faster of the two, but Herta stuck to his guns. Finally, on lap 22, Montoya found a chink in the armor in Turn One and slipped through into third place.

Shortly after, Shigeaki Hattori triggered a full-course caution by crashing his Epson Mercedes/Reynard in Turn Two. It was his second wreck of the day and his fourth since joining Tony Bettenhausen's team at the beginning of the season. The yellows became the catalyst for the first round of pit stops, which saw no change among the leading positions. Kanaan resumed ahead of Franchitti, Montoya, Herta and Adrian Fernandez, who had found a way past Papis on lap 15 and was soon followed by Gil de Ferran.

The green flags waved again at the beginning of lap 27, but only briefly. Tarso Marques, whose Marlboro Mercedes/Penske had lost a couple of laps following an earlier skirmish with Robby Gordon, attempted to regain much of the lost ground with a wildly optimistic move at Turn One. He succeeded only in collecting an innocent Scott Pruett, whose Pioneer Toyota/Reynard had been running smoothly in 16th. Yellow again. Following another cleanup, Franchitti failed to accelerate cleanly out of the Turn 11 hairpin as CART Starter Jim Swintal prepared to wave the green flag. Montoya drew level with the KOOL machine on the long drag race down Shoreline Drive before forging his way past the Scotsman on the way into Turn One.

'I think he just got a bit too much wheelspin,' noted Montoya, 'and I had a better line. I just braked a little bit later and managed to get by.'

The trio of Honda/Reynards ran in nose-to-tail formation for the next dozen laps, in the order Kanaan, Montoya and Franchitti. Herta, Fernandez (driving one of Pat Patrick's new Swift chassis, despite winning at Motegi a week earlier in an updated '97 Reynard) and de Ferran (Valvoline/Cummins Honda/Reynard) were unable to keep pace. Papis, meanwhile, struggled for grip throughout the race and continued to fall back, being passed in quick succession by the Newman/Haas Ford/Swifts of Christian Fittipaldi and Michael Andretti.

The track surface became increasingly treacherous as the asphalt began to break up, especially on the new section. The drivers' predicament was worsened as rubber 'marbles' built up off-line. On lap 45, Kanaan's dream of a maiden victory came to a premature end when he left his braking a fraction too late and speared off into the tire wall at Turn Six.

'I made a mistake,' said Kanaan, who was in tears as he clambered out of his stricken McDonald's car. 'The track was breaking up and I just ran off-line a little bit and lost it.'

'It was okay on-line, but if you got just a little bit off-line [the rubber] was really balling up and [the track was] tearing up,' confirmed Herta. 'I think if you got out there, you weren't coming back.'

Kanaan's demise ensured another full-course caution, prompting the final round of pit stops. Once again, the top positions remained unchanged, Montoya leading Franchitti, Herta, Fernandez and Fittipaldi. Montoya jumped to a big lead on the restart as Franchitti lagged behind due to excessive rubber build-up on his tires. It was

A man to watch

TONY Kanaan has accumulated an enviable watch collection over the years. On Saturday at Long Beach, he persuaded his entire McDonald's Drive-Thru crew to pony up their watches if he could qualify on the pole. The 24-year-old Brazilian lived up to his side of the bargain, so immediately at the end of the session, every crew member handed over the goods.

'Somebody want to buy a Rolex 95?' quipped Kanaan amid widespread hilarity as he arrived at the post-race media conference. 'I have one. I can make you a good deal.'

It was all in jest. Later, Kanaan returned the timepieces, commenting, 'I don't want my guys to be late for the race tomorrow!'

The youngster had earned a reputation as a comedian during his rookie campaign in 1998, but he also indicated his serious aspirations by developing into a regular front-runner with Steve Horne's Tasman Motorsports Group. The partnership, which garnered a PPG-Dayton Indy

Michael C. Brown

Lights Championship crown in '97, remained unchanged for the new season, except for the fact that Horne had relinquished overall responsibility for the financial aspects of the organization following a 'merger' with Jerry Forsythe. The new alliance brought with it a prestigious sponsorship deal with McDonald's Corp.

'McDonald's has given us the opportunity to do more testing – we've done over twice the amount we did last year already,' noted Kanaan, 'and that has made a big difference. As Steve says, we have no excuses this year.'

Kanaan went on to dominate the first half of the 85-lap race, before being caught out by the slippery track conditions in Turn Six. Typically, he made no excuses. 'It was my mistake,' he said. 'Sometimes you learn the hard way. I am very disappointed, but you learn from your mistakes. I won't make the same mistake again. What happened today hurt, but I proved to myself that I can run up there.'

Right: Adrian Fernandez picked up more valuable PPG Cup points to consolidate his strong start to the season.

Far right: Christian Fittipaldi hustles through the new section of track in front of the Aquarium of the Pacific.

Below far right: Bryan Herta wasn't altogether happy with his Ford/Reynard, but the Shell team maximized its potential to salvage third place.

Below right: Scott Pruett enjoyed a good run until assaulted by Tarso Marques.

all for naught, though, as PJ Jones brought out the yellow flags one more time on lap 55, when he half-spun and stalled Pat Patrick's Visteon Ford/Swift in Turn One while attempting to pass Greg Moore (Player's Mercedes/Reynard) for tenth position.

Franchitti didn't make the same mistake at the next restart. Even so, he was no match for Montoya.

'I was just trying hard to keep Juan in sight,' said Franchitti, 'but I didn't have the car to do it. I was struggling coming off a couple of key corners.'

Likewise, Herta was in no position to challenge the two leaders. 'It felt like I was stuck in third place all weekend,' he said. 'I just didn't have anything for Juan or Dario. I'm happy because I didn't have a car to finish any higher than third today, and that's what we managed.'

Franchitti's hopes of tracking down Montoya received a boost on lap 78, when the yellows waved for a fifth time after Cristiano da Matta's MCI WorldCom Toyota/Reynard found the same tire wall as close buddy Kanaan. Four laps remained at the final restart, but Montoya coped with the pressure like a true veteran and was never seriously threatened.

Fernandez finished fourth, earning valuable PPG Cup points, as did Fittipaldi, who had risen impressively from

11th on the grid to fifth. Gil de Ferran took sixth, after trading places a couple of times with Andretti in the closing stages. He made his decisive move after the final restart on lap 82.

'I got a good run on him and when we got to the braking area [at Turn One], I thought, "That's my chance,"' related de Ferran, 'so I went really deep [on the brakes] and he went deeper, and I thought, "There's no way you're going to make it, pal!"'

Sure enough, Andretti had to settle for seventh, chased by Moore, who took advantage of a slip by the hapless Papis on the final corner. A similarly disgruntled Jimmy Vasser completed the top ten after a torrid afternoon in the second Target Honda/Reynard.

'After the last pit stop, the car got loose on me,' explained Vasser. 'I held onto my position, but I'm not real happy.'

Teammate Montoya, of course, picked up the slack, much to his employer's delight. 'We had a couple of problems in the first two races and I think we let him down,' declared Ganassi. 'I knew he had the talent for the kind of drive he had today; what I didn't know is that he had the mental toughness to put these early challenges behind him so quickly and just focus on the job at hand.'

Jeremy Shaw

Montoya's rapid rise

FROM the first moment Juan Montoya stepped aboard one of Chip Ganassi's Target Honda/Reynards, there was never any doubt that he would develop into a front-runner. The youngster was immediately impressive, both with his pace and his maturity behind the wheel.

In the formative stages of his career, Montoya had displayed more than his share of youthful aggression. He was introduced to karting at a young age by his father, Pablo, who had taken up the sport at the age of 30, after becoming a successful architect in his native Colombia. The younger Montoya soon began to win, and after traveling to Europe for a couple of World Championship races, he set his sights on a career in auto racing. He competed first in his homeland, then tackled the North American Barber Saab (now Dodge) Pro Series in 1994. He won twice during his rookie campaign. Europe beckoned again, however, and in '95 he joined Paul Stewart Racing to contest the British and European Formula Vauxhall/Opel series. After graduating through Formula 3, Montoya really set tongues a-wagging with his performances in Formula 3000. He won the title at his second attempt, in '98, and cemented his future with a series of excellent tests for the Formula 1 Winfield Williams team.

The departure of former World Champion Jacques Villeneuve to the new British American Racing team, at the conclusion of the '98 season, left Williams in a quandary. Ultimately, however, rather than plump for a rookie to partner new recruit Ralf Schumacher, the team selected twice PPG Cup champion Alex Zanardi. Montoya was 'traded' to Target/Chip Ganassi Racing on a three-year contract.

When Montoya first tested a Champ Car, toward the end of 1998, Chief Engineer Morris Nunn predicted that the Colombian could win as early as Long Beach. His forecast was perfect.

The most striking feature of Montoya's maiden victory was the manner in which he put behind him the disappointment of the previous week in Japan, where a potential victory had been snatched away due to a fuel miscalculation. 'What happened last week in Japan, we just let it go,' he said, with remarkable sangfroid. 'This weekend, we put it all together. Now we're just going to try to keep on winning.'

FEDEX CHAMPIONSHIP SERIES • ROUND 3

With palms and the 'Queen Mary' as a backdrop, Dario Franchitti weaves between the cement walls.

LONG BEACH SNIPPETS

• GUALTER SALLES *(right)* made a welcome return to the Champ Car fray after concluding a last-minute deal to drive Payton/Coyne Racing's ex-Arnd Meier/Davis Racing Ford/Lola T98/00. The familiar bright yellow car had not turned a wheel in anger since the final race of the '98 season at California Speedway. Salles, meanwhile, had not driven a Champ Car since Road America in the previous fall. Unfortunately, his race ended early due to wing damage following an on-track incident.

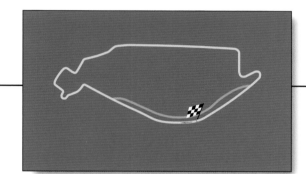

• DuPont Engineering Polymers and Tone Brothers (the second largest spice producer in the United States) were confirmed as being new associate sponsors of **PATRICK RACING'S** Visteon Ford/Swift, driven by PJ Jones.

• Gil de Ferran's Valvoline/Cummins Honda/Reynard was again the top contender running on **GOODYEAR TIRES**. The Brazilian driver emerged triumphant from a lengthy battle with Michael Andretti to finish in fifth position. It was enough to move him to equal second place (with Adrian Fernandez) in the PPG Cup standings, six points adrift of Greg Moore.

• **LAURIE GERRISH** resigned as Manager of Team Gordon only a couple of days before the race took place at Long Beach.

• Exactly one year after the Initial Public Offering of **CART SHARES** on the New York Stock Exchange, several team owners – including Roger Penske, Barry Green and Pat Patrick – created a stir by selling a substantial portion of their investment. Fellow team owner Dale Coyne played down the process, however, explaining, 'It's just a change of ownership. It's not like a country printing money; we're just selling [the stock] to somebody else. And obviously Wall Street's taken note of that because [the share price] hasn't taken a hit.' Coyne, incidentally, chose not to sell any of his own stock.

• Marlboro Team Penske rookie **TARSO MARQUES** didn't exactly cover himself with glory when he tangled with two other cars in Turn One. However, he did gain victory in the inaugural Mercedes-Benz Grand Prix of Orange, a 49-mile race that took place on a brand-new, state-of-the-art 'Virtual Reality' simulator at the Penske Racing Center's grand opening on the previous Thursday, in nearby Orange, California. Marques was presented with a pair of teammate Al Unser Jr.'s racing gloves for his efforts!

• **FIRESTONE** presented a $50,000 check to the Target House in Memphis, Tennessee, a soon-to-be-opened residential facility provided for the family members of long-term hospital patients. The tire company also pledged a donation of $50 for each lap that was led during the season by Target/Chip Ganassi drivers Jimmy Vasser and Juan Montoya.

FEDEX CHAMPIONSHIP SERIES • ROUND 3
TOYOTA GRAND PRIX OF LONG BEACH

LONG BEACH STREET CIRCUIT, CALIFORNIA

APRIL 18, 85 laps – 155.04 miles

Place	Driver (Nat.)	No.	Team Sponsors Engine/Car	Tires	Q Speed	Q Time	Q Pos.	Laps	Time/Status	Ave. (mph)	Pts.
1	*Juan Montoya (COL)	4	Target/Chip Ganassi Racing Honda/Reynard 99I	FS	106.966	1m 01.388s	5	85	1h 45m 48.688s	87.915	20
2	Dario Franchitti (GB)	27	Team KOOL Green Honda/Reynard 99I	FS	107.412	1m 01.133s	2	85	1h 45m 51.493s	87.876	16
3	Bryan Herta (USA)	8	Team Rahal Shell Ford Cosworth/Reynard 99I	FS	107.154	1m 01.280s	3	85	1h 45m 55.691s	87.818	14
4	Adrian Fernandez (MEX)	40	Patrick Tecate/Quaker State Ford Cosworth/Swift 010.c	FS	106.642	1m 01.574s	6	85	1h 45m 57.298s	87.796	12
5	Christian Fittipaldi (BR)	11	Newman/Haas Big Kmart Ford Cosworth/Swift 010.c	FS	106.175	1m 01.845s	11	85	1h 45m 57.519s	87.793	10
6	Gil de Ferran (BR)	5	Walker Valvoline/Cummins Honda/Reynard 99I	GY	106.568	1m 01.617s	7	85	1h 46m 02.254s	87.727	8
7	Michael Andretti (USA)	6	Newman/Haas Kmart/Texaco Ford Cosworth/Swift 010.c	FS	105.917	1m 01.966s	13	85	1h 46m 04.282s	87.699	6
8	Greg Moore (CDN)	99	Forsythe Racing Player's/Indeck Mercedes/Reynard 99I	FS	106.378	1m 01.727s	8	85	1h 46m 06.087s	87.675	5
9	Max Papis (I)	7	Team Rahal Miller Lite Ford Cosworth/Reynard 99I	FS	107.044	1m 01.343s	4	85	1h 46m 06.406s	87.670	4
10	Jimmy Vasser (USA)	12	Target/Chip Ganassi Racing Honda/Reynard 99I	FS	106.259	1m 01.796s	9	85	1h 46m 10.816s	87.610	3
11	Richie Hearn (USA)	10	Della Penna Motorsports Budweiser Toyota/Swift 010.c	FS	104.148	1m 03.049s	24	85	1h 46m 12.209s	87.590	2
12	PJ Jones (USA)	20	Patrick Visteon Ford Cosworth/Swift 010.c	FS	105.770	1m 02.082s	15	84	Running		1
13	Mark Blundell (GB)	18	PacWest Racing Group Motorola Mercedes/Reynard 99I	FS	105.988	1m 01.954s	12	84	Running		
14	Mauricio Gugelmin (BR)	17	PacWest Racing Group Hollywood Mercedes/Reynard 99I	FS	105.853	1m 02.033s	14	84	Running		
15	Scott Pruett (USA)	24	Arciero-Wells Racing Pioneer Toyota/Reynard 99I	FS	104.846	1m 02.629s	20	84	Running		
16	Robby Gordon (USA)	22	Team Gordon Panasonic/Menards Toyota/Reynard 98I	FS	104.776	1m 02.671s	21	84	Running		
17	Patrick Carpentier (CDN)	33	Forsythe Racing Player's/Indeck Mercedes/Reynard 99I	FS	105.273	1m 02.375s	17	84	Running		
18	Michel Jourdain Jr. (MEX)	19	Payton/Coyne Racing Herdez/Viva Mexico Ford Cosworth/Lola T97/00	FS	104.349	1m 02.927s	23	82	Out of fuel		
19	Helio Castro-Neves (BR)	9	Hogan Racing Hogan Motor Leasing Mercedes/Lola B99/00	FS	105.248	1m 02.390s	18	76	Running		
20	*Cristiano da Matta (BR)	25	Arciero-Wells Racing MCI WorldCom Toyota/Reynard 99I	FS	105.673	1m 02.139s	16	75	Accident		
21	Paul Tracy (CDN)	26	Team KOOL Green Honda/Reynard 99I	FS	106.180	1m 01.842s	10	48	Suspension		
22	Tony Kanaan (BR)	44	McDonald's Championship Racing Honda/Reynard 99I	FS	107.454	1m 01.109s	1	45	Accident		2
23	Alex Barron (USA)	36	All American Racers Denso/Castrol Toyota/Eagle 997	GY	104.526	1m 02.821s	22	34	Brakes		
24	*Luiz Garcia Jr. (BR)	71	Payton/Coyne Tang Ford Cosworth/Reynard 97I	FS	100.325	1m 05.451s	27	28	Accident		
25	*Tarso Marques (BR)	2	Marlboro Team Penske Mercedes/Penske PC27B	GY	105.133	1m 02.458s	19	24	Accident		
26	*Shigeaki Hattori (J)	16	Bettenhausen Motorsports Epson Mercedes/Reynard 98I	GY	103.208	1m 03.623s	26	21	Accident		
27	Gualter Salles (BR)	34	Payton/Coyne Refricentro Ford Cosworth/Lola T98/00	FS	103.643	1m 03.356s	25	17	Wing damage		

* denotes rookie driver

Caution flags: Laps 23–25, accident/Hattori; laps 27–30, accident/Marques, Castro-Neves and Pruett; laps 46–51, accident/Kanaan; laps 55–56, spin/Jones; laps 77–80, accident/da Matta. **Total:** Five for 19 laps.

Lap leaders: Bryan Herta, 1 (1 lap); Tony Kanaan, 2–45 (44 laps); Juan Montoya, 46–85 (40 laps). **Totals:** Kanaan, 44 laps; Montoya, 40 laps; Herta, 1 lap.

Fastest race lap: Juan Montoya, 1m 02.779s, 104.595 mph on lap 63 (establishes record).

Championship positions: 1 Moore, 39; **2** Fernandez & de Ferran, 33; **4** Andretti, 32; **5** Franchitti, 30; **6** Fittipaldi, 28; **7** Montoya, 23; **8** Vasser, 16; **9** Herta, 15; **10** Papis, 14; **11** Kanaan, 10; **12** Gugelmin, 8; **13** Carpentier, 6; **14** Blundell, Hearn & Gordon, 5; **17** Castro-Neves, 4; **18** Tracy, 2; **19** Jones, 1.

Ω OMEGA
OFFICIAL TIMEKEEPER OF CART

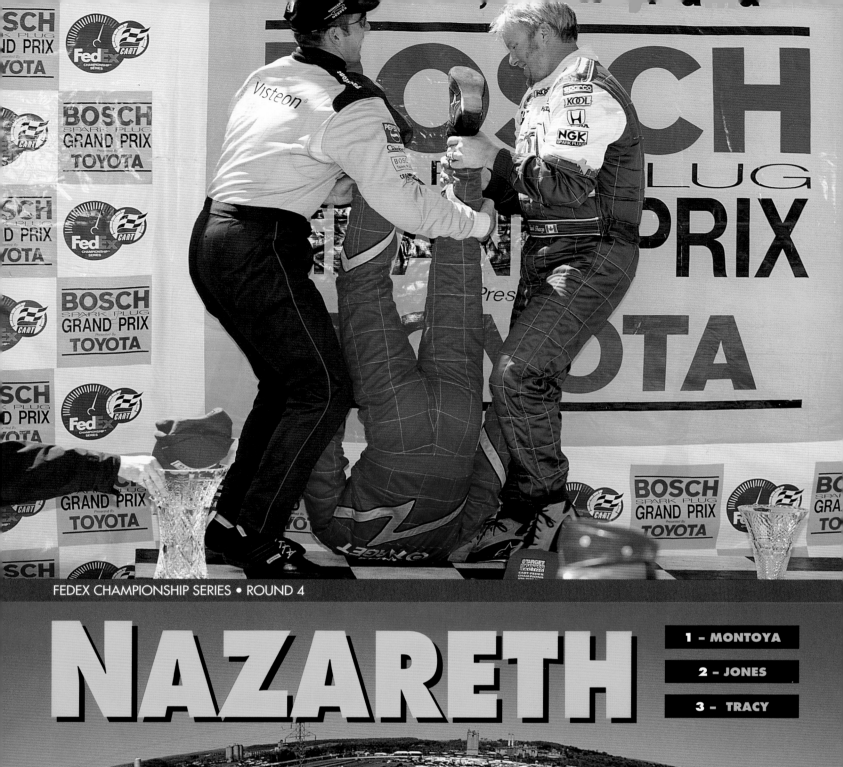

NAZARETH

1 – MONTOYA

2 – JONES

3 – TRACY

Podium finishers Paul Tracy *(right)* and PJ Jones exact a modicum of revenge for Juan Montoya having upset the form book in his rookie season.

Bottom left: Spectators gain a bird's-eye view of the tight Nazareth oval from the Turn Four grandstand.

Below: Cristiano da Matta brought his MCI WorldCom Toyota/Reynard into fourth place, the best result to date for the Japanese engine manufacturer.

IT took a little less than two hours for rookie sensation Juan Montoya to double his total of Champ Car victories after another flawless performance in the Bosch Spark Plug Grand Prix Presented by Toyota at Nazareth Speedway. Montoya followed his Long Beach triumph with a five-second win over a surprising PJ Jones, whose form aboard Pat Patrick's Visteon Ford/Swift was a revelation. In the process, Montoya replaced Greg Moore as the series' points leader, becoming the first rookie to sit atop the PPG Cup standings since Nigel Mansell in 1993. He also became the first CART rookie to win back-to-back races since Mansell turned the trick at Michigan and New Hampshire during his title run.

Youth was more of an advantage than usual at Nazareth, for as the veterans groused about the new CART-mandated smaller wing package, Montoya simply went out and

drove his Target/Chip Ganassi Racing Honda/Reynard faster than anyone else. Smaller wings slashed downforce almost in half, infuriating some drivers and eliciting predictions of dire consequences from others. But the rookie never knew any other way of getting around the tri-cornered, 0.946-mile oval and won the race from pole position.

'I never tried the big wings [at Nazareth], so it makes it a bit easier,' said Montoya after Friday's practice. 'When the car is handling well, it's okay, but [finding] the fine-point of the car is very critical.'

Montoya's win was the third on the mile ovals for Ganassi following Jimmy Vasser's 1998 sweep of the Nazareth and Milwaukee races, which

gave the team its first-ever victories on the smaller tracks. The young Colombian's dominance began on Saturday as he sped to the pole. He continued his spectacular form on race day under picture-perfect weather conditions, jumping immediately to a 1.7-second advantage over Helio Castro-Neves' Hogan Motor Leasing Mercedes/Lola. However, the Brazilian soon began to reel in the leader and, by lap six, they were in the nose-to-tail formation they would follow for most of the following 150 circuits.

The smaller wings slowed the cars (Montoya's pole speed was 11 mph adrift of Carpentier's 1998 clocking), but didn't make for much in the way of competitive passing. Jones and Max Papis (Miller Lite Ford/Reynard) took advantage of a slip by Patrick Carpentier (Player's/Forsythe Mercedes/Reynard) on lap 18 to make the only green-flag position changes among the

QUALIFYING

Qualifying times are always close at Nazareth Speedway, and this year was no exception. Lap times, of course, were significantly slower than in '98, due to the adoption of much smaller superspeedway-type wings, but the top four contenders in practice – Juan Montoya, Helio Castro-Neves, Patrick Carpentier and Dario Franchitti – were separated by only 0.077 seconds, and all but Dennis Vitolo were within one second of the brilliant rookie's best of 19.715 seconds.

Montoya's effort ensured that he would have the final attempt in the one-at-a-time qualifying session. The young Colombian took full advantage, his first full-speed lap being a microscopic 0.001 second quicker than Castro-Neves, who had edged out Franchitti only moments earlier. His task completed, Montoya immediately backed off and cruised into the pits without even bothering to complete his second lap.

"It was a bit of a surprise because I thought I went into Turn Two a little bit slow," related Montoya. "Then when I went across the line, they said I was on the pole, and I said, 'Oh, thank you!'"

Castro-Neves was relatively content with the second starting spot for his Hogan Motor Leasing Mercedes/Lola, the best qualifying attempt of his career. "I'm very happy being on the front row," he said. "The key tomorrow [for the race] is going to be patience."

Team KOOL Green's Dario Franchitti and Paul Tracy lined up alongside each other on row two, ahead of a resurgent Mark Blundell (PacWest Racing Motorola Mercedes/Reynard), who was delighted to secure by far his best ever starting position on a one-mile oval.

"I feel pretty good," said the Englishman. "We have a good balance and the Motorola team has been working very hard. I think things are really coming together and that we're well on our way to capturing our winning ways from 1997."

Patrick Carpentier qualified alongside on row three, again eclipsing his highly vaunted Player's/Forsythe Mercedes/Reynard teammate, Greg Moore, while Max Papis (fastest of the Ford contingent in Team Rahal's Miller Lite Reynard) and PJ Jones (Visteon Ford/Swift) made up row four.

Michael C. Brown

Lola's comeback

DESPITE getting shut out of the points for the third time in the first four races of the FedEx Championship Series, rejuvenated chassis manufacturer Lola Cars International demonstrated that it was definitely a force to be reckoned with at the Nazareth Speedway event.

Helio Castro-Neves was fastest in Friday's practice (172.357 mph) and missed pole position by a scant 0.001 second when nipped by Target/Chip Ganassi Racing's Juan Montoya in qualifying. It was Lola's first front-row start since Michael Andretti captured the Vancouver pole in 1996. The 23-year-old Brazilian ran a strong race, too, before a pair of late-race miscues culminated in a Turn Three crash. Before the trouble, Castro-Neves was Montoya's nemesis, riding on the Colombian's tail for most of the day. A lap-170 spin resulted in a stalled engine, costing the Hogan car any chance of claiming victory. Then a sticking throttle on the next restart sent the #9 Lola spinning into the wall.

'We just have to keep running and running and be comfortable in the car,' said Castro-Neves. 'The Lola is a good car. Especially in Japan, we found a good setup and we've been going well ever since.'

Michel Jourdain Jr. also produced some fireworks aboard Payton/Coyne Racing's Ford Cosworth-powered Herdez/Viva Mexico Lola. A crash during Saturday's practice consigned him to the backup car, but Jourdain never skipped a beat. On a track where very few passes were made, the #19 car eclipsed four drivers, including Bryan Herta and Tony Kanaan, in the first nine laps. Jourdain later snared Paul Tracy and Mauricio Gugelmin, climbing from 22nd to as high as 13th before being caught out by an ill-timed caution period.

'It was the best car that I ever had in Champ Car racing,' said Jourdain, who remains the youngest competitor in the FedEx Championship Series at 22 years of age. 'We were unfortunate with our pit strategy. Our last pit stop was under green, and two laps later the yellow waved, so everyone else was able to pit during the caution. It was a shame. That affected us a lot. However, I am very pleased because the car was good and the team worked well together.'

top eight runners until Castro-Neves passed Montoya for the lead on lap 39.

After being trapped behind Al Unser Jr., who was struggling to stay on the lead lap in his Marlboro Mercedes/ Penske PC27B, Montoya had to give way to an outrageous maneuver around the outside line in Turn Two by Castro-Neves. A half-dozen laps later, however, the inspired Brazilian relinquished the lead to Montoya during the first round of pit stops, which took place during a full-course caution after Unser made heavy contact with the Turn Three wall. Fortunately, he did not inflict any further injury on the right ankle he had broken in a crash at Homestead.

'We were running just ahead of the #4 [Montoya] and #9 [Castro-Neves] cars and we were holding our own,' explained Unser. 'I picked up some understeer and just got in too deep on the entry to Turn Three. The front brakes locked up and I went straight into the wall.'

Montoya and Castro-Neves resumed their battle at the front on the restart, followed by a gaggle of pursuers led by Dario Franchitti (KOOL Honda/Rey-

nard) and Jones. The leaders pulled away to nearly a six-second lead on lap 75, but Jones was not deterred. Enjoying by far the most competitive race of his Champ Car career, he used a backmarker to help him get around Franchitti for third place on the 97th lap and set sail for the front.

By lap 139, the battle for the lead had developed into a three-way affair. A handful of laps later, when Montoya was held up again by lapped cars in Turn Two, Castro-Neves took full advantage of the situation and dived brilliantly into the lead. As the front-runners sped downhill toward Turn Three, Montoya attempted to redress the balance, which forced Castro-Neves to adopt a defensive line to the inside. Jones, following closely behind, saw his opportunity and motored to the outside of Montoya to take second. A little more than a couple of hundred yards later, however, Jones got into Turn One a mite too hot and looped his car. There was no contact, but it was enough to bring out the yellow.

'I was real loose at that point in traffic and got into the kink a little bit

PJ Jones drove the race of his life for Pat Patrick, surviving a mid-race spin to finish an excellent second.

Bottom: Helio Castro-Neves resumes after a pit stop, but not quite quickly enough to protect his lead from Juan Montoya.

Overleaf: Paul Tracy flashes around the Nazareth Speedway oval during a practice run. The Canadian overcame an early spin in the race to score third place for Team KOOL Green.

on lap 155. The Lola driver lost his bid for a podium finish 15 laps later, when he spun at the exit of the final corner while seeking to repass Jones. Castro-Neves lost a lap after stalling the engine, then crashed for good in Turn Three shortly after the restart.

'In Turn Two, it felt like the throttle stuck a little bit, but then it was okay, so I figured it was me,' he related. 'I touched the brake; it was fine. I let everybody go, because I wanted to go for the fastest race lap, and as I headed toward Turn Three and lifted off, the throttle stuck [again] and when I hit the brakes, the pedal went straight to the floor. The next thing I knew, I was in the wall.'

It was an ignominious end to an otherwise brilliant performance.

After a lengthy cleanup, the final 27 laps boiled down to little more than a high-speed parade. Montoya enjoyed the luxury of a pair of lapped cars between himself and Jones at the restart. Jones was further burdened when his car became loose in the closing stages of the race. Under the circumstances, he was delighted with the outcome, as he moved up to ninth in the points race.

'During the first few oval races, I was not that comfortable with the car,' said Jones. 'I may have been relying on [teammate] Adrian's [Fernandez] setup a bit too much. This weekend, we were in totally different cars [Fernandez ran

his '97 Reynard again, while Jones went with the Swift 010.c] and I think that allowed me to work on it.'

Tracy drove a strong second half of the race to claim the final podium spot. Standing 13th at lap 139, the Canadian driver shrewdly waited for the leaders to pit, which helped him make up track positions when others were caught up by the yellow flag. Strong pit-lane work got the Team KOOL Green machine back in the fray in fourth position, which became third when Castro-Neves fell out. Earlier, Tracy had caught a break when he saved his car from harm during a lap-11 spin.

'My car picked up a bit of a push and I made an adjustment with the weight-jacker, and suddenly the car turned into a John Deere,' related Tracy. 'I was mowing the grass on the front straight! The second stint, the

car was only okay, but we caught a break – a break I haven't had in a long time – with the yellow just before the last stop.'

Rookie Cristiano da Matta drove a fine race to finish fourth in Arciero-Wells Racing's MCI WorldCom Toyota/Reynard, securing the engine manufacturer's best finish to date. The 1998 PPG-Dayton Indy Lights champion made his way to the front from 17th on the grid and earned his first-ever Champ Car points. Fernandez overcame a stalled engine on his second pit stop to finish fifth in his Patrick Racing Tecate/Quaker State Ford/Reynard. Michael Andretti and Christian Fittipaldi drove their Newman/Haas machines to sixth and seventh, while the unfortunate Franchitti battled back to the lead lap before finishing eighth.

Jeremy Shaw/Eric Mauk

On a wing and...

T O a man, CART drivers will band together and fight anything they believe diminishes their safety in their race cars. But not everybody believed that the new CART-mandated superspeedway wings were detrimental to safety. Some, like Newman/Haas pilot Michael Andretti, welcomed the change, while others vehemently spoke against it.

'If you want to watch carnage, I think [the race] is going to be interesting,' declared points leader Greg Moore after Friday's practice. 'If you want to watch motor racing, it's going to be boring, because there's just no way to pass out there. I think it's ridiculous to run with these wings.'

CART Vice President of Competition J Kirk Russell fired back by confirming that team owners, drivers and equipment suppliers had all agreed upon the need to slow the cars down on the one-mile ovals.

Happily, the predicted gloom and doom never materialized, as the event was relatively incident-free. There were five caution flags during the 225-lap race, including three for no-contact spins. The total was down from the 1998 race, which saw six accidents bring out yellow flags.

Passing room, however, appeared to have been sacrificed for safety's sake, as much of the green-flag racing was done in the same order. During the 169 laps run under the green banner, only five position changes were recorded among the top six. Helio Castro-Neves slipped past Juan Montoya twice during the race, the only times all day that a leader lost his advantage at full speed.

Not that there wasn't close racing. Castro-Neves and Montoya negotiated the 0.946-mile oval nose-to-tail for much of the race, but overtaking was a problem.

'It was tough to pass out there,' acknowledged Andretti, who finished sixth. 'But no more than usual. It's always tough to pass at Nazareth. I still think the smaller wings are the way to go. I had a really good race car and it would have been great if the straightaways were a little longer, which is why I think we'll see a lot more passing when we get to Milwaukee.'

too hot; the car got sideways,' explained a chastened Jones. 'Once I did, I was just focusing on keeping the engine running.'

Somehow, Jones contrived to prevent his car from collecting the wall, but not before Montoya had scooted by to reclaim second place. During the subsequent pit stops, Castro-Neves was a bit too hasty in attempting to leave his pit stall, losing precious seconds as he reapplied the brakes while the refueling process was completed. Montoya, meanwhile, hit his marks perfectly and got back into the race in first place.

The timing of the caution could not have been worse for front-runners Dario Franchitti and Mark Blundell (Motorola Mercedes/Reynard), who had been embroiled in a close battle for fourth, and defending race champion Vasser, all of whom had made pit stops shortly before Jones spun. Consequently, all had lost a lap to the leaders and, effectively, were out of contention for the win.

Amazingly, Jones emerged still in third place after being serviced and, undaunted, he promptly zipped past Castro-Neves when the race restarted

Michael C. Brown

NAZARETH SNIPPETS

• CART Chairman and CEO Andrew Craig was joined by U.S. Transportation Secretary Rodney E Slater, National Highway Traffic Safety Administration (NHTSA) Executive Dr. Ricardo Martinez and Ford Racing Marketing Manager Sam Scott at a Friday press conference at Nazareth Speedway. Former PPG Cup champions Michael Andretti and Jimmy Vasser also were present to announce a new initiative aimed at delivering **ROAD SAFETY MESSAGES** to the American public. 'As a father of two, and with another on the way, I realize how important this is to my family,' said Andretti. 'Especially as my kids get a little older.'

• Tony Bettenhausen's team withdrew its Epson entry for **SHIGEAKI HATTORI** after the Japanese rookie spun and hit the wall on the exit of Turn Three after a mere dozen laps of practice on Friday.

• Alex Barron's Denso/Castrol All American Racers Toyota/Eagle *(right)* was the fastest of those carrying **GOODYEAR TIRES** on raceday. The talented sophomore set the sixth-fastest race lap (and fastest of the Toyota-powered entries) en route to a career-best ninth-place finish, earning his first points of the year.

• AL UNSER JR.'s return to competition with Marlboro Team Penske was little short of disastrous. Driving with a carbon fiber brace to support his healing left knee, he qualified 23rd, faster than only Robby Gordon, who also struggled. Unser was a promising fifth in the race-morning warmup, but eventually crashed heavily on lap 45.

• **DENNIS VITOLO** crashed his Nicorette/Nicoderm CQ Ford/Reynard heavily during qualifying on Saturday, causing him to sit out Sunday's event. The 42-year-old Floridian complained of a severe headache following Sunday morning's warmup, and was diagnosed as having 'post-concussive-like' symptoms by CART's on-site doctors, Terry Trammell and Chris Pinderski.

• Teams employed a variety of **AERODYNAMIC DEVICES** in an attempt to claw back some of the downforce lost due to the newly mandated wing package. McDonald's Championship Racing perhaps came up with the most brazen solution – small winglets that protruded from the bodywork just forward of the front suspension. The appendages were deemed legal by CART Technical Director Kirk Russell because the surface of the 'KRAs' (for Kirk Russell Agitators!) consisted simply of a flat plane.

• Tino Belli and veteran Tony Cicale shared the **RACE ENGINEERING DUTIES** for Team KOOL Green's Paul Tracy following the departure of John Dick, who resurfaced at the Nazareth Speedway event working with the Arciero-Wells Racing team on Scott Pruett's Pioneer Toyota/Reynard.

FEDEX CHAMPIONSHIP SERIES • ROUND 4
BOSCH SPARK PLUG GRAND PRIX PRESENTED BY TOYOTA

NAZARETH SPEEDWAY, PENNSYLVANIA

APRIL 18, 225 laps – 212.850 miles

Place	Driver (Nat.)	No.	Team Sponsors Engine/Car	Tires	Q Speed	Q Time	Q Pos.	Laps	Time/Status	Ave. (mph)	Pts.
1	*Juan Montoya (COL)	4	Target/Chip Ganassi Racing Honda/Reynard 99I	FS	173.755	19.600s	1	225	1h 46m 13.527s	120.225	22
2	PJ Jones (USA)	20	Patrick Visteon Ford Cosworth/Swift 010.c	FS	170.810	19.938s	8	225	1h 46m 18.630s	120.129	16
3	Paul Tracy (CDN)	26	Team KOOL Green Honda/Reynard 99I	FS	172.935	19.693s	4	225	1h 46m 19.407s	120.115	14
4	*Cristiano da Matta (BR)	25	Arciero-Wells MCI WorldCom Toyota/Reynard 99I	FS	167.739	20.303s	17	225	1h 46m 19.832s	120.107	12
5	Adrian Fernandez (MEX)	40	Patrick Tecate/Quaker State Ford Cosworth/Reynard 97I	FS	170.630	19.959s	9	225	1h 46m 29.928s	119.917	10
6	Michael Andretti (USA)	6	Newman/Haas Kmart/Texaco Ford Cosworth/Swift 010.c	FS	168.920	20.161s	14	225	1h 46m 30.246s	119.911	8
7	Christian Fittipaldi (BR)	11	Newman/Haas Big Kmart Ford Cosworth/Swift 010.c	FS	169.915	20.043s	12	225	1h 46m 34.151s	119.838	6
8	Dario Franchitti (GB)	27	Team KOOL Green Honda/Reynard 99I	FS	173.154	19.668s	3	225	1h 46m 35.363s	119.815	5
9	Alex Barron (USA)	36	All American Racers Denso/Castrol Toyota/Eagle 997	GY	167.434	20.340s	18	224	Running		4
10	Scott Pruett (USA)	24	Arciero-Wells Racing Pioneer Toyota/Reynard 99I	FS	165.933	20.524s	21	224	Running		3
11	Jimmy Vasser (USA)	12	Target/Chip Ganassi Racing Honda/Reynard 99I	FS	170.025	20.030s	11	224	Running		2
12	Greg Moore (CDN)	99	Forsythe Racing Player's/Indeck Mercedes/Reynard 99I	FS	170.237	20.005s	10	224	Running		1
13	Max Papis (I)	7	Team Rahal Miller Lite Ford Cosworth/Reynard 99I	FS	171.489	19.859s	7	224	Running		
14	Patrick Carpentier (CDN)	33	Forsythe Racing Player's/Indeck Mercedes/Reynard 99I	FS	171.636	19.842s	6	224	Running		
15	Gil de Ferran (BR)	5	Walker Racing Valvoline/Cummins Honda/Reynard 99I	GY	169.054	20.145s	13	224	Running		
16	Michel Jourdain Jr. (MEX)	19	Payton/Coyne Racing Herdez/Viva Mexico Ford Cosworth/Lola T97/00	FS	164.458	20.708s	22	224	Running		
17	Mark Blundell (GB)	18	PacWest Racing Group Motorola Mercedes/Reynard 99I	FS	172.217	19.775s	5	223	Running		
18	Mauricio Gugelmin (BR)	17	PacWest Racing Group Hollywood Mercedes/Reynard 99I	FS	168.302	20.235s	15	222	Running		
19	Robby Gordon (USA)	22	Team Gordon Panasonic/Menards Toyota/Reynard 98I	FS	162.986	20.895s	24	220	Running		
20	Richie Hearn (USA)	10	Della Penna Motorsports Budweiser Toyota/Swift 010.c	FS	166.452	20.460s	19	212	Oil pressure		
21	Helio Castro-Neves (BR)	9	Hogan Racing Hogan Motor Leasing Mercedes/Lola B99/00	FS	173.746	19.601s	2	175	Accident		
22	Bryan Herta (USA)	8	Team Rahal Shell Ford Cosworth/Reynard 99I	FS	167.896	20.284s	16	77	Handling		
23	Tony Kanaan (BR)	44	McDonald's Championship Racing Honda/Reynard 99I	FS	166.273	20.482s	20	51	Throttle		
24	Al Unser Jr. (USA)	2	Marlboro Team Penske Mercedes/Penske PC27B	GY	164.125	20.750s	23	44	Accident		
DNS	Dennis Vitolo (USA)	34	Payton/Coyne Racing Nicorette Ford Cosworth/Reynard 97I	FS	no speed	no time	–	–	Accident in qualifying		
DNS	*Shigeaki Hattori (J)	16	Bettenhausen Motorsports Epson Mercedes/Reynard 98I	GY	no speed	no time	–	–	Accident in practice		

* denotes rookie driver

Caution flags: Laps 11–16, spin/Tracy; laps 45–58, accident/Unser Jr.; laps 145–153, spin/Jones; laps 170–175, spin/Castro-Neves; laps 178–198, accident/Castro-Neves. **Total:** Five for 56 laps.

Lap leaders: Juan Montoya, 1–38 (38 laps); Helio Castro-Neves, 39–49 (11 laps); Montoya, 50–144 (95 laps); Castro-Neves, 145–148 (4 laps); Montoya, 149–225 (77 laps); **Totals:** Montoya, 210 laps; Castro-Neves, 15 laps.

Fastest race lap: Helio Castro-Neves, 21.106s, 161.357 mph on lap 19.

Championship positions: 1 Montoya, 45; 2 Fernandez, 43; 3 Moore & Andretti, 40; 5 Franchitti, 35; 6 Fittipaldi, 34; 7 de Ferran, 33; 8 Vasser, 18; 9 Jones, 17; 10 Tracy, 16; 11 Herta, 15; 12 Papis, 14; 13 da Matta, 12; 14 Kanaan, 10; 15 Gugelmin, 8; 16 Carpentier, 6; 17 Blundell, Hearn & Gordon, 5; 20 Castro-Neves & Barron, 4; 22 Pruett, 3.

RIO

1 – **MONTOYA**

2 – **FRANCHITTI**

3 – **FITTIPALDI**

FEDEX CHAMPIONSHIP SERIES • ROUND 5

Taking full advantage of the draft at the start, Juan Montoya makes a brilliant move to slip inside front-row starters Christian Fittipaldi and Dario Franchitti in Turn One. Gil de Ferran tries to make it four abreast on the outside, before wisely deciding not to press the issue.

Bottom left: The top contenders, Montoya and Franchitti, battle it out with bubbly.

Left: The rain doesn't dampen the enthusiasm of Brazilians Moreno, Castro-Neves and Gugelmin.

Below left: PJ Jones finds solace in the garage area while waiting for the storm to pass.

QUALIFYING

When the South American rains washed away much of the allotted practice time for the GP Telemar Rio 200, the clock became the enemy of every CART team in the paddock. To give its mechanics a head start, the Newman/Haas team began working with the basic setup from last year's Rio race for Christian Fittipaldi's Big Kmart Ford Cosworth/Swift. Never mind that the team had switched from the 1998 Goodyear tires to this season's Firestone Firehawks, nor that the car ran just 78 laps in last year's event before dropping out with a fuel system malady.

Fittipaldi was second quickest in Friday's practice, trailing only the Team KOOL Green Honda/Reynard of Dario Franchitti, which earned the car a coveted late-session qualifying attempt. The time saved paid off in the last hours of preparation for Friday's qualifying, as Fittipaldi was the strongest of three drivers who consecutively broke the track record, allowing him to claim his first career pole. His lap set a track standard of 174.002 mph (38.565 seconds) for the Emerson Fittipaldi Speedway at Nelson Piquet International Raceway.

'It's nice to be starting first here; now we need to make sure we do all the correct changes,' said Fittipaldi. 'My lap was fast, and then in [Turn] Four, I got a little bit of a push. The car has been running good since this morning.'

Gil de Ferran (Walker Racing Valvoline/Cummins Honda/Reynard) began the onslaught on the record books with just four cars left in the qualifying line. Then Juan Montoya claimed the track record, but held it for less than a minute before Fittipaldi took to the track. Franchitti made the final attempt at the pole, but fell a scant 0.009 second short.

Rain and an early-session accident by Gualter Salles shortened the qualifying period, causing three drivers to be added to the back of the grid for Saturday's race. Mauricio Gugelmin, Robby Gordon and Luiz Garcia Jr. all waived their initial attempts in the morning, and when the session ran too long for a second try, the trio was allotted the 25th, 26th and 27th positions in the starting field.

stop. Problems on cold tires prevented him from making a move on Montoya, but Fittipaldi earned his eighth career podium appearance with his third-place finish.

Although Montoya pulled out a two-second lead in the opening laps, Fittipaldi and Franchitti gradually reduced his advantage, despite the fact that the Scot's 'speed-shift' had pitched, forcing him to lift off the throttle on each up-shift. Gil de Ferran led the chase in fourth with Derrick Walker's Valvoline/Cummins Honda/Reynard, followed by fellow Brazilian Tony Kanaan, who jumped from seventh on the grid to fifth inside the first couple of laps with Jerry Forsythe's McDonald's Honda/Reynard. Once again, Montoya's teammate, Jimmy Vasser, was overshadowed by the Colombian youngster, but he held onto sixth place until sidelined by an electrical glitch after just 23 laps. It was only the second time in 58 races – dating back to Vancouver in '95 – that he had been put out of a race by a mechanical problem.

'The law of averages affects even Chip Ganassi sometimes,' said Vasser philosophically. 'My guys have allowed me to finish most races over the years, so I'm not really concerned.'

Five laps later, Michael Andretti, who, like Vasser, had endured a frustrating start to the season, posted the second retirement of the day when his Kmart/Texaco Swift's Ford Cosworth engine expired. Andretti, in contrast to teammate Fittipaldi, had qualified only 16th following a troubled practice session and had made up only two positions in the first 28 laps.

'The engine problems in practice hurt us in qualifying and, ultimately, in the race,' said Andretti. 'The Ford Cosworth is very reliable, so this was an unusual weekend. I'd rather have this happen when I am running 14th than another weekend.'

The resulting caution spelled problems for two more of the lead-lap cars. De Ferran dropped from fourth to 14th after an airjack failed during his pit stop, while Paul Tracy's Team KOOL Green Honda/Reynard was assessed a drive-through penalty after his foot slipped off the clutch and he inadvertently clipped one of his own crewmen. After paying for his violation, Tracy had fallen from ninth to 21st.

Helio Castro-Neves became the first of the home-grown drivers to bow out, vacating his Hogan Motor Leasing Mercedes/Lola after a turbo fire erupted on lap 32. Fellow countrymen Mauricio Gugelmin (Hollywood Mercedes/Reynard) and Cristiano da Matta

Photos: Barry Hathaway

O N the cusp of reaching heights that few first-year drivers attain in any racing series, Champ Car *wunderkind* Juan Montoya seemed remarkably centered prior to the GP Telemar Rio 200. While everyone else was watching for Montoya to become the first rookie ever to win three straight races in the series, the Colombian driver seemed unencumbered by thoughts of setting a record.

'I hope to earn a few points and prove that the past two races [victories at Long Beach and Nazareth] weren't accidents,' he said.

That calm facade melted away when the green flag waved over the Emerson

Fittipaldi Speedway. Instructed by team owner Chip Ganassi to be patient in the early stages, Montoya, who started third, pounced on the field in the first turn and assumed the lead. The youngster made the move pay off, as he led 93 of the 108 laps and won his third consecutive FedEx Championship Series event.

'Chip [Ganassi] said to take it easy at the start, but I saw a chance and I just went for it,' said Montoya. 'After that, it got pretty close. We were all running at the same pace, and after the second pit stop, it got a bit exciting.'

The race was exciting from the get-go for the Brazilian fans, who saw one

of their own, 28-year-old Christian Fittipaldi, lead the way to the green flag after claiming his first career pole. The pilot of the Newman/Haas Racing Big Kmart Ford Cosworth/Swift held the advantage for an extra circuit after CART Starter Jim Swintal's yellow flag signaled a field out of proper alignment, necessitating a restart on the second lap.

Fittipaldi soon fell behind Montoya, but didn't fall far. The Sao Paolo native traded positions with Dario Franchitti (Team KOOL Green Honda/Reynard) for the entire race, tumbling out of the top three only briefly during a late green-flag pit

Juan Montoya and Dario Franchitti don't have time to admire the spectacular views in Rio as they speed past the pits at over 200 mph.
Photo: Kazuli Saito

Insets: Al Unser Jr., still recuperating from a crash in the opening race, earned his first PPG Cup point of the season; Riding pillion Rio-style; Max Papis (right) is clearly impressed.

Barry Hathaway

Photos: Kazuki Saito

FEDEX CHAMPIONSHIP SERIES • ROUND 5

Safety systems

RESPONDING to the spectator deaths at the 1998 U.S. 500 and the May 1 Indy Racing League event at Lowe's Motor Speedway in Charlotte, Championship Auto Racing Teams Chairman and CEO Andrew Craig announced that CART would require its teams to run wheel and suspension tethers – or 'Energy Absorbing Restraints' (EARs) – beginning with the FedEx Championship Series' next race at Gateway International Raceway, Madison, Illinois.

'Safety is the priority in racing,' said Craig. 'This is part of the continuous evolution of the safety systems for fans, teams and officials.'

The EARs were designed to follow the same guidelines set down for Formula 1 World Championship cars, with the exception that, initially, the Champ Cars were required to tether only the front wheels due to a shortage of materials. The new edict utilized FIA (Federation Internationale de l'Automobile) rule 10.3.4: 'In order to prevent a wheel from becoming separated [from the car] in the event of all suspension members connecting to the car failing, cables must be fitted which connect each wheel/upright assembly to the main structure of the car. Under such circumstances, the design of the cable must be such that no wheel may make contact with the driver's head.'

Manufacturers from both the CART and IRL camps worked jointly to build the restraint systems. 'We've worked with the IRL from the beginning,' said Reynard's Bruce Ashmore. 'This is for safety and not for politics.'

(MCI WorldCom Toyota/Reynard) were also early arrivals in the paddock: Gugelmin with a broken radiator on the 63rd lap; da Matta with turbo problems after 81 circuits.

The battle up front was still with Fittipaldi and Franchitti, while Kanaan and Patrick Carpentier (Player's/Indeck Mercedes/Reynard) gave chase in fourth and fifth positions. It nearly became only a three-car skirmish on lap 49, when Franchitti got a bit closer than he would have liked to the Turn One wall. Looking for a way around Montoya, he almost discovered the route to the transporter.

'I was trying pretty hard, experimenting with how early I could come off the brakes,' he explained. 'I went wide in Turn One, got up in the marbles, and the car just didn't want to come back down. I was very close to hitting the wall.'

'Dario had a close moment, but I think God did not want him to hit the wall today,' added the close-following Fittipaldi with a chuckle.

Fittipaldi took second place, but any hope of further progress was interrupted by a full-course caution after Scott Pruett's engine expired. The leaders elected not to head for the pits, since a fuel stop at that stage would not have taken them to the finish, although others dashed in looking for a new plan. When the green flag waved, it was more of the same as Montoya pulled away from the field.

The order remained unchanged until the second round of fuel stops began on lap 73. Fittipaldi and Franchitti each led the race briefly during the cycle, which ended with an out-of-sequence Al Unser Jr. showing the way. It was the first race the Penske driver had led since Vancouver in 1998. The former series champion had Tracy, Robby Gordon and Richie Hearn riding with him, although Adrian Fernandez put everyone back on the same schedule after brushing the wall with Pat Patrick's Tecate/Quaker State Ford/Reynard, bringing out a caution flag on lap 84.

The yellow banner remained in place as four more laps were washed away by a brief drizzle, after which Montoya pointed the field toward the restart. The fun didn't last long, however, as Gordon spun his Panasonic Toyota/Reynard in Turn One just three laps later. In the process, he nearly collected Michel Jourdain Jr.'s Lola. The subsequent caution period reduced the race to a seven-lap shootout, which Montoya claimed with ease, followed by Franchitti, Fittipaldi and Team Rahal's Max Papis, who built on strong pit work to post a career-high fourth-place finish.

'Track position was all important today,' said Franchitti. 'We were trying to conserve fuel and I was able to go two or three more laps than Juan, which I thought was an advantage. Our biggest problem was on the restarts after my shifter broke. It's nice to have the points, but I'd rather be in that [Montoya's] seat.'

Kanaan and Carpentier were next, chased by PJ Jones, who brought his Visteon Ford/Swift home seventh after starting 16th. Tarso Marques earned his first-ever CART points with a ninth-place finish for Marlboro Team Penske, while Roberto Moreno scored in his first race as a replacement for the injured Mark Blundell in the Motorola Mercedes/Reynard. His 11th-place finish secured the first series points for the Brazilian since Laguna Seca in 1997.

But all eyes were on the young Colombian after the race, Montoya having stamped his name in the record book as the first-ever rookie to win three straight Champ Car events. His trio of consecutive victories was also the first since Target/Ganassi's Alex Zanardi had won four in a row [Detroit, Portland, Cleveland and Toronto] in 1998.

Montoya's triple play was the 11th in CART history, and in nine of the previous ten instances, the driver went on to win the season championship. Only Paul Tracy failed to take the title after winning three consecutive races in '97. Notably, Montoya gained his three wins on three different types of track, demonstrating the youngster's versatility. The street course of Long Beach was little trouble, nor was the oddly-shaped short oval at Nazareth. The 'roval' of Rio, so named because of its two high-speed corners and two technically-demanding, braking corners, also offered little challenge to the calm Colombian.

Eric Mauk

Under pressure

Michael C. Brown

ALL of the Brazilian drivers felt the pressure of returning to Rio de Janeiro for a Champ Car race, but none carried the load that Christian Fittipaldi had to deal with. Not only was his Uncle Emerson the promoter, but the family name also flew majestically above the Emerson Fittipaldi Speedway at Nelson Piquet International Raceway, site of the GP Telemar Rio 200. Rains dampened the spirits and washed away Thursday's practice, leaving the pilot of the Newman/Haas Racing Big Kmart Ford/Swift 010.c to ponder winning in his home country.

'As a Brazilian, I only have one chance to do well at home. My mother [Suzy] has been involved with the race since it started in 1996, and my uncle [Emerson] is the promoter,' declared Fittipaldi. 'Above all, I would like to do well for myself and my team.'

A Sao Paolo native, the 28-year-old Fittipaldi saw his day end early in 1998 when a fuel problem closed the books after 78 laps. Christian responded to the pressure with the second-fastest practice time, and followed that up with a record qualifying effort for Rio of 35.565 seconds (174.002 mph) to win his first CART pole position.

'It's definitely very nice to be here [as the pole sitter], but tomorrow will be a completely different day,' said Fittipaldi in the post-qualifying press conference. '[The race] is not going to be easy.'

Fittipaldi relinquished his advantage at the first corner of the race, but never let leaders Juan Montoya and Dario Franchitti out of sight. A miss on the downforce settings cost the Newman/Haas car any chance of making a late-lap pass, but Fittipaldi was right there at the end to earn a third-place finish. That gave him the eighth podium of his career while vaulting him into third place in the FedEx Championship Series points race.

'I wanted to be as quick as these other two guys, but we messed up on the level of downforce,' admitted Fittipaldi. 'I was quicker than them on the straights, but not in the corners. On the restarts, I was all over the place. It took about three laps to get the tires up to speed. I'm not happy finishing third, because I thought I had a better shot at the win, but it was important to score points.'

RIO SNIPPETS

• Long known as an owner willing to give a young driver a chance, JOHN DELLA PENNA surprised no one when he announced a new incentive program for the champion of the South American Formula 3 Championship. Della Penna, the only Latin American owner in the CART series, announced that he would offer a Champ Car test to the 1999 champion. 'The F3 championship is the top open-wheel series in Latin America,' said Della Penna, who was born and raised in Argentina. 'And it's the place where some of the guys that are currently running in Champ Cars get their start, including Helio Castro-Neves and Christian Fittipaldi.'

• MARK BLUNDELL's streak of 51 consecutive starts in the FedEx Championship Series came to an end at Rio when ROBERTO MORENO (right) took over in the PacWest Racing Motorola Mercedes/Reynard. Blundell crashed hard in a May 4 test session at Gateway International Raceway and was unable to race due to a fracture of his seventh cervical vertebra. He had been nearing the end of the windy session when a gearbox malady caused him to hit the Turn Three wall at the suburban St Louis track.

• The time-honored COMMAND of 'Gentlemen start your engines' came from nearly 200 miles above the Earth as Commander Victor Afanasiev and fellow cosmonaut Sergei Avdeev started the GP Telemar Rio 200 from the Russian space station 'Mir'. It was the first time that a sporting event had been started from outer space. The feat was made possible through the efforts of Omega Timing, the official timekeeper of the CART series and maker of the first and only watch to be worn on the moon.

• Despite finishing in the top five at his home country's race, McDonald's Championship Racing's TONY KANAAN appeared dissatisfied. Starting seventh, Kanaan ran fourth midway through the race before placing fifth. 'Last year, if I was in the top five, I would be celebrating,' said Kanaan. 'This year, it is not good enough. We cannot say that we are having a bad year so far because if it wasn't for Long Beach, we would be top five in the championship right now.' Team President Steve Horne, who sold his ownership of the former Tasman Motorsports outfit to Gerald Forsythe before the season, also withheld any celebratory statements, despite Rio being the team's best finish of the year. 'We had a reasonable day,' he said. 'The car wasn't quite good enough, but we're leaving with some points.'

• Each of the TOP SIX FINISHERS in the GP Telemar Rio 200 either equaled or bettered career- or season-best performances. Rookie Juan Montoya equaled his career best with the win, while Max Papis established a new highlight, as his fourth spot was one better than his previous best, a fifth-place finish at Houston in 1998. Dario Franchitti and Christian Fittipaldi equaled their season bests with finishes of second and third respectively. Tony Kanaan and Patrick Carpentier also registered season bests by taking fifth and sixth positions.

Barry Hathaway

FEDEX CHAMPIONSHIP SERIES • ROUND 5
GP TELEMAR RIO 200

EMERSON FITTIPALDI SPEEDWAY, RIO DE JANEIRO, BRAZIL

MAY 15, 108 laps – 201.312 miles

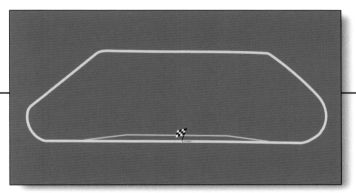

Place	Driver (Nat.)	No.	Team Sponsors Engine/Car	Tires	Q Speed	Q Time	Q Pos.	Laps	Time/Status	Ave. (mph)	Pts.
1	*Juan Montoya (COL)	4	Target/Chip Ganassi Racing Honda/Reynard 99I	FS	173.615	38.651s	3	108	1h 36m 32.233s	125.120	21
2	Dario Franchitti (GB)	27	Team KOOL Green Honda/Reynard 99I	FS	173.962	38.574s	2	108	1h 36m 33.969s	125.082	16
3	Christian Fittipaldi (BR)	11	Newman/Haas Big Kmart Ford Cosworth/Swift 010.c	FS	174.002	38.565s	1	108	1h 36m 36.187s	125.034	15
4	Max Papis (I)	7	Team Rahal Miller Lite Ford Cosworth/Reynard 99I	FS	170.397	39.381s	13	108	1h 36m 37.163s	125.013	12
5	Tony Kanaan (BR)	44	McDonald's Championship Racing Honda/Reynard 99I	FS	172.159	38.978s	7	108	1h 36m 39.269s	124.968	10
6	Patrick Carpentier (CDN)	33	Forsythe Racing Player's/Indeck Mercedes/Reynard 99I	FS	171.872	39.043s	9	108	1h 36m 39.851s	124.956	8
7	PJ Jones (USA)	20	Patrick Racing Visteon Ford Cosworth/Swift 010.c	FS	170.345	39.393s	16	108	1h 36m 40.290s	124.946	6
8	Greg Moore (CDN)	99	Forsythe Racing Player's/Indeck Mercedes/Reynard 99I	FS	171.249	39.185s	10	108	1h 36m 40.537s	124.941	5
9	*Tarso Marques (BR)	3	Marlboro Team Penske Mercedes/Penske PC27B	GY	172.031	39.007s	8	108	1h 36m 42.921s	124.889	4
10	Gil de Ferran (BR)	5	Walker Racing Valvoline/Cummins Honda/Reynard 99I	GY	173.467	38.684s	4	108	1h 36m 43.474s	124.877	3
11	Roberto Moreno (BR)	18	PacWest Racing Group Motorola Mercedes/Reynard 99I	FS	167.254	40.121s	23	108	1h 36m 43.950s	124.867	2
12	Al Unser Jr. (USA)	2	Marlboro Team Penske Mercedes/Penske PC27B	GY	168.573	39.807s	19	108	1h 36m 44.448s	124.857	1
13	Bryan Herta (USA)	8	Team Rahal Shell Ford Cosworth/Reynard 99I	FS	173.346	38.711s	5	108	1h 36m 46.371s	124.815	
14	Robby Gordon (USA)	22	Team Gordon Panasonic/Menards Toyota/Swift 010.c	FS	no speed	no time	26	108	1h 36m 49.703s	124.744	
15	Paul Tracy (CDN)	26	Team KOOL Green Honda/Reynard 99I	FS	170.705	39.310s	12	108	1h 36m 52.447s	124.685	
16	Michel Jourdain Jr. (MEX)	19	Payton/Coyne Herdez/Viva Mexico Ford Cosworth/Lola T97/00	FS	162.594	41.271s	24	107	Running		
17	Gualter Salles (BR)	16	Bettenhausen Motorsports Epson Mercedes/Reynard 98I	GY	167.806	39.989s	21	107	Running		
18	*Luiz Garcia Jr. (BR)	71	Payton/Coyne Tang Ford Cosworth/Reynard 97I	FS	no speed	no time	27	102	Running		
19	Richie Hearn (USA)	10	Della Penna Motorsports Budweiser Toyota/Swift 010.c	FS	169.343	39.626s	18	101	Cooling system		
20	Adrian Fernandez (MEX)	40	Patrick Racing Tecate/Quaker State Ford Cosworth/Reynard 97I	FS	170.129	39.443s	17	83	Accident		
21	*Cristiano da Matta (BR)	25	Arciero-Wells Racing MCI WorldCom Toyota/Reynard 99I	FS	170.393	39.382s	14	81	Turbo		
22	Mauricio Gugelmin (BR)	17	PacWest Racing Group Hollywood Mercedes/Reynard 99I	FS	no speed	no time	25	61	Cooling system		
23	Alex Barron (USA)	36	All American Racers Denso/Castrol Toyota/Eagle 997	GY	167.530	40.055s	22	58	Overheating		
24	Scott Pruett (USA)	24	Arciero-Wells Racing Pioneer Toyota/Reynard 99I	FS	167.836	39.982s	20	49	Turbo		
25	Helio Castro-Neves (BR)	9	Hogan Racing Hogan Motor Leasing Mercedes/Lola B99/00	FS	170.739	39.302s	11	32	Turbo		
26	Michael Andretti (USA)	6	Newman/Haas Kmart/Texaco Ford Cosworth/Swift 010.c	FS	170.375	39.386s	15	28	Engine		
27	Jimmy Vasser (USA)	12	Target/Chip Ganassi Racing Honda/Reynard 99I	FS	172.389	38.926s	6	23	Electrical		

* denotes rookie driver

Caution flags: Lap 1, yellow start; laps 29–35, engine/Andretti; laps 49–54, engine/Pruett; laps 84–89, accident/Fernandez; laps 90–94, moisture; laps 97–101, accident/Jourdain Jr. & Gordon. **Total:** Six for 30 laps.

Lap leaders: Christian Fittipaldi, 1 (1 lap); Juan Montoya, 2–72 (71 laps); Fittipaldi, 73 (1 lap); Dario Franchitti, 74–76 (3 laps); Al Unser Jr., 77–86 (10 laps); Montoya, 87–108. **Totals:** Montoya, 93 laps; Unser Jr., 10 laps; Franchitti, 3 laps; Fittipaldi, 2 laps.

Fastest race lap: Juan Montoya, 38.891s, 172.544 mph on lap 107 (record).

Championship positions: 1 Montoya, 66; 2 Franchitti, 51; 3 Fittipaldi, 49; 4 Moore, 45; 5 Fernandez, 43; 6 Andretti, 40; 7 de Ferran, 36; 8 Papis, 26; 9 Jones, 23; 10 Kanaan, 20; 11 Vasser, 18; 12 Tracy, 16; 13 Herta, 15; 14 Carpentier, 14; 15 da Matta, 12; 16 Gugelmin, 8; 17 Blundell, Hearn & Gordon, 5; 20 Castro-Neves, Marques & Barron, 4; 23 Pruett, 3; 24 Moreno, 2; 25 Unser Jr., 1.

OMEGA
OFFICIAL TIMEKEEPER OF CART

GATEWAY

FEDEX CHAMPIONSHIP SERIES • ROUND 6

QUALIFYING

In searching for his fourth straight win, Target/Chip Ganassi Racing's Juan Montoya started his Motorola 300 weekend in the same fashion as he had when he gained his previous three victories. At each of the last three events, he had started in the top five. This time, he made it four in a row with style by taking the pole in his Honda/Reynard.

Montoya became the first multiple pole winner in the season's six events, after having qualified fastest at the Nazareth oval in Round Four. The feat came as a shock to the 23-year-old Colombian, who figured his qualifying time (25.014 seconds) would put him deeper in the field.

'After I saw the [practice] times, I thought the pole would be in the high 24s. But this morning, we had a problem with the rear shocks, so qualifying was a bit of a lottery as far as the setup goes,' said Montoya. 'When it came to qualifying, the car had so much push, it was a bit of a surprise [to win the pole]. To learn an oval is fairly sim-

ple. There are only two corners. The biggest thing is to get a good car, and we've worked very hard at that.'

Team KOOL Green's Paul Tracy, whose front-row starting spot was his first since claiming the Milwaukee pole in 1997, lined up beside Montoya.

'Things are shaping up. Our short-oval package is coming together. I came here and tested after Nazareth and the car was really good right off the truck,' said Tracy. 'We made a few changes right before qualifying, but we didn't go in the right direction. I felt we had a real shot at the pole.'

Hometown favorite Hogan Racing earned the third position on the grid as Helio Castro-Neves put his St. Louis Sports Mercedes/Lola in the field just ahead of Patrick Carpentier. Tracy's teammate Dario Franchitti earned his fourth straight top-five starting spot in his identical Honda-powered Reynard, flanked in the third row by Greg Moore (Player's/Indeck Mercedes/Reynard).

Michael Andretti pushed his Firestone tires to the limit and reaped the reward with a fine win.

Inset: 'I was this close!' exclaims Helio Castro-Neves, who just failed to find a way past Andretti.
Photos: Kazuki Saito

change during his fourth and final pit stop, he fought off a determined challenge from the Hogan Motor Leasing Mercedes/Lola of Helio Castro-Neves.

'I have to give credit to Firestone,' declared Andretti. 'We decided to try to get track position and not take on tires during our last stop. It was a bit of a gamble, but the tires were excellent.'

Castro-Neves took a different route than Andretti to get to the front. The Brazilian, who started third, missed his pit entirely on his first stop of the day, necessitating another time-consuming attempt that put him out of sequence with the leaders. Castro-Neves was distraught about the error, but team owner Carl Hogan worked wonders to play down the issue, imploring his young charge to remain focused on the race ahead.

After falling as low as 22nd, Castro-Neves moved inexorably forward. He emerged in sixth following his final pit stop and used his ever-improving Lola to maximum effect as he scorched past Dario Franchitti (Team KOOL Green Honda/Reynard), PJ Jones (Visteon Ford/Swift), Max Papis (Miller Lite Ford/Reynard) and a similarly inspired Roberto Moreno, once again filling in for the injured Mark Blundell in the Motorola Mercedes/Reynard.

Castro-Neves took over second place on lap 203 and rapidly erased a deficit of almost two seconds to race leader Andretti. For the final 30 laps, they were never separated by more than a couple of car lengths. Andretti, though, made not the hint of a slip.

'Michael's an excellent driver and he knows how to win,' acknowledged Castro-Neves. 'I tried not to blow it. I wanted to make sure I finished. We proved we had a good car and we'll go to [the next race at] Milwaukee and see what happens.'

Montoya tried to live up to his billing in the early stages of the race, taking the lead from his pole position in search of a CART record-equaling fourth straight victory. His progress was interrupted by a couple of early cautions, however, when Robby Gordon crashed his Panasonic/Johns Manville Toyota/Swift in Turn Three, just 11 laps into the race, and when Tarso Marques (Marlboro Mercedes/Penske) suffered a similar fate on lap 32. Several teams had elected to make pit stops during the earlier caution, so the leading positions were dramatically shuffled when the remainder of the field made their first scheduled pit stops following Marques' demise. Montoya resumed in eighth after taking on fresh tires and a full load of methanol. He became embroiled in a

lengthy battle with Paul Tracy and had climbed to third when his Target team attempted to stretch the fuel load a little too far. Montoya had to coast into the pits on lap 106, costing him a lap and leaving him out of contention. Even so, he fought back to finish as the final car on the lead lap in 11th.

Moreno was one of those who took service during Gordon's incident, and he found himself leading the way after Marques' crash. The PacWest Mercedes/Reynard led for the next 38 laps before yielding to Al Unser Jr., who was running his first race in Marlboro Team Penske's newly acquired Mercedes/Lola. The laps allowed Unser to pass Bobby Rahal for third place on CART's all-time lap leader list (3,113).

As the pit sequence swung back toward the early leaders, Tracy had maneuvered his Team KOOL Green Honda/Reynard to the front. Andretti followed, pursued by Jimmy Vasser's similar Target/Ganassi entry. Tracy's lead vanished in the pits as Andretti brought the field back to green after Mauricio Gugelmin's PacWest Hollywood Mercedes/Reynard ran out of fuel and needed a tow on lap 106.

Andretti kept the lead by default during a lengthy caution (15 laps) caused by an accident between Patrick Carpentier and Bryan Herta on the restart. When the green waved again at lap 130, the Team KOOL Green cars were preparing for an assault on the front-running Newman/Haas Ford/Swift. The plan of attack disintegrated in the Barry Green war room on lap 148, however, when Tracy and Franchitti collided on the entry to Turn Three. The incident occurred when Franchitti attempted to make a pass after Tracy had been held up momentarily by a slower car on the exit of Turn Two.

'Well, I'm not very happy,' said an irate Tracy after making heavy contact with the outside retaining wall. 'Obviously, it's all the more disappointing, considering how well the car was working.'

Franchitti, who, amazingly, managed to save the car after performing a half-spin, was rather more forthcoming: 'I got a run on Paul out of Turn Two. He came down across the track to hold his line. I got alongside him and we turned into the corner, which didn't allow much room. There's a big bump in Turn Three. The front of my car hit the bump and skipped up into his car. After that, I was just hanging on. I feel sorry for Paul because he was running well all day and it's about time that he got a break.'

Castro-Neves, along with Christian

Rookie Juan Montoya may have been the story at the beginning of the Motorola 300 at Gateway International Raceway, but conversation at the end of the afternoon was centered upon 1991 PPG Cup champion Michael Andretti, who guided Newman/Haas Racing's Kmart/Texaco Havoline Ford Cosworth/Swift to another accomplished victory.

The most successful driver in CART history started from 11th on the grid, but wasn't worried about making up ground too quickly. Andretti knew from bitter experience that early speed wouldn't automatically result in a trip to Victory Lane. After all, in 1998,

critical seconds lost in a late-race pit stop had allowed Alex Zanardi to claim the win. This time, while pit-road demons ensnared early leaders, Andretti took advantage of some inspired strategic calls and a typically forceful performance behind the wheel to emerge with his 38th career Champ Car win.

The Newman/Haas team elected not to change tires during its first pit stop on lap 36. The few seconds saved were enough to vault Andretti past four rivals in the closely matched field. Andretti took the lead for the first time on lap 102, and in the closing stages, after once again eschewing a tire

GATEWAY SNIPPETS

• FedEx Championship Series points leader Juan Montoya and Target/Chip Ganassi Racing teammate Jimmy Vasser paid a visit to Memphis, Tenn., a few days prior to the Gateway event to attend the grand opening and dedication of **TARGET HOUSE**, which offers temporary housing for patients of St. Jude Children's Research Hospital and their families. PGA Tour star Tiger Woods and Grammy Award-winning singer Amy Grant also participated in the dedication ceremonies.

• A special sight lit up the Illinois sky Friday evening *(right)* as a Champ Car practice took place **UNDER THE LIGHTS** for the very first time, perhaps in anticipation of a future FedEx Championship Series event at night. The session was universally well received. 'I would love to race these cars at night,' said Richie Hearn. 'I think our cars look really sexy at night!'

• Team Gordon and Della Penna Motorsports literally **EXCHANGED CARS** prior to the race at Gateway, with Della Penna taking delivery of Gordon's ex-Team Rahal Reynard 98I in exchange for a Swift 010.c.

• **AL UNSER JR.** decided to drive Marlboro Team Penske's new Lola B99/00 following a test session the previous Tuesday at Nazareth. His progress was hindered by engine problems on Thursday. He eventually qualified 24th – six places behind teammate Tarso Marques, who was blighted by brake and gear-shift problems on Thursday in his Mercedes/Penske. Good strategy enabled Unser to finish 12th.

(left margin) Barry Hathaway

• Walker Racing crewman **DAVE STEPHENS**, vent man for Gil de Ferran's Valvoline/Cummins Reynard/Honda, was fortunate to escape with no worse than a concussion and extensive bruising when he took a heavy tumble during a botched first pit stop.

• **HOGAN RACING**, based in nearby St. Louis, Mo., entered an arrangement with three local Major League teams – the St. Louis Cardinals (baseball), Rams (football) and Blues (hockey) – with the slogan 'St. Louis Sports' emblazoned on its car's rear wing. 'These St. Louis teams have set a benchmark in sportsmanship and quality sports programs,' said team owner Carl Hogan. 'We're proud to be a member of the St. Louis sports scene.'

• Referring to his miraculous save following contact with teammate Paul Tracy, Team KOOL Green's **DARIO FRANCHITTI** said, 'Every time I get sideways on an oval, I seem to hit the wall, so I decided to work on my technique. I think I improved it today.'

• A three-race winning streak not only gave **JUAN MONTOYA** the series points lead, but it also allowed the Colombian to extricate himself from the CART doghouse. CART Chief Steward Wally Dallenbach announced that he had removed Montoya from the probationary status that the Target/Chip Ganassi driver had been under since the season's second race.

FEDEX CHAMPIONSHIP SERIES • ROUND 6
MOTOROLA 300

GATEWAY INTERNATIONAL RACEWAY, MADISON, ILLINOIS

MAY 29, 236 laps – 299.72 miles

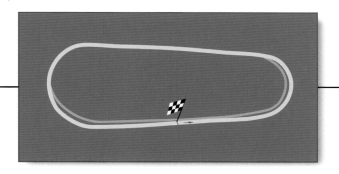

Place	Driver (Nat.)	No.	Team Sponsors Engine/Car	Tires	Q Speed	Q Time	Q Pos.	Laps	Time/Status	Ave. (mph)	Pts.
1	Michael Andretti (USA)	6	Newman/Haas Kmart/Texaco Ford Cosworth/Swift 010.c	FS	180.135	25.381s	11	236	2h 25m 35.829s	123.513	21
2	Helio Castro-Neves (BR)	9	Hogan Racing Hogan Motor Leasing Mercedes/Lola B99/00	FS	182.130	25.103s	3	236	2h 25m 36.158s	123.509	16
3	Dario Franchitti (GB)	27	Team KOOL Green Honda/Reynard 99I	FS	181.450	25.197s	5	236	2h 25m 36.876s	123.499	14
4	Roberto Moreno (BR)	18	PacWest Racing Group Motorola Mercedes/Reynard 99I	FS	178.065	25.676s	19	236	2h 25m 41.564s	123.432	12
5	Max Papis (I)	7	Team Rahal Miller Lite Ford Cosworth/Reynard 99I	FS	179.972	25.404s	13	236	2h 25m 46.806s	123.358	10
6	Greg Moore (CDN)	99	Forsythe Racing Player's/Indeck Mercedes/Reynard 99I	FS	181.436	25.199s	6	236	2h 25m 47.032s	123.355	8
7	Tony Kanaan (BR)	44	McDonald's Championship Racing Honda/Reynard 99I	FS	179.675	25.446s	14	236	2h 25m 52.680s	123.276	6
8	PJ Jones (USA)	20	Patrick Racing Visteon Ford Cosworth/Swift 010.c	FS	179.055	25.534s	16	236	2h 26m 01.598s	123.150	5
9	Christian Fittipaldi (BR)	11	Newman/Haas Big Kmart Ford Cosworth/Swift 010.c	FS	181.163	25.237s	8	236	2h 26m 01.810s	123.147	4
10	Jimmy Vasser (USA)	12	Target/Chip Ganassi Racing Honda/Reynard 99I	FS	180.305	25.357s	10	236	2h 26m 02.360s	123.139	3
11	*Juan Montoya (COL)	4	Target/Chip Ganassi Racing Honda/Reynard 99I	FS	182.778	25.014s	1	236	2h 26m 03.134s	123.129	3
12	Al Unser Jr. (USA)	2	Marlboro Team Penske Mercedes/Lola B99/00	GY	176.532	25.899s	24	235	Running		1
13	Richie Hearn (USA)	10	Della Penna Motorsports Budweiser Toyota/Reynard 98I	FS	175.873	25.996s	25	234	Running		
14	Scott Pruett (USA)	24	Arciero-Wells Racing Pioneer Toyota/Reynard 99I	FS	178.030	25.681s	20	234	Running		
15	*Shigeaki Hattori (J)	16	Bettenhausen Motorsports Epson Mercedes/Reynard 98I	GY	173.609	26.335s	26	229	Running		
16	Alex Barron (USA)	36	All American Racers Denso/Castrol Toyota/Eagle 997	GY	177.429	25.768s	23	212	Electrical		
17	*Cristiano da Matta (BR)	25	Arciero-Wells Racing MCI WorldCom Toyota/Reynard 99I	FS	180.007	25.399s	12	185	Engine		
18	Mauricio Gugelmin (BR)	17	PacWest Racing Group Hollywood Mercedes/Reynard 99I	FS	177.760	25.720s	21	161	Fuel pressure		
19	Paul Tracy (CDN)	26	Team KOOL Green Honda/Reynard 99I	FS	182.195	25.094s	2	147	Accident		
20	Michel Jourdain Jr. (MEX)	19	Payton/Coyne Herdez/Viva Mexico Ford Cosworth/Lola T97/00	FS	177.526	25.754s	22	141	Electrical		
21	Adrian Fernandez (MEX)	40	Patrick Racing Tecate/Quaker State Ford Cosworth/Reynard 97I	FS	181.263	25.223s	7	132	Transmission		
22	Patrick Carpentier (CDN)	33	Forsythe Racing Player's/Indeck Mercedes/Reynard 99I	FS	181.522	25.187s	4	114	Accident		
23	Bryan Herta (USA)	8	Team Rahal Shell Ford Cosworth/Reynard 99I	FS	178.461	25.619s	17	113	Accident		
24	Dennis Vitolo (USA)	34	Payton/Coyne Nicorette-CQ Ford Cosworth/Reynard 98I	FS	166.424	27.472s	27	62	Handling		
25	Gil de Ferran (BR)	5	Walker Racing Valvoline/Cummins Honda/Reynard 99I	GY	179.062	25.533s	15	36	Pit incident		
26	*Tarso Marques (BR)	3	Marlboro Team Penske Mercedes/Penske PC27B	GY	178.134	25.666s	18	31	Accident		
27	Robby Gordon (USA)	22	Team Gordon Panasonic/Menards Toyota/Swift 010.c	FS	181.084	25.248s	9	10	Accident		

* denotes rookie driver

Caution flags: Lap 1, yellow start; laps 11–23, accident/Gordon; lap 24, no restart; laps 32–43, accident/Marques; laps 106–113, tow/Gugelmin; laps 114–129, accident/Carpentier & Herta; laps 148–157, accident/Tracy & Franchitti; lap 158, no restart; laps 185–192, engine/da Matta. **Total:** Nine for 71 laps.

Lap leaders: Juan Montoya, 1–36 (36 laps); Roberto Moreno, 37–74 (38 laps); Al Unser Jr., 75–85 (11 laps); Moreno, 86–89 (4 laps); Paul Tracy, 90–102 (13 laps); Michael Andretti, 103–104, (2 laps); Patrick Carpentier, 105 (1 lap); Greg Moore, 106–109 (4 laps); Andretti, 110–151 (42 laps); Helio Castro-Neves, 152–189 (38 laps); Andretti, 190–236 (47 laps). **Totals:** Andretti, 91 laps; Moreno, 42 laps; Castro-Neves, 38 laps; Montoya, 36 laps; Tracy, 13 laps; Unser Jr., 11 laps; Moore, 4 laps; Carpentier, 1 lap.

Fastest race lap: Helio Castro-Neves, 26.180s, 174.637 mph on lap 165.

Championship positions: 1 Montoya, 69; **2** Franchitti, 65; **3** Andretti, 61; **4** Moore & Fittipaldi, 53; **6** Fernandez, 43; **7** de Ferran & Papis, 36; **9** Jones, 28; **10** Kanaan, 26; **11** Vasser, 21; **12** Castro-Neves, 20; **13** Tracy, 16; **14** Herta, 15; **15** Carpentier & Moreno, 14; **17** da Matta, 12; **18** Gugelmin, 8; **19** Blundell, Hearn & Gordon, 5; **22** Marques & Barron, 4; **24** Pruett, 3; **25** Unser Jr., 2.

OMEGA
OFFICIAL TIMEKEEPER OF CART

MILWAUKEE

1 – TRACY **2 – MOORE** **3 – DE FERRAN**

Crew chief Tony Cotman stands ready to signal Paul Tracy out of the pits following routine service for Team KOOL Green.
Photo: Michael C. Brown

Right: Jimmy Vasser was unlucky not to take the victory after he was brought in to the pits for a splash-and-dash that turned out to be unnecessary.

THE Miller Lite 225 produced enough drama and suspense to uphold the Milwaukee Mile's reputation for close-quarter, high-speed excitement. And in the end, it was a race of redemption, with Paul Tracy ultimately coming out on the favorable end of a high-stakes game of strategy to record his first victory since 1997.

After two seasons of disappointment and frustration, Tracy's fortune turned at last. He earned the win with a daring pit gamble, opting to maintain track position instead of following the race leaders into the pits for a splash of gas in the decisive waning laps. Most of the front-running cars, including race leader Jimmy Vasser, pitted for fuel during a caution period with 15 laps remaining. However, Tracy and his Team KOOL Green crew decided their best chance at the checkered was to stay on track.

Fortunately for those few brave men – Player's/Forsythe drivers Greg Moore and Patrick Carpentier also opted not to pit – PJ Jones brought out another caution on the ensuing restart when he almost collected the wall in Turn Four. Able to conserve even more fuel during the slower yellow laps, Tracy – who was looking for his first victory celebration since 1997 at Gateway International Raceway – was faced with a suspenseful five-lap sprint to the end.

Tracy admitted after the race that he was anything but calm, kool and collected in those final five circuits, being aware of the hard-charging fellow Canadian Moore, who was deftly maneuvering through traffic to position himself for a last-ditch challenge.

'As soon as that green came out, the fuel pressure warning light came on and I thought, "Oh no," because generally when the light comes on, you only have a lap or so before you run out,' said Tracy. 'I don't know how much fuel there was left, but it can't have been much. In a situation like that, you've really got to roll the dice and go for it.'

Several lapped cars straggled in between Tracy's Honda/Reynard and Moore's Mercedes/Reynard, helping Tracy to a hard-fought, 5.88-second margin of victory. Gil de Ferran was third in the Valvoline-sponsored Honda/Reynard of Walker Racing. Carpentier and Patrick Racing's Adrian Fernandez followed, although Fernandez's team launched a successful protest following the race, claiming that Carpentier passed the Tecate/Quaker State Ford/Reynard under caution. The post-race ruling officially scored Fernandez fourth and dropped Carpentier, who was penalized one lap, to ninth in the final standings. Like Carpentier, Target/Chip Ganassi rookie Juan Montoya was found guilty of passing under yellow-flag conditions on lap 210 of the 225-lap event and was scored tenth instead of the sixth place he ran on track.

It's only fitting that pit strategy helped Tracy atop the podium this year at Milwaukee, because it was pit misfortune that cost him a shot at a win there in 1998. He led that race only to

QUALIFYING

A typically exciting qualifying session on the famed Milwaukee Mile saw Helio Castro-Neves save the best for last. The always enthusiastic 24-year-old had tried two different setups on his pair of Hogan Motor Leasing Mercedes/Lolas during practice on Friday, with the result that he preferred the feeling of the backup car. He continued to work with underrated race engineer Casper van der Schoot and topped the practice times on Saturday morning, at 21.869 seconds, an average speed of 169.884 mph, to ensure that he would be the last man onto the track in single-car qualifying.

Castro-Neves rose to the challenge magnificently by posting a time of 21.931 seconds (169.404 mph) to eclipse Jimmy Vasser's previous best.

'I felt a little bit of pressure going into qualifying,' admitted the Brazilian, 'especially because we were fastest this morning. But we're professional and we had to focus, concentrate, and then go for it. I felt so great and so confident once I got in the car that nobody could beat me.'

Vasser lined up second on the grid, having outpaced his rookie teammate, Juan Montoya, for only the second time in seven races.

'We made some changes for qualifying,' said the 1996 PPG Cup champion. 'It's not perfect, but it's better.'

Greg Moore lined up third in Jerry Forsythe's Player's Ltd. Mercedes/Reynard, followed by Dario Franchitti, Montoya and Paul Tracy. The last had bounced back from his disappointment at Gateway one week earlier by posting the fastest time on Friday in his Team KOOL Green Honda/Reynard.

'The cars are so sensitive now, and so critical to setup that one little change of camber or toe [angle] can be the difference between being quickest and being mid-pack,' said Tracy.

Other notable performances were posted by rookie Cristiano da Matta, fastest of the Toyota contingent for the fifth time in seven races with Arciero-Wells Racing's MCI WorldCom Reynard, and Alex Barron, whose Denso/Castrol Toyota/Eagle was comfortably quickest of those running Goodyear tires.

So near, yet so far

HELIO Castro-Neves arrived in Milwaukee with every reason to feel optimistic. A week earlier, he had finished runner-up in the Motorola 300 at Gateway International Raceway. One year ago, driving for Tony Bettenhausen, he recorded the best rookie showing of the season with a second-place finish at Milwaukee.

And his Carl Hogan-owned Mercedes/Lola did not disappoint – at least not immediately. The Milwaukee crowd cheered and embraced Castro-Neves as he captured his first career pole position. It was also Lola's first pole since Andre Ribeiro had claimed top honors for the Tasman team at Toronto in 1996.

Castro-Neves actually earned the pole on his first flying lap – and almost lost it as he attempted to go even faster. 'When I saw 21.9 [on the dash read-out], I thought, "I should try a little bit more,"' he related, 'and when the car was sideways [in Turn One], I thought, "Maybe I shouldn't try so hard!"'

'Oh man, it's the greatest feeling of my life,' he exclaimed, grinning broadly after stepping out of his car. 'Tomorrow [race day] is very important, but I'm going to enjoy today.'

Sadly, that would prove a wise decision.

Castro-Neves immediately parlayed his stellar qualifying run into a race lead through the first 15 laps of the Miller Lite 225, only to have his engine give out. He nursed the car around a few more miles before pulling disconsolately into the pits to retire.

As disappointing as the final result was, Castro-Neves left Milwaukee having received a boost in confidence and given a glimpse of what Champ Car fans can expect from this talented up-and-comer, who could only reason, 'These things happen and you just have to live with it.'

have a stubborn tire cause an extended late-race pit stop, sending him reeling from the points position out of the top ten. He would work his way back to a seventh-place showing, feeling cheated of victory again in what was a common theme for Tracy in the long months between wins. But that, of course, only made this year's Milwaukee Moment that much more rewarding. 'It's been a tough road for a couple of years,' he said with relief, following his 14th career Champ Car win. 'It's hard when you know you and the team have the capability of winning and, for whatever reason, things happen and everything falls through your hand like sand.'

'It's frustrating. You've got to look to the positives each weekend. If you think negative, you're going to have a negative weekend. We came in this weekend with a positive attitude and it paid off for me.'

Although he came up just short, Moore was satisfied with the result. His

car was never among the best in the field, but it ran well enough – and the fuel gamble worked well enough – to land him a runner-up effort.

'We had to gamble at the last pit stop,' Moore recounted, 'and the guys said to me, "Okay, it's time to start saving fuel as best we can." So I went to the leanest setting and with 13 laps to go, I got on the radio and said, "Can we make it to the end?"

'Steve [Challis], my engineer, said, "We're fine." And I guess I was probably a bit terse because I came back and said, "That's not what I asked! Are we going to get to the end?" A couple of laps later, he got back on and said, "We're fine." And I was able to conserve enough fuel and still be quick.'

Preferring to play it safe, Vasser and his Target/Chip Ganassi Racing teammate Montoya had decided to stop for fuel and eliminate any doubt that their Honda/Reynards would be there at the end. It also helped that they had been running up front all day.

Vasser was quicker than Montoya all weekend – a rarity in the early season – and assumed the race lead, at one point by more than three seconds over the Team KOOL Hondas of Tracy and Dario Franchitti. But as the Firestone tires wore and Vasser encountered the grudgingly slow car of Al Unser Jr., by lap 22, his advantage had diminished and the pack closed in.

First Franchitti dashed around Vasser, then Michael Andretti blasted by them both. Andretti's Kmart/Texaco Havoline Ford/Swift started back in 11th position on the grid, but was one of the field's stronger rides on race day, before becoming involved in the second frightening accident of as many weekends.

Andretti and other race leaders made their first pit stops during a caution on lap 62, and it nearly proved disastrous for Newman/Haas Racing. As Andretti's car began to move forward at the end of the stop, the clutch failed to disengage. Team Manager Ed

Nathman frantically attempted to convey to Andretti not to pull away, because the work had not been completed on his car.

Nathman yelled, 'Don't go, Don't go!' into Andretti's radio, but the veteran driver misunderstood the command as, 'Go, Go!' When he dropped the clutch to take off down the pit lane, vent-man Ty Manseau was sent tumbling and was run over, his head being caught by the rotation of the rear wheel. It was a sickening scene, but amazingly Manseau, who was wearing a helmet, was treated at a local hospital and released with nothing more than bruises and a horror story to tell.

Andretti's race was done at that point, but the good to come of the incident involving Manseau (and, one week earlier, Walker Racing's Dave Stephens) was a new CART safety measure requiring all over-the-wall crewmen to wear helmets.

'I've never hit anybody in the pits

before,' said a shaken Andretti after the race. 'I feel terrible. The car was creeping and then I thought they said, "Go." The car was a winner today.

'[After the accident] I was still running quicker than most of the other guys. It's disappointing, but I'm so glad Ty wasn't seriously hurt. That's a big relief.'

Helio Castro-Neves was another to encounter disappointment on race day, despite claiming the first FedEx Championship Series pole position of his young career. Little did the likeable Brazilian know that his fate would maddeningly repeat itself during the summer months.

It was of no great surprise that Castro-Neves won top qualifying honors at Milwaukee, because the track also produced his first Champ Car podium finish in 1998 – the best showing of any CART rookie that season.

It was not to be this time. The Carl Hogan-owned Mercedes/Lola lost power a mere 15 laps into the event,

Michael C. Brown

Paul Tracy snaps winless streak

Right: After a streak of 34 starts without a win, Paul Tracy finally set the record straight at Milwaukee.

Below: Gil de Ferran, trailed here by Roberto Moreno, rose from 16th place on the grid to finish third.

and after continuing for a few laps Castro-Neves retired, wondering what could have happened.

'Everything was working pretty well,' said Castro-Neves. 'The car was handling perfect. Hogan Racing did a fantastic job again. It was a boost problem, but we don't have the specifics yet. These things happen and you just have to live with it.'

Castro-Neves and then Andretti's departure relegated the chase to the Team KOOL Green and Target/Chip Ganassi stables. Vasser led entering the first pit stop, followed closely by Montoya. Then the roles were reversed after the second round of stops. And again entering the final portion of the race. Ultimately, the Target team, however, blinked first and the decision to play it safe at the end was all the opening Tracy needed to restore his standing as winner.

Holly Cain

ALTHOUGH Paul Tracy's driving effort had earned him at least a shot at victory in Milwaukee, he was never sure of the outcome until the checkered flag. And with good reason.

His Team KOOL Green Honda/Reynard had inherited the lead with 15 laps remaining when race leader Jimmy Vasser was called into the pits for a splash of gas. Tracy and his team opted instead for track position. The gamble paid off, but not until he had out-dashed another gas gambler, Greg Moore, in a nerve-racking final five-lap sprint to the checkered flag.

It was an emotional end to a two-year victory drought for the Canadian, who had endured more than his due of bad luck and near-misses before notching his 14th career Champ Car win.

Only a week earlier, Tracy had looked poised for victory when he and teammate Dario Franchitti collided. It had been one misadventure after another.

'When you go from rock-bottom, you kind of feel you can't get any lower and pick yourself up,' revealed Tracy after the win. 'But each weekend we've been building, and trying to build one block at a time.

'This was a rejuvenation of a career. Two years is a long time. You keep scratching your head. You're doing everything right, you make the right decisions on the car, you get yourself into position, and it falls apart.

'It's very frustrating. To get that win again is almost as tough as the first one.'

For team owner Barry Green, Tracy's victory represented a vindication of his decision to hire one of CART's 'Bad Boys', after the Canadian had been dumped by Roger Penske following the '97 season.

'That's a big load off to have Paul win a race,' admitted Green. 'He's taken a lot of hits from people over the last year or so. But we know what he's all about.

'It was his day today. We took a big risk, but we had to do that. We needed a win to get back into the Championship [chase]. It's a proud day for us.'

MILWAUKEE SNIPPETS

• After Walker Racing's vent-man, Dave Stephens, was involved in a dramatic miscue in the pits at Gateway, CART responded immediately by mandating the use of **FULL-FACE HELMETS** for all over-the-wall crew members. Further, the pit-road speed limit was lowered from 60 mph to 50 mph. The measures weren't enough to prevent another frightening accident, however, when Newman/Haas colleague Ty Manseau also was run over. Miraculously, he, too, emerged with relatively minor injuries. 'I saw the [television] replay of the accident and I couldn't believe it,' Manseau said the day after the Milwaukee race. 'I was very lucky. It was a freak accident. The helmet definitely saved me. It's good to know that CART has mandated helmets for tire changers. You never know when this kind of thing can happen.'

Photos: Michael C. Brown

• **TOYOTA'S** development program showed obvious signs of improvement at Milwaukee. Armed with a new Reynard 99I and Toyota's new Phase VI motor, Richie Hearn *(left)* finished out of the points, but did record the tenth-fastest race lap. Earlier in the week, Cristiano da Matta's MCI WorldCom Toyota/Reynard joined Jimmy Vasser's Honda/Reynard in setting the fastest times during a two-day test at Portland International Raceway.

• Paul Tracy's victory represented the 50th for **FIRESTONE** tires since the company's return to Champ Car racing in 1995. Even more impressively, it was the 25th in a row.

• CART Chief Steward **WALLY DALLENBACH** was a busy man following the Miller Lite 225. Not only were Patrick Carpentier and Juan Montoya penalized a lap for passing under yellow, but Christian Fittipaldi was also placed on probation for blocking violations. 'The drivers asked for blocking to be policed and it was outlined with clarity in the pre-race drivers meeting,' explained Dallenbach. 'The blocking maneuvers have escalated in the past several races and we are reacting to it.'

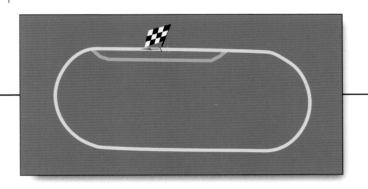

• Target/Chip Ganassi Racing Managing Director **TOM ANDERSON** *(right)* took the unusual step of publicly apologizing to his driver Jimmy Vasser following the race. It was Anderson's call to come in for a splash-and-dash pit stop late in the race, which turned over the lead – and eventually victory – to Paul Tracy. 'I definitely cost him the race,' admitted Anderson. 'We had enough fuel to go [the distance]. Jimmy and [race engineer] Julian [Robertson] had everything working right.'

• Team Gordon received a bit of a surprise on the eve of the race when race engineer **KENNY ANDERSON** announced that he was leaving the CART operation in favor of the Indy Racing League. Anderson returned to Charlotte, N.C., eager to work on the design and development of a brand-new IRL car. He was replaced at Team Gordon by David Cripps, who had been released by Kelley Racing's IRL team following the Indianapolis 500.

FEDEX CHAMPIONSHIP SERIES • ROUND 7
MILLER LITE 225

MILWAUKEE MILE,
WISCONSIN STATE FAIR PARK, W. ALLIS, WISCONSIN

JUNE 6, 225 laps – 232.2 miles

Place	Driver (Nat.)	No.	Team Sponsors Engine/Car	Tires	Q Speed	Q Time	Q Pos.	Laps	Time/Status	Ave. (mph)	Pts.
1	Paul Tracy (CDN)	26	Team KOOL Green Honda/Reynard 99I	FS	166.818	22.271s	6	225	1h 48m 49.169s	128.029	20
2	Greg Moore (CDN)	99	Forsythe Racing Player's/Indeck Mercedes/Reynard 99I	FS	167.858	22.133s	3	225	1h 48m 55.049s	127.913	16
3	Gil de Ferran (BR)	5	Walker Racing Valvoline/Cummins Honda/Reynard 99I	GY	164.564	22.576s	16	225	1h 48m 55.625s	127.902	14
4	Jimmy Vasser (USA)	12	Target/Chip Ganassi Racing Honda/Reynard 99I	FS	168.200	22.088s	2	225	1h 48m 57.106s	127.873	12
5	Adrian Fernandez (MEX)	40	Patrick Racing Tecate/Quaker State Ford Cosworth/Reynard 97I	FS	164.411	22.597s	18	225	1h 48m 59.098s	127.834	10
6	Christian Fittipaldi (BR)	11	Newman/Haas Big Kmart Ford Cosworth/Swift 010.c	FS	165.105	22.502s	13	225	1h 49m 00.420s	127.808	8
7	Dario Franchitti (GB)	27	Team KOOL Green Honda/Reynard 99I	FS	167.843	22.135s	4	225	1h 49m 01.747s	127.780	6
8	Mauricio Gugelmin (BR)	17	PacWest Racing Group Hollywood Mercedes/Reynard 99I	FS	165.186	22.491s	12	225	1h 49m 04.392s	127.731	5
9	Patrick Carpentier (CDN)	33	Forsythe Racing Player's/Indeck Mercedes/Reynard 99I	FS	166.295	22.341s	8	+224	Running		4
10	*Juan Montoya (COL)	4	Target/Chip Ganassi Racing Honda/Reynard 99I	FS	166.960	22.252s	5	+224	Running		4
11	*Cristiano da Matta (BR)	25	Arciero-Wells Racing MCI WorldCom Toyota/Reynard 99I	FS	166.706	22.286s	7	224	Running		2
12	Roberto Moreno (BR)	18	PacWest Racing Group Motorola Mercedes/Reynard 99I	FS	165.798	22.408s	9	223	Running		1
13	Max Papis (I)	7	Team Rahal Miller Lite Ford Cosworth/Reynard 99I	FS	164.491	22.586s	17	222	Running		
14	Alex Barron (USA)	36	All American Racers Denso/Castrol Toyota/Eagle 997	GY	165.776	22.411s	10	222	Running		
15	Michael Andretti (USA)	6	Newman/Haas Kmart/Texaco Ford Cosworth/Swift 010.c	FS	165.739	22.416s	11	222	Running		
16	Michel Jourdain Jr. (MEX)	19	Payton/Coyne Herdez/Viva Mexico Ford Cosworth/Lola T97/00	FS	164.063	22.645s	21	222	Running		
17	Scott Pruett (USA)	24	Arciero-Wells Racing Pioneer Toyota/Reynard 99I	FS	164.601	22.571s	15	222	Running		
18	Tony Kanaan (BR)	44	McDonald's Championship Racing Honda/Reynard 99I	FS	164.135	22.635s	20	221	Running		
19	Al Unser Jr. (USA)	2	Marlboro Team Penske Mercedes/Lola B99/00	GY	163.435	22.732s	22	221	Running		
20	PJ Jones (USA)	20	Patrick Racing Visteon Ford Cosworth/Swift 010.c	FS	164.849	22.537s	14	219	Running		
21	Richie Hearn (USA)	10	Della Penna Motorsports Budweiser Toyota/Reynard 99I	FS	164.237	22.621s	19	219	Running		
22	Dennis Vitolo (USA)	34	Payton/Coyne CQ-Nicorette Ford Cosworth/Reynard 98I	FS	157.164	23.639s	26	212	Running		
23	*Shigeaki Hattori (J)	16	Bettenhausen Motorsports Epson Mercedes/Reynard 98I	GY	162.314	22.889s	24	118	Accident		
24	Robby Gordon (USA)	22	Team Gordon Panasonic/Menards Toyota/Swift 010.c	FS	162.363	22.882s	23	83	Electrical		
25	Bryan Herta (USA)	8	Team Rahal Shell Ford Cosworth/Reynard 99I	FS	161.748	22.969s	25	81	Handling		
26	Helio Castro-Neves (BR)	9	Hogan Racing Hogan Motor Leasing Mercedes/Lola B99/00	FS	169.404	21.931s	1	30	Engine		1

* denotes rookie driver   † denotes penalized one lap for passing under yellow

Caution flags: Lap 1, yellow start; laps 2–7, spin/Jones; laps 62–73, debris; laps 121–130, accident/Hattori; laps 210–216, spin/Moreno; laps 217–219, spin/Jones. **Total:** Six for 39 laps.

Lap leaders: Helio Castro-Neves, 1–14 (14 laps); Jimmy Vasser, 15–46 (32 laps); Dario Franchitti, 47–49 (3 laps); Michael Andretti, 50–65 (16 laps); Paul Tracy, 66–105 (40 laps); Vasser, 106–124, (19 laps); Juan Montoya, 125–208 (84 laps); Vasser, 209–212 (4 laps); Tracy, 213–225 (13 laps). **Totals:** Montoya, 84 laps; Vasser, 55 laps; Tracy, 53 laps; Andretti, 16.laps; Castro-Neves, 14 laps; Franchitti, 3 laps.

Fastest race lap: Helio Castro-Neves, 23.517s, 157.979 mph on lap ten.

Championship positions: 1 Montoya, 73; **2** Franchitti, 71; **3** Moore, 69; **4** Andretti & Fittipaldi, 61; **6** Fernandez, 53; **7** de Ferran, 50; **8** Tracy & Papis, 36; **10** Vasser, 33; **11** Jones, 28; **12** Kanaan, 26; **13** Castro-Neves, 21; **14** Carpentier, 18; **15** Herta & Moreno, 15; **17** da Matta, 14; **18** Gugelmin, 13; **19** Blundell, Hearn & Gordon, 5; **22** Marques & Barron, 4; **24** Pruett, 3; **25** Unser Jr., 2.

OFFICIAL TIMEKEEPER OF CART

PORTLAND

1 – DE FERRAN

2 – MONTOYA

3 – FRANCHITTI

QUALIFYING

Juan Montoya underlined his relish at the start of the 'road course season' (six of the ensuing seven events taking place on road courses of one description or another) with a convincing pole position at Portland International Raceway. Not that unfamiliarity with ovals had prevented the 23-year-old Colombian phenomenon from setting the pace at Nazareth and St. Louis; but at PIR his confidence was palpable. In final qualifying, he duly pulled out all the stops, recovering from some lurid slides to put the pole beyond reach with a lap of 58.193 seconds.

'It's good to start at the front,' confirmed Montoya. 'We struggled this morning [in practice] a lot, and the team has done a good job to give me a good car. Honestly, I'm surprised. I never expected to be that quick.'

Dario Franchitti had been fastest in Saturday morning's free practice, but the expected challenge never materialized in final qualifying, thanks to a bizarre miscue by Team KOOL Green: his final set of rear tires had been mounted back to front, seriously upsetting the car's balance. A frustrated Franchitti had to settle for a lowly 12th on the grid.

Instead, Helio Castro-Neves sprung to the top of the time sheets with a surprising late run less than 0.1 second shy of Montoya's best. The young Brazilian demonstrated once again that, in the right hands, the promise of the renascent Lola chassis wasn't confined to the oval tracks.

Gil de Ferran cited performance gains by Goodyear after qualifying a competitive third, while Bryan Herta went some way to redeeming a truly dismal showing at Milwaukee by completing the second row in Team Rahal's Shell Ford Cosworth/Reynard. Adrian Fernandez, relieved to get his hands at last on a '99 Reynard, claimed fifth spot, barely 0.2 second adrift of the pole-winning time.

Helio Castro-Neves moved Carl Hogan's Mercedes/Lola into the lead with an opportunistic pass at the first corner, chased by Juan Montoya *(hidden)* and Gil de Ferran.
Photos: Kazuki Saito

GIL de Ferran's long overdue victory in the Budweiser/G.I. Joe's 200 was earned in the best traditions of the sport – a triumph in equal measures for outright speed and perfect strategy. Team owner Derrick Walker chose a different tactic to the other front-runners in the closing stages, and while most drivers were instructed to employ a full-lean fuel mixture in the hope of making it to the finish line without requiring a late splash of methanol, de Ferran was subjected to no such inhibitions. 'Go for it,' was the credo. De Ferran rose to the challenge magnificently. He pulled away from his rivals by more than a second per lap, and the gamble paid off, as he was able to make one more pit stop with eight laps remaining and still emerge from the pit lane with his lead intact.

'With about five laps to go, I couldn't help thinking, "What's [going to go wrong] next,"' admitted de Ferran, 'but

I managed to put those thoughts out of my mind because I knew there wasn't much that could go wrong. I had plenty of fuel, five laps to go; there's nothing to worry about.'

Indeed there wasn't. De Ferran duly reeled off the remaining miles to score his first victory since Cleveland in 1996. Pole-sitter Juan Montoya had to be content with second, followed by a third Honda/Reynard in the hands of a charging Dario Franchitti.

Fears that the race might turn into another Montoya benefit – after the apparent anomalies of Gateway and Milwaukee – were quickly dispelled when outside-front-row qualifier Helio Castro-Neves seized the lead from the Colombian with a neatly executed outside pass in the first right-hander of the notorious Festival Curves chicane.

'I just went for it," related Castro-Neves, with a smile, 'and I was very happy because Juan is an aggressive driver, and I wanted to take the lead.'

De Ferran followed in third, while a typically fast start enabled Paul Tracy to jump to fourth, ahead of Bryan Herta and Adrian Fernandez.

Castro-Neves posted a flawless display, lapping consistently in the low 60-second bracket and looking very smooth and composed under pressure. Having checked out from the rest of the field, the two leaders traded fastest laps. Montoya was unable to make a pass, but he remained in hot pursuit right up to the first round of pit stops. Shortly after, however, for the second race in a row, disaster struck the Hogan driver while leading. Almost immediately after his routine first pit stop had been completed on lap 31, a broken valve spring heralded Castro-Neves' imminent retirement.

'It's tough,' said the distraught Brazilian. 'We've worked so hard. The car was great again this weekend and was strong enough to win the race. What can I say?'

Castro-Neves' demise left Montoya with a comfortable lead, despite a slip-up under braking, which caused him to straight-line the Festival chicane on his 'out' lap following his first pit visit. The officials judged that no advantage had been gained in the maneuver, so Montoya escaped penalty and could concentrate on consolidating his advantage over de Ferran and Tracy.

The race continued to be run at a fast pace until lap 47, when Richie Hearn's Budweiser Toyota/Reynard became stranded at the Festival Curves. The subsequent full-course caution had two principal effects: it erased Montoya's 12-second advantage and opened up the possibility of making it to the finish with just one more pit stop.

Of more immediate interest was Montoya's spectacular restart on lap 50. The crowd rose to its feet in unison as the Colombian lost the back end of

Gil de Ferran parlayed excellent strategy by team owner Derrick Walker into a long overdue victory.

De Ferran gains long-awaited victory

ARRIVING in the United States with an impressive European resumé, highlighted by the prestigious British Formula 3 Championship in 1992, Gil de Ferran displayed prodigious talent from the moment he first set foot in a Champ Car. Indeed, he qualified on the provisional pole for his very first race! When he closed out 1995 with an emphatic maiden victory at Laguna Seca, and then out-duelled Alex Zanardi to win at Cleveland halfway through 1996, he was widely touted as obvious champion material.

Certainly, few observers could have imagined that the likeable Brazilian would still be chasing a third career victory nearly three years later. In the interim, he was usually a force to be reckoned with, but a combination of inferior tires, a spate of mechanical failures in 1998, periodic unforced errors and plain bad luck perpetuated an agonizing winless streak stretching to 49 races.

A cerebral, mild-mannered man, de Ferran (below) rarely lets frustration get the better of his natural professionalism; but he could barely hold back the tears after finally ending the drought with a perfectly judged victory in the Budweiser/G.I. Joe's 200.

'It's hard to speak of things from the heart,' he related. 'It's a combination of a lot of effort and not the reward we hoped for in the last few years. This is a day I'll never forget.'

Reflecting on his strong start to the 1999 season, de Ferran, 31, stressed the rejuvenating effect of a long winter break: 'At the end of last year, I was worn down and hardly [drove] in November and December. I spent time with my family and reviewed what we had done in the last few years. I started this year with a clear head.'

At Portland, de Ferran and Walker Racing – which had last tasted victory as long ago as Detroit 1995, with Robby Gordon – both took care of some unfinished business.

his car under hard acceleration out of Turn 12, spun through 180 degrees and straightened out; all while feeding in the power, as per Chip Ganassi's urgent radio instructions: 'Gas it! Gas it!' (As if the Colombian knows any other way!)

De Ferran, in close attendance as they merged onto the pit straightaway, wisely figured that Montoya would spin to the inside of the track and picked his way through the tire smoke to emerge in the lead. Montoya, meanwhile, recovered from the spin completely intact and having given away just one position.

After a few more laps behind the pace car, clearly unfazed by his earlier error, Montoya snatched the lead cleanly from de Ferran going into the Festival Curves. Just behind, Fernandez and Franchitti capitalized on a tardy restart from Herta to move up into fourth and fifth places respectively. Montoya immediately pulled away

from de Ferran who, at this point, was saving fuel after surprisingly poor consumption had forced an earlier-than-planned initial pit stop.

The yellow flags flew again on lap 59, after PJ Jones spun his Visteon Ford/Swift at the Festival Curves. The leaders all elected to take the opportunity of making their second pit stops, albeit slightly earlier than most would have wished. For once, the Ganassi crew fumbled its stop and Montoya was held in his pit box a little longer than de Ferran and Tracy, relegating him to third position. Franchitti benefited from typically sharp pitwork from Team Green to emerge from the pits ahead of Fernandez, so that the order prior to the restart was de Ferran, Tracy, Montoya, Franchitti, Fernandez, Jimmy Vasser and Herta.

De Ferran duly headed the field when green-flag racing resumed on lap 62, while Montoya wasted no time in dispatching Tracy to move up to

Kazuki Saito

Goodyear makes a comeback

REMARKABLY, Gil de Ferran's victory was Goodyear's first on a road course since Michael Andretti won in Vancouver in 1996. Since then, the Akron, Ohio-based company had consistently produced competitive tires for the oval races on the CART schedule (witness Andretti's wins at Homestead in 1997 and 1998), but Firestone invariably had the upper hand elsewhere, often by an appreciable margin. Thus the 11th-hour decision by Newman/Haas Racing to join the Firestone bandwagon immediately prior to the 1999 season, ending a longstanding association with Goodyear, was a surprise more for its timing than its substance.

Walker Racing, meanwhile, opted to remain loyal to Goodyear and willingly took on much of the development work. Benefiting from a tireless and able test driver in Gil de Ferran, and stung by criticism from customers and competitors alike, Goodyear developed a much improved tire that contributed handily to de Ferran's clear-cut victory at Portland International Raceway.

'Goodyear has made the commitment to compete in CART racing by increasing its personnel resources and technology, taking some of the lessons we've learned in other series and utilizing that knowledge to put together a winning product,' declared Perry Bell, Goodyear's CART Operations Manager, who previously had been employed on the American giant's Formula 1 program.

Fuel strategy obviously played a pivotal part in the outcome, but favorable tire performance and wear were key aspects to capitalizing on the daring three-stop strategy, enabling de Ferran to reel off a string of laps in the low 60-second bracket and establish control of the race.

'We both did a lot of work coming into this race,' said de Ferran, after finally ending a 25-race win streak for Firestone. 'We came here twice to test our Goodyear tires and they were perfect. They had a lot of grip and they were consistent throughout the final run. If the tires weren't consistent, I would never have been able to open up that gap.'

Jubilation in the Walker and Goodyear camps after Gil de Ferran's fine victory.

Bottom: A huge sideways 'moment' at a restart on lap 55 cost Bryan Herta a couple of positions and a shot at a podium finish.

the opportunity to make a virtue of necessity. Since even the most assiduous fuel conservation would still leave de Ferran marginal on fuel, why not forget any idea of stretching it to the end and allow him to richen the mixture and put the hammer down? It was a brilliant improvised gamble by the savvy Walker.

'We knew we couldn't make it [on fuel],' admitted Derrick Walker, 'so we just told him to go for it. The guys did their job in the pits and Gil took care of the rest.'

De Ferran, indeed, was up to the challenge, although afterward he admitted to a degree of nervousness once his pit stop had been completed in less than five seconds by the Valvoline/Cummins crew. Ahead lay that agonizing drone along the length of the pit lane while observing the mandatory 50-mph speed limit. It seemed like an eternity.

'As I went down the pit lane, I saw Juan's [crewman] putting the [pit] board out for him, so I thought, "Uh-oh, have we made it?" But we came out in the lead and Derrick came on the radio and said, "Plus eight [seconds]," and so I knew it was okay,' related de Ferran, who eased his pace in the final laps before taking the checkered flag 4.393 seconds clear of a philosophical Montoya.

'Last time [in Milwaukee], we played it the other way round [making a stop in the closing stages] and [the strategy] didn't work,' reflected Montoya, who nevertheless extended his FedEx Championship Series lead to five points over Franchitti. 'This time it didn't play out either, so it's a bit frustrating. But we decided to go our way and his way was better. That's the way it goes.'

Franchitti, too, was relatively content, having driven well from 12th on the grid after a rare error in qualifying by Team KOOL Green.

'I was driving as hard as I could, trying to pick up as many places as I could,' related the Scotsman. 'I'm happy to finish third, considering where we started.'

Fernandez capped a strong debut run in Pat Patrick's Tecate/Quaker State Ford/Reynard by passing Tracy for fourth place on lap 92, thereby recording his best result since April in Long Beach (where he piloted a Swift chassis). Herta managed to hold on for a somewhat disappointing sixth place, while Roberto Moreno's creditable seventh in PacWest Racing's Motorola Mercedes/Reynard represented his fourth consecutive point-scoring finish while acting as substitute for the injured Mark Blundell.

Alex Sabine/Jeremy Shaw

second place. Franchitti also closed in on his teammate and began to apply some pressure. Although clearly faster around much of the track, Franchitti bided his time, clearly mindful of their rather notorious recent encounters as teammates. Finally, on lap 67, the Scot slipped past cleanly at the Festival Curves and promptly caught Montoya, who was being instructed almost on a corner-by-corner basis to lean off the fuel mixture and short-shift.

In fact, this was a familiar refrain from team managers and crew chiefs up and down the pit lane throughout the final stint of the race. If you wanted to make it to the finish, you simply had to economize on fuel in every way possible.

'It's a hard thing to go down the straight at part-throttle,' commented Montoya, who nonetheless obediently heeded the warnings from his pit while making skilful use of track position to keep Franchitti at bay. In much worse trouble was Montoya's teammate, Vasser, who had to cut his pace so drastically that he was demoted from sixth to 13th in a matter of five laps.

Walker, meanwhile, saw in poor fuel mileage combined with ideal track position and a perfectly handling car

Michael C. Brown

PORTLAND SNIPPETS

• The first round of pit stops passed largely without incident. The exception – predictably, perhaps, in view of recent history – was **MICHAEL ANDRETTI**. As the black Kmart/Texaco Havoline Ford/Swift was dropped down from its air jacks, the revs suddenly plummeted and the engine died – a faulty ECU the culprit. Andretti finally got going again after spending no fewer than 83 seconds in the pit lane. He would drive flat-out for the rest of the day, setting the race's fastest lap as he charged from 15th to tenth (and three welcome PPG Cup points) inside the final five laps.

• Former KOOL/Toyota Atlantic standout **MEMO GIDLEY**, 29, made his Champ Car debut (right) for Walker Racing as substitute for the injured Naoki Hattori. Gidley earned the ride following a head-to-head test session with Indy Lights front-runner Guy Smith.

Michael C. Brown

• Cal Wells III and team co-owner Frank Arciero confirmed that **CRISTIANO DA MATTA**, the reigning PPG-Dayton Indy Lights champion and one of the rising stars of the FedEx Championship Series, had agreed to remain with Arciero-Wells Racing through the end of the 2000 season. 'His performance this season, and over the course of his career, has been nothing short of exceptional,' said Wells. 'We're looking forward to building a long, successful relationship with him.'

• An inspired **RICHIE HEARN** took advantage of drying conditions on Friday afternoon to claim the provisional pole aboard John Della Penna's Budweiser Toyota/Reynard. 'It's a tremendous boost for our team, for Toyota, for Budweiser,' commented Hearn. 'The guys have put in long, long hours, and no matter what else happens this weekend, this feels very, very good.'

• Under-utilized Brazilian **GUALTER SALLES** stepped into the All American Racers Denso/Castrol Toyota/Eagle in place of Alex Barron, as team owner Dan Gurney sought a 'second opinion' regarding the capabilities of the unique chassis.

• **MARLBORO TEAM PENSKE** elected to field a pair of cars at Portland, and once again newcomer Tarso Marques outpaced his illustrious teammate, Al Unser Jr. Marques qualified 18th in his Penske PC27B, despite a few delays caused by mechanical problems and inclement weather, and, impressively, set the fifth-fastest race lap. He was on course for a point-scoring finish until involved in minor scrapes with Tony Kanaan and Michael Andretti. Unser, meanwhile, started 26th – the worst qualifying position of his career, apart from the 1995 Indianapolis 500, for which he failed to qualify – and finished 16th in his Lola B99/00.

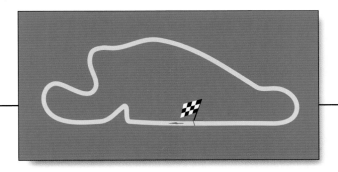

FEDEX CHAMPIONSHIP SERIES • ROUND 8
BUDWEISER/G.I. JOE'S 200
PRESENTED BY TEXACO/HAVOLINE

PORTLAND INTERNATIONAL RACEWAY, PORTLAND, OREGON

JUNE 20, 98 laps – 192.962 miles

Place	Driver (Nat.)	No.	Team Sponsors Engine/Car	Tires	Q Speed	Q Time	Q Pos.	Laps	Time/Status	Ave. (mph)	Pts.
1	Gil de Ferran (BR)	5	Walker Racing Valvoline/Cummins Honda/Reynard 99I	GY	121.504	58.339s	3	98	1h 47m 44.560s	107.457	21
2	*Juan Montoya (COL)	4	Target/Chip Ganassi Racing Honda/Reynard 99I	FS	121.808	58.193s	1	98	1h 47m 48.953s	107.384	17
3	Dario Franchitti (GB)	27	Team KOOL Green Honda/Reynard 99I	FS	120.876	58.642s	12	98	1h 47m 49.556s	107.374	14
4	Adrian Fernandez (MEX)	40	Patrick Racing Tecate/Quaker State Ford Cosworth/Reynard 99I	FS	121.452	58.364s	5	98	1h 47m 58.128s	107.232	12
5	Paul Tracy (CDN)	26	Team KOOL Green Honda/Reynard 99I	FS	121.370	58.403s	6	98	1h 48m 04.853s	107.121	10
6	Bryan Herta (USA)	8	Team Rahal Shell Ford Cosworth/Reynard 99I	FS	121.462	58.359s	4	98	1h 48m 12.491s	106.995	8
7	Roberto Moreno (BR)	18	PacWest Racing Group Motorola Mercedes/Reynard 99I	FS	120.944	58.609s	11	98	1h 48m 13.010s	106.986	6
8	Max Papis (I)	7	Team Rahal Miller Lite Ford Cosworth/Reynard 99I	FS	121.043	58.561s	10	98	1h 48m 14.628s	106.960	5
9	Patrick Carpentier (CDN)	33	Forsythe Racing Player's/Indeck Mercedes/Reynard 99I	FS	121.300	58.437s	8	98	1h 48m 14.948s	106.954	4
10	Michael Andretti (USA)	6	Newman/Haas Kmart/Texaco Havoline Ford Cosworth/Swift 010.c	FS	120.791	58.683s	14	98	1h 48m 26.471s	106.765	3
11	*Cristiano da Matta (BR)	25	Arciero-Wells Racing MCI WorldCom Toyota/Reynard 99I	FS	120.699	58.728s	15	98	1h 48m 26.477s	106.765	2
12	Jimmy Vasser (USA)	12	Target/Chip Ganassi Racing Honda/Reynard 99I	FS	121.370	58.403s	7	98	1h 48m 27.945s	106.741	1
13	Greg Moore (CDN)	99	Forsythe Racing Player's/Indeck Mercedes/Reynard 99I	FS	120.800	58.679s	13	98	1h 48m 29.448s	106.716	
14	Christian Fittipaldi (BR)	11	Newman/Haas Big Kmart Ford Cosworth/Swift 010.c	FS	121.213	58.479s	9	98	1h 48m 36.604s	106.599	
15	Tony Kanaan (BR)	44	McDonald's Championship Racing Honda/Reynard 99I	FS	120.549	58.801s	17	98	1h 48m 43.608s	106.485	
16	Al Unser Jr. (USA)	2	Marlboro Team Penske Mercedes/Lola B99/00	GY	118.553	59.791s	26	98	1h 48m 44.249s	106.474	
17	Robby Gordon (USA)	22	Team Gordon Panasonic/Menards Toyota/Swift 010.c	FS	119.830	59.154s	20	98	1h 48m 44.533s	106.469	
18	*Tarso Marques (BR)	3	Marlboro Team Penske Mercedes/Penske PC27B	GY	120.404	58.872s	18	97	Running		
19	*Memo Gidley (USA)	15	Walker Racing Alpine Honda/Reynard 98I	GY	119.615	59.260s	25	97	Running		
20	Michel Jourdain Jr. (MEX)	19	Payton/Coyne Herdez/Viva Mexico Ford Cosworth/Lola T97/00	FS	119.646	59.245s	24	96	Running		
21	PJ Jones (USA)	20	Patrick Racing Visteon Ford Cosworth/Swift 010.c	FS	119.652	59.242s	23	95	Running		
22	Richie Hearn (USA)	10	Della Penna Motorsports Budweiser Toyota/Reynard 98I	FS	119.775	59.181s	21	95	Running		
23	*Luiz Garcia Jr. (BR)	71	Payton/Coyne Racing Tang Ford Cosworth/Reynard 97I	FS	118.333	59.902s	27	95	Running		
24	Scott Pruett (USA)	24	Arciero-Wells Racing Pioneer Toyota/Reynard 99I	FS	120.236	58.954s	19	43	Engine		
25	Mauricio Gugelmin (BR)	17	PacWest Racing Group Hollywood Mercedes/Reynard 99I	FS	120.586	58.783s	16	42	Turbo		
26	Helio Castro-Neves (BR)	9	Hogan Racing Hogan Motor Leasing Mercedes/Lola B99/00	FS	121.622	58.282s	2	40	Engine		
27	Gualter Salles (BR)	36	All American Racers Denso/Castrol Toyota/Eagle 997	GY	119.765	59.186s	22	10	Transmission		
28	*Shigeaki Hattori (J)	16	Bettenhausen Motorsports Epson Mercedes/Reynard 98I	GY	114.092	62.129s	28	8	Driver retired		

* denotes rookie driver

Caution flags: Laps 47–50, spin/Hearn; laps 51–53, yellow restart; laps 59–61, spin/Jones. **Total:** Three for 10 laps.

Lap leaders: Helio Castro-Neves, 1–30 (30 laps); Juan Montoya, 31–50 (20 laps); Gil de Ferran, 51–54 (4 laps); Montoya, 55–59 (5 laps); de Ferran, 60–98 (39 laps). **Totals:** de Ferran, 43 laps; Castro-Neves, 30 laps; Montoya, 25 laps.

Fastest race lap: Michael Andretti, 59.749s, 118.636 mph, on lap 91 (record).

Championship positions: 1 Montoya, 90; **2** Franchitti, 85; **3** de Ferran, 71; **4** Moore, 69; **5** Fernandez, 65; **6** Andretti, 64; **7** Fittipaldi, 61; **8** Tracy, 46; **9** Papis, 41; **10** Vasser, 34; **11** Jones, 28; **12** Kanaan, 26; **13** Herta, 23; **14** Carpentier, 22; **15** Castro-Neves & Moreno, 21; **17** da Matta, 16; **18** Gugelmin, 13; **19** Blundell, Hearn & Gordon, 5; **22** Marques & Barron, 4; **24** Pruett, 3; **25** Unser Jr., 2.

OMEGA
OFFICIAL TIMEKEEPER OF CART

CLEVELAND

1 – MONTOYA

2 – DE FERRAN

3 – ANDRETTI

Whatever the conditions, Juan Montoya was the master of Cleveland.

Right: Gualter Salles lit up Saturday's practice session with a massive blaze on his AAR Toyota/Eagle. The Brazilian makes a hasty exit.

Bottom: Patrick Carpentier and newcomer Memo Gidley explore different lines on the Burke Lakefront Airport circuit.

THE Medic Drug Grand Prix of Cleveland Presented by Firstar provided further testimony that – whether oval or road course, rain or shine – Juan Montoya is more than a match for any challenge that the FedEx Championship Series, his fellow drivers and the weather can throw at him.

In his most convincing performance to date, the precociously talented Colombian stamped his authority on the Burke Lakefront Airport from the outset. He put not a wheel wrong during a torrential mid-race downpour and withstood a determined challenge from Gil de Ferran before pulling away to win by a comfortable ten-second margin. In the process, he not only consolidated his lead in the PPG Cup point standings, but also erased any lingering doubts there may have been about his ability to capture the title at the first time of asking.

After the final restart, when Montoya ducked inside de Ferran to retake a lead he would not surrender, the outcome of the race was never really in doubt. But the latter stages were enlivened by a furious scrap for the lower placings. Eventually, Michael Andretti pulled clear of a snarling pack of cars to salvage 14 points from a hard afternoon's work, much of it spent locked in combat with longtime nemesis Paul Tracy.

The chief concern up and down the pit lane, as the 27-car field circulated slowly behind the pace car prior to the start, was not the elements, but a more traditional Cleveland headache:

QUALIFYING

Shrugging off a hefty Friday practice accident that consigned him to his backup car for the balance of the weekend, Juan Montoya uncorked another sensational lap in final qualifying to extend Target/Chip Ganassi Racing's string of consecutive poles at Cleveland to four.

The fact that this was the 23-year-old rookie's first acquaintance with the unique Burke Lakefront Airport circuit did not prevent him from topping the timing charts after a mere eight laps of running on Friday, then clocking the only sub-57-second time of the weekend en route to his fourth pole of the season on Saturday afternoon.

'It's a fun track,' reckoned Montoya. 'It's very challenging. The most difficult corner [Turn Eight] is the only one that has a wall. I hit it yesterday. I nearly hit it today, but almost doesn't count, so it's okay!'

Gil de Ferran, who likewise sat on the pole on his maiden visit to the makeshift airfield venue, back in 1995, had to settle for the outside front-row starting spot on this occasion. The Portland winner set the pace in Friday's qualifying, but fell a couple of tenths short on Saturday: 'We did one good lap on our second set of tires and got close to Juan, but we couldn't get it done. After that, I didn't get another chance.'

Early pace-setter Michael Andretti was forced to sit out the final eight minutes of qualifying as penance for bringing out the red flag with an 'off' during Friday afternoon's session. 'You could see [track conditions] improving almost minute by minute. It was kind of frustrating watching guys pick me off when I was on the pole,' admitted Michael, after being demoted to third. Needless to say, the '91 PPG Cup champion and Cleveland winner loomed as a major threat on race day.

Bryan Herta, showing his customary road-course form, qualified a strong fourth for Team Rahal, while Roberto Moreno posted a splendid late effort to vault from 12th on the provisional grid to fifth in the Motorola/PacWest Mercedes/Reynard. Languishing in tenth place was Dario Franchitti, the Scot setting his time in the spare #27 Team KOOL Green Honda/Reynard after enduring 'a pretty bad weekend so far', in which he had struggled to find a rhythm and crashed twice.

negotiating the first corner without incident. The ultra-wide main runway funnels into a narrow hairpin, and the temptation to make a banzai move often proves too much for midfield qualifiers anxious to make up a host of 'free' places. On this occasion, however, everyone managed to squeeze through and a pile-up was averted,

although a minor skirmish knocked the unfortunate Bryan Herta into a spin that relegated him to the tail of the field, nullifying his strong qualifying effort.

Having played the start to perfection, Montoya wasted no time in opening out a small lead over fellow front-row starter de Ferran. Just

behind, Andretti soon found himself under pressure from a charging Tracy, who made up four places on the opening lap. Also making rapid progress was Helio Castro-Neves, the Brazilian catapulting from an unrepresentative 17th qualifying spot into the thick of the midfield action by lap two. Alas, the luckless Hogan driver would fall victim to yet more engine problems.

Behind Montoya and de Ferran, Andretti and Tracy continued to wage a fierce battle over third place, while Roberto Moreno, once again doing sterling duty as substitute for the injured Mark Blundell, ran fifth. Dario Franchitti was not so fortunate, succumbing to mechanical woes after a miserable weekend that dealt his championship chances a major blow.

The gap between the two leaders grew to as much as five seconds by lap 16, whereupon de Ferran turned up the wick and began to whittle away at the deficit. The Brazilian set what was to stand as the fastest lap of the race on lap 27, trimming Montoya's advantage to less than two seconds before peeling into the pits at the end of the next tour. The latter was able to squeeze an extra three laps out of his first tank of fuel, although any bearing this might have had on the race's outcome was swiftly negated by an altogether more dramatic development.

No sooner had Moreno become the last of the front-runners to take on routine service on lap 32 than a deluge engulfed the Burke Lakefront Airport circuit. The skies had been darkening

Cleveland CART races to continue

A COUPLE of days after the race, promoter International Management Group announced that it had failed to reach an agreement with CART to continue to host a round of the FedEx Championship Series at the Burke Lakefront Airport. Instead, IMG had inked a deal to host a round of the rival Pep Boys Indy Racing League in 2000.

Financial considerations proved to be the stumbling block between IMG and CART, which insisted on a substantially increased sanctioning fee. The IRL was more than happy to conclude a deal for a significantly lower sum.

One of the stipulations of switching allegiance to the IRL, however, required a considerable expenditure in converting the existing layout into an oval configuration. Furthermore, the changes needed approval of the Federal Aviation Authority, operators of the airport site, which is situated on the shores of Lake Erie and in close proximity to downtown.

The decision not to renew the contract with CART received an overwhelmingly negative response from race fans and the local business community. That fact, allied to the potential costs and persistent rumors of a

possible rapprochement between CART and the IRL, eventually caused the FAA and city officials, led by Mayor Michael R. White, to block the IRL initiative.

'The FAA and city of Cleveland have been extremely cautious to make any pavement changes on Burke's airfield which are not directly related to Burke's airport operations,' confirmed Mayor White in early September.

'The recent installation and investment of an instrument landing system and planning for expansion at Burke gives the city additional reason to withhold approval of IMG's request for airfield pavement changes.

'Based upon both the airfield-related concerns and reports of merger discussions, the city is immediately stopping all work on legislative and FAA approvals for an IRL-sanctioned race at Burke Lakefront Airport.'

Shortly afterward, IMG and CART confirmed that they had patched up their differences and the event – one of the most popular on the schedule – would continue into the next millennium.

ominously since flag-fall; had the precipitation begun even 30 seconds earlier, Moreno's miserly fuel consumption would have paid handsome dividends, as he could have switched directly onto wet tires. Instead, he took on a fresh set of slicks and had little option but to stop again three laps later.

In an instant, the track was awash, and cars were spinning every which way – including de Ferran's Valvoline/Cummins Honda/Reynard. 'The engine actually died, but somehow, just before the tire wall, I managed to bump it and restarted the thing again and snaked it around. I guess that was

kind of lucky,' admitted the Brazilian driver sheepishly.

Andretti, who had just served a drive-through penalty for exceeding the pit lane speed limit (by all of 1 mph!), led the charge back onto the pit lane for grooved rubber. Several others elected to remain on slicks, hoping the shower would quickly pass. Forsythe Championship Racing's Tony Kanaan never made it back to his Drive-Thru Crew, losing control in Turn Eight and making heavy contact with the outside wall.

'It was my mistake... My guys called me in, but I couldn't come in on the

lap I was supposed to. Michael [Andretti] and, I believe, Cristiano [da Matta] were in front of me. There was a lot of spray and I couldn't see to come in,' explained the ever candid Champ Car sophomore, who had just moved into the top ten, having started a lowly 19th.

Almost simultaneously, the wall-lined turn – treacherous even in dry conditions – claimed Jimmy Vasser's Target/Chip Ganassi Racing Honda/Reynard and rookie Tarso Marques' Marlboro Team Penske Mercedes/Lola, bringing out the full-course yellows on lap 34.

A lengthy pace-car interlude ensued while the debris was cleared and the worst of the standing water was allowed to drain. Even so, keeping 850 horsepower under control on a surface that bore more resemblance to a skating rink than a race track proved no easy matter and, among the race's 16 survivors, few didn't admit to a heart-stopping moment or two.

The proceedings eventually resumed under sunny skies on lap 50, whereupon Montoya took off in the lead again. This time, however, de Ferran launched an immediate counter-attack, his Goodyear rain tires working a treat

On Goodyear's home turf, less than an hour from its base in Akron, Ohio, Gil de Ferran earned the company another podium finish.
Photo: Michael C. Brown

in the damp, but drying, conditions. The Walker Racing man took advantage of a perfect run through the chicane before the pits to dive inside Montoya's similar Honda/Reynard going into Turn One on lap 58. The maneuver elicited a huge cheer from the packed main grandstands.

Montoya's Firestones were beginning to suffer. 'When it was really wet, the car was good, [but] as it started to dry out, my rear tires started going away,' said the eventual winner. 'I didn't want to change to dry tires too early. I said two laps before we pitted that I could go to slicks, but I stayed out because I didn't want to spin off.'

De Ferran made full use of his superior traction, romping away at the rate of two seconds a lap before pitting for slicks on lap 62, by which time Montoya had fallen into the clutches of Paul Tracy.

Sadly for the enthusiastic crowd, the prospect of an enthralling chase was dashed when Fernandez crashed in Turn Eight on lap 64, bringing out the pace car once more. The cleanup this time was quick. And Montoya, on cold Firestones, was simply too good for his Goodyear-shod rival.

'I just couldn't get the tires up to temperature quick enough,' said de Ferran, 'and he was gone before I could blink.'

Montoya, indeed, made a perfect restart, dispatching de Ferran easily into Turn One and taking off into the distance with nary a backward glance. Try as he might, the Brazilian was unable to get close enough to challenge again.

Andretti appeared to have a shot at catching de Ferran for second, until an obscure software glitch caused his Ford Cosworth engine to cut momentarily on the back straight on lap 78,

costing him close to ten seconds. The handicap could have been far greater, but for quick thinking by Andretti, who immediately hit the computer reset button inside his cockpit, clearing the problem.

'Considering everything that happened, I'll take third,' said Andretti with a resigned smile.

In the remaining minutes, all eyes settled on a furious dogfight between Herta, Tracy and Al Unser Jr. After initially making little headway, Herta had driven well to move back into contention following his first-lap spin in Team Rahal's Shell Ford/Reynard,

Unser impresses in the wet

AL Unser Jr. enjoyed by far his most competitive outing of the season, finishing a racey fifth. The twice PPG Cup Champion, who had suffered a broken leg in an accident with rookie Naoki Hattori in the first race of the year, at Homestead, causing him to miss the next two events, once again piloted Marlboro Team Penske's Lola chassis, which he had debuted at St. Louis in May.

Hitherto, the chassis switch had not produced the desired turnaround in form, still less team owner Roger Penske's elusive 100th win. At Milwaukee and Portland, in particular, Unser's name was to be found embarrassingly far down the time sheets. New teammate Tarso Marques' impressive eighth place on the grid at Rio and fifth-fastest race lap at Portland (both in a Penske PC27B chassis) represented the height of the team's achievements thus far in 1999.

At Cleveland, however, Unser qualified solidly in the midfield and used his wealth of experience to good effect in the changeable conditions on race day. After dropping a couple of places at the start, he settled into 14th amid a long line of cars. Crucially, he was among the first (along with Michael Andretti and Robby Gordon) to take on wet-weather tires when the rain arrived, pitting on lap 32. Most of the front-runners delayed their stops at least one further lap and had to contend with the downpour while still circulating on slicks.

Some of this advantage was relinquished when visibility problems obliged Unser to make an unscheduled stop for a replacement visor immediately before the restart. But the 37-year-old veteran – who, aside from a masterful victory in the rain-sodden Molson Indy Toronto of 1990, has never been noted for his wet-weather prowess – climbed through the field impressively in the damp mid-race conditions and spent the waning laps embroiled in a titanic battle over fourth place with Paul Tracy and Bryan Herta.

'It was a good time out there today,' reflected Unser. 'The Marlboro car has been performing well during the race. Now we need to focus on qualifying better.'

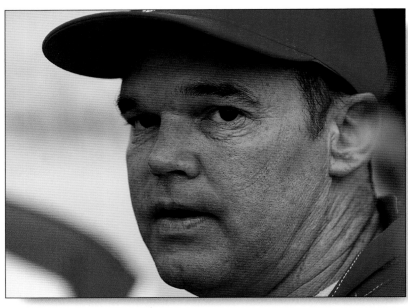

Below: Virtual monsoon conditions forced Roberto Moreno to pit for rain tires merely three laps after his regular stop, costing the Brazilian a better finish than his eventual eighth.

rising all the way to fourth place before encountering the lapped car of Memo Gidley on lap 86. The momentary delay caused Herta to fall behind a grateful Tracy and Unser. Patrick Carpentier and Roberto Moreno were in close attendance, too, completing the unlapped finishers in a race that was halted after 90 of the scheduled 100 laps in accordance with the two-hour time limit, which applies to all road-course events.

In any case, by this point, Montoya was long gone. It had been another masterful performance from the youngster, who moved into a commanding 25-point lead over de Ferran in the PPG Cup standings as the Champ Car teams looked forward to a rare weekend off before back-to-back July races at Road America, Toronto and Michigan Speedway.

Alex Sabine/Jeremy Shaw

CLEVELAND SNIPPETS

• TONY BETTENHAUSEN was obliged to skip his first CART event since Laguna Seca in 1990 – ending a streak of 142 starts as either a driver or entrant – after he was unable to find sponsorship (or a funded driver) for his '98 Mercedes/Reynard. (Japanese rookie Shigeaki Hattori's deal with Epson covered only 13 of the season's 20 races.)

• ROBBY GORDON (right) used his wealth of experience in the changeable weather conditions, moving as high as fourth place before a cut tire forced him to make an unscheduled pit stop. 'That was the most fun I've had in a CART race since Japan,' enthused Gordon, who ultimately brought his Panasonic/Menards/Johns Manville Toyota/Swift home in ninth.

Michael C. Brown

• TARSO MARQUES was initially set to race a Penske PC27B chassis, but after struggling on Friday (due to a faulty shock absorber, it transpired), the decision was made to install him in teammate Al Unser Jr.'s spare Lola B99/00.

• Rookie MEMO GIDLEY earned his first PPG Cup points with a promising drive to 11th aboard Walker Racing's Alpine Honda/Reynard. The Toyota Atlantic graduate lost two places at the start, falling to 21st, but passed three cars during the opening stint and kept his wits about him during the mid-race cloudburst. He also set a very respectable 13th fastest lap. 'He's doing a very good job,' praised team manager Rob Edwards. 'He just needs miles.'

• Richie Hearn raced the latest TOYOTA PHASE VI ENGINE at Cleveland, although not by choice. The lightweight, compact powerplant had yet to fulfil expectations, and the Della Penna Motorsports team had intended to race its '98 Reynard, fitted with the older RV8D engine, as used by all the other Toyota teams. Unfortunately, that car was badly damaged in a crash on Friday.

• MAX PAPIS would like nothing more than to erase the Cleveland weekend from his memory completely. He struggled over the Burke Lakefront Airport's bumps with Team Rahal's Miller Lite Ford/Reynard, qualified a dismal 22nd, lost two laps by spinning in the wet and, strangely, never came remotely close to the pace of teammate Bryan Herta. 'I felt embarrassed this weekend,' admitted the Italian driver. 'But we'll be back at the front for Elkhart Lake. I am sure of that.'

• Having competed at Cleveland on four previous occasions, GIL DE FERRAN was asked (somewhat curiously) during Saturday's post-qualifying press conference what advice he would give Juan Montoya on tackling the notorious first turn at the start. De Ferran pondered the question for a fraction of a second before replying impishly, 'None.' Not for the first time, Chip Ganassi's young charge demonstrated on Sunday that he was in scant need of help from an old hand...

FEDEX CHAMPIONSHIP SERIES • ROUND 9
MEDIC DRUG GRAND PRIX OF CLEVELAND
PRESENTED BY FIRSTAR

BURKE LAKEFRONT AIRPORT, CLEVELAND, OHIO

JUNE 27, 90 laps – 189.54 miles

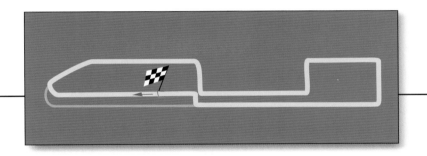

Place	Driver (Nat.)	No.	Team Sponsors Engine/Car	Tires	Q Speed	Q Time	Q Pos.	Laps	Time/Status	Ave. (mph)	Pts.
1	*Juan Montoya (COL)	4	Target/Chip Ganassi Racing Honda/Reynard 99I	FS	133.448	56.813s	1	90	2h 01m 04.277s	93.931	22
2	Gil de Ferran (BR)	5	Walker Racing Valvoline/Cummins Honda/Reynard 99I	GY	132.971	57.017s	2	90	2h 01m 14.881s	93.795	16
3	Michael Andretti (USA)	6	Newman/Haas Kmart/Texaco Havoline Ford Cosworth/Swift 010.c	FS	132.457	57.238s	3	90	2h 01m 16.974s	93.768	14
4	Paul Tracy (CDN)	26	Team KOOL Green Honda/Reynard 99I	FS	131.682	57.575s	8	90	2h 01m 22.126s	93.701	12
5	Al Unser Jr. (USA)	2	Marlboro Team Penske Mercedes/Lola B99/00	GY	130.481	58.105s	14	90	2h 01m 23.486s	93.684	10
6	Bryan Herta (USA)	8	Team Rahal Shell Ford Cosworth/Reynard 99I	FS	132.051	57.414s	4	90	2h 01m 24.031s	93.677	8
7	Patrick Carpentier (CDN)	33	Forsythe Racing Player's/Indeck Mercedes/Reynard 99I	FS	131.762	57.540s	6	90	2h 01m 24.873s	93.666	6
8	Roberto Moreno (BR)	18	PacWest Racing Group Motorola Mercedes/Reynard 99I	FS	131.904	57.478s	5	90	2h 01m 27.979s	93.626	5
9	Robby Gordon (USA)	22	Team Gordon Panasonic/Menards Toyota/Swift 010.c	FS	127.576	59.428s	24	89	Running		4
10	Richie Hearn (USA)	10	Della Penna Motorsports Budweiser Toyota/Reynard 99I	FS	127.069	59.665s	25	88	Running		3
11	*Memo Gidley (USA)	15	Walker Racing Alpine Honda/Reynard 98I	GY	129.326	58.624s	21	88	Running		2
12	Christian Fittipaldi (BR)	11	Newman/Haas Big Kmart Ford Cosworth/Swift 010.c	FS	131.106	57.828s	11	88	Running		1
13	Gualter Salles (BR)	36	All American Racers Denso/Castrol Toyota/Eagle 997	GY	126.963	59.715s	26	88	Running		
14	*Luiz Garcia Jr. (BR)	71	Payton/Coyne Tang Ford Cosworth/Reynard 97I	FS	126.449	59.958s	27	87	Running		
15	PJ Jones (USA)	20	Patrick Racing Visteon Ford Cosworth/Swift 010.c	FS	130.337	58.169s	16	86	Running		
16	Max Papis (I)	7	Team Rahal Miller Lite Ford Cosworth/Reynard 99I	FS	128.928	58.805s	22	86	Running		
17	Scott Pruett (USA)	24	Arciero-Wells Racing Pioneer Toyota/Reynard 99I	FS	130.018	58.312s	18	70	Engine		
18	Greg Moore (CDN)	99	Forsythe Racing Player's/Indeck Mercedes/Reynard 99I	FS	131.760	57.541s	7	64	Exhaust		
19	Adrian Fernandez (MEX)	40	Patrick Racing Tecate/Quaker State Ford Cosworth/Reynard 99I	FS	130.862	57.936s	12	63	Accident		
20	*Cristiano da Matta (BR)	25	Arciero-Wells Racing MCI WorldCom Toyota/Reynard 99I	FS	130.798	57.964s	13	37	Suspension		
21	Mauricio Gugelmin (BR)	17	PacWest Racing Group Hollywood Mercedes/Reynard 99I	FS	131.632	57.597s	9	34	Accident		
22	Tony Kanaan (BR)	44	McDonald's Championship Racing Honda/Reynard 99I	FS	129.370	58.604s	19	33	Accident		
23	Jimmy Vasser (USA)	12	Target/Chip Ganassi Racing Honda/Reynard 99I	FS	130.342	58.167s	15	33	Accident		
24	*Tarso Marques (BR)	3	Marlboro Team Penske Mercedes/Lola B99/00	GY	127.669	59.385s	23	32	Accident		
25	Dario Franchitti (GB)	27	Team KOOL Green Honda/Reynard 99I	FS	131.616	57.604s	10	19	Throttle linkage		
26	Helio Castro-Neves (BR)	9	Hogan Racing Motor Leasing Mercedes/Lola B99/00	FS	130.277	58.196s	17	19	Linkage		
27	Michel Jourdain Jr. (MEX)	19	Payton/Coyne Herdez/Viva Mexico Ford Cosworth/Lola T97/00	FS	129.350	58.613s	20	2	Transmission		

*denotes rookie driver

Caution flags: Laps 34–49, accident/Marques, Vasser and Kanaan; laps 64–67, accident/Fernandez. **Total:** Two for 20 laps.

Lap leaders: Juan Montoya, 1–30 (30 laps); Roberto Moreno, 31 (1 lap); Montoya, 32 (1 lap); Moreno, 33–34 (2 laps); Montoya, 35–57 (23 laps); Gil de Ferran, laps 58–61 (4 laps); Paul Tracy, 62 (1 lap); Michael Andretti, 63 (1 lap); de Ferran, 64–68 (5 laps); Montoya, 69–90 (22 laps). **Totals:** Montoya, 76 laps; de Ferran, 9 laps; Moreno, 3 laps; Tracy, 1 lap; Andretti, 1 lap.

Fastest race lap: Gil de Ferran, 58.790s, 128.961 mph, on lap 27.

Championship positions: 1 Montoya, 112; **2** de Ferran, 87; **3** Franchitti, 85; **4** Andretti, 78; **5** Moore, 69; **6** Fernandez, 65; **7** Fittipaldi, 62; **8** Tracy, 58; **9** Papis, 41; **10** Vasser, 34; **11** Herta, 31; **12** Jones & Carpentier, 28; **14** Kanaan & Moreno, 26; **16** Castro-Neves, 21; **17** da Matta, 16; **18** Gugelmin, 13; **19** Unser Jr., 12; **20** Gordon, 9; **21** Hearn, 8; **22** Blundell, 5; **23** Marques & Barron, 4; **25** Pruett, 3; **26** Gidley, 2.

OMEGA
OFFICIAL TIMEKEEPER OF CART

ROAD AMERICA

Brazilian breakthrough

Photos: Kazuki Saito

PRIOR to his triumph in the Texaco/Havoline 200, Christian Fittipaldi had become the most experienced active Champ Car performer without a win to his name. His previous best result in 70 starts had been second, achieved on two occasions – at the 1995 Indianapolis 500, during his rookie campaign with Walker Racing, and at Detroit in '96, when he led most of the way before a slight slip in the closing stages allowed Newman/Haas teammate Michael Andretti to snatch the victory.

Since then, the 28-year-old Brazilian, who now makes his home in Miami, Florida, had struggled through two-and-a-half seasons filled with one disappointment after another. Twice he had been sidelined by injury. He missed seven races in '97, following a terrifying crash in Surfers Paradise, Australia, where he suffered a badly broken leg, and one race in '98, after being rendered briefly unconscious by a heavy impact at Milwaukee. He accumulated a handful of top-five finishes during that two-year period, but only rarely was a match for Andretti.

There had been rumors to suggest that Fittipaldi's place in the team was in serious jeopardy, especially after he had scored precisely half the number of PPG Cup points earned by Andretti in '98. Ultimately, though, team co-owner Carl Haas kept faith with the man who beat Alex Zanardi in the final, pivotal race of the 1991 European Formula 3000 Championship. Fittipaldi responded by finishing among the top ten in each of the first seven races in '99, including three top-five results.

His overdue maiden victory thoroughly vindicated Haas' decision. 'He has more talent than people give him credit for,' said Haas. 'He has been on the verge all season, and I am just so happy for him.'

Fittipaldi was equally delighted after securing his first win in over seven years. 'I am very happy for the team and all the sponsors that stayed behind me through two very tough seasons,' he declared, 'and I am also happy for my parents, who have given me great support through all my racing years.'

Juan Montoya set the pace for most of the Texaco/Havoline 200, but Christian Fittipaldi gave dogged chase and ended up with the victory.

Below: After taking the pole, Michael Andretti was forced to settle for second best on race day in the wake of his Newman/Haas teammate.

QUALIFYING

Michael Andretti has always enjoyed competing at Elkhart Lake's Road America. He had qualified among the top five in all but one of his previous eight appearances at the Wisconsin road course, but, surprisingly, had to wait until 1998 before snaring his first pole. Clearly he enjoyed the experience. This time, his Kmart/Texaco Havoline Ford Cosworth/Swift 010.c was fastest in every practice and qualifying session, although he had an enthralling back-and-forth tussle with series leader Juan Montoya before clinching his first pole of the 1999 campaign.

First one protagonist, then the other held the top spot during the final half-hour on Saturday afternoon. As the minutes ticked away, Andretti ducked into the pits for a spring change. He emerged with enough time for just one quick lap to regain the pole from Montoya, who had gone fastest with less than two minutes remaining. Andretti responded magnificently.

'I have to give credit to Ford on this one,' said Andretti, after snatching the 32nd pole of his career. 'The engine was perfect. I mean this is the best engine I have ever had. We were just flying down the straightaways.'

Montoya also improved on his final lap, but wound up just 0.139 second shy in Chip Ganassi's Target Honda/Reynard.

'I thought I had it,' declared Montoya, 'but I got to the Carousel and I had too much push. I just tried to carry a bit too much speed.

'I think Michael did a good job anyway,' added the young Colombian. 'It's alright, it's a long race.'

Gil de Ferran also got in on the act. The Brazilian was fastest for a few moments in the waning stages, but then had to sit and watch from the sidelines after his Valvoline/Cummins Honda/Reynard ran out of fuel in Turn One.

'I should be happy,' said de Ferran, 'but somebody made a miscalculation and we ran out of fuel when we thought we had plenty. It's a shame. The guys really got the car up to speed and the car was very, very good today.'

CHRISTIAN Fittipaldi rode a little good fortune, excellent strategy and a perfectly set up Big Kmart Ford Cosworth/Swift to a long overdue maiden Champ Car victory in the Texaco/Havoline 200 at Road America. It was no more than he deserved. Three years earlier, Fittipaldi had seen a potential victory slip through his fingers due to an engine failure in the closing stages. This time, he was perfectly positioned to profit when PPG Cup points leader Juan Montoya suffered a rare mechanical problem on his Target/Chip Ganassi Racing Honda/Reynard. And just to make race promoter Carl Haas' day complete, Michael Andretti finished second to secure the first 1-2 punch for Newman/Haas Racing since Detroit in 1996.

'I feel sorry for Juan, but unfortunately it wasn't his day,' said Fittipaldi. 'All of us who finished on the podium have had problems this year, and fortunately for us it happened to him today and we were able to make very good use of it.'

Teammate Andretti was equally philosophical after finishing just 1.060 seconds behind Fittipaldi and vaulting to second in the FedEx Championship Series points table: 'You hate to see anyone in that position [endure a mechanical problem], but after you have been in that position a few times,

you feel like it is just evening the score a little bit.'

A couple of hours earlier, Montoya, too, had been in the mood to even the score, when he responded to being out-qualified by Andretti with an outrageous around-the-outside maneuver in Turn One to grasp the lead at the start. Unfortunately, it was for naught, as the race was red-flagged following a couple of incidents during a wild opening lap. The biggest fracas took place in Turn One, where Helio Castro-Neves, who had been restricted to 20th on the grid due to another engine failure, misjudged his entry speed and took out an innocent Memo Gidley (Alpine Honda/Reynard) and Max Papis (Miller Lite Ford/Reynard). A half-mile farther down the track, an error by rookie Cristiano da Matta

deposited both his MCI WorldCom Toyota/Reynard and Brazilian countryman Mauricio Gugelmin's Hollywood Mercedes/Reynard in the gravel trap. The complete restart gave Andretti time to ponder the manner in which he had been usurped by Montoya. 'I got a good start,' reflected the pole-sitter, 'but he just came flying past me. I've just got to make sure it doesn't happen again.'

Andretti being overtaken twice around the outside of the first turn by a rookie? Mostly likely, one could have been given some fairly good odds against that occurrence in Las Vegas. Nevertheless, Montoya clearly wasn't about to stand on ceremony. Andretti might well be the most successful driver in CART history, with 38 wins, but so what?

1 - FITTIPALDI

2 - ANDRETTI

3 - FERNANDEZ

Juan Montoya powers through
Thunder Valley, once again displaying
his class before Target/Chip Ganassi
Racing's Honda/Reynard was
sidelined by a transmission problem.
Photo: Kazuki Saito

Longer race a success

PRIOR to the first qualifying session, officials from Championship Auto Racing Teams and Road America announced that the Texaco/Havoline 200 would be extended from the traditional 50 laps of the challenging 4.048-mile road course to 55. The change had been made in an effort to ensure that the race would not be dominated by fuel strategy. By extending the distance, all cars would be obliged to make three pit stops for fuel, thereby eliminating the practice of running as lean as possible to complete the distance with just two stops.

'Our goal at Road America has always been to give our fans the best racing possible,' said Jim Haynes, President of the popular Wisconsin road course. 'Too many times, the outcome here was decided primarily by which team got the best fuel mileage. By lengthening the race slightly, we have made this a three-stop race for everyone, which allows more teams to be racing full bore at the finish. That means more exciting racing.'

'We feel it puts a better emphasis on full-out racing than fuel management,' added CART Vice President of Competition Kirk Russell. 'It reduces your temptation to base your race strategy on fuel management.'

The decision was welcomed universally by fans, teams and drivers, including Michael Andretti, who finished a close second to Newman/Haas teammate Christian Fittipaldi.

'It made for a much better race,' confirmed Andretti. 'We were all able to run our engines without worrying about conserving.'

'The only problem,' he added, 'was that Christian decided to lean his [fuel mixture] out a little bit [before his first pit stop], which allowed him to go an extra lap, which is basically how he managed to pass me. In doing that, he was coming out of the pits in front of me because I was coming out of the pits later on cold tires, and he was making up a lot of time. So they did a better strategy there, and that's how they won the race.'

Race winner Christian Fittipaldi is flanked by teammate Michael Andretti and Adrian Fernandez amid the sylvan setting of Victory Lane.

Kazuki Saito

made not even a hint of an error in the closing stages.

'After [Montoya] broke, I knew all I had to do was bring my toy home and not make any mistakes in the last couple of laps,' declared Fittipaldi, before adding with a mischievous grin, 'I knew I just needed to keep running strong because Michael just started racing yesterday and doesn't have much experience!'

Gil de Ferran had kept close company with the two Newman/Haas Swifts until his Valvoline/Cummins Honda/Reynard succumbed to engine failure on lap 42. Dario Franchitti (Team KOOL Green Honda/Reynard) was running fifth until he, too, suffered engine maladies, as did PacWest teammates Gugelmin and Roberto Moreno, who also posted strong performances.

Thus Fernandez took advantage of the high rate of attrition to complete a 1-2-3 sweep for Ford Cosworth, despite his earlier miscue and the fact that he lost more time when he stalled the engine during his final stop. 'Overall, it was a good day for us to come back from all the problems we had to finish where we did,' he reflected.

Once again, Moore was the best-placed of the Mercedes-powered cars, finishing fourth after turning some very quick laps in the closing stages with Jerry Forsythe's Player's Reynard. Papis survived another difficult weekend for Team Rahal to emerge with useful fifth-place points following a steady drive in his Miller Lite Ford/Reynard. Tony Kanaan (McDonald's Honda/Reynard) was the only other unlapped finisher.

The last few laps were rather processional as the depleted field made its way toward the checkered flag. Try as he might, Andretti was unable to make any impression on Fittipaldi's lead – until the final lap, when the Brazilian eased off and coasted home to a popular triumph.

'I have been waiting for this day for quite some time,' said Fittipaldi, whose last victory had come in the final race of the 1991 Formula 3000 Championship, when he beat Alex Zanardi to clinch the title. 'This is even sweeter, because in 1996 I had a nice race here with Michael before my car stopped [with a blown engine while running ahead of Andretti] four laps from the end. But that's racing. Sometimes you need a little bit of luck. The same way Michael was a little lucky three years ago [when Al Unser Jr. also suffered an engine failure while leading just two corners from the finish line], I was a little lucky today.'

Jeremy Shaw

In fact, when the race was restarted following a 35-minute delay, Montoya confounded any doubters by repeating his audacious pass. Furthermore, he promptly proceeded to leave the entire field floundering in his wake. He completed the first lap a full 2.1 seconds clear of Andretti, then extended his advantage to 3.4, 4.0, 4.7, 5.4 and 6.1 seconds throughout the opening half-dozen laps. No one else was in the same league.

The lead had stretched to nine seconds before Montoya made the first of three scheduled pit stops, on lap 15. The service was completed with the usual alacrity by Simon Hodgson's crew, whereupon Montoya employed his usual astonishing pace on cold tires to increase the margin by another couple of seconds by the time all of the leaders had taken on fresh tires and fuel.

Fittipaldi, who had tailed Andretti dutifully until the pit stops, had taken the opportunity to run a lean fuel mixture, thus enabling him to extend his fuel window by one lap. The extra hot lap allowed him to resume ahead of Andretti after taking on service, although the veteran American quickly redressed the balance in Turn One before Fittipaldi's new tires had got up to temperature. An inspired Adrian Fernandez also got in on the act by demoting Fittipaldi to fourth with a bold move in Turn Three on lap 19.

In fact, Fernandez was a contender all weekend in Pat Patrick's Tecate/Quaker State Ford/Reynard. But the Mexican very nearly negated all his hard work when he misjudged an attempt to pass Andretti on lap 23 and slid into the rear of the second-placed car in Turn Five.

'My car was working really good and I thought I had a good shot at him. But when I went to brake, I locked the rear wheels and got into the back of him. Thankfully, we were both able to continue,' related Fernandez, who resumed after a quick spin that cost him just one position.

Montoya, meanwhile, continued to hold a handsome lead. But then his lap times began to show uncharacteristic inconsistency. On lap 27, he, too, performed a quick spin under braking for Turn Five.

Later, it transpired that there had been a problem with the gear change.

'I lost third gear after the first pit stop,' explained Montoya. 'For a while, it was okay. I figured out a way to quickly downshift from fourth to second, skipping over third with just a blip. One time, though, I did it too fast and caught first gear in Turn Five, instead of second, and spun right around.'

Montoya quickly gathered it all together and continued, albeit with a much reduced lead. Even more impressively, he contrived to regain a consistent rhythm and retained his lead after making his second pit stop on lap 31.

Andretti, running in second place, some five seconds adrift of the young Colombian, also made for the pits on lap 31. Fittipaldi stretched his fuel a lap farther again and, for a second time, the Brazilian emerged from the pit lane with the advantage. Only on this occasion, he was able to maintain his position.

'Unfortunately, he's a good learner,' said Andretti, 'and he did a better job on his out-lap on cold tires, and I wasn't able to get a run on him.'

Once into second place, Fittipaldi began to edge closer to Montoya, who continued to be afflicted by the gearbox difficulty and was forced to make all his gear changes – upshifts and downshifts – while the engine was under load on the exits from the corners. It was a remarkable performance by the youngster, who maintained his lead through his final pit stop on lap 46 and seemed to have the race in hand until the gearbox failed completely just three laps later.

'The car was brilliant,' he confessed after limping back to the pits. 'Without that [problem] we'd have beaten them by ages.'

Montoya's demise with just seven laps remaining handed the race on a silver platter to Fittipaldi, who withstood the pressure from Andretti and

ROAD AMERICA SNIPPETS

• A few days before the race at Road America, **LOLA CARS INTERNATIONAL** hosted a reception at the grand opening of its brand-new Technical Center, incorporating a state-of-the-art 50-percent wind tunnel and a seven-post dynamic test rig, in Huntingdon, England.

• **PATRICK CARPENTIER** emerged unscathed from a massive accident at Turn One on Friday, when he locked the rear brakes of his Player's Mercedes/Reynard, slid sideways into the gravel trap, then rolled five times before coming to rest against the tire barrier. 'There's not much you can do when you're sideways at 200 mph,' reported the French-Canadian. 'The only thing I saw after that was sky...then gravel...sky...gravel...'

• **MARK BLUNDELL** *(below)* fully intended to drive the PacWest team's Motorola Mercedes/Reynard after missing the previous five races while recuperating from a teardrop flexion compression (burst fracture) of his seventh cervical vertebra. He had been cleared to

Jamie Squire/Allsport

drive by his doctors earlier in the week and tested briefly on the Putnam Park road course near Indianapolis on Wednesday. Everything was going to plan. Upon further examination by CART Chief Orthopedic Consultant Dr. Terry Trammell, however, Blundell was advised to delay his return until Detroit. 'Obviously, it's very frustrating, but I've got to be realistic,' said Blundell. 'It's not a question of me not doing the next few Champ Car races; it's a question of the next 50 years of my life.'

• **MICHEL JOURDAIN JR.** finally put a sequence of misfortunes behind him to enjoy a trouble-free race in Payton/Coyne Racing's Herdez/ Viva Mexico Ford/ Lola. At 22, still the youngest driver in the CART arena, Jourdain *(right)* finished in a career-high seventh place.

Jon Ferrey/Allsport

• Christian Fittipaldi's maiden victory represented the first win for **SWIFT** on a road course – and, amazingly, the first for an American-built Champ Car since Johnny Rutherford took the checkered flag at Mid-Ohio on July 13, 1980, aboard Jim Hall's Chaparral 2K.

• With Jimmy Vasser sliding into a gravel trap while attempting to pass Bryan Herta on lap 16, and teammate Juan Montoya succumbing to gearbox woes, it was the first time neither **TARGET/CHIP GANASSI** car had reached the finish since Toronto in '95.

• CART rookie **MEMO GIDLEY** was a sensational fourth fastest in the provisional qualifying session. Sadly, he was prevented from maintaining his position on Saturday by persistent engine problems with Walker Racing's Alpine Honda/Reynard. Similar woes brought about his retirement after only three laps of the race.

FEDEX CHAMPIONSHIP SERIES • ROUND 10
TEXACO/HAVOLINE 200

ROAD AMERICA,
ELKHART LAKE, WISCONSIN

JULY 11, 55 laps – 222.64 miles

Place	Driver (Nat.)	No.	Team Sponsors Engine/Car	Tires	Q Speed	Q Time	Q Pos.	Laps	Time/Status	Ave. (mph)	Pts.
1	Christian Fittipaldi (BR)	11	Newman/Haas Big Kmart Ford Cosworth/Swift 010.c	FS	144.692	1m 40.716s	4	55	1h 37m 00.799s	137.697	20
2	Michael Andretti (USA)	6	Newman/Haas Kmart/Texaco Havoline Ford Cosworth/Swift 010.c	FS	145.428	1m 40.206s	1	55	1h 37m 01.859s	137.671	17
3	Adrian Fernandez (MEX)	40	Patrick Racing Tecate/Quaker State Ford Cosworth/Reynard 99I	FS	144.452	1m 40.883s	5	55	1h 37m 18.226s	137.286	14
4	Greg Moore (CDN)	99	Forsythe Racing Player's/Indeck Mercedes/Reynard 99I	FS	144.209	1m 41.053s	8	55	1h 37m 20.196s	137.239	12
5	Max Papis (I)	7	Team Rahal Miller Lite Ford Cosworth/Reynard 99I	FS	143.005	1m 41.904s	14	55	1h 37m 35.292s	136.885	10
6	Tony Kanaan (BR)	44	McDonald's Championship Racing Honda/Reynard 99I	FS	143.388	1m 41.632s	10	55	1h 37m 59.233s	136.328	8
7	Michel Jourdain Jr. (MEX)	19	Payton/Coyne Herdez/Viva Mexico Ford Cosworth/Lola T97/00	FS	142.428	1m 42.317s	18	54	Running		6
8	Robby Gordon (USA)	22	Team Gordon Panasonic/Menards Toyota/Swift 010.c	FS	140.592	1m 43.653s	23	54	Running		5
9	Al Unser Jr. (USA)	2	Marlboro Team Penske Mercedes/Lola B99/00	GY	142.059	1m 42.583s	19	54	Running		4
10	Richie Hearn (USA)	10	Della Penna Motorsports Budweiser Toyota/Reynard 99I	FS	140.288	1m 43.878s	24	54	Running		3
11	Paul Tracy (CDN)	26	Team KOOL Green Honda/Reynard 99I	FS	143.861	1m 41.298s	9	54	Running		2
12	Mauricio Gugelmin (BR)	17	PacWest Racing Group Hollywood Mercedes/Reynard 99I	FS	143.118	1m 41.824s	13	54	Running		1
13	*Juan Montoya (COL)	4	Target/Chip Ganassi Racing Honda/Reynard 99I	FS	145.227	1m 40.345s	2	49	Transmission		1
14	Gil de Ferran (BR)	5	Walker Racing Valvoline/Cummins Honda/Reynard 99I	GY	144.921	1m 40.557s	3	41	Engine		
15	Bryan Herta (USA)	8	Team Rahal Shell Ford Cosworth/Reynard 99I	FS	143.353	1m 41.657s	12	41	Steering		
16	Helio Castro-Neves (BR)	9	Hogan Racing Hogan Motor Leasing Mercedes/Lola B99/00	FS	141.829	1m 42.749s	20	38	Transmission		
17	PJ Jones (USA)	20	Patrick Racing Visteon Ford Cosworth/Swift 010.c	FS	141.756	1m 42.802s	21	36	Accident		
18	Dario Franchitti (GB)	27	Team KOOL Green Honda/Reynard 99I	FS	144.345	1m 40.958s	7	34	Turbo		
19	Roberto Moreno (BR)	18	PacWest Racing Group Motorola Mercedes/Reynard 99I	FS	142.544	1m 42.234s	16	31	Engine		
20	Gualter Salles (BR)	36	All American Racers Denso/Castrol Toyota/Eagle 997	GY	139.369	1m 44.563s	25	31	Engine		
21	*Cristiano da Matta (BR)	25	Arciero-Wells Racing MCI WorldCom Toyota/Reynard 99I	FS	143.357	1m 41.654s	11	19	Transmission		
22	Patrick Carpentier (CDN)	33	Forsythe Racing Player's/Indeck Mercedes/Reynard 99I	FS	142.505	1m 42.262s	17	17	Engine		
23	Jimmy Vasser (USA)	12	Target/Chip Ganassi Racing Honda/Reynard 99I	FS	144.367	1m 40.943s	6	15	Accident		
24	*Luiz Garcia Jr. (BR)	71	Payton/Coyne Tang Ford Cosworth/Reynard 97I	FS	137.211	1m 46.207s	26	13	Engine		
25	Scott Pruett (USA)	24	Arciero-Wells Racing Pioneer Toyota/Reynard 99I	FS	141.471	1m 43.009s	22	6	Engine		
26	*Memo Gidley (USA)	15	Walker Racing Alpine Honda/Reynard 98I	GY	142.904	1m 41.976s	15	3	Engine		

*denotes rookie driver

Caution flags: None.

Lap leaders: Juan Montoya, 1–31 (31 laps); Greg Moore, 32–33 (2 laps); Montoya, 34–48 (15 laps); Christian Fittipaldi, 49–55 (7 laps).
Totals: Montoya, 46 laps; Fittipaldi, 7 laps; Moore, 2 laps.

Fastest race lap: Helio Castro-Neves, 1m 42.108s, 142.719 mph on lap 24.

Championship positions: 1 Montoya, 113; **2** Andretti, 95; **3** de Ferran, 87; **4** Franchitti, 85; **5** Fittipaldi, 82; **6** Moore, 81; **7** Fernandez, 79; **8** Tracy, 60; **9** Papis, 51; **10** Vasser & Kanaan, 34; **12** Herta, 31; **13** Jones & Carpenter, 28; **15** Moreno, 26; **16** Castro-Neves, 21; **17** Unser Jr. & da Matta, 16; **19** Gugelmin & Gordon, 14; **21** Hearn, 11; **22** Jourdain Jr., 6; **23** Blundell, 5; **24** Marques & Barron, 4; **26** Pruett, 3; **27** Gidley, 2.

OMEGA
OFFICIAL TIMEKEEPER OF CART

TORONTO

1 – FRANCHITTI   2 – TRACY   3 – FITTIPALDI

Intense first-corner action as pole-sitter Gil de Ferran leads Dario Franchitti. Behind, Christian Fittipaldi dives to the inside of teammate Michael Andretti, while Jimmy Vasser and Paul Tracy are wheel to wheel on the outside line.

Inset: Paul Tracy and Dario Franchitti celebrate the first-ever 1-2 finish for Team KOOL Green.

D ARIO Franchitti finally enjoyed a trouble-free race in the Molson Indy Toronto, winning handsomely at the third time of asking, after two years when victory appeared to be on the cards only to slip away through minor indiscretions. The 26-year-old Scot took control of proceedings with an opportunistic pass of pole-sitter Gil de Ferran partway around the opening lap and was never seriously threatened, leading all 95 laps in copybook fashion to become the eighth different winner in 11 FedEx Championship Series events.

'It's about time we finished a race here,' quipped a relieved Franchitti, after reclaiming second place in the PPG Cup standings. 'I've made it difficult for myself the last couple of years. Today, it was kind of myself against the track. The most eventful part of the race was the start. Somebody hit me – I think it was Christian [Fittipaldi] – but I was going to say thank you because it knocked me into the clear. Then I managed to get past Gil at Turn Three, and after that the car was awesome all the way.'

Paul Tracy ensured a perfect result for Team KOOL Green by finishing second, only 2.624 seconds behind Franchitti. The local favorite could not match the form of his teammate, but did his own championship chances a power of good with another mature drive, which put him in the points for the fifth consecutive time. 'It was Dario's day,' declared Tracy. '[But] to

come from sixth to second is exactly what we needed. It was a great day for our team. You couldn't ask for a better finish here at home in Canada.'

Effectively, the race was decided within the opening mile – but Franchitti almost didn't make it that far. After a clean getaway from the pole, de Ferran duly led the field into Turn One, while Franchitti was fortunate to survive a bump from a fast-starting Christian Fittipaldi.

'I had a run on Michael [Andretti] and I just went down the inside,' related Fittipaldi. 'I had to brake pretty deep and locked up the wheels, and then I started sliding. I just nudged [Franchitti] and I was lucky, and he was lucky also, and I managed to get away with it. It was close, but that's the way it always is at the start of the race.'

Jimmy Vasser took advantage of the slight kerfuffle to slip ahead of Fittipaldi's Big Kmart Ford/Swift coming out of the first corner. Then, as the field arrived at the braking area for Turn Three, at the end of Lakeshore Boulevard, Franchitti saw an opportunity to dive inside de Ferran. He didn't need a second invitation. The Scotsman emerged from the hairpin in the lead and immediately set about stamping his authority on the race, pulling away inexorably from the pursuing pack.

Also on the move in the early stages was Tony Kanaan in his McDonald's Honda/Reynard. Kanaan had ceded a

Two KOOL for Team Green

B ARRY Green enjoyed a banner day at the Molson Indy Toronto as Dario Franchitti and Paul Tracy provided his team with its first ever 1-2 finish in Champ Car competition. It was the perfect birthday present for the Australian-born team owner, who had turned 47 the day before.

If victory in the 1995 Indy 500 and the series title with Jacques Villeneuve rank most assuredly as the highlights of Green's career, the 1-2 sweep in Toronto represented an important milestone. It signaled the arrival of Team KOOL Green as a bona fide two-car outfit capable of taking on the might of Target/Chip Ganassi Racing on an equal basis.

For Franchitti, in particular, it was a weekend of firsts. The Scotsman chalked up his first win of '99 and finally broke his Toronto jinx of the previous two years. He also vaulted from fourth to second in the PPG Cup standings. Tracy, meanwhile, registered his fourth top-five finish in five races, the first time he had put together a streak of good results since joining Team KOOL Green at the end of '97, after having been fired by Roger Penske. The Las Vegas-resident Canadian had drawn all manner of criticism during a torrid '98 campaign, but had bounced back strongly, especially since the arrival of veteran race engineer/strategist Tony Cicale.

'It was a great team effort,' commented Tracy on Sunday afternoon. 'It's a great feeling for me because it's my wife Lisa's birthday, it's Barry Green's birthday, and besides, Dario and I finished one-two. This kind of finish is what we have been working toward for the last year and a half. Team KOOL Green – the team we have here – may be showing the Ganassi boys around the track pretty soon.'

Added Franchitti, 'It's always nice to win, and when your teammate is second, the entire team – both crews – can enjoy the moment. That's why we're here racing. That's why Team KOOL Green is a two-car team.'

Photos: Michael C. Brown

QUALIFYING

Gil de Ferran confirmed the recent strides made by Goodyear in its road-course tire development by securing his second pole position of the season. After climbing out of Derrick Walker's Valvoline/Cummins Honda/Reynard with ten minutes of final qualifying still remaining, de Ferran opted to watch the balance of the session from the pit wall, waiting for someone to usurp him from the top of the timing charts. No one did.

'It was a bit of a nail-biting session for us, really,' related the Brazilian. 'I went out and I thought to myself, "If it's going to happen, it's either now or not at all." I kind of threw caution to the wind and went for it, and the car responded very, very well.'

Dario Franchitti had started from the pole in each of his previous appearances at the popular Canadian venue, only for his race to end prematurely on both occasions – in 1998 within tantalizingly close reach of a maiden Champ Car victory. In view of this depressing trend, the Scotsman was content to settle for the outside front-row starting spot after setting the pace in practice on Friday. 'I'm looking for a change of luck tomorrow,' he declared.

Toronto has always been a happy hunting ground for Michael Andretti, but the American was disappointed to be only third on the grid after running into traffic on what he claimed were his fastest laps. 'Basically, I didn't get a clear lap the whole session when the tires were at their best,' complained Andretti. 'I had a real quick one that I know would have been [good enough for] the pole; there's no question in my mind. Through Turn One, for instance, I was already three-tenths up on my best.'

Jimmy Vasser was fourth quickest in the leading Target/Chip Ganassi Racing Honda/Reynard, while Tony Kanaan also showed well to line up seventh in his similar McDonald's car. Greg Moore was a distant tenth, 1.261 seconds off the pace, but nonetheless fastest of the Mercedes-Benz contingent, amply demonstrating the handicap of the tiny E3 unit's 'light switch' power delivery around the tortuous Exhibition Place street circuit.

Adrian Fernandez, on a brilliant charge, slides past Tony Kanaan in Turn One on lap 53.

Below right: Scott Pruett enjoyed his best run of the season to date, finishing a strong seventh.

position at the start to the Player's Mercedes/Reynard of Greg Moore, who had leapfrogged ahead of several cars to emerge in sixth place from tenth in the starting lineup. But before long, the Brazilian sophomore was filling the mirrors of Michael Andretti's Swift, which had made an uncharacteristically tardy departure from the second row. Kanaan passed Andretti for seventh in Turn One on lap four, before displacing Moore a handful of laps later at Turn Three.

Franchitti created a comfortable four-second cushion in the course of the first seven laps, then was content to settle into a rhythm and adjust his pace to that of his pursuers. The first brief interruption to his serene progress came on lap 12, when Andretti ploughed into the back of Moore under heavy braking at the end of Lakeshore Boulevard, prompting the first of five full-course cautions. Andretti was out of the race, suspension broken. Moore was able to resume a lap down, although yet another inauspicious appearance in his Canadian homeland continued with another spin in Turn Three (initiated by contact with Al Unser Jr.), before finally being curtailed by a blown engine on lap 67.

Franchitti motored into the distance once more at the restart, while Kanaan continued his bold charge, slicing inside Tracy at Turn One. The hometown boy returned the favor, however, with an equally incisive maneuver under braking for Turn Three a couple of laps later, and soon edged away. A little farther up the road, Vasser and Fittipaldi became engaged in a protracted battle for third place, which was resolved eventually in the Brazilian's favor when he exhibited a fine piece of precision driving to sneak inside the Target car – a matter of only inches from the Turn Three wall – on lap 25. 'Man, that was close!' exclaimed Fittipaldi afterward.

An incident between Richie Hearn and Cristiano da Matta in Turn One – the upshot of an ill-judged passing attempt by Hearn – enabled the frontrunners to make their first scheduled stops under caution on lap 31. Montoya, however, made life difficult for himself by running over an air hose in the adjacent McDonald's pit stall, incurring an automatic penalty that relegated him to the tail end of those on the lead lap.

The running order took on a novel complexion at this point, as a group of cars that had stopped under the earlier yellow, headed by Roberto Moreno's Motorola Mercedes/Reynard, remained out on the circuit. Franchitti retained

his lead, but now had Moreno acting as a buffer between himself and de Ferran, while Fittipaldi was stuck in sixth behind Mauricio Gugelmin and PJ Jones.

Montoya, meanwhile, embarked on a rapid march through the field, progressing as far as Max Papis' 11th-placed Miller Lite Ford/Reynard before encountering any delay. The championship leader spent the next dozen laps frantically looking for a way around the Italian, who was making full use of the track width in his efforts to keep the Target/Chip Ganassi Racing Honda/Reynard at bay. Montoya accused Papis of blocking over the radio, whereupon Chip Ganassi pleaded with the officials to assess a penalty. CART rules, however, dictate that a driver is allowed to make one move across the track in defense of his position. Weaving is deemed unacceptable. Papis, while driving 'defensively', did not appear to be contravening the rules, so the officials declined Ganassi's exhortation.

An increasingly frustrated Montoya finally lost a place to Michel Jourdain Jr., then collided with the Mexican while trying to redress the balance on lap 60. Both cars went out on the spot.

'Once we came out of the corner [Turn Three], I didn't see him on the left and we touched,' explained Montoya, whose weekend as a whole served as a timely reminder of his mortal status.

The ensuing full-course caution was somewhat ill-timed for chief interloper Moreno, who had just taken on a fresh complement of fuel and tires under green-flag conditions and now had to watch the leading contenders make their final stops under yellow. Nevertheless, the Brazilian was able to resume in fourth when the order settled down and held the position to the finish, thereby matching his best result of the year at Gateway.

'Our game was fuel strategy, and it was perfect today,' summed up a delighted Moreno.

The last bout of pit stops gave rise to another penalty. The offender this time was de Ferran who, in his haste to rejoin, had misjudged his wheel-spinning exit and clipped one of the tires in Fittipaldi's neighboring pit box. As with Montoya earlier, de Ferran was sent to the back of the pack. The Brazilian's misery was completed moments later when he spun on oil, deposited by Moore's detonated Mercedes engine, and came to a rest at Turn Three.

Kanaan's day had taken a turn for the worse, too, when he was forced to

Fernandez shows fire

UNLIKE, say, Juan Pablo Montoya, the name of Adrian Fernandez does not readily attract superlatives. But the underrated Mexican, whose maiden Champ Car victory came in harrowing circumstances at Toronto in '96 (when popular rookie Jeff Krosnoff and course worker Gary Avrin were killed in a freak accident), drove a truly sensational race to climb from 23rd to sixth in Pat Patrick's Tecate/Quaker State Ford Cosworth/Reynard.

Fernandez was third fastest in Saturday morning's free practice, but was hobbled by an engine problem early in the final qualifying session. The team elected to withdraw his Friday time and instead wheel out the backup car, an updated '97 Reynard. (In fact, it was the same chassis – 97I-010 – with which Scott Pruett had claimed the pole at Michigan Speedway in '97.) Unfortunately, a problem with the telemetry led Fernandez to run out of fuel after only three laps and meant that he did not post a representative time; hence his uncharacteristic starting position.

'It really is a shame,' said Fernandez. 'We made a huge improvement in the [primary car] this morning, and I think we had a top-five car for sure...maybe a pole car, but we'll never know.'

On Sunday, Fernandez began to charge from the outset. Remarkably, he was up to 13th inside the first dozen laps, before taking the opportunity to pit during the first caution. He resumed 19th and continued to make excellent progress, despite needing two more stops and losing time due to a problem in changing the right front wheel on his final visit to the pit lane.

'The car was very good at the beginning,' noted Fernandez, who passed 17 cars for position on a track where overtaking opportunities are at an acknowledged premium. 'I was making a lot of passes and gaining confidence all day. I was taking chances because I had nothing to lose. To drive the car from 23rd and finish sixth was a great accomplishment. It was a tough day, but a rewarding one.'

Photos: Michael C. Brown

Max Papis claimed his fifth top-five finish of the 1999 campaign and his second in a row.

Below: Sporting a fresh allegiance to Woody Woodpecker on the nose of his Walker Racing entry, Memo Gidley drove well to 12th, despite making an extra pit stop due to a puncture.

stand on the brakes while avoiding Papis shortly after the penultimate restart, badly flat-spotting his right front tire. The resulting vibration caused Kanaan to fall back to eighth place, behind Adrian Fernandez and Scott Pruett, before the tire suddenly let go in the last turn with only four laps remaining.

Otherwise, the closing stages were rather uneventful. The sellout crowd of more than 72,000 was denied a grandstand finish to match last year's barnstormer – Franchitti made sure of that. Tracy moved up to second by virtue of especially good service from his pit crew, followed by an opportunistic move past countryman Patrick Carpentier, whose Player's Mercedes/Reynard was running to a slightly different pit-stop strategy. Fittipaldi emerged in third and kept pace with

Tracy as the race drew toward its conclusion, but was unable to dent the Team KOOL Green formation.

Behind the stalwart Moreno, Papis overcame a lackluster qualifying effort to finish fifth for the second week running, while Fernandez produced perhaps the drive of the race as he hauled his '97 Ford/Reynard up to sixth place from 23rd on the grid.

The day, though, belonged to Franchitti. The Scotsman won a rousing reception from the appreciative Canadian crowd, despite upstaging Ontario native Tracy.

'It means a lot to win here,' said Franchitti. 'It's such a fantastic crowd because they give me so much support. To finally win a race in front of them is pretty awesome. A one-two finish, what more could you ask for?'

Alex Sabine/Jeremy Shaw

TORONTO SNIPPETS

• **SCOTT PRUETT** posted by far his most impressive performance since joining Arciero-Wells Racing at the conclusion of the '98 season, qualifying 11th in his Pioneer Toyota/Reynard – two places ahead of gifted young teammate Cristiano da Matta – and finishing a strong seventh.

• **DENNIS VITOLO** *(right)* received a last-minute call to drive the #71 Payton/Coyne entry, after regular pilot Luiz Garcia Jr. cried off only a day before the start of official practice!

• After **GREG MOORE** pulled off the track at the end of Lakeshore Boulevard, the official reason for the retirement of his Player's Mercedes/Reynard was listed as 'cooling system'. Coincidentally, course workers spent the next five laps of a full-course caution mopping up a huge oil slick in precisely the same location.

• Walker Racing Data Acquisition Engineer **CHUCK MATTHEWS** gave his crew a scare on Friday morning when he collapsed in the pit lane. Thankfully, after a thorough examination by the CART Safety Team, Matthews was diagnosed as suffering nothing worse than heat exhaustion.

Michael C. Brown

• Perry Bell, Goodyear's CART Operations Manager, was elated after seeing Gil de Ferran score Goodyear's second pole of the season – and first on a road or street circuit. 'The **GOODYEAR EAGLES** are definitely proving a force to be reckoned with,' declared Bell. 'Following our finish at Long Beach, we felt our tire was a little conservative, so we tested at Sebring to address that issue.' Clearly, the work had paid off.

• Road America winner **CHRISTIAN FITTIPALDI** proudly sported one of Wally Dallenbach's trademark cowboy hats in Toronto, his prize for becoming the seventh driver to win a race after being placed on probation by CART's Chief Steward. Fittipaldi posted another strong finish, vaulting to third in the points table.

• **JUAN MONTOYA** never really got to grips with the demanding Exhibition Place street circuit – or, more particularly, the constant surface changes between asphalt and concrete. 'It's a little frustrating for him,' declared Race Engineer Morris Nunn, 'because he loves to mash the gas. You should see the steering wheel motions [on the telemetry]! The other interesting thing is that [teammate] Jimmy [Vasser] is braking later on most of the corners. He's having a hard time coming to terms with that,' added Nunn with a broad grin.

FEDEX CHAMPIONSHIP SERIES • ROUND 11
MOLSON INDY TORONTO

EXHIBITION PLACE,
TORONTO, ONTARIO, CANADA

JULY 18, 95 laps – 166.725 miles

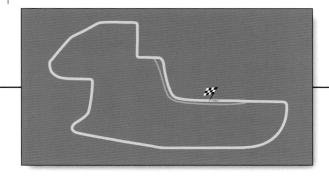

Place	Driver (Nat.)	No.	Team Sponsors Engine/Car	Tires	Q Speed	Q Time	Q Pos.	Laps	Time/Status	Ave. (mph)	Pts.
1	Dario Franchitti (GB)	27	Team KOOL Green Honda/Reynard 99I	FS	110.102	57.383s	2	95	1h 56m 27.550s	85.897	21
2	Paul Tracy (CDN)	26	Team KOOL Green Honda/Reynard 99I	FS	109.300	57.804s	6	95	1h 56m 30.174s	85.865	16
3	Christian Fittipaldi (BR)	11	Newman/Haas Big Kmart Ford Cosworth/Swift 010.c	FS	109.384	57.760s	5	95	1h 56m 34.537s	85.811	14
4	Roberto Moreno (BR)	18	PacWest Racing Group Motorola Mercedes/Reynard 99I	FS	107.550	58.745s	17	95	1h 56m 38.285s	85.765	12
5	Max Papis (I)	7	Team Rahal Miller Lite Ford Cosworth/Reynard 99I	FS	107.259	58.904s	18	95	1h 56m 43.030s	85.707	10
6	Adrian Fernandez (MEX)	40	Patrick Racing Tecate/Quaker State Ford Cosworth/Reynard 97I	FS	106.221	59.480s	23	95	1h 56m 50.453s	85.616	8
7	Scott Pruett (USA)	24	Arciero-Wells Racing Pioneer Toyota/Reynard 99I	FS	108.091	58.451s	11	95	1h 56m 51.806s	85.600	6
8	Jimmy Vasser (USA)	12	Target/Chip Ganassi Racing Honda/Reynard 99I	FS	109.520	57.688s	4	95	1h 57m 00.944s	85.489	5
9	Al Unser Jr. (USA)	2	Marlboro Team Penske Mercedes/Lola B99/00	GY	105.573	59.845s	25	95	1h 57m 02.659s	85.468	4
10	PJ Jones (USA)	20	Patrick Racing Visteon Ford Cosworth/Swift 010.c	FS	106.763	59.178s	20	95	1h 57m 03.565s	85.457	3
11	Patrick Carpentier (CDN)	33	Forsythe Racing Player's/Indeck Mercedes/Reynard 99I	FS	108.037	58.480s	12	95	1h 57m 04.028s	85.451	2
12	*Memo Gidley (USA)	15	Walker Racing Alpine Honda/Reynard 98I	GY	107.702	58.662s	15	95	1h 57m 09.661s	85.382	1
13	Robby Gordon (USA)	22	Team Gordon Panasonic/Menards Toyota/Swift 010.c	FS	106.584	59.277s	22	95	1h 57m 15.713s	85.309	
14	Mauricio Gugelmin (BR)	17	PacWest Racing Group Hollywood Mercedes/Reynard 99I	FS	107.579	58.729s	16	95	1h 57m 19.377s	85.265	
15	Bryan Herta (USA)	8	Team Rahal Shell Ford Cosworth/Reynard 99I	FS	108.333	58.320s	9	93	Running		
16	Richie Hearn (USA)	10	Della Penna Motorsports Budweiser Toyota/Reynard 99I	FS	106.653	59.239s	21	93	Running		
17	Tony Kanaan (BR)	44	McDonald's Championship Racing Honda/Reynard 99I	FS	109.042	57.941s	7	92	Accident		
18	Dennis Vitolo (USA)	71	Payton/Coyne Tang Ford Cosworth/Reynard 97I	FS	101.956	1m 01.968s	27	82	Transmission		
19	Gil de Ferran (BR)	5	Walker Racing Valvoline/Cummins Honda/Reynard 99I	GY	110.565	57.143s	1	71	Accident		1
20	Greg Moore (CDN)	99	Forsythe Racing Player's/Indeck Mercedes/Reynard 99I	FS	108.178	58.404s	10	66	Engine		
21	Michel Jourdain Jr. (MEX)	19	Payton/Coyne Herdez/Viva Mexico Ford Cosworth/Lola T97/00	FS	107.079	59.003s	19	59	Accident		
22	*Juan Montoya (COL)	4	Target/Chip Ganassi Racing Honda/Reynard 99I	FS	108.637	58.157s	8	59	Accident		
23	*Shigeaki Hattori (J)	16	Bettenhausen Motorsports Epson Mercedes/Reynard 98I	GY	103.050	1m 01.310s	26	56	Accident		
24	*Cristiano da Matta (BR)	25	Arciero-Wells Racing MCI WorldCom Toyota/Reynard 99I	FS	108.007	58.496s	13	29	Accident		
25	Gualter Salles (BR)	36	All American Racers Denso/Castrol Toyota/Eagle 997	GY	106.058	59.571s	24	25	Transmission		
26	Michael Andretti (USA)	6	Newman/Haas Kmart/Texaco Havoline Ford Cosworth/Swift 010.c	FS	109.594	57.649s	3	11	Accident		
27	Helio Castro-Neves (BR)	9	Hogan Racing Hogan Motor Leasing Mercedes/Lola B99/00	FS	107.937	58.534s	14	10	Transmission		

* denotes rookie driver

Caution flags: Laps 12–16, accident/Andretti & Moore; laps 30–34, accident/Hearn & da Matta; laps 37–39, spin/Moore; laps 60–66, accident/Montoya & Jourdain Jr.; laps 71–75, spin/de Ferran. **Total:** Five for 25 laps.

Lap leader: Dario Franchitti, 1–95 (95 laps). **Total:** Franchitti, 95 laps.

Fastest race lap: Dario Franchitti, 59.361s, 106.434 mph on lap 88.

Championship positions: 1 Montoya, 113; **2** Franchitti, 106; **3** Fittipaldi, 96; **4** Andretti, 95; **5** de Ferran, 88; **6** Fernandez, 87; **7** Moore, 81; **8** Tracy, 76; **9** Papis, 61; **10** Vasser, 39; **11** Moreno, 38; **12** Kanaan, 34; **13** Jones & Herta, 31; **15** Carpentier, 30; **16** Castro-Neves, 21; **17** Unser Jr., 20; **18** da Matta, 16; **19** Gugelmin & Gordon, 14; **21** Hearn, 11; **22** Pruett, 9; **23** Jourdain Jr., 6; **24** Blundell, 5; **25** Marques & Barron, 4; **27** Gidley, 3.

U.S. 500

FEDEX CHAMPIONSHIP SERIES • ROUND 12

Kanaan makes amends

TONY Kanaan's weekend at Michigan Speedway didn't start out too auspiciously, as an engine failure moments before the conclusion of practice on Friday afternoon pitched him (relatively lightly) into the wall in Turn Four. 'I almost saved it,' related Kanaan, with a chuckle, 'but not quite!'

A fresh engine was installed in the repaired car on Saturday, only for it to be plagued by a lack of oil pressure as well. Kanaan duly switched to the backup McDonald's Honda/Reynard for the remainder of the weekend. The 24-year-old Brazilian overcame the setbacks to qualify a respectable 11th. 'I think we took the best out of the car that we could,' he said. 'I was full throttle both laps. I don't think this car is as good as the primary, but we'll make it that way for tomorrow. It's going to be a long race, and I think we will have a consistent car.'

Sure enough, the 1997 PPG-Firestone Indy Lights champion (and '98 CART Rookie of the Year) was a contender throughout the 250-lap race, rising as high as third before losing a lap to the leaders due to an unscheduled pit stop to replace a damaged Gurney flap on lap 79. 'At the time, I thought, "Okay, there's still a long way to go, anything can happen,"' he related.

There was another problem, too. 'I lost my radio about lap ten. [The crew] could talk to me, but I couldn't hear them. They said that was a good thing,' he laughed.

After mounting a magnificent comeback to score his first Champ Car victory, Kanaan was justifiably elated. He was also relieved, especially after speaking to his mom, Miriam, at home in Brazil, by cell-phone while in Victory Circle. 'She says I always crash!,' said Kanaan, amid much hilarity in the ensuing press conference, referring to a call immediately after the previous weekend's race in Toronto. 'After the race [in Canada], I get a phone call: "You crash! Again!" I said it wasn't my fault. I said, "Hey, I had a tire blow, it wasn't my fault!"'

At Michigan, he more than made amends.

Kazuki Saito

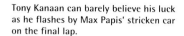

Tony Kanaan can barely believe his luck as he flashes by Max Papis' stricken car on the final lap.

Below: Juan Montoya and Michael Andretti duke it out for the lead in the early stages of the race, while their pursuers are content to remain in single-file formation.

QUALIFYING

The usual cast of characters found its way to the top of the speed charts during two days of official practice at Michigan Speedway. FedEx Championship Series points leader Juan Montoya emerged fastest on Friday, with a lap at 231.258 mph in Chip Ganassi's Target Honda/Reynard. Once again, the lack of any previous experience on a new type of race track – in this case, an unforgiving high-banked, two-mile oval – proved absolutely no handicap whatsoever.

Adrian Fernandez, a familiar front-runner on the superspeedways, upped the ante on Saturday morning, posting a scintillating best of 233.146 mph, and thus it was he who would anchor the traditional one-at-a-time qualifying session later in the day.

Speeds, as usual, were slightly slower than in practice, where drivers take full advantage of the massive draft provided by the Handford Device. Even so, both Montoya and Fernandez managed to exceed the 229-mph barrier – albeit not by enough to eclipse the earlier best of Jimmy Vasser, who secured his first pole of the season.

'I wasn't flat all the way around,' revealed Vasser, 'but sometimes that's not the quickest way around. We had the car a little free and I had to back out of it a little in Turn One and Two.'

Fernandez came within 0.023 second on his first flying lap, but any hope he had of snaring the pole was dashed when he encountered a touch too much push (understeer) in Turn One.

'I knew if I kept my foot flat, I was going to hit the wall, like I did last year in Fontana, and I didn't think it was worth it and decided to just bring it home,' related Fernandez with a wry smile.

Montoya shared row two with Michael Andretti in the Kmart/Texaco Havoline Ford/Swift. Scott Pruett was a remarkable fifth fastest in Arciero-Wells Racing's steadily improving Pioneer Toyota/Reynard.

'Today was a huge step forward for us,' said Pruett after securing the best starting position to date for Toyota. 'We've had a great car all weekend, and the guys on the crew pulled really hard to get the car ready for me today. They've all done an amazing job, and I'm really proud to be a part of this with them.'

MAX Papis was in complete control of the U.S. 500 Presented by Toyota. The likeable 29-year-old Italian had driven flawlessly and seemed set for a well-deserved maiden Champ Car victory until, cruelly, a miscalculation by Team Rahal saw his Miller Lite Ford Cosworth/Reynard run out of fuel midway around the very last lap.

Even then, the drama wasn't over. Tony Kanaan, who had driven equally impressively aboard Jerry Forsythe's McDonald's Honda/Reynard, momentarily – and instinctively – eased off the gas when he saw Papis slow abruptly on the entry to Turn Three. The hesitation almost cost the Brazilian his chance at a first victory. Juan Montoya was closing fast. Kanaan, however, quickly buried his right foot once more and crossed the finish line a scant 0.032 second in front.

'I didn't have much time to think about it, but I saw this red car getting bigger in my mirrors and I thought, "Hey, not today man!"' reflected Kanaan after winning at an average speed of 186.097 mph.

While Montoya had to be content with second, Paul Tracy gained the final podium position after squeezing ahead of Michael Andretti on the final turn. Dario Franchitti and Adrian Fernandez also were close together, leaving the unfortunate Papis to coast home a disconsolate seventh.

All seven had been in the thick of the battle since the opening stages of the 250-lap contest, which began with another demonstration of the effectiveness of the Handford Device. A positive side-effect of the low-downforce, high-drag rear wing (which was introduced in 1998 to cut the escalation in speed on the superspeedway ovals) ensures a strong 'draft' and some spectacular slipstreaming action. Sure enough, Montoya and Andretti, who qualified alongside each other on the second row of the grid, swept past front-row occupants Jimmy Vasser and Fernandez within the opening half mile and proceeded to trade positions with metronomic regularity throughout the first 20 laps.

'It was great, a lot of fun,' said Montoya. 'Usually when you pass someone, you pass someone, but here, 300 yards down the road, here we go, he passes you again and there's nothing you can do about it. You've got to be patient. It's very difficult to understand, but at the beginning of the race, you're fighting with people who won't be around at the end, and you don't believe all that effort is for nothing.'

Ultimately futile it may have been,

Photos: Michael C. Brown

FEDEX CHAMPIONSHIP SERIES • ROUND 12

Anti-clockwise from bottom left: **Paul Tracy**'s crew replenish his fuel; as a squirt of water dissipates any spilled fuel, Jimmy Vasser is given a hand out of his pit box; Michael Andretti receives fuel and fresh tires; Al Unser Jr. performs a burn-out to put some heat into his Goodyear rubber.

Papis sidelined by electronics glitch

A PRODUCTIVE test session for Team Rahal, in preparation for the U.S. 500, left Max Papis in a positive frame of mind. His confidence was not misplaced. Papis qualified a strong fifth in his Miller Lite/Harley-Davidson Ford Cosworth/Reynard, ran among the leaders from the start and then made his move to the front shortly after the first full-course caution.

Papis remained in control for most of the race, although his eventual misfortune of running out of fuel on the final lap could be traced to his final two pit stops, when the electronic dashboard suddenly froze. On the first occasion, under yellow, he was able to hit the reset button and continue, but crucial fuel consumption data had been lost. The next time it happened, though, was immediately after his final stop on lap 221.

'It was [under] green flag and I didn't want to try [the reset button] then,' said Papis. 'Maybe the engine would have died. So I didn't

know our fuel meter [readout], and neither did my guys [in the pits].'

The engineers, however, completed their calculations by hand and reckoned Papis had enough fuel to make it to the end. But he didn't, quite. 'I am devastated for Max,' said team owner Bobby Rahal. 'I have not seen anyone dominate here at Michigan like that in a long, long time. He had them covered, and everyone in the place knew it. Max had the race won today. We lost it for him.'

The contrasting fortunes of Papis and Kanaan could not have been more extreme. While Kanaan celebrated the joy of victory, poor Papis was left to ponder what might have been. To his enormous credit, the Italian remained upbeat: 'We did a great job today, and they know we can win. I am happy for Tony. He is a great guy and a good friend. I think we will get our chance to win again very soon. Today, God didn't want to give it to me. Next time, it's going to be even better.'

Michael C. Brown

but for the remarkably small crowd – estimated at 50,000 – it provided tremendous entertainment, especially with a host of other battles being waged throughout the 26-car field.

Fernandez and Vasser were content to run third and fourth, while Papis, Tracy, Kanaan, Franchitti and, surprisingly, the two Arciero-Wells Toyota/Reynards of Scott Pruett (who qualified a sensational fifth) and Cristiano da Matta were embroiled in a mighty scrap in their mirrors. Al Unser Jr., too, moved quickly up into contention, rising from 17th to tenth inside the first dozen laps in his Marlboro Mercedes/Penske. Alex Barron, making his debut for Marlboro Team Penske, also made good progress, following close behind his team leader.

Montoya was the first of the leaders to make a scheduled pit stop – on lap 35, while running second to Andretti. Tracy was the last man onto the pit road, on lap 38, after leading a couple of laps in his Team KOOL Green Honda/Reynard. Thus the status quo was restored, with Andretti still occupying the lead spot.

One by one, however, several contenders fell by the wayside. The ever unfortunate Helio Castro-Neves went out after 47 laps with electrical problems in Hogan Racing's Mercedes/Lola.

Gil de Ferran, who had struggled with the balance of his Valvoline/Cummins Honda/Reynard, lost control in Turn Two (shortly after going one lap down) and hit the wall on lap 60. During the ensuing first full-course caution of the day, 1998 U.S. 500 winner Greg Moore's Player's Mercedes/Reynard succumbed to transmission woes, while Mauricio Gugelmin's similar Hollywood car was retired due to overheating.

Bryan Herta (Shell Ford/Reynard) and Roberto Moreno (Motorola Mercedes/Reynard) both called it a day after struggling with extreme handling difficulties. Barron, who lost a lap due to an air jack failure at his first stop, was halted later by an engine failure.

On lap 77, misfortune hit Kanaan when his rear wing's Gurney flap worked loose. Two laps later, after receiving the black flag, the Brazilian was into the pits for repairs. He resumed a lap down in 15th.

Coincidentally, Papis was making his move to the front. He passed Andretti for second place on lap 80. Four laps later, he swept past Montoya to lead a FedEx Championship Series event for the first time in his three-year career. Not content with that, Papis soon began to edge clear of the pursuing pack. By lap 100, his advantage had grown to some 3.7 seconds,

which he maintained through his third scheduled pit stop on lap 106.

'The Miller Lite car was so good today,' declared Papis. 'We could pull away from the pack and lead. I could drive anywhere and the car was fantastic.' Sure enough, running what was for him a comfortable pace, at around 223/224 mph, Papis extended his lead to more than ten seconds before the caution flags flew for the second time on lap 136. PJ Jones, a couple of laps off the pace in the Visteon Ford/Swift, had hit the wall in Turn Two. Andretti grasped the lead during the ensuing round of pit stops, but Papis soon reasserted himself and, following a brief tussle with Tracy, he began to edge clear once more.

He did so again after the final caution of the day, on lap 184 when Pruett suffered an identical accident to de Ferran and Jones by understeering into the wall in Turn Two. Thankfully, Pruett also emerged unscathed from his broken Pioneer Toyota/Reynard.

The caution came at the perfect moment for Kanaan and Unser who, like the Brazilian, had lost a lap after making an unscheduled pit stop. Both were in need of service when Pruett hit the wall. All of the leaders had visited the pit lane immediately prior to the caution, thereby enabling Kanaan and

Unser to regain the lead lap. Then they were able to make their own pit stops and rejoin at the back of the pack for the restart, which came on lap 194.

For Unser, sadly, it was a moot point. Ten laps later, his race was over, engine broken.

'We had a good run going today,' recounted Unser. 'The great thing about a 500-mile race is you can work with the car all day and get ready for the stretch run. It's really a shame we lost power, because the Marlboro car was really hooked up today.'

Papis, meanwhile, was untroubled at the front of the field. There were myriad changes of position among his pursuers – particularly between Andretti and Franchitti, who exchanged places regularly – but no one could hold a candle to the Italian. He maintained an advantage of 3.8 seconds when he pulled onto the pit lane for his final routine service on lap 221.

Quite suddenly, however, came a challenge from an unlikely source. Kanaan had charged hard after regaining the lead lap, progressing from ninth on lap 195 to fifth before the final round of pit stops. He continued to set some fast laps, enjoying six laps in the lead, before making his own final fuel stop on lap 228. That spurt enabled him to resume in second, and for the next ten laps he edged ever closer to the race leader.

The gap dwindled to 1.1 seconds on lap 239, at which point Kanaan was being implored by his crew to turn up the wick, richen the fuel mixture and continue to chase down the leader. But Kanaan's radio hadn't been functioning properly since the early stages. He could hear Steve Horne, but was unable to communicate any response, other than by hand signals as he sped past the pits at better than 230 mph. In the heat of battle, Kanaan mistook the message and instead reasoned that, with the end drawing near, he should run a *leaner* mixture to ensure better fuel consumption.

Papis was unaware of Kanaan's predicament. And with the pressure eased, he was able to stretch his lead again to more than three seconds. Then came that fateful final half lap.

'I feel sorry for Max,' said Kanaan graciously, 'but that's the way races are. I don't think many people were feeling sorry for me in Long Beach, when I crashed [after leading from the pole]. But I do feel sorry. He was in control of the race. I was pretty happy with second place, coming from a lap down. But today wasn't Max's day; it was my day.'

Jeremy Shaw

MICHIGAN SNIPPETS

• **JIMMY VASSER** boasted new Superman colors *(below)* on Chip Ganassi's Target Honda/Reynard, courtesy of an arrangement concluded by Action Performance, DC Comics and Warner Bros. Consumer Products. The '96 PPG Cup champion qualified on pole and was in contention to win but for a miscue during what should have been his final pit stop. He was obliged to make one more pit visit and eventually finished a lap down in ninth.

• Following an impressive test carried out at Michigan Speedway by Alex Barron, **MARLBORO TEAM PENSKE** reverted to its own Penske PC27B chassis. Both Barron, who made an impressive debut for the team, and Al Unser Jr. ran strongly until felled by mechanical woes.

• John Cummiskey, who spent ten years with Marlboro Team Penske before leaving after the recent race at Cleveland, resurfaced at Michigan as Chief Mechanic for Hogan Racing. Among other **PERSONNEL MOVES**, Brad Filbey, who was Hiro Matsushita's Chief Mechanic at Arciero-Wells Racing in '97 and who subsequently worked with Toyota Racing Development, had joined Team Gordon as Crew Chief.

Michael C. Brown

• PacWest Racing Group's **100TH CHAMP CAR RACE** did not go according to plan. Bruce McCaw's team had assembled an enviable record in previous 500-mile races, but neither Mauricio Gugelmin (who, coincidentally, also was making his 100th start) nor Roberto Moreno made it to the halfway mark.

• Three **TOYOTA-POWERED CARS** ran among the top dozen for much of the race, although none was around at the finish line. Scott Pruett crashed and Arciero-Wells teammate Cristiano da Matta succumbed to engine failure. Richie Hearn, meanwhile, salvaged one PPG Cup point for being classified 12th with John Della Penna's Budweiser entry, despite dropping out due to electrical problems in the closing stages.

• A spectacular *Detroit News* 100 PPG-Dayton Indy Lights race saw Austrian **PHILIPP PETER** edge Dorricott-Mears Racing teammate Casey Mears to the finish line by just 0.002 second – or approximately six inches. It was the closest finish in CART history.

U.S. 500
PRESENTED BY TOYOTA

MICHIGAN SPEEDWAY,
BROOKLYN, MICHIGAN

JULY 25, 250 laps – 500 miles

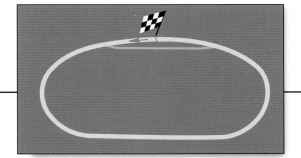

Place	Driver (Nat.)	No.	Team Sponsors Engine/Car	Tires	Q Speed	Q Time	Q Pos.	Laps	Time/Status	Ave. (mph)	Pts.
1	Tony Kanaan (BR)	44	McDonald's Championship Racing Honda/Reynard 99I	FS	227.029	31.714s	11	250	2h 41m 12.362s	186.097	20
2	*Juan Montoya (COL)	4	Target/Chip Ganassi Racing Honda/Reynard 99I	FS	229.321	31.397s	3	250	2h 41m 12.394s	186.097	16
3	Paul Tracy (CDN)	26	Team KOOL Green Honda/Reynard 99I	FS	227.790	31.608s	8	250	2h 41m 20.815s	185.935	14
4	Michael Andretti (USA)	6	Newman/Haas Kmart/Texaco Havoline Ford Cosworth/Swift 010.c	FS	229.168	31.418s	4	250	2h 41m 20.868s	185.934	12
5	Dario Franchitti (GB)	27	Team KOOL Green Honda/Reynard 99I	FS	227.790	31.608s	9	250	2h 41m 21.499s	185.922	10
6	Adrian Fernandez (MEX)	40	Patrick Racing Tecate/Quaker State Ford Cosworth/Reynard 99I	FS	229.438	31.381s	2	250	2h 41m 21.883s	185.914	8
7	Max Papis (I)	7	Team Rahal Miller Lite Ford Cosworth/Reynard 99I	FS	228.231	31.547s	6	250	2h 41m 22.705s	185.898	7
8	Christian Fittipaldi (BR)	11	Newman/Haas Big Kmart Ford Cosworth/Swift 010.c	FS	225.996	31.859s	16	250	2h 41m 27.772s	185.801	5
9	Jimmy Vasser (USA)	12	Target/Chip Ganassi Racing Honda/Reynard 99I	FS	229.606	31.358s	1	249	Running		5
10	Patrick Carpentier (CDN)	33	Forsythe Racing Player's/Indeck Mercedes/Reynard 99I	FS	226.922	31.729s	12	248	Running		3
11	Dennis Vitolo (USA)	34	Payton/Coyne CQ-Nicoderm Ford Cosworth/Reynard 98I	FS	221.682	32.479s	23	232	Running		2
12	Richie Hearn (USA)	10	Della Penna Motorsports Budweiser Toyota/Reynard 99I	FS	223.748	32.179s	20	207	Electrical		1
13	Al Unser Jr. (USA)	2	Marlboro Team Penske Mercedes/Penske PC27B	GY	225.854	31.879s	17	206	Engine		
14	Scott Pruett (USA)	24	Arciero-Wells Racing Pioneer Toyota/Reynard 99I	FS	228.593	31.497s	5	183	Accident		
15	Gualter Salles (BR)	36	All American Racers Denso/Castrol Toyota/Eagle 997	GY	221.076	32.568s	24	146	Engine		
16	PJ Jones (USA)	20	Patrick Racing Visteon Ford Cosworth/Swift 010.c	FS	222.195	32.404s	22	132	Accident		
17	*Cristiano da Matta (BR)	25	Arciero-Wells Racing MCI WorldCom Toyota/Reynard 99I	FS	227.740	31.615s	10	126	Electrical		
18	Alex Barron (USA)	3	Marlboro Team Penske Mercedes/Penske PC27B	GY	225.275	31.961s	18	120	Engine		
19	Roberto Moreno (BR)	18	PacWest Racing Group Motorola Mercedes/Reynard 99I	FS	226.693	31.761s	13	113	Handling		
20	Bryan Herta (USA)	8	Team Rahal Shell Ford Cosworth/Reynard 99I	FS	227.834	31.602s	7	92	Suspension		
21	Michel Jourdain Jr. (MEX)	19	Payton/Coyne Herdez/Viva Mexico Ford Cosworth/Lola T97/00	FS	no speed	no time	26	80	Driveshaft		
22	Mauricio Gugelmin (BR)	17	PacWest Racing Group Hollywood Mercedes/Reynard 99I	FS	226.209	31.829s	14	64	Overheating		
23	Greg Moore (CDN)	99	Forsythe Racing Player's/Indeck Mercedes/Reynard 99I	FS	223.575	32.204s	21	63	Transmission		
24	Gil de Ferran (BR)	5	Walker Racing Valvoline/Cummins Honda/Reynard 99I	GY	226.202	31.830s	15	59	Accident		
25	Helio Castro-Neves (BR)	9	Hogan Racing Hogan Motor Leasing Mercedes/Lola B99/00	FS	224.916	32.012s	19	47	Electrical		
26	Robby Gordon (USA)	22	Team Gordon Panasonic/Menards Toyota/Swift 010.c	FS	220.089	32.714s	25	33	Handling		

* denotes rookie driver

Caution flags: Lap 1, yellow start; laps 60–70, accident/de Ferran; laps 136–143, accident/Jones; laps 184–192, accident/Pruett. **Total:** Four for 29 laps.

Lap leaders: Jimmy Vasser, 1 (1 lap); Juan Montoya, 2–7 (6 laps); Michael Andretti, 8 (1 lap); Montoya, 9–18 (10 laps); Andretti, 19–36 (18 laps); Paul Tracy, 37–38 (2 laps); Andretti, 39–70 (32 laps); Montoya, 71–72 (2 laps); Andretti, 73 (1 lap); Montoya, 74 (1 lap); Andretti, 75 (1 lap); Montoya, 76–83 (8 laps); Max Papis, 84–105 (22 laps); Andretti, 106–107 (2 laps); Papis, 108–139 (32 laps); Andretti, 140–144 (5 laps); Papis, 145–147 (3 laps); Dario Franchitti, 148 (1 lap); Papis, 149–151 (3 laps); Franchitti, 152 (1 lap); Andretti, 153 (1 lap); Papis, 154–177 (24 laps); Franchitti, 178 (1 lap); Andretti, 179–182 (4 laps); Papis, 183–220 (38 laps); Montoya, 221 (1 lap); Franchitti, 222 (1 lap); Tony Kanaan, 223–228 (6 laps); Papis, 229–249 (21 laps); Kanaan, 250 (1 lap). **Totals:** Papis, 143 laps; Andretti, 65 laps; Montoya, 28 laps; Kanaan, 7 laps; Franchitti, 4 laps; Tracy, 2 laps; Vasser, 1 lap.

Fastest race lap: Jimmy Vasser, 31.778s, 226.572 mph on lap 236.

Championship positions: 1 Montoya, 129; 2 Franchitti, 116; 3 Andretti, 107; 4 Fittipaldi, 101; 5 Fernandez, 95; 6 Tracy, 90; 7 de Ferran, 88; 8 Moore, 81; 9 Papis, 68; 10 Kanaan, 54; 11 Vasser, 44; 12 Moreno, 38; 13 Carpentier, 33; 14 Jones & Herta, 31; 16 Castro-Neves, 21; 17 Unser Jr., 20; 18 da Matta, 16; 19 Gugelmin & Gordon, 14; 21 Hearn, 12; 22 Pruett, 9; 23 Jourdain Jr., 6; 24 Blundell, 5; 25 Marques & Barron, 4; 27 Gidley, 3; 28 Vitolo, 2.

OMEGA
OFFICIAL TIMEKEEPER OF CART

DETROIT

1 – FRANCHITTI   2 – TRACY   3 – MOORE

Dario Franchitti uses every inch of the difficult Detroit street course on his way to victory.

Below left: The impassive Scotsman contemplates a reprieve for his hopes of lifting the PPG Cup trophy.

Below middle: Paul Tracy relives the race with wife Lisa.

Below: Tony Kanaan overcame a minor pit lane miscue to salvage a top-six finish.

TEAM KOOL Green earned its second 1-2 finish in three races when Dario Franchitti led Paul Tracy to the checkered flag in a caution-plagued Tenneco Automotive Grand Prix of Detroit. Unlike the Molson Indy Toronto, however, where Franchitti was in complete control, this time he had to rely on the misfortune of erstwhile FedEx Championship Series leader Juan Montoya, who took the pole and led convincingly until lap 44, when his team made a crucial error.

Team owner Ganassi, responsible for relaying the strategic decisions to the young Colombian, initially instructed Montoya not to make a pit stop when the double yellow flags were displayed to warn of a stalled car out on the course. It was the wrong call. By the time the team realized its error, Montoya was past the pit entrance. And all the other contenders were making their way onto the pit lane.

Rather than make a pit stop next time around, which would have relegated Montoya to the back of the pack, a new plan was quickly formulated. It involved running flat out at the restart in the hope of building enough of a lead to enable the Colombian to make his final pit stop and still salvage a good result. The ploy might have worked. Montoya rejoined in eighth, with plenty of time remaining, only to be involved in a couple of incidents, the second of which saw his Target Honda/Reynard parked heavily against the wall.

Thus did Franchitti take the checkered flag. Sadly, however, the anticipated duel between Franchitti and Tracy never materialized, as the race finished – under yellow – four laps shy of the scheduled 75-lap distance in accordance with CART's two-hour rule, which applies to all road- and street-course events. It was an unsatisfactory conclusion.

'I told the guys on the radio it was a pretty ugly way to win a race, but we'll take it any way we can,' concluded Franchitti, who had been in full fuel-conservation mode following his earlier-than-anticipated final pit stop. 'We saved enough fuel that we'd be able to run full-rich the last six laps to defend ourselves, but as matters turned out, we didn't need to because the race ended on a yellow. It's a nice feeling to know nobody can pass you, but I don't much like to take checkered flags at 20 mph.'

Two hours earlier, Montoya made full use of his fifth pole of the season by jumping into the lead at the start. Fellow front-row qualifier Tracy followed dutifully in second, while Franchitti snuck ahead of Gil de Ferran's Valvoline/Cummins Honda/Reynard at the first corner. Tony Kanaan got away fast, too, slipping past Roberto Moreno

QUALIFYING

The Raceway on Belle Isle is a temporary circuit with omnipresent cement walls and a broad spectrum of turns that provide a stern test for the drivers. Perhaps it should have come as no surprise, therefore, to see the name of Juan Montoya atop the grid sheet come Saturday afternoon.

Target/Chip Ganassi Racing sent its young charger out in each of his two Target Honda/Reynards on Friday morning, intent on evaluating two slightly different setups. Montoya preferred the feel of his backup car, whereupon Simon Hodgson's crew routinely transferred the spring/shock settings to his primary machine in time for qualifying. Montoya posted the second fastest time on Friday afternoon, just 0.093 second adrift of the similar Firestone-shod KOOL Honda/Reynard of Paul Tracy. Then he turned the tables on Saturday to secure his fifth pole of the season. It was a spectacular lap, the Colombian rookie clearly on the ragged edge and even sending up a shower of magnesium sparks as his left rear wheel snagged the wall on the exit of Turn 13 on his fastest lap.

Tracy confessed to not making best use of his second set of tires in the final session. Under the circumstances, he was content to qualify on the front row.

'When the tires were fresh, I really pushed hard to get through [Turns] One and Two really well, and then I made mistakes on three consecutive laps and that pretty much used up that set of tires,' he declared. 'The car was better today. I just didn't catch the tires when I had to.'

Gil de Ferran was third fastest – the only Goodyear representative among the top 15 – followed by Dario Franchitti, who rebounded well from a calamitous Friday qualifying session, during which he crashed his primary car, then suffered a fuel pump failure in his backup KOOL Honda/Reynard. Tony Kanaan was sixth for the McDonald's team, with only Roberto Moreno standing in the way of a Honda/Reynard clean sweep of the top five positions on the starting grid. Moreno's performance was especially meritorious, given the fact that he was only invited to drive Newman/Haas Racing's #11 Big Kmart Ford Cosworth/Swift a couple of days before the race.

Jimmy Vasser rejoins in exuberant style following a routine pit stop.

Below left: Greg Moore and Jan Magnussen (in car) found the Turn 13 wall in practice.

Kazuki Saito

(this time at the wheel of Newman/Haas Racing's Big Kmart Ford/Swift, following an injury sustained by Christian Fittipaldi in testing) at the first turn and promptly executing a brave outside-line maneuver to displace de Ferran into Turn Three. A little farther back, there was disaster for Max Papis, whose Miller Lite Ford/Reynard was nerfed into the tire wall at Turn One, following inadvertent contact with Patrick Carpentier.

After three laps behind the PPG pace car, Montoya underlined his superiority by rapidly easing away from Tracy, who fought off a determined challenge from teammate Franchitti at the restart. The margin between first and second increased by a half-second per lap for the first five laps, then by as much as a second each circuit as Montoya stamped his authority on the proceedings.

On lap 12, having tired of being held up by his teammate, Franchitti made a move to the inside under braking for Turn Three. Tracy wisely offered no resistance.

'I had to let Dario go because I was struggling with my tires,' related the Canadian. 'I thought we'd get him later on in the race.'

Montoya continued to ease away from Franchitti, but not nearly so quickly. By lap 24, when the pace car emerged following a scrape in Turn Three between Jan Magnussen (who had been installed in Pat Patrick's Visteon Ford/Swift in place of PJ Jones) and Robby Gordon, the lead stood at 9.3 seconds. The full-course caution negated that advantage, of course, but Montoya maintained his lead after the first round of pit stops. Franchitti and Tracy still followed, while Greg Moore vaulted from eighth to fourth by virtue of excellent work in the pits by the Player's/Forsythe team, led by Crew Chief Chris Schofield.

The race was restarted briefly on lap 28, whereupon Carpentier and Mauricio Gugelmin tangled under braking for Turn Three to ensure another appearance by the pace car. The caution was extended once more when de Ferran made an embarrassing and totally uncharacteristic error by spinning into the wall while running in fifth behind the pace car.

'It was completely my fault,' admitted the Brazilian. 'I must apologize to the Walker Racing team. I was trying to get the tires as warm as I could and I just lost it.'

The mishap elevated Kanaan (who, uncharacteristically for the Drive-Thru crew, had lost a couple of positions during the pit stops) to fifth, followed

Trading places

THE complexion of the FedEx Championship Series changed radically during the two weeks that separated races held less than 80 miles apart at Michigan Speedway and the Raceway on Belle Isle. Firstly, Christian Fittipaldi, who was placed fourth in points after the U.S. 500, crashed while testing at Gateway International Raceway on the Monday prior to the Tenneco Automotive Grand Prix of Detroit. Knocked unconscious for a few minutes, Fittipaldi was expected to miss only one race. However, subsequent tests showed that he had suffered a subdural hematoma (blood clot) and he was ruled out for six to eight weeks.

Next came Friday morning's opening practice at Detroit, where Adrian Fernandez, fifth in the points table, crashed in Turn Two and suffered a fracture to the radius bone in his right arm. He underwent surgery at Methodist Hospital in Indianapolis on Friday evening and would miss a total of three races. The injuries to Fittipaldi and Fernandez cost each a legitimate shot at winning the coveted PPG Cup.

While Patrick Racing opted not to replace Fernandez for the remainder of the Detroit weekend, Newman/Haas Racing asked Roberto Moreno – who, ironically, had completed his duties as substitute for Mark Blundell at the U.S. 500 – to pilot Fittipaldi's Big Kmart Ford/Swift during his Brazilian countryman's recuperation.

Moreno further enhanced his reputation as Champ Car racing's 'Super Sub' by promptly out-qualifying teammate Michael Andretti. He lost three positions during the first round of pit stops, but continued to run strongly in sixth until being punted off by Juan Montoya in the closing stages. Moreno lost a lap and finished an unrepresentative 14th.

Blundell *(above, displaying Motorola's new Digital DNA livery)*, meanwhile, saw his first checkered flag – indeed his first racing flags of any kind – in 11 weeks when he returned to action aboard PacWest Racing's Motorola Mercedes/Reynard. Although a worthy ninth fastest in provisional qualifying, he fell to 16th on the grid. A puncture in the opening laps dropped him to the back of the field, and he spent the rest of the day clawing his way back to finish tenth, turning the sixth-fastest lap in the process.

by Michael Andretti (Kmart/Texaco Havoline Ford/Swift) and Jimmy Vasser, who had started way back in 12th with the second Target Honda/Reynard. Moreno lay ninth after also losing ground during his first pit stop.

Again, Montoya romped clear at the restart, but only for another eight laps until the yellows waved once more after a promising run by Memo Gidley in Dale Coyne's Herdez Ford/Lola ended with gearbox failure (only one lap after teammate Michel Jourdain Jr. succumbed to similar woes). Then came the miscue that cost him an almost certain victory.

When the race was restarted, on lap 47, Montoya remained at the head of the field on a partial load of fuel. Everyone else had topped off their supply of methanol and was good to go the distance. Ganassi, in contact over the radio, told Montoya not to worry. Sure enough, the young Colombian rocketed away from his pursuers at a prodigious rate. In just 12 laps, the lead over a closely matched Franchitti, Tracy and Moore had increased to more than 15 seconds. It wasn't enough for Montoya to hold onto the lead after making his second and final stop for fuel, but he rejoined in eighth. All was not yet lost.

In his haste to make up ground, however, Montoya made contact with

Moreno in Turn Three while attempting to wrest sixth place on lap 63. Both cars spun, and Moreno lost a lap before he could rejoin.

'I never even saw Montoya coming,' said the disgruntled Brazilian. 'I was way ahead of him going into the corner. There was no way he was going to pass me there without getting a better run on me.'

After yet another brief caution, Montoya, who had lost merely one position, snuck past Helio Castro-Neves at the ensuing restart. But he was prevented from making any more progress by another full-course caution after fellow rookie Cristiano da Matta crashed his 12th-placed MCI WorldCom Toyota/Reynard heavily on the exit of Turn Two. Da Matta was unhurt, but a lengthy clean-up was required, during which the CART officials determined that the race would be concluded at the two-hour mark.

To complicate matters further, Franchitti called in to his pit to say that the pace car was leaking fuel. A lap or two later, the offending Ford Mustang was flagged into the pits. Unfortunately, several drivers took that as the signal that the race was about to be restarted.

'The pace car came in and everyone started going [for a restart],' said Montoya, 'but everyone didn't know whether it was going green or not.' It

wasn't. In fact, a backup pace car already had been despatched. It was due to pick up the field in Turn Two. Montoya didn't make it that far. He had accelerated in anticipation of the green, only to have to arrest his progress abruptly when he realized there would be no restart. Castro-Neves, following close behind, was caught totally unaware.

'People started to speed up, and the team told me that it was going to go green,' said Castro-Neves, 'but I never knew they were bringing another pace car onto the track. By the time I knew that the track was still yellow, I had already hit Juan.'

Montoya's car was punted into the wall and out of the race. Castro-Neves continued with his left-front wheel knocked badly awry. The race, however, was concluded under yellow, so the Brazilian nursed Carl Hogan's stricken Mercedes/Lola around for two more laps and was credited with a seventh-place finish!

Thus Montoya emerged with no points. Franchitti, meanwhile, took the victory and a narrow championship lead. 'That was unbelievable,' admitted the Scotsman. 'It's great to be leading the championship now, but the time to do it is after the last race at Fontana. I hope we can keep it until then.'

Jeremy Shaw

New horizons. Roger Penske *(top)* and
Al Unser announced that they would
be parting company at season's end.
Photos: Michael C. Brown

DETROIT SNIPPETS

• After an impressive test during the winter at Sebring, **GONZALO RODRIGUEZ** *(below)* was invited to contest a couple of races in a second Marlboro Team Penske entry, beginning in Detroit. The talented Uruguayan, a leading contender in the European-based FIA Formula 3000 Championship with Team Astromega, had not driven the team's Lola B99/00 chassis before, but looked immediately at home in the car and comfortably outpaced veteran teammate Al Unser Jr.

• **JAN MAGNUSSEN** replaced the out-of-favor PJ Jones in Patrick Racing's Visteon Ford/Swift. The Dane, however, produced no great improvement, crashing on Saturday and winding up 22nd on the grid out of 26 starters. He clashed with Robby Gordon in the race, before setting a worthy seventh-fastest lap behind Juan Montoya, Greg Moore, Dario Franchitti, Paul Tracy, Jimmy Vasser and Mark Blundell. 'The key is to qualify better because I feel we can race with these guys. It is fun to be back in Champ Cars; I absolutely love it,' said Magnussen, who contested four races for the Hogan Penske team in 1996, following Emerson Fittipaldi's retirement due to an injury.

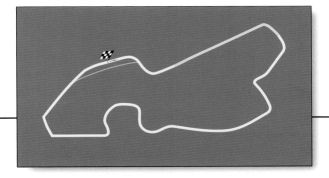

• **PATRICK CARPENTIER** was fortunate to escape serious injury when he clashed on lap 28 with Mauricio Gugelmin, whose car climbed over the French-Canadian's and, quite literally, landed on Carpentier's head. Nevertheless, a cervical muscle strain precluded Carpentier from competing in the following weekend's race at Mid-Ohio.

• **NAOKI HATTORI** returned to action for the first time since suffering a badly broken leg in the series opener at Homestead. The Japanese rookie, who tested at Mid-Ohio before making his decision, never looked comfortable in the car, qualified last, but ran all day to finish a lap down.

• Hattori's return to Derrick Walker's Alpine Honda/Reynard left **MEMO GIDLEY** on the sidelines...but only briefly, for the promising Californian rookie was quickly invited to drive for Payton/Coyne Racing, following the decision by Luiz Garcia Jr. to seek greener pastures. Gidley, 29, was installed in a second Herdez/Viva Mexico Ford/Lola and again performed well, overcoming some mechanical problems on Friday and rising as high as 14th in the race, before being felled by a gearbox failure.

• Newman/Haas Racing co-owner **PAUL NEWMAN** was invited to drive one of the PPG Pace Cars, enjoying himself enormously until depositing the Toyota Supra into a tire barrier! Oops.

Kauki Saito

FEDEX CHAMPIONSHIP SERIES • ROUND 13

TENNECO AUTOMOTIVE GRAND PRIX OF DETROIT

THE RACEWAY ON BELLE ISLE, DETROIT, MICHIGAN

AUGUST 8, 71 laps – 166.566 miles

Place	Driver (Nat.)	No.	Team Sponsors Engine/Car	Tires	Q Speed	Q Time	Q Pos.	Laps	Time/Status	Ave. (mph)	Pts.
1	Dario Franchitti (GB)	27	Team KOOL Green Honda/Reynard 99I	FS	114.451	1m 13.792s	4	71	2h 02m 24.662s	81.643	20
2	Paul Tracy (CDN)	26	Team KOOL Green Honda/Reynard 99I	FS	114.733	1m 13.611s	2	71	2h 02m 24.797s	81.641	16
3	Greg Moore (CDN)	99	Forsythe Racing Player's/Indeck Mercedes/Reynard 99I	FS	114.099	1m 14.020s	7	71	2h 02m 25.192s	81.637	14
4	Michael Andretti (USA)	6	Newman/Haas Kmart/Texaco Havoline Ford Cosworth/Swift 010.c	FS	114.070	1m 14.039s	8	71	2h 02m 26.133s	81.626	12
5	Jimmy Vasser (USA)	12	Target/Chip Ganassi Racing Honda/Reynard 99I	FS	113.585	1m 14.355s	12	71	2h 02m 27.256s	81.614	10
6	Tony Kanaan (BR)	44	McDonald's Championship Racing Honda/Reynard 99I	FS	114.195	1m 13.958s	6	71	2h 02m 28.314s	81.602	8
7	Helio Castro-Neves (BR)	9	Hogan Racing Hogan Motor Leasing Mercedes/Lola B99/00	FS	112.466	1m 15.095s	18	71	2h 02m 29.464s	81.589	6
8	Scott Pruett (USA)	24	Arciero-Wells Racing Pioneer Toyota/Reynard 99I	FS	112.519	1m 15.059s	17	71	2h 02m 31.412s	81.568	5
9	Bryan Herta (USA)	8	Team Rahal Shell Ford Cosworth/Reynard 99I	FS	113.788	1m 14.222s	11	71	2h 02m 31.873s	81.563	4
10	Mark Blundell (GB)	18	PacWest Racing Group Motorola Mercedes/Reynard 99I	FS	112.793	1m 14.877s	15	71	2h 02m 32.892s	81.551	3
11	Gualter Salles (BR)	36	All American Racers Denso/Castrol Toyota/Eagle 997	GY	110.469	1m 16.452s	25	71	2h 02m 33.882s	81.540	2
12	*Gonzalo Rodriguez (URG)	3	Marlboro Team Penske Mercedes/Lola B99/00	GY	112.557	1m 15.034s	16	71	2h 02m 39.135s	81.482	1
13	Richie Hearn (USA)	10	Della Penna Motorsports Budweiser Toyota/Reynard 99I	FS	111.640	1m 15.650s	21	71	2h 02m 40.493s	81.467	
14	Roberto Moreno (BR)	11	Newman/Haas Big Kmart Ford Cosworth/Swift 010.c	FS	114.338	1m 13.865s	5	70	Running		
15	Al Unser Jr. (USA)	2	Marlboro Team Penske Mercedes/Lola B99/00	GY	111.870	1m 15.495s	20	70	Running		
16	*Naoki Hattori (J)	15	Walker Racing Alpine Honda/Reynard 98I	GY	109.676	1m 17.005s	26	70	Running		
17	*Juan Montoya (COL)	4	Target/Chip Ganassi Racing Honda/Reynard 99I	FS	114.773	1m 13.585s	1	68	Accident		2
18	Jan Magnussen (DK)	20	Patrick Racing Visteon Ford Cosworth/Swift 010.c	FS	111.495	1m 15.749s	22	68	Running		
19	*Cristiano da Matta (BR)	25	Arciero-Wells Racing MCI WorldCom Toyota/Reynard 99I	FS	112.980	1m 14.753s	14	65	Accident		
20	*Memo Gidley (USA)	71	Payton/Coyne Herdez/Viva Mexico Ford Cosworth/Lola T97/00	FS	110.585	1m 16.372s	24	42	Transmission		
21	Michel Jourdain Jr. (MEX)	19	Payton/Coyne Herdez/Viva Mexico Ford Cosworth/Lola T97/00	FS	111.409	1m 15.807s	23	41	Transmission		
22	Gil de Ferran (BR)	5	Walker Racing Valvoline/Cummins Honda/Reynard 99I	GY	114.456	1m 13.789s	3	32	Accident		
23	Patrick Carpentier (CDN)	33	Forsythe Racing Player's/Indeck Mercedes/Reynard 99I	FS	113.991	1m 14.090s	9	27	Accident		
24	Mauricio Gugelmin (BR)	17	PacWest Racing Group Hollywood Mercedes/Reynard 99I	FS	113.318	1m 14.530s	13	27	Accident		
25	Robby Gordon (USA)	22	Team Gordon Panasonic/Menards Toyota/Swift 010.c	FS	112.457	1m 15.101s	19	23	Accident		
26	Max Papis (I)	7	Team Rahal Miller Lite Ford Cosworth/Reynard 99I	FS	113.799	1m 14.215s	10	0	Accident		
NS	Adrian Fernandez (MEX)	40	Patrick Racing Tecate/Quaker State Ford Cosworth/Reynard 99I	FS	no speed	no time	–	–	Withdrawn		

* denotes rookie driver

Caution flags: Laps 1–2, accident/Papis & Carpentier; laps 23–26, accident/Magnussen & Gordon; laps 28–32, accident/Gugelmin & Carpentier; laps 33–34, accident/de Ferran; laps 44–45, tow/Gidley; laps 63–64, accident/Montoya & Moreno; laps 66–68, accident/da Matta; laps 69–71, accident/Montoya. **Total:** Eight for 23 laps.

Lap leaders: Juan Montoya, 1–58 (58 laps); Dario Franchitti, 59–71 (13 laps). **Totals:** Montoya, 58 laps; Franchitti, 13 laps.

Fastest race lap: Juan Montoya, 1m 15.701s, 111.565 mph on lap 49 (record).

Championship positions: 1 Franchitti, 136; **2** Montoya, 131; **3** Andretti, 119; **4** Tracy, 106; **5** Fittipaldi, 101; **6** Fernandez & Moore, 95; **8** de Ferran, 88; **9** Papis, 68; **10** Kanaan, 62; **11** Vasser, 54; **12** Moreno, 38; **13** Herta, 35; **14** Carpentier, 33; **15** Jones, 31; **16** Castro-Neves, 27; **17** Unser Jr., 20; **18** da Matta, 16; **19** Gugelmin, Pruett & Gordon, 14; **22** Hearn, 12; **23** Blundell, 8; **24** Jourdain Jr., 6; **25** Marques & Barron, 4; **27** Gidley, 3; **28** Vitolo & Salles, 2; **30** Rodriguez, 1.

OMEGA
OFFICIAL TIMEKEEPER OF CART

MID-OHIO

1 – MONTOYA

2 – TRACY

3 – FRANCHITTI

Eventual winner Juan Montoya leads
Paul Tracy and Dario Franchitti
immediately after the only full-
course caution of the day.
Photo: Michael C. Brown

QUALIFYING

Dario Franchitti arrived at the Mid-Ohio Sports Car Course eager to build on the mid-season momentum that had catapulted him to the top of the PPG Cup standings with seven rounds remaining. He went the right way about it in Friday afternoon's provisional qualifying session, circulating the picturesque 2.258-mile road circuit in just 1 minute, 5.347 seconds to eclipse the best efforts of his rivals by nearly half a second.

Franchitti confessed to being a little taken aback himself when he saw the time. 'The track didn't feel as good today as when we tested here,' he observed. 'I looked at the dash and saw a [one minute] 5.3 and I thought, "Where the hell did that come from?"'

The Scotsman reckoned it would take a substantial improvement on Saturday to secure the pole. As it transpired, however, the final qualifying session was all but washed out by persistent rain, so Friday's times dictated the starting order. Franchitti's second pole in as many years at Mid-Ohio was assured.

Lining up alongside the championship leader was another acknowledged Mid-Ohio master. Bryan Herta had never started lower than third in four previous visits, although a dramatic tire blowout in 1997 and a contentious first-corner collision with Franchitti in 1998 had deprived him of a finishing record to match. 'I want to run a full race and get a good result,' he declared, pointedly. 'We haven't been able to do that the last two years here.'

The front-row starters played down the prospects of another territorial dispute at the Esses. 'I don't have any concerns about the start. The thought process isn't any different here from the other 19 races,' insisted Herta, whose Shell Reynard was the only Ford Cosworth interloper among five Honda-powered cars.

Paul Tracy pronounced himself satisfied with third on the grid, while Tony Kanaan posted his best qualifying effort since claiming the pole at Long Beach in April to annex fourth. Kanaan, whose Forsythe Championship Racing team is based in nearby Hilliard, Ohio, approached Sunday's race in a confident frame of mind, following two productive pre-race tests at the demanding parkland track. Jimmy Vasser and perennial Goodyear interloper Gil de Ferran would share row three.

JUAN Montoya expunged the painful memories of Detroit's tribulations with a consummate drive to victory in the Miller Lite 200 at the Mid-Ohio Sports Car Course. The Colombian's fifth triumph of the season matched the record for a rookie (established by Nigel Mansell in 1993) and moved him to within a solitary point of Dario Franchitti in the battle for the FedEx Championship Series.

Montoya's success came as a stunning blow to his championship rival, who controlled the first two-thirds of the event before hitting trouble in the shape of a deflating tire. Franchitti's predicament compelled him to make an early second pit stop, thereby delivering a clear track to Montoya, who already had forged ahead of the second Team KOOL Green Honda/Reynard of Paul Tracy. Chip Ganassi's driver responded by reeling off a pair of inspired laps prior to his own final visit to the pits, paving the way for a sizeable lead when he rejoined. Thereafter, it was game over for his pursuers. The Target car simply motored into the distance, pulling away to win by a comfortable 10.927 seconds.

Montoya's performance was all the more remarkable for the fact that he had struggled to find any kind of pace on Friday. When final qualifying was washed out, he was obliged to start a relatively lowly eighth on the grid.

'Whoa, what a day!' he exclaimed. 'After all the trouble we had on Friday, I can't believe we came so far so fast, especially with the rain on Saturday. It really means a lot to me that Chip has a team that can help me so much.'

As usual at Mid-Ohio, the starting signal was given midway down the long back straightaway, rather than on the short chute in front of the pits. Franchitti, intent on avoiding a replay of last year's first-lap mishap, successfully converted his pole position into a clear advantage turning into the Esses. Bryan Herta and Tracy followed in his wheel tracks, while Jimmy Vasser made it past Tony Kanaan for fourth.

The first significant shuffle came on lap three, when Tracy relieved Herta of second in an audacious maneuver around the outside under braking for Turn Four. Shortly after, Kanaan capitalized on a missed gear change by Vasser to reclaim fourth. Next in line

Montoya back on target

JUAN Montoya was relieved to return to the winner's circle at Mid-Ohio after seeing his best-laid championship plans go awry in previous weeks, most notably in Detroit, where a high-level miscommunication robbed him of a seemingly assured victory. The Colombian had amassed a paltry 19 points since outdistancing the competition at Cleveland at the end of June. Three races without a win amounted to a barren spell by his lofty standards.

'Last week in Detroit was really hard for me. We had the fastest car, but made a mistake and took no points,' said Montoya, after emphatically redressing the balance in the Miller Lite 200. 'This win was exactly what we needed.'

Montoya's accomplishment was especially meritorious for the fact that he had struggled to find a workable balance on his Target/Chip Ganassi Racing Honda/Reynard during Friday's practice and qualifying sessions, and was consigned to a meager eighth on the grid when rain sluiced away his hopes of improving on Saturday. Veteran race engineer Morris Nunn elected to install a brand-new setup on the #4 car after his young charge expressed continued dissatisfaction in Sunday morning's half-hour warmup. The results were spectacular, although it would take a true team effort to procure victory from such a distant starting spot.

'Morris did a great job,' praised Montoya. 'We came to Mid-Ohio with high hopes after we had a very good test here, but I just couldn't drive the car. At one point, I actually told my crew, "This car is dangerous to drive!" We made some changes for qualifying, but we were still way off. I never expected to win.'

Nunn reiterated his high rating of Montoya. 'To me, he's the quickest guy out there,' enthused the Englishman. 'It's a gift, the raw natural talent he has. It was beautiful to see what he did today because of the bonus I'm going to make!'

Paul Tracy took advantage of Dario Franchitti's misfortune to finish ahead of his KOOL Honda/Reynard teammate.

Below: Gil de Ferran once again proved to be fastest of the Goodyear contingent.

---

quo resumed after Roberto Moreno's stop on lap 32.

'I was a lot quicker than the guys in front of me,' explained Montoya. 'I sat there in traffic, lifting at the end of the straights and getting the slipstream as best I could. I went an extra lap on fuel and turned [the fuel mixture] to full rich and went for it with nobody in the way. It was a pretty good in-lap. Then the guys did a fantastic pit stop...and I came out in third place.'

Ahead lay only Franchitti and Tracy. Catching them, however, looked like a tall order. The gap to Tracy alone stood at more than 12 seconds on lap 33. But that served only to inspire Montoya, who was reveling in the transformed handling of his chassis – and in the clear road with which he was now presented. He simply put his head down and set about whittling away the deficit, homing in on the lead pair at the rate of a second per lap.

'Chip told me over the radio, "You're catching them quickly,"' related Montoya, 'so I just pushed harder.'

Even Tracy was impressed: 'Juan was able to catch us, which was quite surprising because I thought we were running a pretty good pace.'

Franchitti, though, was grappling with the effects of a slowly deflating right rear tire. It was all he could do to retain a tenuous lead over Tracy's sister car.

'It was down to about 10 psi,' related Franchitti. 'The car became a handful. It was bottoming in a lot of places and oversteering through the left-handers and understeering through the right-handers.'

He had another complaint, too. 'What can I say about the backmarkers? They were just atrocious. I don't know what PJ Jones was playing at. He was a lap down and wouldn't get out of the way. So that was disappointing,' fumed Franchitti.

By lap 52, the three leaders were in virtual nose-to-tail formation. Montoya was poised for a challenge. His task was halved at a stroke when Franchitti's slow puncture forced the Scot to pit for a new set of Firestone radials on lap 55, three laps earlier than originally planned. Tracy now assumed the lead, only for Montoya to take a leaf out of the Canadian's book by pulling off a bold outside pass under braking for Turn Four on the very next lap.

'It was a clean pass,' acknowledged Tracy. 'I got into the [previous] Keyhole [turn] a little too deep, slid a bit wide, picked up some dirt on my tires, and Juan got a run on me down the straight.'

Having worked so hard to get to the front, Montoya was determined to make the most of his opportunity. Tracy pulled onto the pit lane on the 57th lap, but again the Target car stayed out for one more circuit. Once more, the extra lap on hot tires and with a low fuel load was to prove decisive. Montoya duly emerged in front after taking on service. Franchitti's early stop, meanwhile, had been especially costly, dropping the erstwhile leader to third behind Tracy.

were Helio Castro-Neves in Hogan Racing's Mercedes/Lola and Gil de Ferran's Goodyear-shod Honda/Reynard, the two Brazilians having swapped positions at the start, followed by Montoya, Max Papis and Michael Andretti. The top ten runners continued in that order to the first round of pit stops. Franchitti enjoyed a small, but comfortable, cushion over his teammate who, in turn, steadily drew clear of the knot of cars fighting over third place, headed by Herta, who was struggling for traction aboard his Shell Ford/Reynard.

Somewhat unexpectedly, Montoya failed to provide any relief from this stalemate throughout the first stint – a measure of the difficulty of overtaking around Mid-Ohio's serpentine layout. Instead, the Colombian displayed a maturity beyond his years by taking the opportunity to conserve fuel. The strategy paid off handsomely. He was able to stay out a lap longer than his immediate rivals and, assisted by typically slick work from his crew, leapfrogged past de Ferran, Castro-Neves, Vasser, Kanaan and Herta to emerge in third place when the status

Michael C. Brown

Cristiano da Matta leads Robby Gordon and Richie Hearn through the Esses. All three Toyota-powered cars finished among the points.

Immediately after the pit stops came the only full-course yellow of the day, after Al Unser Jr. and Luiz Garcia Jr. spun in separate incidents, and Tony Kanaan ran out of fuel and was stranded out on the course. The same fate had befallen the McDonald's driver just before his first scheduled stop, sending him to the tail of the field and negating his solid run in fourth place. A faulty fuel system was to blame.

The closing laps were merely a formality as Montoya romped away from the Team KOOL Green machines, which held station to the flag.

'Paul and I were running the same pace,' said Franchitti. 'They told me to get on the radio and we would discuss it if Paul was holding me up, but he wasn't. I just couldn't get close enough to him.'

Tracy said of his third runner-up finish in four races, 'We're running very consistent races and scoring points, but we need to get up on that top rung a little more if we want to contend for the championship.'

Franchitti garnered a couple of extra points for snaring the pole and leading most laps, but he considered that third place was poor reward for his weekend's work: 'It's obviously nice to be on the podium, but from the way the day started to the way it ended, it's disappointing.'

Vasser added to Ganassi's cheer with a strong run to fourth, setting second-fastest lap of the race as he pulled to within striking distance of Franchitti in the closing stages. The 1996 PPG Cup champion had been promoted a place when the unfortunate Herta succumbed to a blown engine just 11 laps from home, and might have finished even higher had he been able to muster better fuel mileage. Papis salvaged some points for Team Rahal, profiting from a fortuitously timed (and ultra-rapid) second pit stop, which coincided with the caution, to vault from eighth to fifth in his Miller Lite Ford/Reynard. De Ferran prevailed over Castro-Neves for sixth, having found a way past his younger compatriot on lap 67. Andretti could manage only a distant eighth in his Kmart/Texaco Havoline Ford/Swift, hampered by a lack of overall grip.

In truth, it was largely a processional race, with little in the way of on-track passing for position. As so often during the season, Montoya's performance provided the highlight. The brilliant young rookie had given his championship aspirations a much-needed fillip on a day when his chief rival might have least expected it.

AlexSabine/Jeremy Shaw

Toyota continues forward march

TOYOTA had endured a steep learning curve since joining the Champ Car ranks in 1996. Its original RV8A power unit proved overweight, underpowered and, above all, chronically unreliable. The 1997 version was scarcely an improvement. Both Toyota teams, All American Racers and Arciero-Wells Racing, were obliged to conduct an inordinate number of unscheduled engine changes in the course of that season. There appeared little cause for optimism.

But Toyota had always insisted it would take time for the development program to bear fruit. It affirmed the seriousness of its intentions by hiring some high-quality personnel and expanding the scope of its Japanese involvement toward the end of '97. The arrival of the RV8C engine, superseded in mid-season by the more powerful RV8D model, signaled a quantum leap forward.

Toyota standard-bearer Max Papis served notice of progress with a splendid fifth place at Houston, underscored by second-fastest race lap, in addition to a handful of other points-paying finishes, while AAR's Alex Barron gave the manufacturer its first – albeit brief – taste of the lead in Vancouver, almost pulling off a stunning upset.

The momentum was carried over into 1999, when rookie Cristiano da Matta qualified a remarkable sixth for his debut race at Homestead and then delivered Toyota's best-ever race result with a fine run to fourth at Nazareth. Da Matta's veteran Arciero-Wells teammate, Scott Pruett, later set a new qualifying benchmark by lining up fifth for the U.S. 500 at Michigan.

At Mid-Ohio, it was Robby Gordon's turn to make history. The Californian's strong form on Friday ensured that a Toyota-powered car finally broke into the top ten on the grid at a road course event.

'I'm happy to be the one to help [Toyota] reach that goal,' commented Gordon. 'The motor has slowly been creeping up on the rest of the field. More and more you're noticing us up in the fast group on Saturday afternoons.'

CART's only owner/driver guided his Panasonic-backed Swift to an equally competitive tenth-place finish in the race, one spot behind da Matta. Pruett and Richie Hearn further attested to Toyota's recent strides by clocking the eighth and ninth fastest laps respectively, putting a phalanx of Mercedes and Ford-Cosworths in the shade.

MID-OHIO SNIPPETS

• When inhospitable weather conditions on Saturday effectively put paid to final qualifying, CART organized a special **AUTOGRAPH SESSION** wherein all the Champ Car drivers were available, next to their hospitality trailers, to appease the fans who were otherwise prevented from seeing their heroes in action. The session was extremely well received by fans and drivers alike.

• Pat Patrick's team, which a year earlier had celebrated a historic 1-2 finish in the Miller Lite 200, was left to rue its **DOWNWARD SPIRAL** after PJ Jones, sitting in for the injured Adrian Fernandez, was unable to get to grips with his '97 Reynard in the limited practice time. Jones spun off during the only dry qualifying session, started 21st and finished 15th. Jan Magnussen, newly installed in a '98 example, fared little better, crossing the line directly in front of his teammate in 14th.

• PacWest's **MARK BLUNDELL** had more reason than most to be depressed by Saturday's inclement weather. The Englishman, who had returned to the fray in Detroit after a lengthy injury timeout, had been a heartening third quickest in provisional qualifying on Friday, only for his time to be scratched when his Motorola Mercedes/Reynard fell foul of the two-inch ground-clearance rule in technical inspection, relegating him to the tail end of the starting order.

Photo: Michael C. Brown

• **LUIZ GARCIA JR.** *(below)* drove a second Hogan Motor Leasing Mercedes/Lola. The Brazilian Indy Lights graduate, who had abruptly quit the Payton/Coyne team after seven outings, qualified toward the rear of the field, but ran respectably in the race before retiring due to clutch failure after 56 laps.

• A couple of days before making the trip to Ohio from his home in Fort Lauderdale, Florida, **GIL DE FERRAN** was invited to throw out the ceremonial first pitch prior to the Florida Marlins' home game against the San Francisco Giants. 'It's a big honor,' said de Ferran. 'My family enjoyed it, too, which made it an even better experience.' Incidentally, the Marlins won 8-7.

• Brazilian hero **EMERSON FITTIPALDI**, who gained three victories at Mid-Ohio before hanging up his helmet in 1996, was a welcome visitor in his role as manager/mentor for Helio Castro-Neves.

• Remarkably, **HONDA-POWERED** cars filled five of the top six places in both qualifying and the race. It was a graphic demonstration that the Japanese concern still held the upper hand, despite intense competition from Ford Cosworth in particular (whose entrants routinely registered the highest speed-trap figures throughout the season).

FEDEX CHAMPIONSHIP SERIES • ROUND 14
MILLER LITE 200

MID-OHIO SPORTS CAR COURSE, LEXINGTON, OHIO

AUGUST 15, 83 laps – 186.446 miles

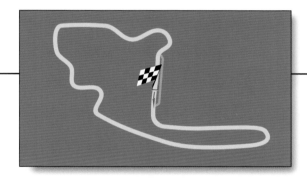

Place	Driver (Nat.)	No.	Team Sponsors Engine/Car	Tires	Q Speed	Q Time	Q Pos.	Laps	Time/Status	Ave. (mph)	Pts.
1	*Juan Montoya (COL)	4	Target/Chip Ganassi Racing Honda/Reynard 99I	FS	122.840	1m 06.174s	8	83	1h 42m 03.808s	109.606	20
2	Paul Tracy (CDN)	26	Team KOOL Green Honda/Reynard 99I	FS	123.336	1m 05.908s	3	83	1h 42m 14.735s	109.411	16
3	Dario Franchitti (GB)	27	Team KOOL Green Honda/Reynard 99I	FS	124.394	1m 05.347s	1	83	1h 42m 16.121s	109.386	16
4	Jimmy Vasser (USA)	12	Target/Chip Ganassi Racing Honda/Reynard 99I	FS	122.994	1m 06.091s	5	83	1h 42m 18.536s	109.343	12
5	Max Papis (I)	7	Team Rahal Miller Lite Ford Cosworth/Reynard 99I	FS	122.557	1m 06.316s	9	83	1h 42m 23.707s	109.251	10
6	Gil de Ferran (BR)	5	Walker Racing Valvoline/Cummins Honda/Reynard 99I	GY	122.916	1m 06.133s	6	83	1h 42m 27.490s	109.184	8
7	Helio Castro-Neves (BR)	9	Hogan Racing Hogan Motor Leasing Mercedes/Lola B99/00	FS	122.909	1m 06.137s	7	83	1h 42m 28.905s	109.159	6
8	Michael Andretti (USA)	6	Newman/Haas Kmart/Texaco Havoline Ford Cosworth/Swift 010.c	FS	122.306	1m 06.463s	11	83	1h 42m 35.107s	109.049	5
9	*Cristiano da Matta (BR)	25	Arciero-Wells Racing MCI WorldCom Toyota/Reynard 99I	FS	121.972	1m 06.645s	14	83	1h 42m 35.680s	109.038	4
10	Robby Gordon (USA)	22	Team Gordon Panasonic/Menards Toyota/Swift 010.c	FS	122.510	1m 06.352s	10	83	1h 42m 36.630s	109.022	3
11	Greg Moore (CDN)	99	Forsythe Racing Player's/Indeck Mercedes/Reynard 99I	FS	119.390	1m 08.086s	25	83	1h 42m 37.070s	109.014	2
12	Richie Hearn (USA)	10	Della Penna Motorsports Budweiser Toyota/Reynard 99I	FS	122.133	1m 06.557s	12	83	1h 42m 39.125s	108.977	1
13	Mark Blundell (GB)	18	PacWest Racing Group Motorola Mercedes/Reynard 99I	FS	no speed	no time	26	83	1h 42m 39.583s	108.969	
14	Jan Magnussen (DK)	20	Patrick Racing Visteon Ford Cosworth/Reynard 98I	FS	121.585	1m 06.857s	15	83	1h 42m 46.933s	108.839	
15	PJ Jones (USA)	40	Patrick Racing Tecate/Quaker State Ford Cosworth/Reynard 97I	FS	120.898	1m 07.237s	21	83	1h 42m 47.502	108.829	
16	Roberto Moreno (BR)	11	Newman/Haas Big Kmart Ford Cosworth/Swift 010.c	FS	121.318	1m 07.004s	19	83	1h 42m 48.373	108.814	
17	Scott Pruett (USA)	24	Arciero-Wells Racing Pioneer Toyota/Reynard 99I	FS	121.313	1m 07.007s	20	82	Running		
18	Gualter Salles (BR)	36	All American Racers Denso/Castrol Toyota/Eagle 997	GY	121.527	1m 06.889s	16	82	Running		
19	*Naoki Hattori (J)	15	Walker Racing Alpine Honda/Reynard 98I	GY	120.785	1m 07.300s	23	82	Running		
20	Mauricio Gugelmin (BR)	17	PacWest Racing Group Hollywood Mercedes/Reynard 99I	FS	121.452	1m 06.930s	17	76	Engine		
21	Bryan Herta (USA)	8	Team Rahal Shell Ford Cosworth/Reynard 99I	FS	123.493	1m 05.824s	2	72	Engine		
22	*Memo Gidley (USA)	71	Payton/Coyne Herdez/Viva Mexico Ford Cosworth/Lola T97/00	FS	122.094	1m 06.578s	13	69	Engine		
23	Tony Kanaan (BR)	44	McDonald's Championship Racing Honda/Reynard 99I	FS	123.190	1m 05.986s	4	58	Fuel system		
24	*Luiz Garcia Jr.(BR)	21	Hogan Racing Hogan Motor Leasing/Tang Mercedes/Lola B99/00	FS	119.471	1m 08.040s	24	56	Clutch		
25	Al Unser Jr. (USA)	2	Marlboro Team Penske Mercedes/Lola B99/00	GY	120.799	1m 07.292s	22	56	Spin		
26	Michel Jourdain Jr. (MEX)	19	Payton/Coyne Herdez/Viva Mexico Ford Cosworth/Lola T97/00	FS	121.327	1m 06.999s	18	54	Transmission		

* denotes rookie driver

Caution flags: Laps 59-64, spins/Garcia & Unser Jr. **Total:** One for six laps.

Lap leaders: Dario Franchitti, 1-54 (54 laps); Paul Tracy, 55 (1 lap); Juan Montoya, 56-83 (28 laps). **Totals:** Franchitti, 54 laps; Montoya, 28 laps; Tracy, 1 lap.

Fastest race lap: Juan Montoya, 1m 06.788s, 121.710 mph on lap 76 (record).

Championship positions: 1 Franchitti, 152; **2** Montoya, 151; **3** Andretti, 124; **4** Tracy, 122; **5** Fittipaldi, 101; **6** Moore, 97; **7** de Ferran, 96; **8** Fernandez, 95; **9** Papis, 78; **10** Vasser, 66; **11** Kanaan, 52; **12** Moreno, 38; **13** Herta, 35; **14** Castro-Neves & Carpentier, 33; **16** Jones, 31; **17** da Matta & Unser Jr., 20; **19** Gordon, 17; **20** Pruett & Gugelmin, 14; **22** Hearn, 13; **23** Blundell, 8; **24** Jourdain Jr., 6; **25** Marques & Barron, 4; **27** Gidley, 3; **28** Vitolo & Salles, 2; **30** Rodriguez, 1.

CHICAGO

FEDEX CHAMPIONSHIP SERIES • ROUND 15

On target

CHICAGO Motor Speedway, the product of a new partnership between CART team owner/entrepreneur Chip Ganassi and horse racing diehard Charles Bidwill III, opened to rave reviews for the Target Grand Prix. Built at a cost of $60 million on the site of a historic horse racing track (Sportsman's Park), just a few miles west of the Windy City's downtown district, the brand-new facility attracted a full-house crowd of 70,000 fans.

The dominating feature at CMS is an imposing, 150-foot high, state-of-the-art grandstand (topped by 42 skyboxes) that runs virtually the length of the front straightaway and offers magnificent views from virtually every seat. Equally impressive are the concession areas beneath the main structure, which are expansive and easily accessible. There is also an indoor, air-conditioned Expo area adjacent to Turn One, offering yet more creature comforts, which are so lacking at most auto racing venues.

There was no shortage of side shows and attractions for the fans, too, including air displays, a beach volleyball competition on the infield and a magnificent fireworks show both before and after the main event.

Even the drivers were impressed with the super-smooth 1.029-mile oval, which comprises long straightaways and wide corners banked at only six degrees. 'This track is good for our cars,' declared Bryan Herta after qualifying. 'We can really race here. Some tracks aren't suited for our cars, but this one is terrific. I think Sunday's race will be good.'

It was, with plenty of close racing and an exciting battle for the lead that raged virtually throughout the 225 laps. The result, of course, was especially satisfying for Ganassi, who saw his young rookie charge, Juan Montoya, blast through from tenth on the grid to take the victory.

Said Ganassi, 'To win the Target Grand Prix – with Target cars – how much better can it get?'

Photo: Michael C. Brown

JUAN Montoya chalked up another accomplished victory in the inaugural Target Grand Prix at Chicago Motor Speedway. With his second triumph in as many weeks, he established a new record for rookie wins, surpassing Nigel Mansell's tally of five set in 1993. He also wrested back a slender advantage in the PPG Cup point standings over Dario Franchitti, who limited the damage by finishing a strong second, a scant three-quarters of a second in arrears. Meanwhile, a controversial collision between Michael Andretti and Paul Tracy effectively distilled the title chase to a two-way contest with five races remaining.

As at Mid-Ohio, Montoya left himself with plenty of work to do on Sunday after struggling to come to terms with understeer throughout practice and qualifying. Once again, race engineer Morris Nunn worked his Midas touch with a battery of overnight setup changes, which ensured that the #4 Target Honda/Reynard was handling to its driver's taste when it mattered most.

'This morning, when we went out for the warmup, the car was so much better,' related Montoya. 'Morris and the guys stayed pretty late last night and they made the right changes. The car was just flying all day long.'

The pre-race festivities, capped by an impressive fireworks display, finally gave way to the 'Gentlemen, start your engines' command shortly before two o'clock. It promised to be an intriguing race, given both the novelty of the starting order and the unknown quantities that inevitably attend the first event at a new venue. Chief among these was the question of whether a secondary groove would develop outside the preferred racing line to allow side-by-side racing through the corners; or whether, as many feared (and perhaps even a few hoped), passing opportunities would hinge on the role of lapped traffic.

Somewhat unnecessarily, it took no less than four attempts to get the race under way. The original start was waved off when Max Papis stole a slight march on the competition. Mark Blundell was the culprit on the next two occasions, lagging behind his fellow front-row starter and bunching up the rest of the pack.

When the 26-car field was finally unleashed, Papis stormed away into an immediate lead over Blundell, whose Motorola Mercedes/Reynard soon developed a lurid oversteer condition and tumbled down the order. Franchitti duly took over second place, having

QUALIFYING

Max Papis had been cruelly denied a first Champ Car victory in the U.S. 500 Presented by Toyota in July, but a month later, in the FedEx Championship Series' very next visit to an oval track, the ebullient Italian bounced back to claim his first career pole. Papis set the pace in two of the three official practice sessions in Team Rahal's Miller Lite Ford Cosworth/Reynard and earned the right to go last in the suspenseful one-car-at-a-time qualifying session. He did not disappoint. Papis' first timed lap was a hair slower than surprise pacesetter Mark Blundell, but he turned up the wick on lap two to edge the Englishman with a best lap of 162.559 mph (22.788 seconds).

'On the first lap, I saw 22.81 on my dash and I knew it wasn't enough,' said Papis (above, being congratulated by Bobby Rahal). 'I used all of the road in Turns Three and Four, and it was good enough. It feels good to win an oval pole, since I come from Italy and we are road racers. It was very intimidating back in 1996 when I first raced on an oval. Now I have learned a lot from people like Gordon Coppuck [his race engineer at Arciero-Wells Racing], Bobby [Rahal] and [current race engineer] Tim Reiter.'

Blundell, who came within 0.025 second of his first pole, had to be content with a place on the outside of the front row, equaling his best set both at Toronto and Road America in 1997.

'I'm still second, which is good,' he related, 'but it's a little frustrating not to pull it off.'

Jimmy Vasser upheld the Target team's honor at the Target Grand Prix, setting the third fastest time to ensure there would be three different engine manufacturers – Ford, Mercedes and Honda – represented at the front of an intensely close grid. In fact, Dario Franchitti, Helio Castro-Neves and Patrick Carpentier also were within 0.1 second of the pole-sitter, with Bryan Herta a mere 0.101 second adrift in seventh.

'The car was pretty good,' said Herta. 'That was the fastest lap I've run all weekend. After the tough summer we've had on the ovals, my engineer, Ray Leto, and I went over all of the oval setups for the past several years and we found some things that helped us this week.'

made light work of Jimmy Vasser on the first lap. Ominously, however, Montoya was already up to fifth by lap seven, before being detained in a lengthy battle with the Hogan Racing Mercedes/Lola of Helio Castro-Neves.

Papis stretched his lead to three seconds by lap 22 and continued to hold the upper hand through most of the opening stint. Franchitti remained in touch, though, and began to make some headway when the rear brakes on the leader's Miller Lite Ford/Reynard started to overcook, which in turn drove up the rear tire temperatures and provoked oversteer in the tight corners. Montoya, meanwhile, finally found a way past Castro-Neves for fourth on lap 47, and slipped ahead of teammate Vasser with little ado a handful of laps later.

Impressive as the Colombian's progress was, it paled in comparison to Michael Andretti's meteoric march up the lap chart. Andretti had qualified a lowly 18th, but cracked the top ten as early as lap 29 and followed Montoya past Vasser on lap 52 to move into fourth place. His Newman/Haas Ford/Swift patently was the fastest car on the track amid the frenetic traffic that is a fact of life in any short-oval race. Before long, both Montoya and Andretti were breathing down the necks of the race leaders. Montoya picked off Franchitti on lap 58, then

effortlessly outbraked Papis into Turn One to claim the lead a half-dozen laps later – only to find Andretti hot on his heels.

A fascinating needle match was now in prospect, but the intervention of a full-course yellow (to tow in Greg Moore's stricken Player's Mercedes/Reynard) promptly shifted the focus of activity onto the pit lane.

The routine stops saw a significant shuffle among the top ten. Papis and Castro-Neves each slipped back three positions, rejoining in sixth and eighth respectively, while Paul Tracy vaulted from ninth to fourth courtesy of outstanding service from Team KOOL Green. Then Franchitti made a good fist of the restart to breeze past Andretti into Turn One and reclaim second place.

A pair of protracted full-course cautions served to break up the middle stages of the race. The first came on lap 86 when Jan Magnussen's Visteon Ford/Reynard made heavy contact with the wall in Turn One after being nudged by Roberto Moreno's Big Kmart Ford/Swift in a dispute over 11th place.

At the restart, Franchitti got a run on Montoya through Turns One and Two, then made an opportunist dive to the inside at the end of the back straightaway. Barely a cigarette paper's width separated both the front and

rear wheels of the two Honda/Reynards as they swung through Turn Three, but Franchitti held his nerve and nosed ahead in Turn Four.

Almost simultaneously, a similar tussle between Tracy and Andretti for third culminated in both cars careening backward into the outside wall. Tracy had taken over the place going into Turn One, only to drift wide in the middle of the corner and lose momentum, which allowed Andretti to mount a counter-attack as they sped along the back straightaway. The Canadian was still narrowly ahead at the entry to Turn Three and began to make for the apex on his normal line, but Andretti, carrying plenty of speed down on the inside, had already earmarked the same piece of asphalt for his own use. With neither driver prepared to concede an inch, contact was inevitable.

Predictably, each blamed the other for the incident, although Andretti was the more outspoken. 'It's unbelievable – normal Paul Tracy driving,' he raged to ABC Sports pit reporter Gary Gerould. 'What was he thinking? Does he have a death wish? That was so blatant. He was swerving at me all the way down the straightaway, and when we got to the corner, he pinched me down and I had nowhere to go. He took both of us out.'

'It looked to me like we were going for the same piece of real estate,' proffered Tracy. 'I was about half a car length in front of Michael heading into the corner. I knew he was there, but I didn't think he was far enough alongside to outbrake me. This track is such a one-line place that you've got to turn in sometime.'

Vasser, who was holding a watching brief in fifth place at the time and was the principal beneficiary of the accident, perhaps had the best vantage point from which to pass judgment. 'I had a front-row seat for the Paul Tracy/Michael Andretti ego contest, and I thought it was a little early [in the race] for that,' remarked the '96 PPG Cup champion with a wry smile.

It was left to Franchitti and Montoya to stage a tense and exciting duel throughout the latter half of the 225-lap event, which was completed without any further cautions. The pivotal moment came on lap 127, when Franchitti was slightly delayed behind Raul Boesel's AAR Toyota/Eagle. Montoya seized the opportunity to forge ahead in Turn One, bringing the crowd to its feet.

Thereafter, the pair was rarely separated by more than a few car lengths,

Ticket to ride

A SENSATIONAL new promotional tool was unveiled during the Target Grand Prix weekend – a two-seater Champ Car that had been commissioned by Target/Chip Ganassi Racing and was driven by none other than Mario Andretti.

In fact, the car started life as Reynard 98I-020 and was raced successfully by Jimmy Vasser during the '98 season. The car's achievements included a front-row starting position at Gateway and a third-place finish in Toronto before it was assigned to testing duties. Since then, it had been extensively reworked by Dave Pendergraph's Performance By Design engineering business.

Right: Mario Andretti returned to the cockpit to give several company executives the ride of a lifetime aboard the two-seater.

Below: Michael Andretti and Paul Tracy charged through the field, but later collided and crashed on the entry to Turn Three.

The original suspension components had been retained and the car was still fitted with a 1998-spec Honda HRK engine. The bulk of the alterations, of course, were in the cockpit area, which had been lengthened by 12 inches to accommodate the extra passenger, who sat directly behind the driver, legs akimbo. The standard 35-gallon fuel cell had been replaced by a more suitable 12-gallon receptacle, and thus the overall weight distribution was affected only minimally.

'It handles very nice,' said Andretti after his first shakedown laps in the two-seater, which looked slightly incongruous, but was maintained to full-race standards by a small crew led by the vastly experienced Gary Neal. 'It feels very secure, very safe; it really does. Actually, I'm not surprised, I wouldn't expect any different. It's prepared perfectly, not a glitch.'

Several executives from Target and other team sponsors – plus ABC Sports pit reporter Gary Gerould – were treated to high-speed, two-lap tours of the track during the weekend, with Andretti circulating impressively and consistently in the mid-25-second range.

'Talk about heightening your appreciation!' declared a wide-eyed Gerould, grinning broadly, after stepping from the two-seater. 'There's no ride like that at Disneyland, that's for sure. You think you have an appreciation for what these guys do, but...'

Summarized Andretti, 'It's a real booster for our sport. People have no idea what the drivers have to deal with – how physical it is. Of course, I'm out there by myself, I don't have 26 or 27 other guys to worry about, but at least it gives them an idea.'

although the reluctance of the track surface to generate more than one line ensured that Montoya's lead was less in jeopardy than his narrow cushion suggested. The Colombian's only real problem came in the closing stages as he searched, in vain, for a way around PJ Jones, who steadfastly refused to go a lap down aboard Patrick Racing's Tecate/Quaker State Ford/Reynard.

'Most of the race traffic was no problem,' said Montoya, 'until I got to PJ. He's always in the way.'

For Franchitti, the bogeyman was Moreno, who, after losing two laps following his early skirmish with Magnussen, shadowed the #27 Team KOOL Green Honda/Reynard and proceeded to split the two leaders inside the final ten laps. The maneuver effectively put paid to Franchitti's challenge and allowed Montoya to breathe a little easier in the final minutes. Nevertheless, the latter's 0.783-second winning margin was an accurate reflection of a particularly evenly matched contest between the two principal championship rivals.

Vasser, Papis and Castro-Neves completed the top five, the trio blanketed by just half a second as they crossed the line. Vasser was relieved finally to make the podium in 1999, but felt that he might have given his teammate a run for his money had he not spent a large portion of the race bottled up behind Robby Gordon's lapped Toyota/Eagle. Vasser remonstrated angrily with his fellow Californian afterward.

Papis was obliged to conserve fuel in the closing stages, having made an earlier final pit stop than the other front-runners, while Castro-Neves was delighted to log a third consecutive points-paying finish after suffering appalling mechanical reliability for most of the year.

Jeremy Shaw

CHICAGO SNIPPETS

• Several drivers were **HEAVILY CRITICIZED** after the race, accused of failing to heed the blue 'move-over' flag, with PJ Jones singled out as the worst offender. CART Chief Steward Wally Dallenbach also earned the wrath of several leading contenders. 'Guys are supposed to give a little lift when they see the blue flag. I just don't understand why things aren't being done, [and why] black flags aren't being thrown,' said Dario Franchitti. Added Jimmy Vasser, 'I'm just a little surprised and confused why something wasn't done, when we stand up in the drivers' meeting and talk about it for hours on end. Wally told us what he was going to do [in the event of blocking] and he didn't do it.'

• Formula 1 team owner **FRANK WILLIAMS** (right) was an interested observer, paying his first visit to a Champ Car event in more than 15 years. Williams was a guest of Chip Ganassi.

Michael C. Brown

• PacWest Racing Group owner Bruce McCaw confirmed on race day that he had negotiated a **NEW CONTRACT** with primary sponsor Motorola for the 2000 FedEx Championship Series, and that 39-year-old Englishman Mark Blundell would continue at the wheel of the #18 Motorola Mercedes/Reynard for a fourth consecutive season. 'We're very pleased to extend our relationship with a proven winner like Mark Blundell,' said McCaw. 'Mark has been an excellent ambassador for both Motorola and PacWest, and plays a major role in the continuing development of our organization.'

• For the first time in CART's 20-year history, two **EAGLE CHASSIS** finished among the points. Raul Boesel, making his debut for Dan Gurney's All American Racers team, ran steadily to 12th after taking over from Gualter Salles. New customer Robby Gordon, who had driven Reynards and Swifts earlier in the year, enjoyed a strong run to tenth in his first outing in a similar Eagle 997.

• Some idea of the intensity of the **COMPETITION** could be gleaned from the morning warmup practice session, when all 26 starters were covered by just 0.8 second. (Luiz Garcia Jr. did not take up his position after crashing Hogan Racing's Mercedes/Lola heavily in qualifying.)

• **JAN MAGNUSSEN** drove both a Reynard 97I and a Swift 010.c for Patrick Racing during practice, before deciding to concentrate on the Reynard. The Dane did well on his oval debut, running as high as tenth before tangling with Roberto Moreno.

• **PATRICK CARPENTIER** made a welcome return to the #33 Player's/Indeck Mercedes/Reynard after missing the Miller Lite 200 at Mid-Ohio due to neck ligament injuries sustained in the accident with Mauricio Gugelmin in Detroit. Carpentier started and finished a respectable sixth.

FEDEX CHAMPIONSHIP SERIES • ROUND 15
TARGET GRAND PRIX
PRESENTED BY SHELL

CHICAGO MOTOR SPEEDWAY, CICERO, ILLINOIS

AUGUST 22, 225 laps – 231.525 miles

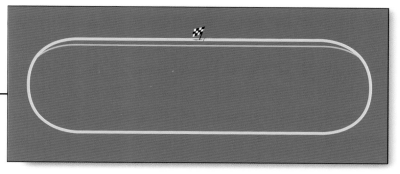

Place	Driver (Nat.)	No.	Team Sponsors Engine/Car	Tires	Q Speed	Q Time	Q Pos.	Laps	Time/Status	Ave. (mph)	Pts.
1	*Juan Montoya (COL)	4	Target/Chip Ganassi Racing Honda/Reynard 99I	FS	160.357	23.101s	10	225	1h 53m 38.704s	122.236	21
2	Dario Franchitti (GB)	27	Team KOOL Green Honda/Reynard 99I	FS	162.296	22.825s	4	225	1h 53m 39.487s	122.222	16
3	Jimmy Vasser (USA)	12	Target/Chip Ganassi Racing Honda/Reynard 99I	FS	162.331	22.820s	3	225	1h 53m 54.483s	121.954	14
4	Max Papis (I)	7	Team Rahal Miller Lite Ford Cosworth/Reynard 99I	FS	162.559	22.788s	1	225	1h 53m 54.659s	121.950	13
5	Helio Castro-Neves (BR)	9	Hogan Racing Hogan Motor Leasing Mercedes/Lola B99/00	FS	162.246	22.832s	5	225	1h 53m 55.039s	121.944	10
6	Patrick Carpentier (CDN)	33	Forsythe Racing Player's/Indeck Mercedes/Reynard 99I	FS	161.884	22.883s	6	225	1h 54m 00.055s	121.854	8
7	PJ Jones (USA)	40	Patrick Racing Tecate/Quaker State Ford Cosworth/Reynard 97I	FS	158.633	23.352s	14	225	1h 54m 03.237s	121.798	6
8	Bryan Herta (USA)	8	Team Rahal Shell Ford Cosworth/Reynard 99I	FS	161.842	22.889s	7	224	Running		5
9	Roberto Moreno (BR)	11	Newman/Haas Big Kmart Ford Cosworth/Swift 010.c	FS	161.222	22.977s	8	223	Running		4
10	Robby Gordon (USA)	22	Team Gordon Panasonic/Menards Toyota/Eagle 997	FS	156.317	23.698s	21	223	Running		3
11	Tony Kanaan (BR)	44	McDonald's Championship Racing Honda/Reynard 99I	FS	158.159	23.422s	15	222	Running		2
12	Raul Boesel (BR)	36	All American Racers Denso/Castrol Toyota/Eagle 997	GY	155.732	23.787s	22	222	Running		1
13	Gil de Ferran (BR)	5	Walker Racing Valvoline/Cummins Honda/Reynard 99I	GY	156.561	23.661s	19	221	Running		
14	*Cristiano da Matta (BR)	25	Arciero-Wells Racing MCI WorldCom Toyota/Reynard 99I	FS	161.019	23.006s	9	220	Running		
15	Dennis Vitolo (USA)	34	Payton/Coyne Nicoderm CQ Ford Cosworth/Reynard 98I	FS	150.751	24.573s	26	220	Running		
16	Richie Hearn (USA)	10	Della Penna Motorsports Budweiser Toyota/Reynard 99I	FS	153.220	24.177s	23	220	Running		
17	*Naoki Hattori (J)	15	Walker Racing Alpine Honda/Reynard 98I	GY	152.294	24.324s	25	217	Running		
18	Michel Jourdain Jr. (MEX)	19	Payton/Coyne Herdez/Viva Mexico Ford Cosworth/Lola T97/00	FS	156.324	23.697s	20	197	Engine		
19	Mauricio Gugelmin (BR)	17	PacWest Racing Group Hollywood Mercedes/Reynard 99I	FS	159.762	23.187s	12	187	Transmission		
20	Scott Pruett (USA)	24	Arciero-Wells Racing Pioneer Toyota/Reynard 99I	FS	159.124	23.280s	13	178	Engine		
21	Mark Blundell (GB)	18	PacWest Racing Group Motorola Mercedes/Reynard 99I	FS	162.381	22.813s	2	142	Cooling system		
22	Michael Andretti (USA)	6	Newman/Haas Kmart/Texaco Havoline Ford Cosworth/Swift 010.c	FS	156.906	23.609s	18	98	Accident		
23	Paul Tracy (CDN)	26	Team KOOL Green Honda/Reynard 99I	FS	157.006	23.594s	17	98	Accident		
24	Jan Magnussen (DK)	20	Patrick Racing Visteon Ford Cosworth/Reynard 98I	FS	157.179	23.568s	16	85	Accident		
25	Al Unser Jr. (USA)	2	Marlboro Team Penske Mercedes/Lola B99/00	GY	152.357	24.314s	24	64	Engine		
26	Greg Moore (CDN)	99	Forsythe Racing Player's/Indeck Mercedes/Reynard 99I	FS	160.017	23.150s	11	62	Turbo		
NS	*Luiz Garcia Jr.(BR)	21	Hogan Racing Hogan Motor Leasing/Tang Mercedes/Lola B99/00	FS	no speed	no time	–	–	Withdrawn		

* denotes rookie driver

Caution flags: Laps 1–2, yellow start; laps 64–73, tow/Moore; laps 74–75, yellow restart; laps 86–97, accident/Magnussen; laps 99–112, accident/Andretti and Tracy; lap 113, yellow restart. **Total:** Six for 41 laps.

Lap leaders: Max Papis, 1–63 (63 laps); Juan Montoya, 64–98 (35 laps); Dario Franchitti, 99–126 (28 laps); Montoya, 127–164 (38 laps); Franchitti, 165–166 (2 laps); Montoya, 167–225 (59 laps). **Totals:** Montoya, 132 laps; Papis, 63 laps; Franchitti, 30 laps.

Fastest race lap: Roberto Moreno, 23.687s, 156.390 mph on lap 195 (establishes record).

Championship positions: 1 Montoya, 172; **2** Franchitti, 168; **3** Andretti, 124; **4** Tracy, 122; **5** Fittipaldi, 101; **6** Moore, 97; **7** de Ferran, 96; **8** Fernandez, 95; **9** Vasser, 94; **10** Papis, 91; **11** Kanaan, 64; **12** Castro-Neves, 43; **13** Moreno, 42; **14** Carpentier, 41; **15** Herta, 40; **16** Jones, 37; **17** da Matta, Unser Jr. & Gordon, 20; **20** Pruett & Gugelmin, 14; **22** Hearn, 13; **23** Blundell, 8; **24** Jourdain Jr., 6; **25** Marques & Barron, 4; **27** Gidley, 3; **28** Vitolo & Salles, 2; **30** Rodriguez & Boesel, 1.

OMEGA
OFFICIAL TIMEKEEPER OF CART

VANCOUVER

1 – MONTOYA
2 – CARPENTIER
3 – VASSER

FEDEX CHAMPIONSHIP SERIES • ROUND 16

QUALIFYING

Team KOOL Green set the pace on Friday, Paul Tracy topping the timing charts in morning practice and teammate Dario Franchitti earning the provisional pole later in the day. The following morning, it was the turn of 'Super Sub' Roberto Moreno to take a taste of the glory for Newman/Haas Racing, followed by Mark Blundell, who gave the PacWest team a much-needed shot in the arm. Final qualifying, though, saw Juan Montoya back on top when it mattered most. The series leader's progress had been blunted by engine problems in both practice sessions, obliging him to use the spare Target Honda/Reynard. This proved to be no more than a minor inconvenience. Montoya duly claimed his fifth pole of the campaign.

'I think the day was good,' said the Colombian with characteristic understatement. 'The car felt much better. We had some problems this weekend, which cost a lot of time.'

PJ Jones turned out to be the surprise of qualifying. The Californian set the eighth-best time on Friday, substituting for injured buddy Adrian Fernandez in Pat Patrick's Tecate/Quaker State Ford/Reynard, and on Saturday proved that it was no fluke by annexing the outside front-row starting position.

'I'm happy for Tecate, Quaker State and Adrian,' said Jones. 'He deserves a lot of credit. If it wasn't for him, I wouldn't have this opportunity.'

Several drivers had hoped to improve their times in the waning moments, but were prevented from doing so when Jones nosed lightly into the tire wall at Turn Three, bringing the session to a premature close. The red flag, though, was good news for Tracy, who already had gotten the best from his tires. Franchitti, meanwhile, ended up fourth after what he described as a 'dreadful session'.

'It was just horrible. We went almost as fast this morning with full tanks and 30 laps on the tires,' declared Franchitti who, to make matters worse, failed to notice the warning flags and slid heavily into Jones' parked car.

Blundell and Moreno also were within 0.1 second of Jones on the closely-matched grid, while Gil de Ferran, Michael Andretti, Greg Moore and Mauricio Gugelmin completed the top ten.

Fresh chance for PJ Jones

PJ Jones had much to prove when he was invited to drive Adrian Fernandez's Tecate/Quaker State Ford Cosworth/Reynard after the Mexican had suffered a broken right wrist when he crashed during practice at Detroit. Jones had been unceremoniously dumped by Patrick Racing after a dozen races in the sister Visteon entry, despite the fact that he had scored a fine second-place finish at Nazareth and was lying a respectable 14th in the points table. Nevertheless, his close friendship with Fernandez led to a fresh opportunity with the team.

Jones, who had endured a tough time with the recalcitrant Visteon Swift, struggled initially at Mid-Ohio when he was installed in Fernandez's '97 Reynard. Matters were much improved at Chicago, where he finished a strong seventh. Then came his front-row starting position in Canada.

'It's really satisfying,' admitted Jones. 'It's been a real confidence tester all year. I never really had the support behind me. I have been asking to get in the Reynard all year. We were not that good in Mid-Ohio, but everyone else tested there and we didn't, so we were a little behind there too.'

Added Fernandez, 'This is fantastic. He needed that big-time. He has been going through a lot of things during the year, and I am really happy for him. He is really starting to communicate well with [race engineer] John [Ward], and that takes some time. It takes a few races. I am very proud of him. I am proud because he is driving my car and he has my sponsors up on the front row.'

Unfortunately, the team erred on race day by electing not to adopt a full rain setup, despite the track being completely saturated prior to the start. Jones *(below)* struggled from the get-go. He was passed by Paul Tracy at the start and slipped quickly to fourth, where he remained until sliding into the escape road at Turn One on lap 25. Jones later crashed after a gamble on switching to slick tires failed to pay off.

'I'm disappointed because the car was strong all weekend,' concluded Jones. 'The crew did a fantastic job preparing the car. We just didn't get any luck with the weather and missed a little on the race setup.'

Come rain or shine, Juan Montoya was the man in Vancouver. The race began on a sodden track behind the pace car *(left)*, but was concluded in glorious sunshine *(below left)*, with the Colombian still out in front.

FOR the second time during his sensational rookie campaign, Juan Montoya completed a hat-trick of victories when he stormed home in treacherous conditions to win the tenth annual Molson Indy Vancouver. The Colombian's latest success was his seventh of the season, equaling the rookie record set by Nigel Mansell in 1993 and taking him to within one win of the single-season record held jointly by Michael Andretti (set in '91) and Al Unser Jr. ('93). More importantly, Montoya extended his championship advantage to 23 points over Dario Franchitti, who made a mistake while challenging for the lead and fell to a disappointing tenth-place finish.

'This was a really good day for us,' said a delighted Montoya. 'Having this [championship] lead in my pocket feels really good.'

Montoya qualified Chip Ganassi's Target Honda/Reynard on pole for the fifth time, but wasn't happy in the Sunday morning warmup, on a wet track, setting only the 17th-fastest time more than two seconds adrift of pace-setter Tony Kanaan. Once again, veteran race engineer Morris Nunn came to the rescue, and a few judicious modifications to the setup transformed the car for the race. The rain returned with a vengeance prior to the start. Indeed, the track became flooded in several locations, leading CART Chief Steward Wally Dallenbach to decree that the race would be started behind the pace car. Moments before the green flag was due to be displayed after nine slow laps, however, Michael Andretti caused another delay when, inexplicably, he spun his Kmart/Texaco Havoline Ford Cosworth/Swift.

'I just lost it,' said an embarrassed Andretti, who fell a lap down before being restarted by the CART Safety Team. 'It was a stupid, stupid mistake. It cost us a podium finish for sure.'

With 11 laps in the books, the order finally was given for Starter Jim Swintal to wave the green flag. Montoya took full advantage of unimpeded vision as he romped clear of the field, which was led by Paul Tracy, who elicited a huge cheer from the partisan Canadian crowd by slicing past surprise front-row qualifier PJ Jones on the back straightaway. Incredibly, Montoya was almost three seconds to the good by the time he splashed around to complete the first lap of full-fledged competition. Next time by, though, he was greeted once again by crossed yellow flags, signaling another full-course caution after Al Unser Jr., running a distant 22nd, had tagged the

wall. Already, the two most experienced drivers were out of contention.

Once again Montoya stamped his authority on the proceedings when the race was restarted, completing lap 17 a massive three seconds clear of Tracy,

then extending his margin to 4.4 and 5.4 seconds over the next two laps. By now, the rain had abated, however, and soon Tracy's KOOL Honda/Reynard began to whittle away at the deficit. Between laps 30 and 35, the

gap diminished rapidly from 4.2 seconds to just a car length or so.

'When the track started drying out, I started losing the rear tires,' declared Montoya, 'and I was a bit concerned because I didn't see any more rain coming.'

Roberto Moreno had emerged a strong third in the Big Kmart Ford/Swift, having passed Mark Blundell's Motorola Mercedes/Reynard on lap 28. Franchitti, meanwhile, having started fourth, lost three positions in the early stages as he struggled to cope with excessive oversteer. Fortunately, his car's handling improved as the track began to dry and he, too, passed the struggling Blundell.

All eyes, though, were on Tracy, who brought the crowd to its feet with a magnificent pass for the lead in Turn Seven on the 36th lap. Unfortunately, little more than a mile later, Tracy undid all his good work by spinning in Turn Three. His car sustained a bent rear-suspension toe-link, although he continued in third behind Montoya and Moreno.

Moments later, the yellow flags waved again after Bryan Herta, having already inadvertently punted off teammate Max Papis, locked up and spun while attempting to pass Mauricio Gugelmin in Turn Eight.

All of the leaders seized the opportunity to make pit stops during the ensuing full-course caution. Montoya took on fresh wet tires and a full load of methanol, resuming once again in the lead. Moreno, though, had a problem as he attempted to leave his pit. The engine died momentarily and had to be refired. Despite a lengthy delay, Moreno lost only two positions – to Tracy and Franchitti – but later spun, losing any hope of a podium finish.

Surprisingly, Jones and Greg Moore, both of whom had fallen off the lead lap due to separate incidents, opted to switch to dry tires during their otherwise routine pit stops. Both, however, soon retired after making contact with the omnipresent concrete walls.

'We made the change just a little too early,' admitted Moore. It was the fourth time in four Champ Car appearances that the local boy from Maple Ridge, B.C., had failed to finish in front of his home crowd.

Fortunately for Canadian-funded Player's/Forsythe Racing, Moore's teammate Patrick Carpentier took up the slack. After qualifying 11th, he worked his way past the two PacWest drivers, Blundell and Gugelmin. Sundry errors by other fancied contenders enabled him to move up to fifth, behind Moreno, following the pit stops.

Left: Jimmy Vasser parlayed a sensible drive into his second successive third-place for Target/Chip Ganassi Racing.

Above: Cristiano da Matta hustles his M WorldCom Toyota/Reynard through the revised Turn 12/13 complex.

Below and right: Patrick Carpentier delighted both himself and the Canadian crowd by scoring his best-ever road-course finish in a Champ Car.
Photos: Michael C. Brown

Montermini makes his mark

ANDREA Montermini made a solid impression while making his debut aboard Dan Gurney's All American Racers Denso/Castrol Toyota/Eagle. It was the 35-year-old Italian's first Champ Car ride since contesting seven races for the unheralded Project Indy and Euromotorsport teams in 1993 and '94, the highlight of which was a fine run to fourth (after starting sixth) at Detroit in '93.

Since then, Montermini had made an unsuccessful bid to secure a full-time ride in Formula 1 and had raced only sporadically in sports car events. Nevertheless, he had not given up hope of resurrecting his career in North America and gave a fine account of himself during a midsummer test with Tony Bettenhausen's team. His aspirations with the Indianapolis-based organization foundered due to a lack of finance, but after a good word from Bettenhausen, Gurney agreed to give the personable Italian a try.

After merely a brief run in the Eagle at Buttonwillow Raceway Park in California earlier in the week, Montermini faced a steep learning curve upon his arrival in Vancouver. He was 22nd on the provisional grid, within a half-second of the best Toyota qualifying time, which represented a respectable effort. On Saturday afternoon, however, he did himself no favors by clipping the wall at the apex of Turn Three, which sent him heavily into the wall on the opposite side of the track. The incident restricted him to 25th on the final grid.

After switching to the backup Eagle 997 on Sunday morning, Montermini completed more laps than anyone in the damp conditions, ultimately setting the seventh-fastest time. He shone in the early stages of the race, too, climbing to 16th before indulging in a quick spin, which dropped him back to 22nd. Montermini rose as high as eighth before damaging the rear suspension in the closing stages when he clipped the wall at Turn 12. The resulting handling problems caused him to slip to a nonetheless respectable 11th place at the finish.

'On wet tires, we were fourth or fifth quickest,' said Montermini proudly. 'The setup we worked up this morning was good. I had fun.'

Michael C. Brown

'At first the car had a little too much push,' related Carpentier, 'but it got better as the race progressed.'

Richie Hearn, who had started 21st, ran sixth after team owner John Della Penna employed a creative strategy that entailed making a pit stop during the long early caution period. The Budweiser Toyota/Reynard duly stayed out on the track when everyone else pitted on lap 38. Hearn made his second visit to pit lane on lap 54, falling as low as 15th, but took full advantage of the drying conditions to take on dry-weather tires.

Montoya, meanwhile, took off into a commanding lead yet again. Initially, Tracy held off Franchitti, despite worsening oversteer caused by the bent rear suspension. On lap 50, though, Jones – on slick tires – slithered wildly through Turn 12 and inadvertently was nudged into the wall by Tracy. The Canadian lost valuable momentum, which allowed Franchitti to get a run on his teammate. Franchitti completed the pass in Turn One.

The gap between Montoya and Franchitti remained at around seven seconds until lap 55, when Moore's attempt to maintain the pace on slick tires ended abruptly in Turn Seven. The crash precipitated yet another full-course caution, which allowed Franchitti to close up onto Montoya's tail. Glimpsing an opportunity to make up some ground in the championship standings, Franchitti made an ill-judged bid for the lead at Turn Four on the restart during lap 60. He nosed alongside Montoya briefly before pirouetting across the track and into the wall.

'It wasn't a clever move,' admitted the chastened Scotsman, who was fortunate to be able to continue. 'It's disappointing, but there's nobody to blame but me. We worked pretty hard to get back up to second place... very frustrating.'

Even worse for Team KOOL Green, Tracy slid into the wall at Turn 12 on the very same lap.

'The car was really poor in handling and I was just trying to stay on the track,' explained Tracy, referring to the damaged suspension following his earlier brush with the wall. 'Over there in the last chicane, it broke.'

Montoya was left with an easy run to the checkered flag, which, due to the frequent cautions, was shown at the two-hour mark rather than the scheduled distance of 90 laps. As it turned out, he might have struggled in the late stages, as at this point the track was almost completely dry – at least on the optimal racing line. Several drivers on slick tires harbored hopes of making significant progress in the waning laps, but their aspirations were thwarted by yet another caution – the seventh of the day – after Michel Jourdain Jr. was punted into the wall by an impatient Jan Magnussen.

Only seven minutes remained following the cleanup. Those contenders still on wet tires, including Montoya, found their rubber disintegrating badly as time ticked by, but a couple of quick laps gave him enough of a margin to cruise home comfortably ahead of Carpentier.

'It's very gratifying because it's contracts time,' grinned the French-Canadian, still seeking to finalize a deal for 2000, after equaling his career-best result. 'Also, it's great because it's at home in Canada, so it feels really good.'

Jimmy Vasser drove a typically sensible race to third, making no mistakes as he rose steadily through the field after a dismal time in qualifying left him languishing in 16th. Gugelmin secured his best result of the year, fourth in his Hollywood Mercedes/Reynard, while Cristiano da Matta drove a fine race to fifth in the MCI WorldCom Toyota/Reynard, followed closely by Hearn and Magnussen.

'It was fun. I had a great time. We hit the strategy just right by switching to slicks. Unfortunately, those last couple of yellows killed us. I could have been on the podium without those,' mused Hearn.

Jeremy Shaw

VANCOUVER SNIPPETS

• **PAUL TRACY** set the second-fastest time in Friday qualifying, but the time was disallowed after his car failed the 'two-inch rule' (the minimum permitted distance between the reference plane on the bottom of the chassis and the lowest edge of the sidepod) in routine technical inspection.

• In response to **SAFETY CONCERNS**, several areas of the Concord Pacific Place temporary circuit had been modified since the initial running of the Molson Indy event on the eastern side of False Creek in 1998. Most notably, Turns One and Two had been widened, the pit exit road having been moved around the corner; and the final corner, Turn 12, had been made significantly slower due to the incorporation of a preceding slow chicane. In addition, the tight Turn Five chicane had been replaced by a fast sweeper that led onto a long back straightaway.

• Helio Castro-Neves *(right)* experienced another fraught weekend. After suffering no fewer than **FIVE ENGINE FAILURES**, Hogan Racing erred on Saturday afternoon in attempting to send out its Brazilian charge in a car that had been officially withdrawn from competition during qualifying on Friday. Much to car owner Carl Hogan's chagrin, Castro-Neves was not permitted to leave the pit lane. After starting an unrepresentative 26th, Castro-Neves drove a fine race to finish eighth, despite losing two positions on the final lap as his badly worn wet-weather tires proved no match for the slicks of Richie Hearn and Jan Magnussen.

• Officials of Player's Ltd. and Forsythe Racing hosted a press conference prior to provisional qualifying to announce that three **CANADIAN DRIVERS** - David Empringham, 34, Lee Bentham, 29, and Alexandre Tagliani, 26 - would audition for the ride being vacated by Greg Moore, who confirmed at Detroit that he would conclude his lengthy association in favor of a ride with Marlboro Team Penske in 2000.

• Roberto Moreno was presented with an **OMEGA SPEEDMASTER** watch in Vancouver, his prize for setting fastest lap of the race in the previous FedEx Championship Series race at Chicago Motor Speedway. Moreno, however, immediately passed the watch along to Newman/Haas race engineer Todd Bowland. 'He's the one who won it for me,' said Moreno, 'so he deserves it.'

• **MEMO GIDLEY** earned a PPG Cup point after finishing 12th in one of Payton/Coyne Racing's two Herdez/Viva Mexico Ford/Lolas. Gidley ran as high as eighth inside the final ten laps, before being forced to ease his pace due to a deflating left rear tire.

• **ANDREA MONTERMINI** became the fourth different driver (joining Alex Barron, Gualter Salles and Raul Boesel) to score points during the season aboard Dan Gurney's AAR Denso/Castrol Toyota/Eagle.

Michael C. Brown

FEDEX CHAMPIONSHIP SERIES • ROUND 16
MOLSON INDY VANCOUVER

CONCORD PACIFIC PLACE, VANCOUVER, B.C., CANADA

SEPTEMBER 5, 74 laps – 131.794 miles

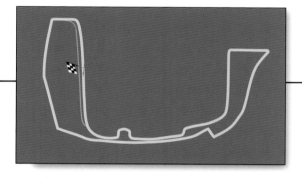

Place	Driver (Nat.)	No.	Team Sponsors Engine/Car	Tires	Q Speed	Q Time	Q Pos.	Laps	Time/Status	Ave. (mph)	Pts.
1	*Juan Montoya (COL)	4	Target/Chip Ganassi Racing Honda/Reynard 99I	FS	105.730	1m 00.641s	1	74	2h 01m 08.183s	65.279	22
2	Patrick Carpentier (CDN)	33	Forsythe Racing Player's/Indeck Mercedes/Reynard 99I	FS	104.282	1m 01.483s	11	74	2h 01m 15.768s	65.211	16
3	Jimmy Vasser (USA)	12	Target/Chip Ganassi Racing Honda/Reynard 99I	FS	103.655	1m 01.855s	16	74	2h 01m 16.147s	65.207	14
4	Mauricio Gugelmin (BR)	17	PacWest Racing Group Hollywood Mercedes/Reynard 99I	FS	104.282	1m 01.483s	10	74	2h 01m 21.226s	65.162	12
5	*Cristiano da Matta (BR)	25	Arciero-Wells Racing MCI WorldCom Toyota/Reynard 99I	FS	103.453	1m 01.976s	17	74	2h 01m 22.184s	65.153	10
6	Richie Hearn (USA)	10	Della Penna Motorsports Budweiser Toyota/Reynard 99I	FS	102.550	1m 02.522s	22	74	2h 01m 22.475s	65.151	8
7	Jan Magnussen (DK)	20	Patrick Racing Visteon Ford Cosworth/Reynard 98I	FS	102.717	1m 02.420s	21	74	2h 01m 23.426s	65.142	6
8	Helio Castro-Neves (BR)	9	Hogan Racing Hogan Motor Leasing Mercedes/Lola B99/00	FS	100.870	1m 03.563s	26	74	2h 01m 23.500s	65.142	5
9	Tony Kanaan (BR)	44	McDonald's Championship Racing Honda/Reynard 99I	FS	103.719	1m 01.817s	15	74	2h 01m 24.848s	65.129	4
10	Dario Franchitti (GB)	27	Team KOOL Green Honda/Reynard 99I	FS	105.191	1m 00.952s	4	74	2h 01m 27.200s	65.108	3
11	Andrea Montermini (I)	36	All American Racers Denso/Castrol Toyota/Eagle 997	GY	101.279	1m 03.306s	25	74	2h 01m 42.201s	64.975	2
12	*Memo Gidley (USA)	71	Payton/Coyne Herdez/Viva Mexico Ford Cosworth/Lola T97/00	FS	102.854	1m 02.337s	20	74	2h 01m 43.850s	64.960	1
13	Scott Pruett (USA)	24	Arciero-Wells Racing Pioneer Toyota/Reynard 99I	FS	103.774	1m 01.784s	14	74	2h 01m 47.464s	64.928	
14	Michael Andretti (USA)	6	Newman/Haas Kmart/Texaco Havoline Ford Cosworth/Swift 010.c	FS	104.833	1m 01.160s	8	73	Running		
15	Roberto Moreno (BR)	11	Newman/Haas Big Kmart Ford Cosworth/Swift 010.c	FS	105.150	1m 00.976s	6	71	Running		
16	*Luiz Garcia Jr.(BR)	21	Hogan Racing Hogan Motor Leasing/Tang Mercedes/Lola B99/00	FS	104.426	1m 03.844s	27	71	Running		
17	Michel Jourdain Jr. (MEX)	19	Payton/Coyne Herdez/Viva Mexico Ford Cosworth/Lola T97/00	FS	103.260	1m 02.092s	18	64	Accident		
18	Paul Tracy (CDN)	26	Team KOOL Green Honda/Reynard 99I	FS	105.258	1m 00.913s	3	59	Accident		
19	Mark Blundell (GB)	18	PacWest Racing Group Motorola Mercedes/Reynard 99I	FS	105.182	1m 00.957s	5	59	Accident		
20	Greg Moore (CDN)	99	Forsythe Racing Player's/Indeck Mercedes/Reynard 99I	FS	104.310	1m 01.467s	9	52	Accident		
21	PJ Jones (USA)	40	Patrick Racing Tecate/Quaker State Ford Cosworth/Reynard 97I	FS	105.321	1m 00.877s	2	49	Accident		
22	Robby Gordon (USA)	22	Team Gordon Panasonic/Menards Toyota/Eagle 997	FS	103.240	1m 02.104s	19	41	Accident		
23	Max Papis (I)	7	Team Rahal Miller Lite Ford Cosworth/Reynard 99I	FS	104.249	1m 01.503s	12	39	Accident		
24	Bryan Herta (USA)	8	Team Rahal Shell Ford Cosworth/Reynard 99I	FS	104.105	1m 01.588s	13	35	Accident		
25	Al Unser Jr. (USA)	2	Marlboro Team Penske Mercedes/Lola B99/00	GY	102.060	1m 02.822s	24	12	Accident		
26	Gil de Ferran (BR)	5	Walker Racing Valvoline/Cummins Honda/Reynard 99I	GY	105.110	1m 00.999s	7	12	Accident		
27	*Naoki Hattori (J)	15	Walker Racing Alpine Honda/Reynard 98I	GY	102.345	1m 02.647s	23	4	Brakes		

* denotes rookie driver

Caution flags: Laps 1–8, rain/standing water; laps 9–10, spin/Andretti; laps 13–15, accident/Unser Jr.; laps 37–45, accident/Herta; laps 55–58, accident/Moore; laps 60–63, accident/Blundell & Tracy; laps 64–67, accident/Jourdain Jr. **Total:** Seven for 31 laps.

Lap leaders: Juan Montoya, 1–35 (35 laps); Paul Tracy, 36 (1 lap); Montoya, 37–74 (38 laps). Totals: Montoya, 73 laps; Tracy, 1 lap.

Fastest race lap: Juan Montoya, 1m 11.441s, 89.747 mph on lap 69.

Championship positions: 1 Montoya, 194; **2** Franchitti, 171; **3** Andretti, 124; **4** Tracy, 122; **5** Fittipaldi, 101; **6** Moore, 97; **7** de Ferran, 96; **8** Fernandez, 95; **9** Vasser, 94; **10** Papis, 91; **11** Kanaan, 68; **12** Carpentier, 57; **13** Castro-Neves, 48; **14** Moreno, 42; **15** Herta, 40; **16** Jones, 37; **17** da Matta, 30; **18** Gugelmin, 26; **19** Hearn, 21; **20** Unser Jr. & Gordon, 20; **22** Pruett, 14; **23** Blundell, 8; **24** Jourdain Jr. & Magnussen, 6; **26** Marques, Barron & Gidley, 4; **29** Vitolo, Salles & Montermini, 2; **32** Rodriguez & Boesel, 1.

OMEGA
OFFICIAL TIMEKEEPER OF CART

The Master of Monterey, Bryan Herta, crests the hill approaching the Corkscrew en route to the second Champ Car victory of his career. Both have come at Laguna Seca.
Photo: Michael C. Brown

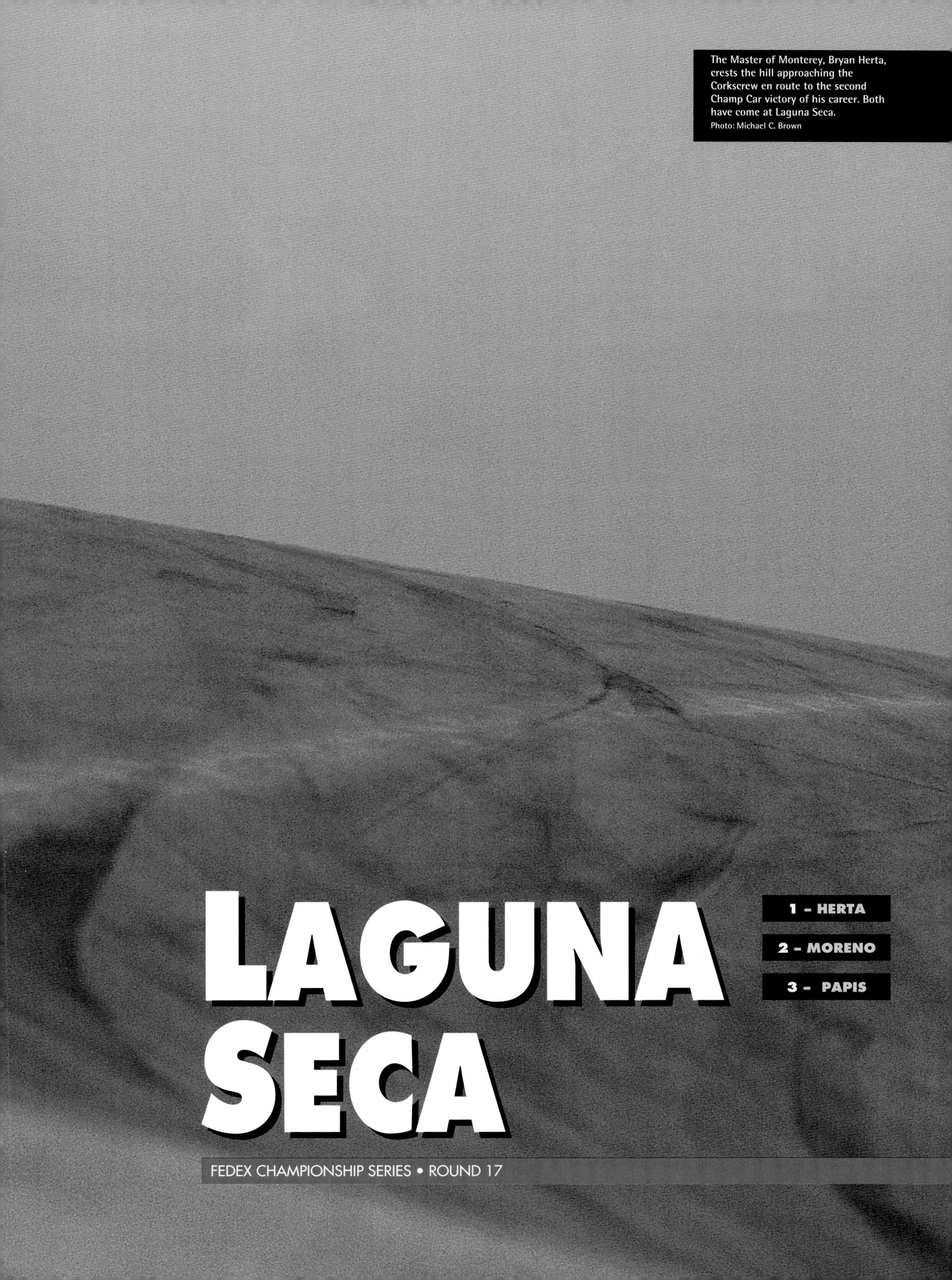

LAGUNA SECA

1 - HERTA

2 - MORENO

3 - PAPIS

FEDEX CHAMPIONSHIP SERIES • ROUND 17

Photo left: Allsport US

QUALIFYING

Bryan Herta wasted little time in asserting his authority, overcoming a couple of niggling problems in the first practice session to set the second fastest time. Then he produced a sensational lap to annex the provisional pole with Team Rahal's Shell Ford/Reynard. Herta emerged fully 0.404 second quicker than his nearest challenger, but reckoned there was even more to come.

'Pretty good,' he summarized. 'I made a mistake or two. There's a bit more in it. I'm not going to go a half-second quicker, but I think there's a couple of tenths. Having said that, I really nailed a couple of corners, so it was definitely a good lap.'

When the final qualifying session was canceled out of respect for Gonzalo Rodriguez, Herta's third successive Champ Car pole at Laguna Seca was assured.

Tony Kanaan also overcame a disappointing sequence of results to annex the outside front-row position in the McDonald's Honda/Reynard.

'Sometimes we do a good job in practice, and we put on new tires and the car isn't as good as it should be,' he related. 'We got it right today.'

Max Papis chose a slightly different setup to Herta and couldn't match his teammate's time, but the Italian was still fleet enough to secure a place on row two of the grid alongside Greg Moore, who was fastest of the Mercedes-Benz contingent.

Michael Andretti was relatively content with fifth on the grid, considering the fact that his Newman/Haas team had not tested on the demanding road course since switching to Firestone tires immediately before the first race of the season.

'Even after 16 years of racing at Laguna Seca for Newman/Haas Racing, we really didn't have much data for this race, so we were behind,' said Andretti. 'You can't imagine how different the car reacts to certain setup changes on a different type of tires.'

Mauricio Gugelmin continued his recent resurgence by qualifying sixth, ahead of Adrian Fernandez, who performed well for Patrick Racing despite missing the previous four races due to injury. Scott Pruett also posted a good effort: eighth in the fastest of the Toyota-powered cars.

Roberto Moreno, under intense pressure from Max Papis in the closing stages, secured a career-best finish.

Below left: Max Papis compounded team owner Bobby Rahal's joy by taking third.

BRYAN Herta banished all thoughts of what thus far had been a disappointing season by scoring a dominant victory in the Honda Grand Prix of Monterey Featuring the Shell 300. The 29-year-old American continued his remarkable sequence of success at Laguna Seca Raceway by qualifying on the pole for the third year in a row, then repeated his 1998 triumph by leading throughout the 83-lap race. Sadly, Herta's magnificent performance on a gloriously sunny September afternoon was overshadowed by the death of popular Uruguayan Gonzalo Rodriguez who, making only his second appearance in a Champ Car, crashed his Marlboro Mercedes/Lola at the Corkscrew turn during practice on Saturday morning and succumbed to his injuries.

'Obviously, after the crappy season we've had, we really needed this win,' said Herta, 'but it pales into insignificance when one considers what happened yesterday. That was a tragic accident, so it certainly puts a damper on our day.'

Herta stamped his authority on the proceedings from the outset, making full use of the seventh pole of his Champ Car career by catapulting Team Rahal's Shell Ford Cosworth/Reynard into the lead when the green flag was waved. Fellow front-row qualifier Tony Kanaan led the chase in Jerry Forsythe's McDonald's Honda/Reynard.

'It was a great start – no dramatics – which, when you start from the pole, is exactly what you want,' said Herta.

Teammate Max Papis slotted into third in the Miller Lite Ford/Reynard, followed by Michael Andretti (Kmart/Texaco Havoline Ford/Swift), who snuck ahead of Greg Moore's Player's Mercedes/Reynard when the Canadian attempted (and failed) to execute a brave maneuver around the outside of Papis at Turn Two. Adrian Fernandez, making a welcome return to Pat Patrick's Tecate/Quaker State Ford/Reynard after missing the previous four races due to a broken right arm, ran sixth after ousting Mauricio Gugelmin's Hollywood Mercedes/Reynard at the start. The biggest mover, meanwhile, was Paul Tracy, who rose from 11th to seventh in his Team KOOL Green Honda/Reynard, followed by Gugelmin and the second KOOL car of Dario Franchitti, who also made a smart getaway, rising three places at the expense of Scott Pruett, Gil de Ferran and Helio Castro-Neves.

The two leaders soon began to edge clear of Papis in third place, Kanaan remaining within a second or so of Herta in the early stages. The gap

Tragedy in practice

GONZALO Rodriguez, 27, from Montevideo, Uruguay, was fatally injured in a crash during practice. Rodriguez, a front-runner in the European-based Formula 3000 Championship for the previous three seasons, was competing in only his second Champ Car event for Marlboro Team Penske. He had placed a promising 12th on his debut in Detroit.

Rodriguez was running mid-pack times in his Mercedes/Lola when he locked his brakes at the top of the hill, prior to the Corkscrew. His car careened straight on, traversed a short gravel trap and slammed headlong into a concrete barrier lined by a single wall of tires. The car vaulted over the barrier before landing upside down.

The practice session was halted soon after the crash occurred, and even though no official announcement was made for almost three hours, word began to filter down to the pit lane concerning the apparent severity of the incident. At 12 noon, after Rodriguez's family in South America had been informed of the tragedy, CART Director of Medical Affairs Dr. Steve Olvey made the following statement: 'It is with deep regret that I announce that driver Gonzalo Rodriguez was fatally injured this morning in the crash that occurred. He was pronounced dead at 10.10 a.m. at the Community Hospital of the Monterey Peninsula by Dr. Robert Keaney and myself. He died of massive head and neck injuries as a result of the crash.'

Added CART Chairman and Chief Executive Officer Andrew Craig, 'On behalf of Championship Auto Racing Teams, on behalf of all our drivers and everybody involved both in the FedEx Championship Series and Laguna Seca Raceway, I express my deepest sympathy to Gonzalo's family and friends on this very, very sad day. Gonzalo was a talented young race car driver who had the potential for a great racing career. No words can alleviate the sadness of his family and friends, but we send them our deepest sympathy at this tragic time.'

reached as high as 2.7 seconds on lap 20, by which time Papis trailed by a further 6.1 seconds. In effect, this was a two-horse race.

'Everything was good,' said Herta. 'We were able to do whatever we needed to do. If we needed to save fuel, we saved fuel. If we needed to pick up the pace, we were able to pick up the pace. It's rare you have a day like this.'

The Californian continued to lead a high-speed procession that saw no more changes of position among the top nine during the first 24 laps. The only significant alteration to the order came on lap 14, when Gil de Ferran fell from tenth to 15th.

'I was adjusting the [fuel] mixture and knocked off the ignition switch,' explained the Brazilian sheepishly. 'I knew right away what had happened, but it took a couple of tries to get the engine to restart.'

De Ferran rejoined behind Pruett, Jimmy Vasser, Castro-Neves, Roberto Moreno and a surprisingly low-placed Juan Montoya. The FedEx Championship Series points leader was suffering a rare off weekend and, after qualifying a distant 16th, was unable to make any significant progress.

'We were really struggling with the car,' admitted Montoya, who nonetheless salvaged an eighth-place finish. 'In the race, I didn't want to push the car too hard and make any mistakes. But we leave here with some points for the championship and now we'll get ready for Houston.'

The first pit stops came on lap 25 – slightly earlier than originally planned – during the first of only two full-course cautions after Castro-Neves' Hogan Motor Leasing Mercedes/Lola was stranded by a broken throttle cable. The leading positions again remained unchanged, with Herta ahead of Kanaan, Papis, Andretti, Moore and Fernandez.

One lap after the restart, Fernandez made a bold move to the inside of Moore under braking for the Turn Two hairpin. It was perfectly judged. Moore attempted to close the door, but too late. Fernandez had filled the gap already and was through into fifth, despite momentary contact, which forced Moore wide and enabled Tracy also to pass his fellow Canadian.

Three laps later, Franchitti tried to make a similar move on Moore. This time, however, the Scotsman wasn't completely alongside when Moore turned into the corner. Contact again. Neither protagonist survived. Franchitti retired to the pits with broken suspension, while Moore lasted only a few more laps before succumbing to a damaged gearbox oil line.

'There aren't too many places to pass on this track, so you have to make your own opportunities and take advantage of any openings,' claimed Franchitti. 'I had practiced that move a couple of times. I got a good run and Greg left the door open, so I went for it. I was alongside and committed; it was too late to back off when we made contact.'

Vasser and Moreno gratefully picked up another couple of positions, followed by Pruett, who had lost two places during the pit stops.

Up ahead, however, there was no change. Once more Herta and Kanaan

A record of success

Michael C. Brown

Bryan Herta acknowledges the applause from the crowd as team boss Bobby Rahal holds the winner's trophy.

BRYAN Herta, as usual, was on scintillating form when the FedEx Championship Series visited Laguna Seca Raceway. For some peculiar reason – which he claims not to understand – the American has enjoyed an amazing record of success at the scenic and demanding road course situated close to the California coastline, a couple of hours south of San Francisco. He won on his debut at the track in the Barber Saab (now Dodge) Pro Series in 1991. Also he gained victory from the pole in two Indy Lights races in '92 and '93. And in five Champ Car appearances, he has never failed to qualify on the front row of the grid.

'It feels good to be back at Laguna,' said the 29-year-old Herta. 'We had a good test session here earlier this year, so I thought we'd have a chance for the pole again. It's important to do well right now after the tough year we've had. We still have a chance to make the season worthwhile with a win and a couple of podium finishes. Other than Montoya's wins, Dario [Franchitti] has two and there are a lot of single race winners.

So another win here would help our season.'

Sure enough, Herta repeated his maiden Champ Car victory, scored one year earlier, by leading from flag to flag in his Shell Ford Cosworth/Reynard.

'My car was almost perfect,' he reflected. 'The only problem that I had was toward the end of the second stint when I started to slide around a bit and lose the rear end. But I came in [to the pits] and put a fresh set of Firestones on for the finish and it was good at the end.'

Herta remained under pressure from Roberto Moreno in the closing stages of the race, but judged his pace perfectly before taking the checkered flag a comfortable 1.825 seconds ahead of the Brazilian.

Regarding his remarkable string of success at Laguna Seca, Herta said, 'If there is a reason, I don't know what it is, and I don't really care. I'm just happy to have a place like this where I've experienced some success, and I hope it will continue.'

great job getting me restarted. What saved me was the gap we had on fourth place.'

Papis resumed ahead of Moreno, whose Newman/Haas crew performed service fast enough for him to rejoin in front of Vasser. The unfortunate Fernandez and Tracy fell from fourth and fifth to sixth and seventh after making their stops immediately before the caution.

The most dramatic moment of the race came at the restart on lap 61, when Herta made his only mistake of the day as he attempted to jump clear of Andretti at Turn 11 prior to the green flag.

'I know Michael and he is just a bulldog,' related Herta, 'and I knew that if he had a shot on the first lap, he was going to try it. So I was trying to get a good gap on him and I just got a little too deep into the corner. I locked up. Michael almost hit me. It was close.'

Herta just managed to maintain control and emerged with his lead intact. Andretti, however, mirrored Herta in braking a fraction too late, which effectively killed his momentum on the exit of the corner. He was duly swamped, crossing the start/finish line virtually three abreast with a hungry Papis and Moreno. Worse was to come for Andretti, as Papis tried to carry too much speed into Turn Two, forcing him wide and enabling Moreno to vault from fourth place up to second. Vasser also managed to slip past Andretti in the confusion.

Moments later in Turn Three, Andretti tried to repass Vasser, but succeeded only in careening into the side of the Californian's Target Honda/Reynard. The innocent Vasser was done for the day, retiring to the pits with a holed radiator. Andretti resumed in 13th and eventually finished a disappointed tenth. The final 20 laps were an anticlimax. Moreno hustled hard after Herta, but never looked likely to pass. Nevertheless, 'Super Sub' was delighted to finish a career-best second, ahead of Papis, Tracy and the plucky Fernandez, who battled hard with his still-painful right arm.

Bryan Herta's victory was thoroughly well deserved.

'Roberto was pushing me at the end, but I was able to answer whatever he threw at me,' said Herta, who established a new CART record by becoming the tenth different race winner in a single season, eclipsing the previous mark of nine set in 1985 and repeated in 1995. 'After [the final restart miscue], I just said to myself, "No mistakes." I just stayed focused and kept on.'

Jeremy Shaw

---

quickly put some distance between themselves and Papis, who this time remained under pressure from Andretti.

The next mishap came, ironically, on lap 44, when Kanaan's #44 McDonald's car slowed abruptly as it swept downhill from the Corkscrew turn. The Brazilian had been stricken by a broken gear shift linkage.

'I'm really disappointed,' said

Kanaan. 'I don't think we had a car to pass Bryan on the race track, but I was saving a lot of fuel and the car was very good after the first pit stop. I think we could have finished well.'

Herta led teammate Papis by over seven seconds by the time both made their way onto the pit lane – again under yellow-flag conditions – after Robby Gordon spun his Toyota/Eagle

to a halt at the top of the Corkscrew. Larry Ellert's crew serviced Herta with its usual efficiency, enabling him to maintain his advantage. Andretti, though, moved up to second after Papis hit difficulties.

'I went to drop the clutch on the exit and the engine stalled,' said Papis, who was fortunate not to lose more than one position. 'The guys did a

LAGUNA SECA SNIPPETS

• Rookie Shigeaki Hattori's CART license was **REVOKED** by Chief Steward Wally Dallenbach prior to the race on Sunday after the Japanese driver had spun and caused red-flag stoppages in every session. 'The driver's performance did not meet the standards of a Champ Car competitor,' said Dallenbach.

• Once again PacWest Racing was **OUT OF LUCK**. Mauricio Gugelmin was fastest in the first practice session and qualified a strong sixth, representing his second-best starting position of the season. He lost a couple of positions at the first turn, but remained in eighth until being punted by Dario Franchitti in Turn Three on lap 28. The Brazilian lost a dozen positions and spent the remainder of the race in company with teammate Mark Blundell, who started 20th after spinning off early in the only qualifying session. Gugelmin finished 11th, one place ahead of Blundell, who survived a couple of scrapes along the way. The Englishman also set second-fastest race lap. 'We had a very good car today,' concluded Blundell. 'We just had a bit of the Sunday afternoon blues.'

Michael C. Brown

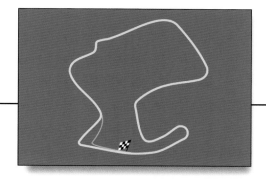

• **ROBBY GORDON** started the first session in a Swift chassis, before switching to his newer Eagle for the final 20 minutes. A problem with a steering arm mounting obliged him to revert to the Swift for qualifying, but he was reunited with the Eagle on Sunday morning and opted to stick with the car for the race. Unfortunately, his day ended early following a couple of off-track excursions.

• Fourth place for Paul Tracy was enough to clinch Honda's third **CART MANUFACTURER'S CHAMPIONSHIP** in four years.

• **SCOTT PRUETT** (left) recorded the best starting position yet for Toyota on a road course (eighth) and equaled his best finish of the season (seventh), despite some excitement at the first corner. '[Paul] Tracy made contact with me on one side and I made contact with someone else on the other side, then I was up in the air,' related Pruett. 'Next thing I knew, I was in 11th.'

• Inevitably, following the tragic accident on Saturday, there was talk concerning **SAFETY STANDARDS** at the scenic and challenging road course. An additional tire wall was constructed between the edge of the track and the cement wall at the Corkscrew prior to the continuation of on-track activities, but the drivers expressed themselves generally satisfied with the facility. 'I think no matter how good we make any track that it can always be better,' said Bryan Herta, who also sits on the Safety Committee. 'There will always be things that we don't realize until something happens and it shows us an area that we need to improve. I guess if you are going to ask any of us, sure, it can always be safer, but I think the tracks in the series have made great strides in safety.'

FEDEX CHAMPIONSHIP SERIES • ROUND 17
HONDA GRAND PRIX OF MONTEREY FEATURING THE SHELL 300

LAGUNA SECA RACEWAY, MONTEREY, CALIFORNIA

SEPTEMBER 12, 83 laps – 185.154 miles

Place	Driver (Nat.)	No.	Team Sponsors Engine/Car	Tires	Q Speed	Q Time	Q Pos.	Laps	Time/Status	Ave. (mph)	Pts.
1	Bryan Herta (USA)	8	Team Rahal Shell Ford Cosworth/Reynard 99I	FS	117.903	1m 08.334s	1	83	1h 49m 20.898s	101.924	22
2	Roberto Moreno (BR)	11	Newman/Haas Big Kmart Ford Cosworth/Swift 010.c	FS	115.984	1m 09.465s	14	83	1h 49m 22.723s	101.986	16
3	Max Papis (I)	7	Team Rahal Miller Lite Ford Cosworth/Reynard 99I	FS	116.911	1m 08.914s	3	83	1h 49m 24.516s	101.868	14
4	Paul Tracy (CDN)	26	Team KOOL Green Honda/Reynard 99I	FS	116.147	1m 09.367s	11	83	1h 49m 28.942s	101.799	12
5	Adrian Fernandez (MEX)	40	Patrick Racing Tecate/Quaker State Ford Cosworth/Reynard 99I	FS	116.440	1m 09.193s	7	83	1h 49m 36.639s	101.680	10
6	Gil de Ferran (BR)	5	Walker Racing Valvoline/Cummins Honda/Reynard 99I	GY	116.241	1m 09.311s	9	83	1h 49m 37.387s	101.669	8
7	Scott Pruett (USA)	24	Arciero-Wells Racing Pioneer Toyota/Reynard 99I	FS	116.414	1m 09.208s	8	83	1h 49m 38.203s	101.656	6
8	*Juan Montoya (COL)	4	Target/Chip Ganassi Racing Honda/Reynard 99I	FS	115.900	1m 09.515s	16	83	1h 49m 38.763s	101.647	5
9	Patrick Carpentier (CDN)	33	Forsythe Racing Player's/Indeck Mercedes/Reynard 99I	FS	115.972	1m 09.472s	15	83	1h 49m 39.244s	101.640	4
10	Michael Andretti (USA)	6	Newman/Haas Kmart/Texaco Havoline Ford Cosworth/Swift 010.c	FS	116.573	1m 09.114s	5	83	1h 49m 39.744s	101.632	3
11	Mauricio Gugelmin (BR)	17	PacWest Racing Group Hollywood Mercedes/Reynard 99I	FS	116.539	1m 09.134s	6	83	1h 49m 41.428s	101.606	2
12	Mark Blundell (GB)	18	PacWest Racing Group Motorola Mercedes/Reynard 99I	FS	114.995	1m 10.062s	20	83	1h 49m 43.349s	101.577	1
13	*Memo Gidley (USA)	71	Payton/Coyne Herdez/Viva Mexico Ford Cosworth/Lola T97/00	FS	114.482	1m 10.376s	22	83	1h 49m 54.649s	101.403	
14	*Naoki Hattori (J)	15	Walker Racing Alpine Honda/Reynard 98I	GY	113.950	1m 10.705s	25	83	1h 50m 15.129s	101.089	
15	*Luiz Garcia Jr. (BR)	21	Hogan Racing Hogan Motor Leasing/Tang Mercedes/Lola B99/00	FS	113.972	1m 10.691s	24	82	Running		
16	Richie Hearn (USA)	10	Della Penna Motorsports Budweiser Toyota/Reynard 99I	FS	113.492	1m 10.990s	26	82	Running		
17	Jan Magnussen (DK)	20	Patrick Racing Visteon Ford Cosworth/Reynard 98I	FS	114.451	1m 10.395s	23	69	Transmission		
18	Jimmy Vasser (USA)	12	Target/Chip Ganassi Racing Honda/Reynard 99I	FS	115.990	1m 09.461s	13	62	Water leak		
19	Robby Gordon (USA)	22	Team Gordon Panasonic/Menards Toyota/Eagle 997	FS	115.573	1m 09.712s	18	56	Accident		
20	Michel Jourdain Jr. (MEX)	19	Payton/Coyne Herdez/Viva Mexico Ford Cosworth/Lola T97/00	FS	115.003	1m 10.057s	19	53	Transmission		
21	Tony Kanaan (BR)	44	McDonald's Championship Racing Honda/Reynard 99I	FS	117.210	1m 08.738s	2	44	Shift linkage		
22	*Cristiano da Matta (BR)	25	Arciero-Wells Racing MCI WorldCom Toyota/Reynard 99I	FS	115.641	1m 09.671s	17	40	Engine		
23	Greg Moore (CDN)	99	Forsythe Racing Player's/Indeck Mercedes/Reynard 99I	FS	116.681	1m 09.050s	4	32	Transmission		
24	Andrea Montermini (I)	36	All American Racers Denso/Castrol Toyota/Eagle 997	GY	114.582	1m 10.315s	21	31	Accident		
25	Dario Franchitti (GB)	27	Team KOOL Green Honda/Reynard 99I	FS	116.022	1m 09.442s	12	31	Accident		
26	Helio Castro-Neves (BR)	9	Hogan Racing Hogan Motor Leasing Mercedes/Lola B99/00	FS	116.164	1m 09.357s	10	29	Throttle cable		
NS	Gonzalo Rodriguez (URG)	3	Marlboro Team Penske Mercedes/Lola B99/00	GY	no speed	no time	–	–	Withdrawn		
NS	Al Unser Jr. (USA)	2	Marlboro Team Penske Mercedes/Lola B99/00	GY	no speed	no time	–	–	Withdrawn		
NS	*Shigeaki Hattori (J)	16	Bettenhausen Motorsports Epson Mercedes/Reynard 98I	GY	no speed	no time	–	–	Withdrawn		

* denotes rookie driver

Caution flags: Laps 24–26, tow/Castro-Neves; laps 54–60, tow/Gordon. **Total:** Two for ten laps.

Lap leaders: Bryan Herta, 1–83 (83 laps). **Total:** Herta, 83 laps.

Fastest race lap: Tony Kanaan, 1m 10.662s, 114.019 mph on lap 23.

Championship positions: 1 Montoya, 199; **2** Franchitti, 171; **3** Tracy, 134; **4** Andretti, 127; **5** Fernandez & Papis, 105; **7** de Ferran, 104; **8** Fittipaldi, 101; **9** Moore, 97; **10** Vasser, 94; **11** Kanaan, 68; **12** Herta, 62; **13** Carpentier, 61; **14** Moreno, 58; **15** Castro-Neves, 48; **16** Jones, 37; **17** da Matta, 30; **18** Gugelmin, 28; **19** Hearn, 21; **20** Unser Jr., Pruett & Gordon, 20; **23** Blundell, 9; **24** Jourdain Jr. & Magnussen, 6; **26** Marques, Barron & Gidley, 4; **29** Vitolo, Salles & Montermini, 2; **32** Rodriguez & Boesel, 1.

OMEGA

OFFICIAL TIMEKEEPER OF CART

HOUSTON

1 – TRACY
2 – FRANCHITTI
3 – ANDRETTI

FEDEX CHAMPIONSHIP SERIES • ROUND 18

Under the cloudless Houston skyline, Paul Tracy leads teammate Dario Franchitti. The Team KOOL Green pair scored a convincing 1–2 after Juan Montoya slid off course and out of the points.
Photo: Michael C. Brown

Typically close and frenetic midfield action on the streets of Houston, with Naoki Hattori fending off the attentions of Richie Hearn, Jimmy Vasser and the rest of the pack.

Below right: 'It's nice to have the Golden Boot in my hands, rather than up my ass,' joked Tracy, in reference to his error while dueling with Franchitti for the Houston win in '98.

PAUL Tracy took advantage of a rare miscue by Juan Montoya to take an accomplished victory in the Texaco Grand Prix of Houston. And to cap a perfect day for Team KOOL Green, Dario Franchitti overcame some early dramas to finish a strong second in his identical Honda/Reynard. It was the team's third 1-2 finish of the season.

'I just can't say enough about the job the Team KOOL Green crew did with the car,' said Tracy after securing his second win of the season and the 15th of his career. 'Tony Cicale gave me a great car, and Firestone gave us awesome tires. We put a lot of laps on them and they held up.'

In addition, Tracy silenced some of his critics after scoring his first road-course victory since his win at Surfers Paradise in 1995. 'We showed everyone that Paul Tracy is a road racer and not just an oval specialist,' said the excited Canadian.

Franchitti was equally pleased, as Montoya's error ensured that the outcome of the FedEx Championship Series remained undecided. The Colombian rookie, who had celebrated his 24th birthday earlier in the week, had stretched his advantage to a comfortable 29 points after claiming his seventh pole of the season. He romped away at the start, quickly establishing a lead of two seconds over the pursuing Tracy and Bryan Herta, who showed his Laguna Seca triumph was no fluke by qualifying on the front row. Franchitti, meanwhile, after starting fourth, was passed by Max Papis shortly after the start, and soon came under increasing pressure from a string of cars headed by Gil de Ferran. By lap 11, Franchitti was in virtual free-fall, having slipped to 11th place.

Then, incredibly, with double yellow flags being waved (signaling a full-course caution after Helio Castro-Neves had slid into the tire wall at Turn 12), Montoya failed to slow down sufficiently as he approached the scene of the accident. Unsighted by the concrete wall on the inside of the turn, Montoya collided with the Brazilian's stricken car. The impact ripped a wheel from Montoya's Target Honda/Reynard, destroying his hopes of clinching the coveted PPG Cup title. Afterward he placed the blame squarely on his team for failing to provide him with more information.

'Just a miscommunication,' said the Colombian. 'It happened before [at Detroit] and it happened again. There was an incident, but nobody told me where it was. I came around the corner and the car was right in the middle of the race track... It was really disappointing that nobody told me.'

Tracy, though, was able to negotiate the incident without drama.

'I wasn't too far behind him. I saw it,' said the Canadian. '[Team owner] Barry [Green] had told me on the radio there was a car in the wall, so I was prepared for it.'

In stark contrast to Montoya, the full-course caution could not have come at a more opportune time for his only championship rival, Franchitti, who immediately ducked onto the pit lane for a fresh set of Firestone tires.

'I have to say thanks to the guy upstairs,' said Franchitti, casting a glance to the heavens. 'That yellow was timely. [Before the pit stop] I had a car that I couldn't drive. Every time I tried to turn left, it would go right. When I saw Juan in the wall, I thought, "Okay, things are bad, but they could be a hell of a lot worse; I just have to get on with it."'

When the green flags waved again, after 18 laps, Tracy quickly pulled out to a huge lead, assisted by the fact that Herta, unfortunately, picked up a puncture just as the race was restarted. He was obliged to struggle around a complete slow lap before reaching his pit. By the time he resumed, he was a lap down to the leader, Tracy, who continued to stretch his advantage over Papis by as much as a second per lap. Tony Kanaan couldn't find a way past the Italian and, in turn, was being hounded by Jan Magnussen, who was enjoying by far his strongest outing in Pat Patrick's Visteon Ford/Reynard, and the equally impressive Christian Fittipaldi, who was making a welcome return from injury aboard Newman/Haas Racing's Big Kmart Ford/Swift.

Magnussen was the first of the leaders to make a scheduled pit stop, on lap 42. Tracy, meanwhile, despite his prodigious speed, contrived to stretch his fuel load the longest, remaining out in front until lap 48 before taking on service.

By chance, Tracy emerged from the pit lane immediately behind teammate Franchitti, who had run a fast pace since his earlier troubles and had enjoyed three laps in the lead before taking the opportunity to make his final pit stop during another perfectly timed full-course caution. Ironically, the interruption was caused by Montoya's teammate, Jimmy Vasser, who struggled with braking difficulties all weekend and ended up parked against a tire barrier.

As the field circulated behind the pace car, Tracy regained the lead and was pursued by Fittipaldi, who had taken advantage of excellent work in

QUALIFYING

Bryan Herta continued from where he left off at Laguna Seca, posting fastest time in the first practice session on Friday with Team Rahal's Shell Ford/Reynard. Once again, though, Juan Montoya lost no time in acclimating himself to a new race track. In fact, after provisional qualifying, there atop the timing sheet was the youngster's Target Honda/Reynard.

A few spots of rain fell just before the decisive final session on Saturday afternoon. Fortunately, the clouds passed on by before the cars took to the unforgiving street circuit. Lap times tumbled as more rubber was laid down, and Adrian Fernandez set a new standard as he emerged fastest after the first group had completed its 30-minute session. The Mexican was delighted, but under no illusions that his time would stand up once the quicker cars from Friday ventured out.

Sure enough, Montoya quickly reclaimed the top position, only to be eclipsed shortly afterward by Herta. But Montoya was not to be denied, establishing a new track record of 58.699 seconds with two minutes remaining.

'The car was good. It wasn't perfect, but we tried to improve it every time we came into the pits,' said Montoya, who was somewhat underawed by the news that he had tied Nigel Mansell's record of seven poles in a rookie campaign: 'Maybe in ten or 20 years it will mean more and I'll think, "Oh, that's good." Right now, I'm just trying to win the championship.'

Herta was relieved to secure a position on the outside of the front row after struggling to find a clear lap until just before the checkered flag flew. Next up were the two KOOL Honda/Reynards of Paul Tracy and Dario Franchitti, followed by Max Papis in the second Team Rahal entry.

There was plenty more symmetry in the starting order, with two Walker Racing Honda/Reynards in sixth and seventh – Gil de Ferran being marginally faster than an inspired Naoki Hattori – followed by Tony Kanaan's sole McDonald's Honda/Reynard and then a pair each of Patrick Racing Ford/Reynards (Jan Magnussen and Fernandez), Newman/Haas Ford/Swifts (Michael Andretti and Christian Fittipaldi) and Player's/Forsythe Mercedes/Reynards (Greg Moore and Patrick Carpentier).

Out of orders

PAUL Tracy took control of the race following the demise of Juan Montoya, although in the late stages there loomed the prospect of team orders after teammate Dario Franchitti overcame an early problem to run in second place. Team owner Barry Green, however, opted not to ask Tracy to sacrifice his victory to assist Franchitti's bid for the championship.

Perhaps it was just as well the radio call was never made. 'I think I would have said, "Ccchhhrrr, ccchhhrrr, I can't hear you,"' said Tracy, imitating radio interference, with a broad smile.

'I think Dario realized that he had a fortunate day today, getting 16 points, and it was my day today,' continued the Canadian in a more serious vein. 'I was never asked to [pull over]. I like to think I helped Dario by keeping the pressure on Juan and making him make a mistake. That was a big help to the team.'

Perhaps surprisingly, in view of the closeness of the title chase, Franchitti was content to finish second.

'I don't think today was the day for team orders,' he said graciously. 'If I was on his tail, different issue, but he was ten seconds up the road. It really wasn't an issue.'

'Barry said to me, "I hope you're not upset,"' revealed Franchitti. 'But you can only expect so much. Either you win it or you don't.'

By finishing second, Franchitti reduced the deficit to Montoya from a hefty 29 points to a far more manageable 13 points with two races remaining.

'Things are certainly looking a lot better today than they were ten days ago,' declared Franchitti, 'so I'm happy. I think both Juan and I are at the top of our game just now. Mr. Tracy, too, is at the top of his game. Anything's possible. It's going to be exciting. I don't know what's going to happen, but I like to think we can do it.'

Photos: Michael C. Brown

Hattori shows his colors

Michael C. Brown

JAPANESE rookie Naoki Hattori produced a stunning upset as he lined up seventh on the starting grid in Derrick Walker's Alpine Honda/Reynard. It was by far his strongest performance since joining the Champ Car ranks at the beginning of the season.

Hattori, 33, won just about everything there was to win in his homeland, including championships in Formula 3 and Touring Cars, before setting his sights on a career in North America.

He joined Team KOOL Green's Indy Lights program in 1997, with support from Honda, and showed sparks of form during his rookie season. Hattori continued to progress in '98, making three podium appearances, including a best of second in Toronto, before switching to Walker Racing for his graduation into the FedEx Championship Series.

His initiation was painful. After displaying good speed in preseason testing, Hattori qualified a respectable 12th for the opening race, at Homestead, only to lose control between Turns One and Two on the very first lap. His car collected Al Unser Jr.'s Marlboro Mercedes/Penske before slamming heavily into the wall. Both drivers suffered

broken limbs, a double compound fracture of his left leg keeping Hattori out of the action for 20 weeks

He was understandably cautious when making his comeback at Detroit, and remained in considerable pain for several races. At Houston, though, Hattori's true colors shone through as he set the fifth-fastest time in qualifying on Friday.

'We changed the car between this morning and now, and it was a big help for me,' he said in his broken (but improving) English. 'My car is more comfortable and has more traction, which, I think, is very important for this track.'

Hattori maintained his form on Saturday, and while he lost a couple of positions on the first lap of the race, he continued to run in ninth until performing a quick spin. He later slipped down the order before retiring after another incident, and was classified 22nd.

'The car felt good at the start, but once the tires gave up it was terrible,' he related. 'Finally, Scott Pruett hit me and I hit the wall. It took off the front wing and the damage was too much to repair.'

the pits to vault ahead of Kanaan and Magnussen. Franchitti emerged from the pits in fifth, but immediately passed Magnussen at the restart. After another brief caution for some debris (actually a large portion of Naoki Hattori's nosewing), Franchitti continued his forward charge by slipping past Kanaan into Turn One.

Fittipaldi, however, proved a tougher nut to crack. 'Every time I'd make a run at him, he'd block,' declared Franchitti. 'He was very quick on the straights, but not anywhere else.'

By lap 82, the deficit to race leader Tracy had grown to almost ten seconds. Franchitti, anxious to gain as many points as possible in the absence of Montoya, was becoming increasingly desperate. Finally, next time around, he lunged to the inside in Turn Two, a tight right-hander that is certainly not regarded as a 'normal' passing place. Franchitti and Fittipaldi made heavy side-to-side contact. Both cars shed

pieces of bodywork, but, thankfully, no serious damage was caused. They were able to continue.

'He was very lucky,' reckoned Fittipaldi. 'He bumped into me big and it worked out for him today, but it could also not have worked out well for him. If it wouldn't have worked out, he would have thrown the championship away. He was just very, very lucky.'

Franchitti's move was all the more surprising considering the fact that he knew Fittipaldi required one more pit stop before the end of the race.

'I knew he had to pit, but I wanted to see if I had a chance of catching Paul,' explained Franchitti, who had squandered vital championship points in the two most recent races – a blatant error at Vancouver and a questionable move in the subsequent race at Laguna Seca.

In reality, Tracy had matters well and truly under control. It was a masterful performance by the sometimes accident-prone Canadian.

'My car was just perfect. I couldn't have asked for a better car,' said Tracy. Incredibly, despite his pace, Tracy was able to complete the 100-lap distance with only one pit stop. Several other contenders attempted the same strategy, but all except one (Cristiano da Matta, who ran as high as sixth in his MCI WorldCom Toyota/Reynard, but slipped to 11th as he cut his pace dramatically in the closing stages) needed a splash of methanol.

'I was getting 2.3 [miles per gallon] and I only needed 2.1,' revealed Tracy. 'They kept telling me to slow down, but I was still able to pull away.'

'I think that's one of my strengths, making good mileage,' he continued. 'That and looking after the tires. That was key today.'

Even teammate Franchitti was impressed. 'I tried to catch Paul, but he was gone,' said the Scotsman. 'He was driving well, I couldn't catch him.'

Fittipaldi's magnificent comeback netted a seventh-place finish after

stopping for fuel with four laps remaining. Third place was taken by Newman/Haas teammate Michael Andretti, whose crew took a gamble by calling for a pit stop during the early full-course caution.

'I questioned [the decision], as I always do,' admitted Andretti. 'I always holler at them and end up apologizing at the end of the race. Which was okay, because we finished on the podium. I'm not sure we had a podium car today, but we finished there. It was the right call. You can pass on this track, so that made it easier for me. The car was halfway decent, but not as good as Dario's and Paul's. I'll take it.'

Papis and Herta finished fourth and fifth for Team Rahal after posting strong comeback drives – Papis after erroneously being assessed a penalty for speeding in the pit lane, and Herta after overcoming his earlier delay as well as a broken first gear.

Jeremy Shaw/Alex Sabine

HOUSTON SNIPPETS

• A major talking point in the garage area was generated when Indianapolis Motor Speedway President and Indy Racing League founder Tony George formally nixed any hopes of a **RAPPROCHEMENT** between CART and the IRL. 'The Indy Racing League will continue to operate as an independent body and will not be merging or otherwise unifying with CART,' said George in a prepared statement. Most CART insiders were 'disappointed, but not surprised' by George's statement. 'What we need to do is just concentrate on what we're doing,' said Barry Green, who, along with fellow CART team owners Bobby Rahal and Derrick Walker, had been involved in many discussions with George during the previous few months. Added Rahal, 'It's a shame. I think open-wheel racing as a whole – forget what you want to call it – would benefit from a reconciliation, and I'm not going to give up.'

• The return of Christian Fittipaldi to the cockpit of his Big Kmart Ford/Swift meant that the services of CART 'Super Sub' **ROBERTO MORENO** were not required in Texas. The ever-optimistic Brazilian did confirm, however, that he was close to a deal for the 2000 FedEx Championship Series. 'I haven't signed anything yet, but I think you're going to see me racing next year full time,' said Moreno.

Michael C. Brown

• CART Chairman and CEO Andrew Craig announced that the **WINNERS** of both CART-sanctioned feeder series, the PPG-Dayton Indy Lights and KOOL/Toyota Atlantic Championships, in 2000 would be granted fully funded tests in Champ Cars and Indy Lights respectively to assist their graduation opportunities going into the 2001 season.

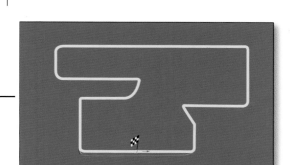

• CART confirmed a new **AERODYNAMIC PACKAGE** for use on all short- and medium-length ovals for next season following criticism of the old superspeedway-type specification that had been employed in 1999. The 'Handford Wing Mk.2' – designed by former Swift Technical Director Mark Handford – will utilize two separate trailing edges that will be used for different venues and ensure slightly more downforce and significantly more drag than the current configuration. The new wing is expected to improve the possibility of overtaking, provide a more stable car for the drivers, and be cheaper for the teams.

• Race engineer **STEVE CHALLIS** (left), who had worked with Greg Moore throughout his racing career, guiding his gifted fellow Canadian to championship titles in Formula Ford, FF2000 and Indy Lights – as well as five Champ Car victories – informed Player's/Forsythe Racing that he would be joining Team KOOL Green for the 2000 season. Challis was promptly told his services would not be required at Houston.

• Michael Andretti's wife, Leslie, gave **BIRTH** to a 7 lb 7 oz baby boy, Lucca Michael, at St. Luke's Hospital in Bethlehem, Pennsylvania, on Thursday, September 16.

FEDEX CHAMPIONSHIP SERIES • ROUND 18
TEXACO GRAND PRIX OF HOUSTON

HOUSTON, TEXAS

SEPTEMBER 26, 100 laps – 152.030 miles

Place	Driver (Nat.)	No.	Team Sponsors Engine/Car	Tires	Q Speed	Q Time	Q Pos.	Laps	Time/Status	Ave. (mph)	Pts.
1	Paul Tracy (CDN)	26	Team KOOL Green Honda/Reynard 99I	FS	93.006	59.106s	3	100	1h 55m 31.263s	78.960	21
2	Dario Franchitti (GB)	27	Team KOOL Green Honda/Reynard 99I	FS	92.891	59.179s	4	100	1h 55m 44.996s	78.804	16
3	Michael Andretti (USA)	6	Newman/Haas Kmart/Texaco Havoline Ford Cosworth/Swift 010.c	FS	91.788	59.890s	11	100	1h 55m 57.124s	78.667	14
4	Max Papis (I)	7	Team Rahal Miller Lite Ford Cosworth/Reynard 99I	FS	92.871	59.192s	5	100	1h 55m 58.795s	78.648	12
5	Bryan Herta (USA)	8	Team Rahal Shell Ford Cosworth/Reynard 99I	FS	93.037	59.086s	2	100	1h 56m 12.201s	78.497	10
6	Mauricio Gugelmin (BR)	17	PacWest Racing Group Hollywood Mercedes/Reynard 99I	FS	90.025	1m 01.063s	23	100	1h 56m 15.426s	78.460	8
7	Christian Fittipaldi (BR)	11	Newman/Haas Big Kmart Ford Cosworth/Swift 010.c	FS	91.673	59.965s	12	100	1h 56m 15.873s	78.455	6
8	Richie Hearn (USA)	10	Della Penna Motorsports Budweiser Toyota/Reynard 99I	FS	91.583	1m 00.024s	15	100	1h 56m 20.125s	78.407	5
9	Tony Kanaan (BR)	44	McDonald's Championship Racing Honda/Reynard 99I	FS	92.159	59.649s	8	99	Running		4
10	Scott Pruett (USA)	24	Arciero-Wells Racing Pioneer Toyota/Reynard 99I	FS	90.656	1m 00.638s	20	99	Running		3
11	*Cristiano da Matta (BR)	25	Arciero-Wells Racing MCI WorldCom Toyota/Reynard 99I	FS	91.260	1m 00.237s	17	99	Running		2
12	Adrian Fernandez (MEX)	40	Patrick Racing Tecate/Quaker State Ford Cosworth/Reynard 99I	FS	91.943	59.789s	10	99	Running		1
13	Jan Magnussen (DK)	20	Patrick Racing Visteon Ford Cosworth/Reynard 98I	FS	92.039	59.727s	9	99	Running		
14	*Memo Gidley (USA)	71	Payton/Coyne Herdez/Viva Mexico Ford Cosworth/Lola T97/00	FS	89.151	1m 01.662s	25	99	Running		
15	Al Unser Jr. (USA)	2	Marlboro Team Penske Mercedes/Penske PC27B	GY	89.000	1m 01.766s	26	98	Running		
16	Greg Moore (CDN)	99	Forsythe Racing Player's/Indeck Mercedes/Reynard 99I	FS	91.670	59.967s	13	98	Running		
17	Gil de Ferran (BR)	5	Walker Racing Valvoline/Cummins Honda/Reynard 99I	GY	92.528	59.411s	6	98	Running		
18	Michel Jourdain Jr. (MEX)	19	Payton/Coyne Herdez/Viva Mexico Ford Cosworth/Lola T97/00	FS	90.362	1m 00.835s	21	98	Running		
19	Patrick Carpentier (CDN)	33	Forsythe Racing Player's/Indeck Mercedes/Reynard 99I	FS	91.654	59.978s	14	78	Engine		
20	Jimmy Vasser (USA)	12	Target/Chip Ganassi Racing Honda/Reynard 99I	FS	91.484	1m 00.089s	16	76	Brakes		
21	Robby Gordon (USA)	22	Team Gordon Panasonic/Menards Toyota/Eagle 997	FS	90.257	1m 00.906s	22	73	Electrical		
22	*Naoki Hattori (J)	15	Walker Racing Alpine Honda/Reynard 98I	GY	92.283	59.569s	7	57	Accident		
23	Andrea Montermini (I)	36	All American Racers Denso/Castrol Toyota/Eagle 997	GY	89.497	1m 01.423s	24	50	Fuel		
24	Mark Blundell (GB)	18	PacWest Racing Group Motorola Mercedes/Reynard 99I	FS	91.204	1m 00.274s	18	46	Transmission		
25	*Juan Montoya (COL)	4	Target/Chip Ganassi Racing Honda/Reynard 99I	FS	93.651	58.699s	1	12	Accident		
26	Helio Castro-Neves (BR)	9	Hogan Racing Hogan Motor Leasing Mercedes/Lola B99/00	FS	90.968	1m 00.430s	19	11	Accident		
NS	*Luiz Garcia Jr.(BR)	21	Hogan Racing Hogan Motor Leasing/Tang Mercedes/Lola B99/00	FS	no speed	no time	–	–	Withdrawn		

* denotes rookie driver

Caution flags: Laps 1–2, yellow start; laps 13–17, accident/Castro-Neves & Montoya; laps 51–56, tow/Montermini; laps 58–60, debris/Hattori. **Total: Four for 16 laps.**

Lap leaders: Juan Montoya, 1–12 (12 laps); Paul Tracy, 13–48 (36 laps); Dario Franchitti, 49–51 (3 laps); Tracy, 52–100 (49 laps). **Totals:** Tracy, 85 laps; Montoya 12 laps; Franchitti, 3 laps.

Fastest race lap: Juan Montoya, 1m 01.018s, 90.091 mph on lap 8 (record).

Championship positions: 1 Montoya, 200; **2** Franchitti, 187; **3** Tracy, 155; **4** Andretti, 141; **5** Papis, 117; **6** Fittipaldi, 107; **7** Fernandez, 106; **8** de Ferran, 104; **9** Moore, 97; **10** Vasser, 94; **11** Herta & Kanaan, 72; **13** Carpentier, 61; **14** Moreno, 58; **15** Castro-Neves, 48; **16** Jones, 37; **17** Gugelmin, 36; **18** da Matta, 32; **19** Hearn, 26; **20** Pruett, 23; **21** Unser Jr. & Gordon, 20; **23** Blundell, 9; **24** Jourdain Jr. & Magnussen, 6; **26** Marques, Barron & Gidley, 4; **29** Vitolo, Salles & Montermini, 2; **32** Rodriguez & Boesel, 1.

OMEGA

OFFICIAL TIMEKEEPER OF CART

SURFERS PARADISE

QUALIFYING

Dario Franchitti was on a mission in Surfers Paradise. The Scot needed every point he could muster in his bid to oust Juan Montoya from the lead in the FedEx Championship. On Friday, Franchitti didn't seem to be much of a challenger, clipping a wall and ending up fifth on the provisional grid, behind teammate Paul Tracy, Michael Andretti, Montoya and Bryan Herta.

'We have a bit of work to do on the KOOL car and I have to do a bit of work, too,' reflected the Scotsman. 'We don't need any big changes, but we need some. I'll huddle up with the engineers and come back stronger tomorrow.'

Franchitti was as good as his word. Third in the morning practice, he made another couple of minor setup changes during final qualifying, then dug deep into his reserves of talent and determination to record a couple of sensationally fast laps. The first, with five minutes remaining, was a 1 minute, 32.218 seconds, easily good enough to move him to the top of the time sheet. The next was even faster – 1 minute, 31.703 seconds. It was a staggering 0.892 second faster than his nearest challenger.

'We've struggled a bit all weekend,' he related, 'and we all worked hard last night getting the thing right. I didn't think there was much more [time] in the car, but Don [Halliday] found it, and I just had to grit my teeth and get on with it.'

Even Herta was impressed. 'We had a decent car and I got a pretty clear lap,' said the Californian. 'Dario's lap was fast. I don't know we could pip him to pole, so I'm pretty happy.'

Scott Pruett was the surprise of qualifying, annexing a magnificent third in Arciero-Wells Racing's Pioneer Toyota/Reynard. He considered the grid placing to be among the most memorable events of his career, and paid tribute to the efforts of Toyota and his team.

Michael Andretti completed the second row of the grid, while Montoya occupied a disappointing fifth place. The Colombian driver had been hindered by braking difficulties and his Target Honda/Reynard's inability to ride the curbs as well as he would have liked.

1 – FRANCHITTI

2 – PAPIS

3 – FERNANDEZ

Dario Franchitti made full use of his hard-earned pole by leaping into an immediate lead. It was a great day for the Team KOOL Green driver, who retook the series lead following Juan Montoya's error.

Pruett's progress

SCOTT Pruett took a while to become properly acclimated to the Arciero-Wells team after his move from Patrick Racing in the fall of '98. Nevertheless, as the season drew toward its conclusion, Pruett suddenly began to display flashes of the old brilliance.

His performance in Surfers Paradise was little short of spectacular. The Pioneer Toyota/Reynard wasn't especially fast on the first day of practice and qualifying, but Pruett was happy with progress. He was even more content on Saturday afternoon after scorching around the demanding 2.795-mile temporary circuit at an average speed of 108.642 mph. It was good enough for third on the starting grid and another 'career best' for Toyota.

'This is, unfortunately, my last street race in CART, but it's nice to go out this way,' said Pruett, who had confirmed a week or so earlier that he would be contesting the 2000 NASCAR Winston Cup Championship with Cal Wells III's Tide-sponsored team. 'We had a good car. It's the best performance ever for Toyota and the team, so it's exciting, especially for my last road-course race.'

'You have some second thoughts [about switching],' he confessed, 'but I've always talked about trying [NASCAR] and this is my chance. I didn't want to look back in ten years and say, "You know what, I should have tried that."'

'This [grid placing] ranks up with the most memorable things I've been able to achieve. Toyota's been working hard and everybody's done a good job.'

Pruett showed the performance was no fluke by taking advantage of Bryan Herta's slip at the start and running strongly in second place throughout the opening stint. The veteran shadowed Dario Franchitti's every move for the first ten laps, before being forced to adopt a fuel conservation strategy that caused him to drop back at upward of one second per lap. A couple of mediocre pit stops also restricted his efforts, such that he finished an unrepresentative ninth.

Photo left: Michael C. Brown Photo far left: Nigel Snowdon

DARIO Franchitti scorched back into contention for the FedEx Championship by virtue of a perfectly judged victory in the Honda Indy 300 at Surfers Paradise, Australia. Juan Montoya, by contrast, endured another nightmare weekend. For the second race in a row, the rookie made a crucial error while well-placed in the closing stages.

This time, after a mediocre qualifying effort had left him a disappointed sixth on the grid, Montoya made his usual rapid progress up the order. By lap 27, he was up in second place, hot on the heels of his championship rival. An epic contest seemed in the offing. Soon afterward, a second round of pit stops shuffled the order and resulted in Montoya's Target Honda/Reynard being separated from Franchitti's similar KOOL car by the Tecate/Quaker State Ford/Reynard of Adrian Fernandez. A dozen laps later, after Franchitti began to stretch out an advantage, Montoya left his braking a touch too late for one of the myriad 90-degree, second-gear corners. An instant later he was parked against a tire barrier, his race over.

'I'm mostly disappointed because we had a winning car and a shot at a spot on the podium,' said Montoya. 'I locked the rear brakes, turned around and tagged the wall.'

Franchitti, meanwhile, made not a hint of an error, cruising home in front of the record-breaking crowd of 102,844. The victory was hugely significant. Not only was it the first for Team KOOL Green principals Barry and Kim Green in their native Australia, but also it was enough to catapult Franchitti into a nine-point lead in the PPG Cup standings with just one race remaining.

'Fantastic!' was how Barry Green described his day. 'To win at home in Australia is just incredible. We've won the Indianapolis 500, but I think this feels even better.'

'A perfect weekend, what can I say?' added Franchitti after securing his third victory of the season. 'I'm so happy, especially to get Barry's first win in Australia.'

After a week of glorious weather on the Queensland Gold Coast, conditions took a dramatic turn once the Champ Car teams had unpacked all their equipment, ready for action. Intermittent rain showers kept the race engineers and drivers guessing on each of the first two days of practice and qualifying, and heavy clouds shrouded the circuit on race morning. There were even a few sprinkles of rain as the huge variety of pre-race proceedings built to a crescendo prior to the 1 p.m. start. Fortunately, the afternoon remained dry.

Franchitti took full advantage of his

Right: Tony Kanaan chases after Michael Andretti (not shown) while under attack from Greg Moore and Cristiano da Matta.

Opposite page: The plethora of high-rise apartments provides a spectacular backdrop for the demanding Surfers Paradise track.

Below right: Curb-hopping is de rigueur in the pursuit of a fast lap time. Juan Montoya *(top)* struggled over the curbs in practice and qualifying, while Bryan Herta *(bottom)* misjudged his line slightly in practice and damaged his Shell car's right front wing.

Photos top & opposite page: Diana Burnett Photos center & bottom: John Morris M/Pix

pole position to jump clear of Bryan Herta's Shell Ford/Reynard at the start. Once again, the one weakness of the Ford Cosworth engine had been exposed – at least in relation to the Honda motor.

'I know the start looked bad,' admitted Herta, who lagged behind as the green flag was waved, 'but I had bad wheelspin. I was surprised they threw the green flag. I couldn't get close to Dario.'

In the recent past, CART Starter Jim Swintal had elected to display the yellow flag if the field was not properly aligned. But not on this occasion. 'We all talked about it in the drivers' meeting,' explained Swintal, 'and this is what we agreed.'

Herta fell instantly to fourth, overhauled both by Scott Pruett, in Arciero-Wells Racing's ever-improving Pioneer Toyota/Reynard, and Franchitti's teammate, Paul Tracy. Soon, though, Tracy was assessed a drive-through penalty for passing Herta (who started directly in front of him) prior to the start/finish line. It was a clear contravention of the regulations.

Green argued that Tracy had no option other than to pass when Herta failed to pick up the pace, but the protest fell on deaf ears. On lap 12, a disgruntled Tracy pulled onto the pit lane. He rejoined in tenth.

'It was unfortunate for Paul,' said CART Chief Steward Wally Dallenbach. 'He was caught behind car number eight. I don't know whether [Herta] was asleep or what. For the record, it was all on [video] tape. We tried to help Paul out, but, unfortunately, we don't have a rule that says if Dallenbach thinks a guy's asleep he can

waive the rule.'

Pruett maintained his qualifying form by remaining in close contact with Franchitti for the first ten laps or so. But then the Scotsman began to edge clear as Pruett was obliged to start saving fuel. By lap 20, the gap had grown to six seconds. Herta remained in third, followed by Fernandez, who passed Montoya at the start and picked off Michael Andretti under braking for the first chicane. Montoya also passed Andretti next time around, leaving the American under pressure from Tony Kanaan.

Franchitti was the first of the leaders to make a routine pit stop, on lap 21. Fernandez stayed out for two more laps, taking advantage of his frugality to hold a brief lead. In fact, he resumed in second before Herta dived to the inside under braking for Speed-stick Turn in front of the ANA Hotel. On the exit of the same corner, Montoya also snuck past Fernandez.

Moments later, the first full-course caution was called after Naoki Hattori, Al Unser Jr. and Richie Hearn all ground to a halt at various points on the track.

Unbeknown to any of the protagonists, however, a local yellow flag had been displayed where Herta made his pass. Accordingly, a few minutes later, while the field circulated behind the pace car, Herta was instructed to fall in line behind Fernandez – and, therefore, behind Montoya, too, who suddenly found himself in second place, right behind Franchitti.

Dallenbach again: 'The local yellow was only out in one corner. Montoya made his pass after that corner, where the green was being shown. Again, it

Testing cuts are well received

D URING the Honda Indy 300 weekend, Championship Auto Racing Teams Senior Vice President of Racing Operations Tim Mayer confirmed that the CART team owners had agreed to a significant cutback in testing for the future. Two-car teams had been allowed to conduct 50 days of testing during the FedEx Championship Series season, but for 2000 and beyond, they would be permitted only 32 days, a mere dozen of them once the racing season was under way. The remaining 20 days would have to be utilized prior to the first race. A one-car team would be permitted 24 days, including eight during the season.

'The decision of the franchise board reflects their strong desire to limit the overall number of test days, particularly during the season,' said Mayer. 'Their primary concern is the number of days on the road that their teams, suppliers and manufacturing partners are required to do in the midst of a very busy schedule. This new set of rules also should limit the overall cost of testing.'

'This is a step in the right direction to reduce the overall emphasis on testing and to focus on our people and our racing,' said Carl Haas, co-owner of Newman/Haas Racing.

The news also was greeted warmly by the various teams.

'It will certainly make it a bit more difficult for rookie drivers, but overall I think it's very good news,' said Steve Ragan, Crew Chief for McDonald's Championship Racing. 'It will definitely save some money and save wear and tear on the boys.'

Nigel Snowdon

Max Papis (under pressure from Helio Castro-Neves) earned a career-high second in Team Rahal's Miller Lite Ford/Reynard.

Below: Characteristically on the limit, Michael Andretti had to pull out all the stops to remain ahead of Tony Kanaan.

was all pretty blatant.'

Franchitti and Montoya quickly pulled away from the pack at the restart, followed by Fernandez, Herta, Pruett (who had lost some ground during the pit stops) and Andretti. The yellows waved again on lap 35, though, after Mark Blundell ended another disappointing weekend against the tire wall after clobbering the lapped car of Naoki Hattori.

In view of the relatively recent round of pit stops, Franchitti, surprisingly, peeled off into the pit lane. Furthermore, everyone except Max Papis, who had been running along in tenth place, followed suit. By making a pit stop at that stage, everyone – including Papis – would be obliged to make one more pit stop before the end of the race. But now Papis had the benefit of track position.

The Italian duly took advantage of his lighter fuel load by pulling away rapidly at the restart. He was chased by Franchitti and Fernandez, who had profited from rapid service by Patrick Racing to leapfrog ahead of Montoya. Papis, running flat out in Team Rahal's Miller Lite Ford/Reynard, established the fastest lap of the race as he edged away to a nine-second lead before making his second pit stop, on schedule, after 46 laps. He rejoined 13th, but had the benefit of knowing that everyone else would require at least a splash more fuel. Sure enough, on lap 50, they had the opportunity to do so during another full-course caution.

Sensationally, the yellow flags were required for none other than Montoya, who misjudged his braking for the left turn off Breaker Street, at the north end of the track, and nosed off into the tire barriers. His race was over.

Suddenly, the race – and, of course, the championship – took on an entirely fresh complexion. Jan Magnussen, who had been running at the bottom end of the top ten, found himself in the lead after Patrick Racing elected to take a gamble by not making a pit stop. Franchitti, after taking on a few gallons of methanol, followed in second, but wasted absolutely no time in sweeping ahead of his former British Formula 3 teammate as soon as the green flags waved for the final time, on lap 54. Franchitti never looked back.

Magnussen maintained second place for nine laps, but had no hope of reaching the finish without a splash of fuel, and duly relinquished his position with four laps remaining. The diminutive Dane fell to 12th before regaining one place when he passed Michel Jourdain Jr. on the final lap.

Papis was left in second. He had nothing for Franchitti in the closing stages, but was still delighted to score the best result of his career.

'Our pit strategy was very good,' said Papis. 'This was the first time this year that Bobby [Rahal] was calling my race. He has a lot of experience and it was a great call.'

Fernandez drove another fine race to finish third, while the unfortunate Herta took fourth, just ahead of Andretti and Kanaan, who enjoyed a fierce battle virtually throughout the 65-lap race.

But the star of the race was Franchitti, who soaked up the pressure and enjoyed a perfect weekend, capitalizing fully on the opportunities with which he was presented.

'We came here with a 13-point deficit and came away with a nine-point lead,' noted the Scotsman. 'You can't ask for any more than that.'

Jeremy Shaw

David Taylor/Allsport

SURFERS SNIPPETS

• Several teams were without **PROMINENT PERSONALITIES** for the trip to Australia. Team Managers Tim Cindric (Team Rahal), Ed Nathman (Newman/Haas Racing) and Steve Newey (Patrick Racing) all remained at home after making clear their intentions of moving elsewhere for the 2000 season. In addition, McDonald's Championship Racing Team Manager Jeff Eischen was relieved of his duties midway through the race weekend. 'It was the hardest thing I've ever had to do,' said team President Steve Horne. 'Jeff and I have been friends for 20 years, but I honestly think this was the best for everyone involved.'

• Just before leaving for Surfers Paradise, **ROGER PENSKE** ended intense speculation by announcing that his team would switch motive power from Mercedes-Benz to Honda for the 2000 season.

• **TONY KANAAN** spent virtually the entire race trying to find a way past Michael Andretti *(right)*, but to no avail. 'Man, that was tough. I've never braked so hard, so late, so many times,' said Andretti with a broad smile. Added Kanaan, 'We had a lot of fun and he played very clean. I would consider this one of my best races this year, even though it wasn't one of our best results. I learned a lot and can use that in the future.'

Kazuki Saito

• Provisional pole-sitter **PAUL TRACY** was unable to defend his front-row starting position after a heavy crash on Saturday morning obliged him to switch to the spare car. Rather than withdraw the primary car's time, Team KOOL Green elected to wait out the final session. Tracy was assessed a drive-through penalty in the early stages of the race, after which his progress was hindered badly by a lack of turbo boost (and, therefore, horsepower). The Canadian ultimately finished close behind Andretti and Kanaan in seventh.

• **ROBBY GORDON** turned in one of the most impressive drives of the race as he charged from 22nd on the grid to eighth. Gordon, who elected to leave his Eagle chassis at home in readiness for the California Speedway season finale, took a bit of time to re-adapt himself to his trusty Swift 010.c, but clearly made excellent headway, as he set the sixth-fastest race lap.

• **GUALTER SALLES** made yet another welcome return – this time aboard Tony Bettenhausen's '98 Mercedes/Reynard. Various dramas drastically restricted the likable Brazilian's track time throughout practice and qualifying, but he made rapid progress on raceday, steering clear of all the dramas and setting a respectable 17th-fastest race lap en route to a well-deserved tenth and three PPG Cup points.

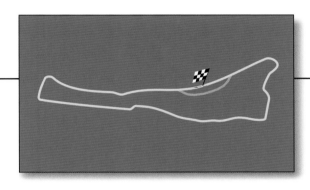

FEDEX CHAMPIONSHIP SERIES • ROUND 19
HONDA INDY 300

SURFERS PARADISE, QUEENSLAND, AUSTRALIA

OCTOBER 17, 65 laps – 181.675 miles

Place	Driver (Nat.)	No.	Team Sponsors Engine/Car	Tires	Q Speed	Q Time	Q Pos.	Laps	Time/Status	Ave. (mph)	Pts.
1	Dario Franchitti (GB)	27	Team KOOL Green Honda/Reynard 99I	FS	109.724	1m 31.703s	1	65	1h 58m 40.726s	91.849	22
2	Max Papis (I)	7	Team Rahal Miller Lite Ford Cosworth/Reynard 99I	FS	107.612	1m 33.503s	11	65	1h 58m 43.335s	91.815	16
3	Adrian Fernandez (MEX)	40	Patrick Racing Tecate/Quaker State Ford Cosworth/Reynard 99I	FS	108.110	1m 33.072s	7	65	1h 58m 48.171s	91.753	14
4	Bryan Herta (USA)	8	Team Rahal Shell Ford Cosworth/Reynard 99I	FS	108.667	1m 32.595s	2	65	1h 58m 51.119s	91.715	12
5	Michael Andretti (USA)	6	Newman/Haas Kmart/Texaco Havoline Ford Cosworth/Swift 010.c	FS	108.311	1m 32.899s	5	65	1h 58m 51.911s	91.705	10
6	Tony Kanaan (BR	44	McDonald's Championship Racing Honda/Reynard 99I	FS	107.923	1m 33.233s	8	65	1h 58m 52.085s	91.702	8
7	Paul Tracy (CDN)	26	Team KOOL Green Honda/Reynard 99I	FS	108.544	1m 32.700s	4	65	1h 58m 52.456s	91.698	6
8	Robby Gordon (USA)	22	Team Gordon Panasonic/Menards Toyota/Swift 010.c	FS	106.333	1m 34.627s	22	65	1h 59m 00.616s	91.593	5
9	Scott Pruett (USA)	24	Arciero-Wells Racing Pioneer Toyota/Reynard 99I	FS	108.642	1m 32.616s	3	65	1h 59m 02.054s	91.574	4
10	Gualter Salles (BR)	16	Bettenhausen Motorsports Mercedes/Reynard 98I	GY	103.013	1m 37.677s	27	65	1h 59m 06.820s	91.513	3
11	Jan Magnussen (DK)	20	Patrick Racing Visteon Ford Cosworth/Reynard 98I	FS	106.930	1m 34.099s	19	65	1h 59m 11.460s	91.454	2
12	Michel Jourdain Jr. (MEX)	19	Payton/Coyne Herdez/Viva Mexico Ford Cosworth/Lola T97/00	FS	106.958	1m 34.074s	18	65	1h 59m 13.774s	91.424	1
13	*Cristiano da Matta (BR)	25	Arciero-Wells Racing MCI WorldCom Toyota/Reynard 99I	FS	107.731	1m 33.399s	10	63	Transmission		
14	*Memo Gidley (USA)	71	Payton/Coyne Herdez/Viva·Mexico Ford Cosworth/Lola T97/00	FS	106.692	1m 34.309s	21	60	Engine		
15	Andrea Montermini (I)	36	All American Racers Denso/Castrol Toyota/Eagle 997	GY	104.702	1m 36.101s	25	56	Misfire		
16	*Juan Montoya (COL)	4	Target/Chip Ganassi Racing Honda/Reynard 99I	FS	108.173	1m 33.018s	6	48	Accident		
17	Greg Moore (CDN)	99	Forsythe Racing Player's/Indeck Mercedes/Reynard 99I	FS	107.554	1m 33.553s	12	46	Electrical		
18	Jimmy Vasser (USA)	12	Target/Chip Ganassi Racing Honda/Reynard 99I	FS	107.078	1m 33.969s	17	44	Fuel pressure		
19	Mark Blundell (GB)	18	PacWest Racing Group Motorola Mercedes/Reynard 99I	FS	106.087	1m 34.847s	23	33	Accident		
20	*Naoki Hattori (J)	15	Walker Racing Alpine Honda/Reynard 98I	GY	106.767	1m 34.243s	20	33	Accident		
21	Helio Castro-Neves (BR)	9	Hogan Racing Hogan Motor Leasing Mercedes/Lola B99/00	FS	107.192	1m 33.869s	16	28	Transmission		
22	Al Unser Jr. (USA)	2	Marlboro Team Penske Mercedes/Penske PC27B	GY	103.661	1m 37.066s	26	22	Throttle		
23	Richie Hearn (USA)	10	Della Penna Motorsports Budweiser Toyota/Reynard 99I	FS	105.207	1m 35.640s	24	21	Transmission		
24	Patrick Carpentier (CDN)	33	Forsythe Racing Player's/Indeck Mercedes/Reynard 99I	FS	107.293	1m 33.781s	15	20	Accident		
25	Christian Fittipaldi (BR)	11	Newman/Haas Big Kmart Ford Cosworth/Swift 010.c	FS	107.526	1m 33.577s	13	3	Fire		
26	Mauricio Gugelmin (BR)	17	PacWest Racing Group Hollywood Mercedes/Reynard 99I	FS	107.879	1m 33.271s	9	1	Transmission		
27	Gil de Ferran (BR)	5	Walker Racing Valvoline/Cummins Honda/Reynard 98I	GY	107.383	1m 33.702s	14	0	Accident		

* denotes rookie driver

Caution flags: Laps 23–26, tow/Unser Jr., Hattori & Hearn; lap 28, accident/Vasser & Blundell; laps 35–36, accident/Hattori & Blundell; laps 50–52, accident/Montoya. **Total:** Four for ten laps.

Lap leaders: Dario Franchitti, 1–21 (21 laps); Adrian Fernandez, 22–23 (2 laps); Franchitti, 24–35 (12 laps); Max Papis, 36–46 (11 laps); Franchitti, 47–50 (4 laps); Jan Magnussen, 51–53 (3 laps); Franchitti, 54–65 (12 laps). **Totals:** Franchitti, 49 laps; Papis, 11 laps; Magnussen, 3 laps; Fernandez, 2 laps.

Fastest race lap: Max Papis, 1m 34.516s, 106.458 mph on lap 44.

Championship positions: 1 Franchitti, 209; **2** Montoya, 200; **3** Tracy, 161; **4** Andretti, 151; **5** Papis, 133; **6** Fernandez, 120; **7** Fittipaldi, 107; **8** de Ferran, 104; **9** Moore, 97; **10** Vasser, 94; **11** Herta, 84; **12** Kanaan, 80; **13** Carpentier, 61; **14** Moreno, 58; **15** Castro-Neves, 48; **16** Jones, 37; **17** Gugelmin, 36; **18** da Matta, 32; **19** Pruett, 27; **20** Hearn, 26; **21** Gordon, 25; **22** Unser Jr., 20; **23** Blundell, 9; **24** Magnussen, 8; **25** Jourdain Jr., 7; **26** Salles, 5; **27** Marques, Barron & Gidley, 4; **30** Vitolo & Montermini, 2; **32** Rodriguez & Boesel, 1.

OMEGA
OFFICIAL TIMEKEEPER OF CART

FONTANA

FEDEX CHAMPIONSHIP SERIES • ROUND 20

Adrian Fernandez parlayed perfect strategy into a well-judged victory.

Bottom left: Juan Montoya and the Ganassi crew did just enough to edge out Dario Franchitti for the PPG Cup title.

THERE was everything to play for when the FedEx Championship Series contenders rolled into Fontana's California Speedway for the Marlboro 500 Presented by Toyota. In addition to the $1 million race winner's purse, there was a similar bag of gold to be claimed either by Juan Montoya or Dario Franchitti, who arrived at the season finale separated by just nine points.

Incredibly, when all was said and done, they were actually tied on points, concluding the closest title-chase in CART history.

The PPG Cup trophy was won, deservedly, by Montoya, by virtue of his seven wins to Franchitti's three. Adrian Fernandez, meanwhile, drove a tactical race to claim victory aboard Patrick Racing's Tecate/Quaker State Ford Cosworth/Reynard.

Tragically, however, what should have been a joyous occasion for both men was overshadowed by news that popular rival Greg Moore had lost his life following a violent accident during the early stages in Turn Two. The huge crowd of more than 90,000 was told that Moore had succumbed to massive head and internal injuries. So were the race teams. At the insistence of Moore's devoted father, Ric, though, the race went on. The drivers themselves did not learn about the fatality until after the checkered flag.

'It's just devastating,' said an emotional Fernandez. 'I won the race, I was so excited, and then when I came into the pits and they told me to pull straight into my pit stall instead of going to Victory Circle, I thought, "What's happening?" Then they told me.

'It's so hard, because Greg was such a good friend of everybody's. We have shared so many good moments inside and outside the race track. The win doesn't matter.'

The loss of a second talented young driver in as many months was tough to bear. It seemed especially cruel given the circumstances of the day. The weather was picture perfect. The grandstands were packed. The championship was up for grabs.

Indeed, the race itself was thoroughly entertaining, as eight different leaders swapped the advantage throughout the 250 laps. The action began right away, although not how surprise pole-sitter Scott Pruett had envisaged. His Pioneer Reynard was fitted with a detuned Toyota RV8D motor for the 500-mile race, and immediately it became apparent that this was no match for the special qualifying-spec engine. Pruett was swallowed by the pack even before Turn One as Max Papis powered into

QUALIFYING

Max Papis – the star of the U.S. 500 at Michigan Speedway in July – shone once again as the series returned to a superspeedway venue. After setting the pace during practice at a remarkable 238.231 mph, the Italian's Miller Lite Ford/Reynard was last in line to have a shot at the pole; but in warm conditions and with an extremely strong wind gusting to over 25 mph, he was unable to match the earlier best of Scott Pruett *(above)*, who duly secured the first-ever pole for Toyota.

Pruett had turned some good laps during practice, showing that his form at Surfers Paradise (where he started third) was no fluke; but even he was surprised to clinch the pole aboard Arciero-Wells Racing's Pioneer Toyota/Reynard.

'The car's been running well all weekend,' said Pruett (who also took the pole at Fontana in 1998, driving a Patrick Racing Ford/Reynard). 'We knew we had to get the car as loose as we could, and it was right on the limit. The first lap it was good. The second lap it went really loose.'

With the wind blowing even stronger as the later runners took to the track, none of the 17 drivers who followed Pruett in the qualifying lineup was able to oust him from the pole.

'It feels great,' he said. 'Everyone on the team and everyone at Toyota has worked so hard. Being my last race in CART [having signed a deal to drive in the NASCAR Winston Cup Championship in 2000], it couldn't be any sweeter.'

Papis earned a place alongside on the front row and remained optimistic for the race. 'Being on the front row is fantastic,' he said, 'and I feel we have a very good car for the race.'

Teammate Bryan Herta also ran well to take fifth on the grid, separated from Papis only by the two Target/Chip Ganassi cars of Juan Montoya and Jimmy Vasser. Montoya's title rival, Dario Franchitti, qualified eighth behind Michael Andretti's Ford/Swift and the fastest Mercedes runner, Patrick Carpentier.

Ganassi to run with Toyota

CONFIRMING a rumor that had been circulating for several months, Chip Ganassi announced at Fontana that his Target Stores-backed team would turn its back on Honda (with which the team clinched an unprecedented fourth consecutive CART championship just two days later) and instead field Toyota engines in the 2000 FedEx Championship Series.

'When you're in this business as long as I have been, you want to be on the leading edge of breaking new ground,' declared Ganassi. 'I have to tell you, I'm pretty pumped up about [the switch]. We're going to continue our winning ways and we're going to do it with Toyota.'

'I think it's time to change the package,' he continued. 'When I met with the people from Toyota, I was impressed. These guys are no strangers to motorsports. We've all been monitoring their progress and I think they're ready to win – and I want to bring them to the winner's circle.

'It's a hunger that I see in their attitude; I see it in their eyes, I see it in the level of commitment they make personally. They're making a huge investment in this formula right now, and I think people that make a huge effort win.'

For Toyota, the new association heralded the start of a formidable challenge.

'For the past three years, we've had the same "Wait until next year" line,' admitted Toyota Motor Sales USA Vice President of Motorsports Jim Aust. 'Well, having Target/Chip Ganassi Racing brings a new perspective.'

Added Toyota Racing Development Vice President Lee White, 'We had to assure [Ganassi] that the product we're going to put in his cars are going to be *the* best. If we couldn't do that, we wouldn't be sitting here right now. Our new RV8E engine is going to be a nuclear-tipped, armor-piercing missile, and in 2000 we absolutely intend to kick the door in.'

With impeccable timing, less than 24 hours later, Scott Pruett claimed Toyota's first-ever pole – at the FedEx Championship Series' fastest circuit. All of a sudden, Ganassi's choice took on a fresh significance...

the lead on the outside line and Montoya dived to the inside.

Michael Andretti, meanwhile, took advantage of the enormous draft provided by the Handford Device rear wing and completed the first lap in second place before diving past Papis' Miller Lite Ford/Reynard into Turn One. Montoya ran third at the end of lap one, followed by Target Honda/Reynard teammate Jimmy Vasser, Dario Franchitti (up three places from eighth on the grid in his similar KOOL car) and Pruett, who slipped farther down the order before succumbing to engine failure after just 48 laps.

'This is definitely not the way I wanted this day to end,' said Pruett. 'The car didn't feel quite right most of the day, and then we started picking up a vibration. Finally, the engine just let go.'

Even at that stage, five other contenders had fallen by the wayside – one, Patrick Carpentier, due to electrical woes and three others because of crashes. First to go was Richie Hearn, who spun luridly off Turn Two on lap four and slammed with sickening force into the inside retaining wall.

'It was simply a turbulence issue. It just gets really unpredictable; you're on a knife-edge out there,' said Hearn after climbing unscathed from his badly damaged Budweiser Toyota/Reynard.

Right away after the restart, Moore wasn't so fortunate. The familiar #99 Player's car had rocketed from 27th to 15th inside the first few laps before spinning off in almost exactly the same location as Hearn. Crucially, Moore's car flipped as it slid over an asphalt access road and onto the grass, then disintegrated as it slammed upside down against the inside retaining wall and cartwheeled along the infield.

A lengthy caution ensued while the gravely injured Canadian was extricated from what remained of his Mercedes/Reynard. Efforts to resuscitate him continued as Moore was flown to nearby Loma Linda University Medical Center, but he was pronounced dead at 1.21 p.m., less than an hour after the accident had occurred.

The race had continued after the cleanup, although it wasn't long before Alex Barron also found the wall in Turn Four in his Marlboro Mercedes/Penske, thankfully without such calamitous consequences. Barron was unhurt.

Only nine of the first 34 laps were run under green-flag conditions. Already, though, Andretti – enjoying his 250th Champ Car start – had made his presence felt. The Kmart/Texaco Havoline Ford/Swift pulled away rapidly at the restart, the veteran extending his advantage to as much as eight seconds before making a second routine pit stop on lap 71. Sadly, he would go no further, halted by a small fire caused by a broken brake-fluid line. Andretti's appalling luck on the superspeedways had struck again.

Coincidentally, Franchitti's championship hopes took a dive when the right rear wheel failed to seat properly during routine service. The Scotsman was obliged to make an additional pit stop. By then, he had lost two laps to the leaders. He was never able to make up the deficit.

Teammate Paul Tracy took up the slack, running confidently in the lead

A recalcitrant retaining nut on Dario Franchitti's right rear wheel cost him the championship.
Photo: Michael C. Brown

Michael C. Brown

Below: Adrian Fernandez and Max Papis are overcome with emotion during the post-race media conference.

for a while before suffering an engine failure. His day, too, was over.

Montoya, meanwhile, ran comfortably among the top four or five. He was never especially happy with his car's handling, but took the lead from Tracy on lap 122 and remained out in front for ten laps before being passed by an inspired Christian Fittipaldi. The Brazilian was showing his best oval-track form since his rookie season in '95, when he finished second at Indianapolis.

Fittipaldi continued to lead the way through the next round of pit stops, which came on lap 158 – again under yellow due to some debris in Turn Two. At the restart, though, it was Papis who moved to the front. The ebullient Italian never pulled far away from Fittipaldi, but he appeared to be in control of the race. At least until lap 201, when the yellow flags flew for the seventh and final time after Mark Blundell's troublesome Motorola Mercedes/Reynard finally ground to a halt due to an electrical failure.

The caution came moments after everybody had made routine pit stops for fuel and fresh tires. Just seven contenders remained on the lead lap: Papis, Montoya, Fittipaldi, Vasser, Fernandez, Mauricio Gugelmin (Holly-wood Mercedes/Reynard) and Al Unser Jr., who drove his Marlboro Mercedes/Penske with gusto, despite being hindered by the Goodyear tires, which caused the car to understeer and, worse, picked up a serious vibration midway through each stint.

As the 'one-lap-to-go-before-the-restart' signal was given, it was apparent that no one could make the finish without a splash-and-go pit stop. That's when Patrick Racing played its trump card – by signaling Fernandez onto the pit lane for a couple more gallons of methanol just before the race was restarted on lap 207. (Unser, incidentally, pursued the same strategy.)

Fittipaldi passed Montoya for second place on lap 213, but could do nothing about Papis, who remained a second or so to the good for the next 30 laps. Montoya followed a similar distance behind in third. Fernandez, meanwhile, was desperately saving fuel – but still running a very respectable pace in sixth.

'It was difficult,' related the Mexican. 'The team felt I could make it to the finish. The engineers gave me the [consumption] numbers I had to do and I was able to do it. It was tough, but that's what it took.'

'We didn't have the car to win the

McGee's moment

ADRIAN Fernandez's victory was the fifth of his career, achieved in his 105th Champ Car start. More significantly, the Mexican's magnificent drive represented an 86th triumph for Chief Mechanic-turned-Team/General Manager Jim McGee. The milestone finally broke the tie he held previously with the legendary George Bignotti.

Tragically, of course, McGee's feeling of satisfaction was outweighed by the death of Greg Moore. '[The record] doesn't mean much,' said McGee simply, 'not compared to what else happened today.'

Nevertheless, it was the crowning moment in a momentous career that had begun more than 40 years earlier, when he and a friend built a car for the Indianapolis 500. Two years later, after moving from Boston, McGee was hired by another celebrated name in Champ Car racing, Clint Brawner. By the mid-1960s, Brawner and McGee were sharing co-chief mechanic duties for the Dean Van Lines team, with which Mario Andretti won a pair of National Championships in 1965 and '66. Three years later, the duo guided Andretti to a third title – and a famous Indianapolis 500 victory – with Andy Granatelli and STP.

More successes followed when McGee joined the Vel's Parnelli 'Super Team' in the early '70s, then moved on to Penske Racing, where he rose to become Team Manager, adding another pair of championships with Tom Sneva and completing the hat-trick (along with another Indy 500 for good measure) with Rick Mears in '79. McGee transferred to Patrick Racing in '81, eventually guiding Emerson Fittipaldi to another Indy 500/CART championship double in '89. Apart from brief spells with the Rahal-Hogan and Newman/Haas teams in the early '90s (which, incidentally, yielded another pair of titles with Bobby Rahal and Nigel Mansell respectively), he remained loyal to Pat Patrick for the next 18 years.

In all, McGee, 62, has presided over a remarkable nine championship-winning teams and four Indy 500 victories.

'There's a lot of satisfaction,' he said with a forced smile, reflecting on his record-breaking day. 'I still enjoy the business, except when you have days like this. Thankfully, they don't come as often as they did years ago...'

Robert Laberge/Allsport

race, to be honest,' he added. 'We had a top-six car, so we had to try something a bit different. It worked out for us.'

Sure enough, when Papis ducked onto the pit lane on lap 237, followed soon afterward by Fittipaldi, Vasser and Montoya, it was Fernandez who emerged in the lead. Papis resumed in second, but Fernandez wasn't to be denied the victory.

All eyes, meanwhile, were on the duel for the championship. Franchitti moved up to ninth, but hadn't been able to conserve enough fuel. On lap 243 he, too, ducked onto the pit lane. He resumed in tenth. Montoya emerged fifth after his final stop, which would have left him two points shy of the title. But Gugelmin had elected to try to stretch his fuel load, and was passed effortlessly by Montoya with four laps remaining.

Thus was the championship decided. However Franchitti had rather more on his mind.

'Today I lost one of the best friends I ever had,' said the emotional Scot. 'Greg and I shared a lot of good times together. The guy was going to be a champion, many, many times over. He was my friend. With what's happened, nothing else matters.'

Jeremy Shaw

FONTANA SNIPPETS

• GREG MOORE *(right)* started from the back of the grid after failing to qualify on Saturday due to an accident in which he was knocked from his motor scooter by a pickup truck in the paddock area. Moore suffered a broken bone in his right hand and several lacerations, which required 15 stitches. He underwent treatment in the CART Medical Center and was given a special dispensation to run a handful of laps on Saturday afternoon, after which he pronounced himself fit to race.

• Team owner Carl Hogan dropped a **BOMBSHELL** on the evening before first practice when he announced that he would close down his Champ Car operation immediately after the season finale. Financial concerns put paid to his effort – specifically the inability to secure a major sponsor to line up alongside his family-owned Hogan Motor Leasing trucking business.

• Goodyear Tire & Rubber Company also was in **WITHDRAWAL MODE**, winding up a desperately disappointing couple of seasons by confirming that it would not return either to the CART FedEx Championship Series or the Pep Boys Indy Racing League in the new millennium.

• Scott Pruett's pole position at Fontana allowed the United States to trim one point from its deficit to leader Brazil in the **NATION'S CUP** competition. It wasn't enough. Christian Fittipaldi's third-place finish on raceday clinched the coveted award by a margin of 271 points to 264 over Team USA, which had been unbeaten in the award's four-year history.

Michael C. Brown

• Former Champ Car driver **STEFAN JOHANSSON** announced his intention to field a car in the 2000 FedEx Championship Series under the banner of Team CAN (Cure Autism Now), a charitable non-profit organization dedicated solely to finding an effective biological treatment, prevention and cure for autism and related disorders. Johansson was joined in the announcement by two long-time CAN spokesmen, actor Anthony Edwards (star of the 'ER' television series) and Artisan Entertainment producer Jonathan Shestack.

• CARA Charities (and joint Chairpersons Dan and Evi Gurney and Michael and Leslie Andretti) hosted **RUNWAY MADNESS II** at Ontario Airport on Friday night. Among the many highlights were joint emcees Paul Page and Parker Johnstone, masquerading as the Blues Brothers, and a hugely amusing Spice Girls impression by Indy Lights drivers Didier Andre, Ben Collins, Mario Dominguez, Jonny Kane and Guy Smith. More than $125,000 was raised for a variety of charitable organizations.

• PPG honored **AL UNSER JR.** with a 'Colorful Character' award, providing a fitting finale to a career that comprised a CART record 273 starts – fifth on the all-time Champ Car list behind Mario Andretti, A.J. Foyt, (his father) Al Unser and Johnny Rutherford – and 31 race wins.

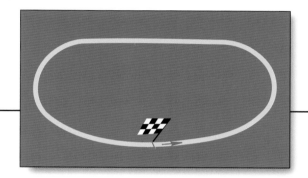

MARLBORO 500
PRESENTED BY TOYOTA

CALIFORNIA SPEEDWAY, FONTANA, CALIFORNIA

OCTOBER 31, 250 laps – 507.25 miles

Place	Driver (Nat.)	No.	Team Sponsors Engine/Car	Tires	Q Speed	Q Time	Q Pos.	Laps	Time/Status	Ave. (mph)	Pts.
1	**Adrian Fernandez (MEX)**	40	Patrick Racing Tecate/Quaker State Ford Cosworth/Reynard 97I	FS	232.535	31.412s	13	250	2h 57m 17.542s	171.666	20
2	**Max Papis (I)**	7	Team Rahal Miller Lite Ford Cosworth/Reynard 99I	FS	234.544	31.143s	2	250	2h 57m 25.176s	171.542	17
3	**Christian Fittipaldi (BR)**	11	Newman/Haas Big Kmart Ford Cosworth/Swift 010.c	FS	232.988	31.351s	9	250	2h 57m 26.385s	171.523	14
4	***Juan Montoya (COL)**	4	Target/Chip Ganassi Racing Honda/Reynard 99I	FS	234.251	31.182s	3	250	2h 57m 31.858s	171.435	12
5	**Jimmy Vasser (USA)**	12	Target/Chip Ganassi Racing Honda/Reynard 99I	FS	234.063	31.207s	4	250	2h 57m 38.248s	171.332	10
6	**Mauricio Gugelmin (BR)**	17	PacWest Racing Group Hollywood Mercedes/Reynard 99I	FS	232.166	31.462s	17	250	2h 58m 01.738s	170.955	8
7	**Al Unser Jr. (USA)**	2	Marlboro Team Penske Mercedes/Penske PC27B	GY	232.899	31.363s	10	249	Running		6
8	**Tony Kanaan (BR)**	44	McDonald's Championship Racing Honda/Reynard 99I	FS	232.839	31.371s	11	249	Running		5
9	**Gil de Ferran (BR)**	5	Walker Racing Valvoline/Cummins Honda/Reynard 99I	GY	232.713	31.388s	12	249	Running		4
10	**Dario Franchitti (GB)**	27	Team KOOL Green Honda/Reynard 99I	FS	233.174	31.326s	8	248	Running		3
11	**Robby Gordon (USA)**	22	Team Gordon Panasonic/Menards Toyota/Eagle 997	FS	232.387	31.432s	15	247	Running		2
12	**PJ Jones (USA)**	20	Patrick Racing Visteon Ford Cosworth/Reynard 98I	FS	229.446	31.835s	23	246	Running		1
13	Michel Jourdain Jr. (MEX)	19	Payton/Coyne Herdez/Viva Mexico Ford Cosworth/Lola T97/00	FS	226.493	32.250s	26	236	Engine		
14	Bryan Herta (USA)	8	Team Rahal Shell Ford Cosworth/Reynard 99I	FS	233.913	31.227s	5	235	Running		
15	Dennis Vitolo (USA)	34	Payton/Coyne Nicoderm CQ Ford Cosworth/Reynard 98I	FS	228.120	32.020s	24	235	Running		
16	Mark Blundell (GB)	18	PacWest Racing Group Motorola Mercedes/Reynard 99I	FS	231.886	31.500s	18	193	Electrical		
17	Raul Boesel (BR)	36	All American Racers Denso/Castrol Toyota/Eagle 997	GY	227.134	32.159s	25	164	Engine		
18	Paul Tracy (CDN)	26	Team KOOL Green Honda/Reynard 99I	FS	231.064	31.612s	19	141	Electrical		
19	*Naoki Hattori (J)	15	Walker Racing Alpine Honda/Reynard 98I	GY	229.474	31.831s	22	124	Electrical		
20	Helio Castro-Neves (BR)	9	Hogan Racing Hogan Motor Leasing Mercedes/Lola B99/00	FS	230.896	31.635s	20	111	Engine		
21	Michael Andretti (USA)	6	Newman/Haas Kmart/Texaco Havoline Ford Cosworth/Swift 010.c	FS	233.256	31.315s	6	71	Oil fire		
22	Scott Pruett (USA)	24	Arciero-Wells Racing Pioneer Toyota/Reynard 99I	FS	235.398	31.030s	1	48	Engine		1
23	*Cristiano da Matta (BR)	25	Arciero-Wells Racing MCI WorldCom Toyota/Reynard 99I	FS	232.365	31.435s	16	32	Engine		
24	Alex Barron (USA)	3	Marlboro Team Penske Mercedes/Penske PC27B	GY	232.410	31.429s	14	27	Accident		
25	Patrick Carpentier (CDN)	33	Forsythe Racing Player's/Indeck Mercedes/Reynard 99I	FS	233.226	31.319s	7	21	Electrical		
26	Greg Moore (CDN)	99	Forsythe Racing Player's/Indeck Mercedes/Reynard 99I	FS	no speed	no time	27	9	Accident		
27	Richie Hearn (USA)	10	Della Penna Motorsports Budweiser Toyota/Reynard 99I	FS	230.328	31.713s	21	3	Accident		

* denotes rookie driver

Caution flags: Laps 4–8, accident/Hearn; laps 10–22, accident/Moore; laps 28–34, accident/Barron; laps 85–90, spin/Vitolo; laps 110–120, engine/Castro-Neves; laps 53–162, debris; laps 201–206, tow/Blundell. **Total:** Seven for 58 laps.

Lap leaders: Max Papis, 1 (1 lap); Michael Andretti, 2–31 (30 laps); Michel Jourdain Jr., 32–36 (5 laps); Paul Tracy, 37–38 (2 laps); Andretti, 39–70 (32 laps); Papis, 71–72 (2 laps); Christian Fittipaldi, 73–74 (2 laps); Papis, 75–114 (40 laps); Tracy, 115–121 (7 laps); Juan Montoya, 122–131 (10 laps); Fittipaldi, 132–163 (32 laps); Papis, 164–196 (33 laps); Fittipaldi, 197–98 (2 laps); Mauricio Gugelmin, 199–200 (2 laps); Papis, 201–236 (36 laps); Fittipaldi, 237–237 (1 lap); Montoya, 238–240 (3 laps); Adrian Fernandez, 241–250 (10 laps). **Totals:** Papis, 112 laps; Andretti, 62 laps; Fittipaldi, 37 laps; Montoya, 13 laps; Fernandez, 10 laps; Tracy, 9 laps; Jourdain Jr., 5 laps; Gugelmin, 2 laps.

Fastest race lap: Christian Fittipaldi, 31.732s, 230.190 mph on lap 224.

Final championship positions: 1 Montoya, 212; **2** Franchitti, 212; **3** Tracy, 161; **4** Andretti, 151; **5** Papis, 150; **6** Fernandez, 140; **7** Fittipaldi, 121; **8** de Ferran, 108; **9** Vasser, 104; **10** Moore, 97; **11** Kanaan, 85; **12** Herta, 84; **13** Carpentier, 61; **14** Moreno, 58; **15** Castro-Neves, 48; **16** Gugelmin, 44; **17** Jones, 38; **18** da Matta, 32; **19** Pruett, 28; **20** Gordon, 27; **21** Unser Jr. & Hearn, 26; **23** Blundell, 9; **24** Magnussen, 8; **25** Jourdain Jr., 7; **26** Salles, 5; **27** Marques, Gidley & Barron, 4; **30** Vitolo & Montermini, 2; **32** Rodriguez & Boesel, 1.

OMEGA
OFFICIAL TIMEKEEPER OF CART

TRIPLE ECHO

by Eric Mauk

Above and below left: Five runner-up finishes set Oriol Servia on course for the PPG-Dayton Indy Lights Championship.

Below: Philipp Peter scored three fine victories for Dorricott-Mears Racing.

Below far right: Casey Mears came so close to stealing the title at the final race.

AFTER the second PPG-Dayton Indy Lights Championship race of the season, a dejected Oriol Servia looked at his crinkled Dorricott-Mears Racing Lola, which he had bounced off the Turn One wall on the Long Beach street course. The wreck had taken the 24-year-old Spaniard out of the race, and while he did finish 12th, gaining a series point, he was already 21 points behind the leaders and didn't feel good about it.

'I just made a mistake. I feel badly for the crew because they gave me a good car,' said Servia. 'I'm confident we'll have other opportunities in other races.'

The statement proved prophetic. Not only did he and his Dorricott-Mears teammates, Casey Mears and Philipp Peter, have other opportunities, but also they capitalized on nearly every one of them in a record-setting season.

Servia led Mears and Peter to the first 1-2-3 sweep in Indy Lights Championship history; but while they easily outdistanced the field (eventual fourth-place finisher Jonny Kane wound up 12 points behind third-place Peter), the trio took vastly different routes to get to the top. In fact, the championship order was not decided until the last laps of the season finale at Fontana, where the race was every bit as wild as the rest of the Lights campaign.

Servia would go on to take the title without winning a race, while the consistent Mears finished second without ever leading a lap. Peter led in just three races, but won all of them to tie Derek Higgins for the most wins in the 1999 campaign.

Nazareth was the starting point of what would be a title run for Servia. He dominated during practice and qualifying, taking Dorricott-Mears' first pole since 1995. A slight let-up for some lapped traffic after 13 circuits allowed early championship contender Airton Dare to sneak by and win the race, but Servia rode Dare's tail for 87 laps to finish second. The event started a run of eight consecutive top-five finishes for Servia – a skein that included three poles and five runner-up finishes.

Mears took over the points lead at the Milwaukee Mile, despite finishing second, just 0.526 second behind Higgins. It was a year of feast or famine for Team Mexico's Higgins, who earned three wins, but managed only one other top-ten finish and wound up seventh in the points.

Mears held serve at Portland as teammate Peter led from start to finish for his second win of the year. Peter also inherited a victory at Long Beach, earning Dorricott-Mears' first triumph since Robbie Buhl took the Detroit checkers in June of 1995.

A Turn One crash at Cleveland's Burke Lakefront Airport took out pole-sitter Didier Andre along with Kane and Tony Renna, clearing the way for Servia to take the points lead with a second-place finish (behind Higgins). Another runner-up finish the following week, this time behind Geoff Boss in Toronto, gave the Miami resident a reason to celebrate his 25th birthday as his points lead grew.

The only problem Servia would have for the rest of the way came in the very last race, and almost cost him the championship. Leading Mears by 14 points at the start of the weekend, Servia's car developed engine trouble early, leaving the points leader to struggle to stay on the lead lap for the rest of the day. Mears, meanwhile, was taking advantage of his golden opportunity and running in the top three, which would have given him the championship.

But in the closing stages, Mears dove into the pits to replace what he thought was a punctured tire. The tire was still holding air, and a subsequent stop two laps later pretty much took him out of contention. Charging through the tightly-bunched field with five circuits remaining, Mears touched another car, lost his front wings and took himself out of the points. A relieved Servia was home free.

'It was the most frustrating race of my life,' said Servia. 'My engine lost much of its power on the fourth or fifth lap. Cars that shouldn't pass me ripped by and there was nothing I could do about it. However, the whole point of this season was to win the championship and that has made it my greatest year in racing.'

Meanwhile, another unlikely scenario was unfolding at the front of the Fontana pack. Johansson Motorsports' first-year pilot Scott Dixon held a 20-point lead over Team KOOL Green's Jonny Kane in the Rookie of the Year standings, but as Kane was earning his team's first-ever Lights victory, Dixon (unlike Mears) did sustain a puncture and finished two laps down. He lost the rookie award by a single point.

Kane had kept his hopes alive the previous week at Laguna Seca, where he placed third, one position behind Dixon, setting the stage for the Fontana heroics.

'We've been fast all year and haven't really got the results we deserved. We knew going into the weekend we needed a lot of luck to get the Rookie of the Year championship,' said Kane. 'That's what my ambition was at the beginning of the year. I'm so pleased to be the first Team KOOL Green guy to win a race. It's a nice way to pay back all the guys and the sponsors for all the help they've been throughout the year.'

Dixon claimed the first win of his career during a strong season for the 19-year-old New Zealander. His roll from the pole at Chicago Motor Speedway earned him a victory and capped a strong oval-course season that included a third at Homestead and a fourth at Milwaukee. Johansson Motorsports teammate Ben Collins finished a season-high second at Fontana to cap a promising rookie campaign for the Briton.

A year of turmoil for Forsythe Championship Racing led to the worst season ever for the organization that won four series titles while flying under the banner of Tasman Motorsports. Jerry Forsythe bought out the Tasman shop early in the year, and it looked to be a promising one as Dare returned to lead a two-car operation that included 1998 Indy Lights Rookie of the Year Guy Smith.

Dare was tied for second place at the halfway point, and dominated the final 87 laps of the Nazareth race for what would be his lone win of the season. Toronto would be the beginning of the end for the young Brazilian, as

Jonny Kane scored Team KOOL Green's first-ever Indy Lights race win.

Below: Scott Dixon, a former champion Down Under in Formula Ford and Formula Holden, is a star in the making.

Bottom: Inconsistency cost three-time winner Derek Higgins a chance at the title.

PPG-DAYTON INDY LIGHTS CHAMPIONSHIP REVIEW

he crashed on the fourth lap after starting second. The accident started a run of four consecutive non-points finishes that saw him plummet to tenth in the point standings.

Smith, meanwhile, righted the ship after a rocky start and wound up topping Dare in the championship. A sixth-place finish at Toronto started a series of four top-six placings in the final six races, including a runner-up effort at Chicago, followed by a pole-winning run at Laguna Seca.

Conquest Racing showed flashes of strength to come, the Eric Bachelart-led team capturing a pair of pole positions with Felipe Giaffone. The team seemingly had its first-ever win in hand at Long Beach...until the Brazilian ran out of fuel with three laps remaining. Rookie Chris Menninga ended the year with three consecutive finishes in the points, thereby boosting spirits in the team's Indianapolis shop.

Team Mexico Quaker Herdez

shocked the circuit by taking the season-opening race at Homestead with Mario Dominguez. Making his first start in the series since 1992, and his first ever on an oval course, Dominguez won wire-to-wire on the 1.5-mile Florida track.

PacWest Racing struggled at times, and threw a few different drivers at the wheel, but ended with a lot of promise for the 2000 campaign. Didier Andre overcame a dismal start to the season, defended his 1998 Laguna Seca victory with a win and followed that with a third at Fontana. American Renna signed for a full-time ride next year with the Bruce McCaw-owned outfit after competing in six races. He finished third at Milwaukee and returned for the season finale to finish a strong sixth. Frenchman Boris Derichebourg also ran two events for the team, scoring points at Laguna Seca.

Ohio-based Lucas Place Motor-sports earned its first victory since

joining the circuit three seasons earlier. Geoff Boss led from flag to flag at Toronto to claim the win, but wound up 12th in the points after earning only one other podium finish. His brother Andy joined the team in 1999, but a season-opening fourth-place finish at Homestead was as high as he would go all season.

Brian Stewart suffered another tough year, despite the fact that

Rodolfo Lavin Jr. and David Pook already had Lights experience under their belts. Lavin matched a career high with his eighth-place finish in Michigan, while Pook took a sixth at Milwaukee. Native Navajo Indian Cory Witherill scored a fine fourth at Fontana, matching his effort of the previous year, but that proved to be far and away his most impressive outing of the season for Genoa Racing.

1999 PPG-DAYTON INDY LIGHTS CHAMPIONSHIP
Final points standings after 12 races:

Pos.	Driver (Nat.), Sponsor(s)-Team	Pts.
1	Oriol Servia (E), Catalonia/RACC/Elf-Dorricott-Mears Racing	130
2	Casey Mears (USA), Sooner Trailer/American Racing Wheels-Dorricott-Mears Racing	116
3	Phillip Peter (A), Red Bull/Remus/ESTEBE-Dorricott-Mears Racing	101
4	Jonny Kane (IRL)*, Team KOOL Green	89
5	Scott Dixon (NZ)*, Diagem/Speedbet-Johansson Motorsports	88
6	Felipe Giaffone (BR), Hollywood/Comet-Conquest Racing	78
7	Derek Higgins (IRL), Quaker State Mexico-Team Mexico Motorsports	76
8	Didier Andre (F), Motorola/PlayStation-PacWest Racing	74
9	Guy Smith (GB), Swift Caravans-Forsythe Championship Racing	71
10	Airton Dare (BR), Banestado-Forsythe Championship Racing	69
11	Mario Dominguez (MEX)*, Herdez/Viva Mexico-Team Mexico Motorsports	66
12	Geoff Boss (USA), Cross Pens/Powerware/Lacoste-Lucas-Place Motorsports	58
13	Ben Collins (GB)*, Hays Home Delivery Services/Diagem-Johansson Motorsports	50
14	Chris Menninga (USA)*, Cambridge Health/Mi-Jack-Conquest Racing	47
15	Andy Boss (USA), Cross Pens/Powerware/Lacoste-Lucas Place Motorsports	32
16	Tony Renna (USA), Motorola-PacWest Racing	22
17	Rodolfo Lavin (MEX), Corona/Modelo-Brian Stewart Racing	19
18	Cory Witherill (USA)*, WSA Health Care-Genoa Racing	17
19	David Pook (USA), Sage & Clay/Quickline-Brian Stewart Racing	16
20	Oswaldo Negri Jr. (BR), Carusi Wheels/ILP-Genoa Racing	6

All drove Lola T97/20 chassis with GM V6 motors and Dayton tires.
* denotes rookie driver

Performance Chart

Driver	Wins	Poles	Fastest laps	Most laps led
Derek Higgins	3	–	1	3
Phillip Peter	3	–	–	2
Jonny Kane	1	2	1	–
Didier Andre	1	1	1	2
Mario Dominguez	1	1	1	1
Geoff Boss	1	1	1	1
Scott Dixon	1	1	–	1
Airton Dare	1	–	–	1
Oriol Servia	–	3	–	–
Felipe Giaffone	–	2	2	1
Guy Smith	–	1	1	–
Casey Mears	–	–	2	–
Tony Renna	–	–	1	–
Rodolfo Lavin	–	–	1	–

Zero-To-30 in 6.6 Years. . .

Greg Moore
1975-1999

Paul Tracy

Adrian Fernandez

Tony Kanaan

Bryan Herta

That isn't the kind of light speed Einstein introduced to the world, but it's plenty fast for the graduates of the PPG-Dayton Indy Lights Championship. Paul Tracy's win in the 1999 Texaco Grand Prix of Houston was the 30th victory for an Indy Lights grad in CART Champ Car competition. The Texas triumph capped a streak Paul started by winning the 1993 Toyota Grand Prix of Long Beach, but drivers from CART's "Official Development Series" were far from finished. Adrian Fernandez scored the 31st career win at the Marlboro 500 to give Indy Lights grads seven victories in 1999. Paul, Adrian, Tony Kanaan, Bryan Herta and the late 1995 champion Greg Moore - the most successful Indy Lights driver in history - all won races in the 1999 FedEx Championship Series. And that's a success rate that not even Einstein would take lightly.

Oriol Servia—1999 Champion
Dorricott—Mears Racing

PPG DAYTON
INDY LIGHTS®
C H A M P I O N S H I P

DREAM TICKET

by Jeremy Shaw

ANTHONY Lazzaro began the 1999 KOOL/Toyota Atlantic Championship as a firm favorite for title honors. He did not disappoint. Indeed, while the 12-race season provided some spectacular competition – the equal of any in the formula's illustrious 26-year history – the 30-something from Acworth, Georgia, took a commanding lead in the point standings during the stages of the season and never looked likely to relinquish his advantage.

'This is a dream come true,' said Lazzaro after clinching the championship with a dominant drive to victory – his fourth of the year – at Laguna Seca with one race remaining. 'It's great that we won the championship, and it's even better that we did it in style.'

In '98, Lazzaro honed Cal Wells III's Precision Preparation Inc./MCI WorldCom Swift 008.a into a formidable weapon in concert with race engineer Gerald Tyler. The combo won three of the final four races. But when Tyler left to pursue an opportunity in the Champ Car ranks with All American Racers during the off-season, Lazzaro had to establish a new rapport with promising young engineer Kyle Brannan. The transition was virtually seamless. Lazzaro finished third in the season opener at Long Beach, then dominated the next two oval races at Nazareth and Gateway,

leading every lap from the pole in both events.

He started from the pole in the next race at Milwaukee, too, only to be involved in a first-lap incident triggered by PPI teammate Andrew Bordin. Lazzaro was obliged to make a sequence of pit stops during the ensuing full-course caution, but fought back to finish fifth. It was a perfect example of his never-say-die attitude. By the season's end, Lazzaro had qualified among the top four and finished among the top six in every race. He led a total of 232 laps, well over three times more than his nearest rival.

Lazzaro was a deserving champion. He was also the consummate professional. He even relinquished the lead in the final race at Houston to Bordin, allowing the Canadian driver to clinch third in the final point standings.

Bordin's season, meanwhile, was filled with frustration. It began with an error while leading at Long Beach and included more than his share of mechanical gremlins. The highlight was a fine victory at Road America to complement his Houston gift. Still only 23, Bordin grew in stature in '99 and has a bright future ahead of him.

Kenny Wilden finished a worthy second after a solid campaign with Michael Shank Racing. The Canadian former sedan champion displayed his intentions by qualifying on pole for the opening round. Unfortunately, he failed to capitalize. A midrace incident left him out of the points and resulted in him playing catch-up for the balance of the year. Wilden bounced back to take a well-deserved victory at Mid-Ohio and went on to add five more podium finishes.

Younger countryman Alexandre Tagliani won at Long Beach and qualified second at Nazareth, only to suffer a suspension failure. The fiercely

ambitious 'Tags' endured another couple of misfortunes and was involved in more than his fair share of scrapes, which explains why he faded from championship contention in the later stages of the season. Still, Tagliani, 27, did enough in a post-season test with the Player's/Forsythe Champ Car team to earn graduation into the FedEx Championship Series for 2000.

Player's teammate Lee Bentham had everything to lose after winning the championship in '98. He never looked like repeating that success and was comprehensively outpaced by Tagliani. Bentham also was a magnet for problems. A measured drive to victory in Milwaukee proved a rare highlight.

Arizona's Buddy Rice was another who endured more than his share of heartbreak. Curiously, the Lynx Racing team took some time to dial in the car to Rice's liking, although the Atlantic sophomore made excellent progress to record three straight podium appearances, at Milwaukee, Montreal and Road America. Sadly, mechanical problems then robbed him of almost certain victories in successive races at Trois-Rivieres and Mid-Ohio.

Ohioan Sam Hornish Jr. emerged as top rookie, capping a promising campaign in a second Mike Shank-prepped car with a beautifully judged victory at Chicago. William Langhorne was even more impressive. A restricted budget meant he was able to contest only the road-course events with George Greco and Malcolm Ross' Active Motorsports team. Langhorne made every one of them count. A brilliant drive to victory in appalling conditions at Vancouver marked him as a man to watch in the future. Other rookies to shine included Nicolas Rondet (who was fast, but prone to mistakes), Elton Julian, Alex Gurney, David Besnard and Rocky Moran Jr. All could do well with the right opportunity.

Top left: Anthony Lazzaro had every reason to smile after a superb season.

Left: Lazzaro was a model of consistency for the PPI/MCI WorldCom team.

Bottom left: Kenny Wilden emerged as a regular contender for Mike Shank's team.

Below center: Buddy Rice reflects on a difficult campaign for Lynx Racing.

Below: After his win at Mid-Ohio, Kenny Wilden shares the limelight with Anthony Lazzaro (left) and Alexandre Tagliani.

Mid-Ohio Sports Car Course

1999 KOOL/TOYOTA ATLANTIC CHAMPIONSHIP
Final point standings after 12 races:

Pos.	Driver (Nat.), Sponsor(s)-Team	Pts.
1	Anthony Lazzaro (USA), Precision Preparation Inc. (PPI)-MCI WorldCom	197
2	Kenny Wilden (CDN), Newcourt/TrizecHahn-Michael Shank Racing	150
3	Andrew Bordin (CDN), Thyssen Steel/Millennium Data/Player's-PPI	121
4	Alexandre Tagliani (CDN), Player's/Indeck-Forsythe Racing	118
5	Buddy Rice (USA), Lynx Racing Scholarship	113
6	Lee Bentham (CDN), Player's/Indeck-Forsythe Racing	71
7	Sam Hornish Jr. (USA)*, APC/Hornish Bros.-Michael Shank Racing	67
8	William Langhorne (USA)*, Black Stone/National MS Society/Active Motorsports	60
9	David Rutledge (CDN), The Keg/Smart Tire/Player's-Forsythe/Binder	58
10	Jean-Francois Veilleux (CDN)*, Miller Lite/NTN Bearings-P-1 Racing	49
11	Nicolas Rondet (F)*, Harmony Schools/Martini Sunglasses-World Speed	40
12	Mike Conte (USA), White/Black Design-Lynx Racing	38
13	Alex Gurney (USA)*, Team KOOL Green	38
14	Rocky Moran Jr. (USA)*, Compaq/Epigram-P-1 Racing	18
15	David Besnard (AUS)*, Kohassett Records/U.S. Print-Hylton Motorsports	16

All drove Swift 008.a chassis with Toyota 4A-GE motors and Yokohama tires.

* denotes rookie driver

Performance Chart

Driver	Wins	Poles	Fastest laps	Most laps led
Anthony Lazzaro	4	5	3*	6
Alexandre Tagliani	2	3	1	2
Andrew Bordin	2	1	1	2
Kenny Wilden	1	2	1	–
Sam Hornish Jr.	1	–	1	–
Lee Bentham	1	–	–	1
William Langhorne	1	–	–	1
Buddy Rice	–	1	3	–
David Rutledge	–	–	2*	–
Nicolas Rondet	–	–	1	–

* Rutledge and Lazzaro set equal-fastest lap at Gateway.

Photos: Michael C. Brown

The 2000 FedEx Championship Series

March 26, Marlboro Grand Prix of Miami Presented by Toyota, Homestead-Miami Speedway, Homestead, Florida

April 9, Bosch Spark Plug Grand Prix Presented by Toyota, Nazareth Speedway, Nazareth, Pennsylvania

April 16, Toyota Grand Prix of Long Beach, Long Beach, California

April 30, Rio 200, Emerson Fittipaldi Speedway, Jacarepagua, Rio de Janeiro, Brazil

May 13, Firestone Firehawk 500, Twin Ring Motegi, Tochigi Prefecture, Japan

June 4, Miller Lite 225, The Milwaukee Mile, West Allis, Wisconsin

June 18, Tenneco Automotive Grand Prix of Detroit, The Raceway on Belle Isle, Detroit, Michigan

June 25, Budweiser/G.I. Joe's 200 Presented by Texaco/Havoline, Portland International Raceway, Portland, Oregon

July 2, Medic Drug Grand Prix of Cleveland Presented by Firstar, Burke Lakefront Airport, Cleveland, Ohio

July 16, Molson Indy Toronto, Canadian National Exhibition Place, Toronto, Ontario, Canada

July 23, Michigan 500 Presented by Toyota, Michigan Speedway, Brooklyn, Michigan

July 30, Target Grand Prix of Chicago, Chicago Motor Speedway, Cicero, Illinois

August 13, Miller Lite 200, Mid-Ohio Sports Car Course, Lexington, Ohio

August 20, Road America 220, Road America, Elkhart Lake, Wisconsin

September 3, Molson Indy Vancouver, Concord Pacific Place, Vancouver, British Columbia, Canada

September 10, Honda Grand Prix of Monterey Featuring the Shell 200, Laguna Seca Raceway, Monterey, California

September 17, Motorola 300, Gateway International Raceway, Madison, Illinois

October 1, Texaco/Havoline Grand Prix of Houston, Houston, Texas

October 15, Honda Indy 300, Surfers Paradise, Queensland, Australia

October 29, Marlboro 500 Presented by Toyota, California Speedway, Fontana, California

Subject to alteration